REVISED ED

Month-By-Month™

WHAT TO DO EACH MONTH TO HAVE A BEAUTIFUL GARDEN ALL YEAR

GARDENING
IN LOUISIANA

Published by
Cool Springs Press
101 Forrest Crossing Boulevard
Franklin, Tennessee, 37064

Cataloging in Publication Data is Available.
ISBN: 1-59186-233-7

First Printing Revised Edition 2006
Printed in the United States
10 9 8 7 6 5 4 3 2 1

Managing Editor: Ramona Wilkes
Designer: James Duncan, James Duncan Creative
Illustrations: Bill Kersey, Kersey Graphics
Production Design: S.E. Anderson

On the cover: Black-eyed Susan (*Rudbeckia hirta*); photo by Tom Eltzroth

Visit the Cool Springs Press website at **www.coolspringspress.net**

Note to reader: The Ultra-Fine Oil brand mentioned in this book is no longer available. You may use any light horticultural oil recommended for year-round use.

PHOTOGRAPHY CREDITS

William Adams: Page 7 (bottom)

Liz Ball: Pages 46, 67 (bottom), 116, 137, 185-187 (top), 198, 202, 246

Paula Biles: Page 242

Tom Eltzroth: Pages 19-21 (top), 26, 32, 34, 44, 53, 62, 65, 67-71 (top), 81, 92, 95-97 (top), 95 (bottom), 101, 108, 112, 139, 155, 159 (bottom), 159-161 (top), 173, 185 (bottom), 204, 207, 211, 212-213 (top), 217, 222, 228, 229, 230-231 (top), 241

Lorenzo Gunn: Pages 7-18 (top)

Pam Harper: Page 191

Rosemary Kautzky: Pages 235, 239, 240

Charles Mann: Pages 132, 140

Anita Nelson: Pages 234, 236

Jerry Pavia: Pages 19 (bottom), 50, 61, 115-118 (top), 127, 163, 178, 209, 244

Neil Soderstrom: Pages 24, 30, 36, 40, 48, 57, 59, 66, 75, 77, 90, 120, 125, 128, 130, 134, 148, 152, 156, 157, 164, 174, 176, 180

Andre Viette: Pages 41 (bottom), 220

David Winger: Page 115 (bottom)

REVISED EDITION

Month-By-Month™
WHAT TO DO EACH MONTH TO HAVE A BEAUTIFUL GARDEN ALL YEAR

GARDENING
in LOUISIANA

DAN GILL

COOL
SPRINGS
PRESS

www.coolspringspress.net

DEDICATION

To the memory of Dr. Bobby Fletcher, whose life inspired all who knew him and to the Louisiana Master Gardeners, for their efforts to educate gardeners around the state.

ACKNOWLEDGEMENTS

Books do not get written without a great deal of support. I would especially like to thank Dr. Joe White, Extension Horticulturist, who spent many hours carefully reviewing the manuscript of this book; Richard Sacher and Jan Goldfield for their information on water gardens; Peggy Cox for information on perennials and herbs; Paul Soniat and the staff and volunteers of the New Orleans Botanical Garden; Doris Cozzens; Annie Coco; and my editor, Ramona Wilkes, whose cheerful attitude and guidance helped make writing this book possible.

CONTENTS

INTRODUCTION
the benefits of a
  gardening schedule 7
gardening in
  louisiana 7–18
  climatic conditions 7
  average freeze dates 8
  average annual
    rainfall amounts 8
  louisiana's gardening
    seasons 8
  soil conditions in
    louisiana 10
  planning the garden 11
  planting 12
  planting in individual
    holes 13
  bed preparation 14

gardening
  techniques 14–17
  the importance of
    fertilization 14
  what are fertilizers? 14
  why we use them 14
  the importance of
    pruning 15
  the importance of
    proper watering 16
  what does "winter
    hardy" really mean? ..16
  how to overwinter
    plants 17
  bringing plants indoors ..17

usda cold hardiness
  zones 18

CHAPTER ONE
annuals 19–40
  introduction 19
  january 22
  february 23
  march 24
  april 26
  may 28
  june 30
  july 32
  august 34
  september 36
  october 38
  november 39
  december 40

CHAPTER TWO
bulbs, corms, rhizomes,
  & tubers 41–66
  introduction 41
  january 44
  february 46
  march 48
  april 50
  may 52
  june 54
  july 56
  august 58
  september 60
  october 62
  november 64
  december 66

CHAPTER THREE
herbs & vegetables ...67–94
  introduction 67
  january 72
  february 74
  march 76
  april 78
  may 80
  june 82
  july 84
  august 86
  september 88
  october 90
  november 92
  december 94

CHAPTER FOUR
lawns 95–114
  introduction 95
  january 98
  february 99
  march 100
  april 102
  may 104
  june 106
  july 108
  august 110
  september 111
  october 112
  november 113
  december 114

CHAPTER FIVE
perennials 115–139
   introduction 115
   january 119
   february 120
   march 122
   april 124
   may 126
   june 128
   july 130
   august 132
   september 134
   october 136
   november 138
   december 139

CHAPTER SIX
roses 140–158
   introduction 140
   january 144
   february 145
   march 146
   april 147
   may 148
   june 150
   july 152
   august 153
   september 154
   october 155
   november 156
   december 158

CHAPTER SEVEN
shrubs 159–184
   introduction 169
   january 162
   february 164
   march 166
   april 168

may 170
june 172
july 174
august 176
september 178
october 180
november 182
december 184

CHAPTER EIGHT
trees 185–210
   introduction 185
   january 188
   february 190
   march 192
   april 194
   may 196
   june 198
   july 200
   august 202
   september 204
   october 206
   november 208
   december 210

CHAPTER NINE
vines, ground covers,
   & ornamental
   grasses 211–228
   introduction 211
   january 214
   february 215
   march 216
   april 218
   may 219
   june 220
   july 222
   august 224
   september 225

october 226
november 227
december 228

CHAPTER TEN
water &
   bog plants 229–248
   introduction 229
   january 232
   february 233
   march 234
   april 236
   may 238
   june 240
   july 242
   august 244
   september 245
   october 246
   november 247
   december 248

about houseplants . . 249–254
louisiana cooperative
   extension service 255
planting charts 256–279
summary of pest
   control options . . . 280–285
glossary 286–290
bibliography 291
botanical name
   index 292–293
common name
   index 294–302
meet the author 303

INTRODUCTION

THE BENEFITS OF A GARDENING SCHEDULE

Gardeners are usually drawn to checklists when reading articles or magazines about gardening. We appreciate seeing what should be done and when in a concise, neat form. Think of this book as a large, expanded checklist. It's full of timely information that relates specifically to the unique growing conditions of Louisiana. It will help you know what to do when, and allow you to develop a schedule for your landscape based on the types of plants you like to grow.

Schedules are appropriate in gardening because seasons are cyclic. The same type of weather generally occurs at about the same time from year to year. The seasons and the weather that they typically bring dictate what should or should not be done in the garden. Plants grow, bloom, die, or are dormant according to the changing seasons, and the same gardening activities are done at about the same time from year to year. Understanding this concept will allow you to better understand how to garden more effectively and efficiently.

But seasons are not the same from one geographical location to another, and gardeners need schedules that are accurate for where they garden. New gardeners do not have the experience to know the rhythm of the seasons, and more knowledgeable gardeners often wish for a clear explanation of what to do at a particular time. This book will help you avoid mistakes by providing a gardening schedule for Louisiana that will help you be a better gardener.

GARDENING IN LOUISIANA
CLIMATIC CONDITIONS

The climate of Louisiana is relatively mild. The United States Department of Agriculture divides the state into two hardiness zones based on the average minimum temperatures experienced during the winter. Most of our state is in zone 8, with average winter lows of 10 to 20 degrees Fahrenheit. Coastal areas around Lake Charles, Lafayette, and New Orleans are in zone 9 and experience average winter lows of 20 to 30 degrees. Despite what the USDA Hardiness Zone Map says, feel free to determine what zone you are in based on what you typically experience. If your typical winter temperatures are below 20 degrees F, then you are in zone 8. If you garden where winter temperatures typically stay above 20 degrees F, you are in zone 9. Our mild climate allows a year-round growing season for flower and vegetable gardens, particularly in the southern part of the state.

INTRODUCTION

AVERAGE FREEZE DATES

Last freeze dates and first freeze dates are of great importance to many garden activities, but it is important to understand that no one knows when the last or first freeze will actually occur during a particular year. Average dates can be helpful, but freezes can and do occur before the average first freeze date and after the average last freeze date. You must use experience and information from knowledgeable local individuals (friends, professional horticulturists, and your parish County Agent with the Louisiana State University Agricultural Center) when making planting decisions.

The first frosts usually occur in northern Louisiana in early to mid-November, in areas south of Alexandria in mid- to late November, and along the Gulf Coast in early to mid-December. Experience shows that first freezes are more likely to occur later rather than earlier than these average dates.

Average last freeze dates are particularly important to gardeners who want to set out tender vegetables and bedding plants in the spring. Northern Louisiana freezes generally end in mid- to late March, freezes in areas south of Alexandria usually end in early to mid-March, and freezes along the Gulf Coast generally end in mid- to late February. Late freezes will occasionally occur after these dates. The conservative gardener should probably consider the frost-free date—when the chance of freezing temperatures is very unlikely—to be about four weeks after the average-last-freeze date. In the New Orleans area, mid- to late March is generally considered the frost-free date, and in Shreveport it would be mid- to late April.

AVERAGE ANNUAL RAINFALL AMOUNTS

Average annual rainfall is abundant, and amounts range from around 50 inches in the northern part of the state to over 60 inches in the New Orleans area and south. Unfortunately, the rain does not appear regularly. Some areas of the state may receive 5 to 10 inches of rain or more in a single rainfall or go for weeks without significant precipitation. Well-drained beds are needed to handle periods of high rainfall, and proper irrigation is important during dry periods, especially during hot weather.

LOUISIANA'S GARDENING SEASONS

According to the calendar, spring, summer, fall, and winter begin and end at the same time everywhere in the United States. Common sense tells us, though, that the dates for spring gardening activities must be very different between Maine and Louisiana.

Spring begins in early to mid-February when deciduous trees like red maples, Japanese magnolias, and Taiwan flowering cherries began to bloom and grow. When the calendar tells us that spring has officially begun, we are about halfway through that season. All Louisiana gardeners need to divide the gardening year in a way that makes sense for us.

The terms spring, summer, fall, and winter carry strong associations with certain types of weather, and that can be a problem for Louisiana gardeners. Winter, for instance, brings to mind a picture of snow-covered dormant gardens with little or no activity. What we actually experience in our state is occasional episodes of cold weather interspersed with extended periods of mild temperatures. Planting and harvesting vegetables, planting hardy annuals, perennials, trees, and shrubs, and controlling weeds and insects continues throughout the season.

To get around those preconceived notions, it would be better to divide the gardening year into seasons that more accurately reflect the weather we have at that time. We can divide the gardening year into a first warm season (spring), a hot

INTRODUCTION

season (summer), a second warm season (fall), and a cool season (winter). There are no sharp boundaries between these seasons, and gardeners must always be aware that unusually high or low temperatures may occur at any time, especially during season transitions.

The first warm season of the year runs from late March through mid-May. This warm season is characterized by mild to warm daytime highs and chilly to cool nights. Light frosts may occur early in this season in north Louisiana. It is a lovely time of the year that is appreciated by gardeners and non-gardeners alike.

After the danger of freezes passes, the first warm season is an excellent time to plant tender annuals and perennials in the landscape. Trees, shrubs, ground covers, and lawns may be fertilized as well to encourage the vigorous growth that takes place in this season. Tender vegetables such as tomatoes, peppers, squash, and snap beans can be planted now. New plantings of trees and shrubs in the landscape should be completed as soon as possible since hot weather is right around the corner.

The first warm season also includes the peak blooming of the spring bulbs and cool-season bedding plants that were planted several months before, such as pansies, dianthus, petunias, snapdragons, and sweet peas. For new bed planting, focus on warm-season plants such as marigolds, periwinkles, lantanas, and zinnias that will bloom for a long time, rather than cool-season plants that will play out as temperatures heat up in May.

May offers a transition into the hot season, which is characterized by brutally hot days in the upper 80s and 90s and warm nights in the mid- to upper 70s. The hot season is our longest season, and it can last through September. High humidity, rainy periods, drought conditions, insects, and diseases combine with heat to make this a stressful time of year for many plants. Numerous trees, shrubs, and perennials that are grown successfully up North cannot be grown

here because they will not tolerate the hot season. Tropical perennials such as hibiscus, gingers, blue daze, banana, and pentas really shine during the hot season, and many gardeners plant them every year even though they are prone to freeze injury.

If there is a down time in our gardens, the hot season is it. In July and August it is so hot that many gardeners retreat to the air-conditioned indoors and spend less time in the garden than at any other season. But in spite of the heat, the hot season is a time of lush growth and abundant flowers from those plants that can deal with it, and it is the season when aquatic gardens put on their best display.

There are a variety of things to do during the hot season. Controlling pests such as weeds, diseases, and insects is an important part of gardening at this time of year. Trees and shrubs grown in containers can be planted in the landscape but will require more care, and their survival is often not as sure as those planted during the cool season. Pruning is important to control the growth of a variety of plants, but avoid heavy pruning on spring-flowering trees and shrubs should not be done after June. Provide irrigation to the landscape during hot, dry periods.

Late September and early October offer a transition into the second warm season, which lasts until mid- to late November. The weather at this time of year is similar to that of the first warm season, generally mild and pleasant. This is not the end of the gardening year as it is in the colder climates that have cold, harsh winters. For us, this time of year celebrates the flowers that are still lingering and looks toward a mild cool season. As the heat diminishes, garden activities become more pleasurable . . . and there is lots to do. Fall crops of tomatoes, squash, cucumbers, and snap beans can be planted in September. Many cool-season vegetables like broccoli, lettuce, cabbage, and turnips can be planted as the weather gets cooler. Flower gardeners can plant cool-season

INTRODUCTION

bedding plants like pansies, snapdragons, and dianthus in October or November. Deciduous trees, shrubs, and perennials begin to lose their leaves in November and finally enter dormancy, but we use so many broadleaf evergreen plants in our landscapes that they rarely look barren.

Late November to early December sees the arrival of the cool season and the possibility of freezing temperatures. Although snow and severe freezes in the teens can occur, harsh weather rarely lasts long. Much of the time the weather is mild with lows above freezing and highs in the 50s, 60s, and even 70s, particularly in the southern part of the state. Tropical plants can be covered or brought in for protection on those occasional freezing nights. The planting of cool-season vegetables and bedding plants can continue. This season is by far the best time to plant hardy trees, shrubs, ground covers, and herbaceous perennials. In early March the cool season makes a transition into the first warm season, bringing us full circle.

SOIL CONDITIONS IN LOUISIANA

The condition and type of soil in which you garden have a profound effect on the health and growth of your plants. One of the most common mistakes novice gardeners make is putting too little effort into learning about their soil and what is needed for proper bed preparation. Soil is the primary source of water and nutrients for the plant and must also provide sufficient air (oxygen) to the root system. Ideally, a soil should be about 25 percent water, 25 percent air, 45 percent minerals (sand, silt, and clay), and 5 percent organic matter.

There are many different kinds of soils in Louisiana, from light sands to loams to heavy clays. A thorough knowledge of the characteristics of the soil in which you garden is necessary for making decisions about vegetable gardening, ornamental beds, and landscaping. If you need to modify the soil, this knowledge is vital to soil improvement, planting, watering, and fertilizing.

Learning about your soil is a matter of experience and talking to individuals who are knowledgeable about the soils in your area. A great place to start is your local LSU AgCenter Extension office. Your County Agent will be able to familiarize you with the characteristics of the soil in your area. In addition, you can have your soil tested by the LSU AgCenter's soil-testing laboratory in Baton Rouge for a modest fee. Kits to submit soil samples for analysis are available at your local Extension office.

A soil sample from each unique area of your landscape should be submitted, especially if you suspect that the soils may be different due to past treatment or location. For example, one sample may be submitted from your front lawn area and another from a rose bed in the front yard, as the soils would have been treated differently over the years. A sample from the back lawn area is probably very similar to the front lawn and does not usually need to be tested.

Take soil from several spots in the area you wish to be tested. Dig down about 6 inches to take a sample, remove any rocks, mulch, grass, or any other material leaving only the soil, and put all the samples in a bucket. Blend them together and remove about a cup to submit to the soil-testing laboratory. Along with the soil, you will submit a form that includes pertinent information such as the plants you are growing or intend to grow in the area.

The test results will tell you the texture of your soil: the relative proportion of sand, silt, and clay. You will also learn the pH of the soil, which reveals how acid or alkaline it is. A pH of 7 is neutral, lower numbers indicate an acid soil condition, and higher numbers mean the soil is alkaline. A pH between 5.5 to 7.5 is generally acceptable for most plants. The pH can be made higher if necessary with the addition of lime or lowered with the addition of sulfur to the soil.

INTRODUCTION

The fertility of the soil is indicated by the levels of phosphorus, potassium, calcium, and magnesium, which should all be medium to high. The fertilizer recommendations you will receive from the laboratory are based on these levels and the types of plants you will grow where the soil sample was taken. The amount of sodium in the soil is also reported. Excessive amounts of sodium are detrimental to plants, so the level should be low or very low. This knowledge can be important to gardeners along the Gulf Coast or those using irrigation water high in sodium.

A test which many horticulturists say is optional, but which you should really have done, is made to determine the percentage of organic matter. Ask your county extension service for help. adequate amounts of organic matter are very important for plant growth. Levels of 2 percent are considered adequate, 5 percent ideal.

PLANNING THE GARDEN

Many gardeners become hopelessly confused when it comes to designing their home landscapes. Landscaping efforts can be disappointing even when you have spent a substantial amount of money. The important thing to know is that developing an attractive, properly functioning landscape is a process.

The first step of the process is to determine the style your garden will have. Look at other gardens and determine the style you are most comfortable with. Gardening and landscaping books and magazines have photographs that can inspire you and help you with decisions. The style you choose is generally a matter of taste, but it should be strongly influenced by the architecture of your house. The style you select will guide the aesthetic elements of the landscape design.

There are two major styles that you might want to consider first. The formal style is characterized by bilateral symmetry, clipped plantings, geometrically shaped plants and beds, orderly rows of plants regularly spaced, traditional garden accents (classical statues for example), a central decorative feature such as a fountain, and "crisp" building materials (smooth painted wood, cut stone, brick). Everything is kept neatly manicured. This style can be very effective, but it can also appear stiff, lifeless, and boring. It is a relatively high-maintenance style.

The second general style is informal. Plants are allowed to develop their natural forms (pruned but not regularly sheared), and they are arranged irregularly in a way that reflects nature. The lines in the landscape and the shape of the beds tend to be curved and flowing. There are few straight edges and no geometric shapes. Building materials are more relaxed and may even be rustic. This style of landscape design is generally less demanding when it comes to maintenance.

As an alternative, or in addition, you may want to use elements of one of the distinct design styles that have developed through many centuries of landscape design. If you have sufficient design skill, you may even be able to combine the features of one style with those of another. Some of the popular ethnic styles are Japanese, Chinese, Spanish, French formal, and English cottage. There are also ecological styles such as desert-like (generally out of place in Louisiana's relatively wet climate), tropical, and native. Get a feel for what suits your taste and the style of your home.

Now you go through the process to develop a landscape design. The following steps will help you organize your thoughts and efforts so that what you end up with is what you want and need.

1. List your needs. Think about yourself and your family, and decide what your landscape should include to provide for their needs. Write the list on paper. It might include such features as privacy, outdoor living area (patio, deck, courtyard, etc.), shade, flower beds, vegetable garden, swimming pool, greenhouse, children's

INTRODUCTION

play area, and storage. Write down all the things you want from your landscape. Be thorough.

2. Study your site. Become familiar with the grounds. Notice the compass directions. Which areas are shady or sunny, wet or dry? Note existing features such as trees, buildings, beds, fences, and walks. Make a simple sketch of the property showing the relevant features. Better yet, create a scale drawing. A scale drawing is much more effective when you actually start to do the design. Most books on landscaping will have directions for doing a scale drawing. Various computer programs are also available to help in this process.

Once the drawing is done, make copies of it to mark up. You will be playing with various ideas and will need copies for trying out those ideas. You may also use tracing paper. Never draw on the original.

3. Diagram your space needs. In this step you decide how much space different activities and areas will need and their location in the landscape. At this time you will see how many things in your list you will actually be able to fit into the landscape. Draw circles or ovals on your scale drawing copy to indicate the size and location of areas: the vegetable garden, the play area, the patio, and so forth. Try several arrangements until the best one is found.

4. Shape the spaces. Now determine the shapes of the areas. You may have indicated a flower bed with an oval to show where and how big it will be; now you decide how it will actually be shaped. Although you don't select the plants at this stage, you decide on the characteristics that the plants should have (size, flowering, color, evergreen, etc.). This is a creative stage that will be guided by the previous steps as well as by the style you have determined for your garden.

5. Select the materials. Now you select the materials that will be chosen to create the landscape. If you listed "privacy" in Step 1, Step 2 determined which view needed to be blocked,

Step 3 determined the location of a privacy screen, Step 4 determined the size of the screen (how tall, how wide), and Step 5 will determine what the screen will be made of. You may choose a ligustrum hedge, a lattice fence, or a brick wall. Let your plan guide you as you select your plants and surfacing materials. Cost will be a factor in these decisions, of course.

PLANTING

Woody plant materials such as trees and shrubs are sold in one of three forms: bare root, balled and burlapped, or container grown. Trees are generally planted into individual planting holes, while shrubs are usually planted in well-prepared beds.

Bare root: Because bare-root plants are so perishable, shipping and selling bare root is the least common method. You should purchase and plant bare-root plants only when they are dormant, generally from December through February. Roses are still sold bare root, and mail-ordered plants are also sometimes shipped bare root.

Never allow the roots to dry out. Plant bare-root plants immediately or as soon as possible after you get them, and be sure they are planted at the same level they were growing previously. This can sometimes be difficult to determine, but look at the stem carefully and you can often detect the original soil line. It is better to plant a little too shallow than too deep.

To plant a bare–root plant properly, make a mound of soil in the bottom of the hole where the plant will be planted, spread the roots over the mound, and fill in with more soil, covering the roots. Water thoroughly to settle them in.

Balled and burlapped: A balled-and-burlapped plant is grown in a field. When it reaches the desired size, it is dug up with a soilball which will be tightly wrapped with burlap and fastened with nails, wrapped with twine, or placed in a wire basket. When it is dug out of the ground, such a

INTRODUCTION

plant loses much or most of its root system and is susceptible to transplant shock. For this reason, balled-and-burlapped plants are best planted during the cooler months of October through March.

Many larger trees and shrubs are sold in this form, although today large trees grown in containers are also available.

Container grown: Container-grown plants are the most common plants for sale. They have well-developed root systems and suffer less transplant shock when planted. For this reason you may plant them virtually year-round, even though it is better to plant them during the milder weather that occurs from October to March.

Avoid planting in the stressful months of June, July, and August whenever possible.

PLANTING IN INDIVIDUAL HOLES

Planting trees properly in individual holes is not difficult, but it can make the difference between success and failure.

1. Whether the tree is balled and burlapped or container grown, dig the hole at least twice the diameter of the rootball and no deeper than the rootball's height.

2. Remove a container-grown tree from its container, and place it gently onto the firm, undisturbed soil in the bottom of the hole. A rootball that is tightly packed with thick encircling roots indicates a rootbound condition. Try to unwrap or open up the rootball to encourage the roots to spread into the surrounding soil. Do not remove the burlap from balled-and-burlapped trees unless it is synthetic burlap (check with the nursery staff when you purchase the tree). Once the tree is in the hole, try to remove any nylon twine or wire basket that may have been used, and fold down the burlap from the top of the rootball. Whether the tree is container grown or balled and burlapped, the top of its rootball should be level with or slightly above the surrounding soil. It is crucial that you do not plant the tree too deep.

3. Pulverize the soil dug out from the hole thoroughly; use this soil, without any additions, to backfill around the tree. Research shows that blending amendments such as peat moss or compost into the fill soil slows establishment; it encourages the roots to grow primarily in the planting hole and delays their spread into the soil beyond. As a tree grows, its roots will grow out well beyond the reach of its branches. Since the roots will spend most of the tree's life growing in native soil outside of the planting hole, they might as well get used to it from the beginning.

4. Add soil around the tree until the hole is half full, then firm the soil to eliminate air pockets—but do not pack it tight. Finish filling the hole, firm again, and then water the tree thoroughly to settle it in. We do not generally add fertilizer to the planting hole, although it is all right to use some slow-release fertilizer in the upper few inches if you like. The use of a root stimulator solution is optional.

5. Stake the tree only if it is tall enough to be unstable—otherwise, staking is not necessary. Do not drive the stakes into place directly against the trunk and tie the tree to it. Two or three stakes should be firmly driven into the ground just beyond the rootball. Tie cloth strips, old nylon stockings, or wire (covered with a piece of garden hose where it touches the trunk) to the stakes and then to the trunk of the tree. Leave the support in place for no longer than nine to twelve months.

6. It is beneficial to keep the area 1 to 2 feet out from the trunk mulched and free of weeds and grass. This encourages the tree to establish faster by eliminating competition from grass roots. It also prevents lawn mowers and string trimmers from damaging the bark at the base of the tree, which can cause stunting or death. The mulch should be about 4 inches deep and pulled back slightly from the base of the tree.

7. Water your tree when the weather is dry. This is the single most important thing you can to

ensure its survival, especially during its first summer. To properly water a tree the first year, turn a hose on to a trickle and lay the end on top of the ground within 6 inches of the trunk. Let the water trickle for about thirty to forty-five minutes. This should be done once or twice a week during hot, dry weather.

BED PREPARATION

Shrubs, ground covers, annuals, and perennials are almost always planted in well-prepared beds. Since their roots are less extensive than trees, amendments are generally added during bed preparation. Soil amendments are materials that are blended with the soil to improve it and can be organic matter (compost, aged manure, finely ground pine bark, peat moss), lime (makes the soil less acid), sulfur (makes the soil less alkaline), sand (for heavy clay soils), and fertilizer. Here are the basic steps for preparing the bed.

1. First, do a thorough job of removing unwanted vegetation in the bed. Weeds or turf-grass may be removed physically or killed with a herbicide such as glyphosate (follow label directions carefully).

2. Next, turn over the soil to a depth of 8 to 10 inches. Spread any desired soil amendment over the turned soil. You will almost always want to add 2 to 3 inches of organic matter and some fertilizer. (Have a soil test done to find out the specific needs of your soil.)

3. Blend the amendments thoroughly into the soil of the bed.

4. Rake, and you're ready to plant.

GARDENING TECHNIQUES
THE IMPORTANCE OF FERTILIZATION

In my conversations with gardeners over the years, I have come to realize that there is, overall, an incomplete understanding of fertilizers—what

they are, what they do, and why we use them. To put things in perspective, using fertilizers properly is an important part of gardening—but it is not a matter of life and death.

WHAT ARE FERTILIZERS?

First of all, fertilizers are not food. Plants make their own food through photosynthesis, which utilizes the energy of the sun to create sugar from carbon dioxide and water. If you need to think of plants eating something, their food is *light.*

To be healthy, plants also require sixteen elements that are essential to their ability to carry on their life processes. These sixteen essential elements are the same for all plants. Plants in laboratory experiments that are completely deprived of any one of the essential elements become very sick or die. That, of course, virtually never happens in the garden since at least some of each essential element is always present. There are times, however, when an essential element may not be present in sufficient quantities for a plant to grow and function to its full potential. That's where fertilizers come in—a fertilizer is a substance added to the plant's environment that provides one or more essential elements.

Of the sixteen essential elements, three of them—carbon, hydrogen, and oxygen—are obtained from water and carbon dioxide. These elements are always available to plants in abundant quantities under normal conditions, and we don't have to worry about them. The other thirteen are almost always absorbed by plants from the soil through their roots (some epiphytic and aquatic plants are exceptions).

WHY WE USE THEM

The thirteen essential mineral elements obtained from the soil are divided into three groups, based on the relative amounts of the elements used by plants. The micronutrients are used in very tiny amounts and include boron, chlorine, copper,

iron, manganese, molybdenum, and zinc. Acid-loving plants often have problems obtaining iron in areas of the state where the soil is alkaline. Micronutrients are also called trace elements.

The secondary elements—calcium, magnesium, and sulfur—are used by plants in larger amounts, and deficiencies can be more common. If your soil is very acid, it is generally going to be low in calcium and possibly magnesium. Gardeners with acid soils often must add dolomitic lime to their gardens to provide calcium and magnesium and make the soil less acid.

Nitrogen (N), phosphorus (P), and potassium (K) are the macronutrients, or primary elements. Although they are no more important to plants than any other essential element obtained from the soil, these nutrients are used in the largest quantities and so are most likely to be in short supply. As a result, gardeners focus on them almost exclusively when using fertilizers. Nitrogen (N), phosphate (which contains phosphorus), and potash (which contains potassium) are represented by the three numbers on a fertilizer's label, indicating the relative amounts of those nutrients contained in the fertilizer.

In summary, we use fertilizers to correct deficiencies in one or more of the essential elements that plants obtain from the soil. The three nutrients most likely to be deficient are nitrogen, phosphorous, and potassium since they are used in the greatest amounts, and most fertilizers focus on providing those nutrients. You do not need a separate fertilizer for every plant you grow. Despite the bewildering array of fertilizer brands and formulations available, it is not that complicated to fertilize properly. Remember, all plants use the same essential elements.

THE IMPORTANCE OF PRUNING

When it comes to gardening, pruning is something that you just have to get used to doing. Plants will never grow exactly the way we want them to and so will need to be shaped. There will always be plants that grow larger than we anticipated and need to be regularly pruned to control size. Dead branches, diseased tissue, and insect infestations may be pruned away for the health of the plant. Then there are special situations such as topiary, espalier, and bonsai where careful selective pruning is used to completely alter the plant's normal growth patterns.

The average gardener is terrified of (well, very concerned about) pruning. The main reason is that most gardeners feel they don't know what they are doing and they are afraid they will damage or kill the plants. You can gain confidence by asking and fully answering two questions before pruning begins.

1. Why, specifically, do I feel this plant needs to be pruned? Or, what specific goal do I want to accomplish and what problem do I need to correct?

2. How, specifically, do I need to prune this plant to accomplish the goal?

There are three basic techniques we use to prune plants: pinching, heading back, and thinning out. Deadheading is another grooming technique that may be placed in the pruning category.

Pinching is done with the thumbnail and forefinger or small garden scissors. The idea is to remove the young, soft growing tip of a shoot.

Pinching encourages branching and produces a fuller, bushier plant.

Heading back involves shortening shoots or branches. Like pinching, it stimulates growth and branching. Heading back is often used to control the size of plants, encourage fullness, rejuvenate older plants, and maintain specific shapes as with topiary and espalier.

Often overutilized by gardeners, careless heading back can destroy the natural form of a plant.

Thinning out removes shoots or branches at their point of origin, either back to a branch fork or back to the main trunk. Thinning can control the

size and shape of a plant while doing a better job of maintaining the plant's natural shape.

Thinning cuts do not stimulate growth and often work with the plant's natural growth patterns to correct problems.

Deadheading is a rather morbid gardening term that refers to the continual removal of faded, unattractive flowers. This is done for a variety of reasons, including keeping the plant more attractive, encouraging more flowers, and preventing self-seeding.

It is usually a tedious process but often worth the effort.

It is generally better to prune lightly regularly than to prune severely occasionally. Do not prune plants when they are under stress. Do not prune plants late in the year when the new growth stimulated will not have time to harden off before freezes. If needed, prune spring-flowering trees and shrubs soon after they finish flowering. Prune most summer-flowering trees and shrubs in February.

THE IMPORTANCE OF PROPER WATERING

Plants must have a constant and regular supply of water to maintain health. Although Louisiana is not a dry state, rainfall does not fall evenly throughout the year. Drought conditions are not uncommon during the hot months of June, July, August, and September, and gardeners will have to irrigate to keep landscape plants in good shape.

Proper watering is a matter of timing and application. Timing is a matter of experience, paying attention to weather conditions, and common sense. Do not allow plants to show water stress (wilting, dull leaf color, burned leaf edges) before you begin watering. During hot weather periods, seven to ten days without rain usually means you should irrigate.

Water must be applied slowly over time to penetrate the soil 4 to 6 inches deep and to thoroughly irrigate a landscape. During especially dry periods, watering landscape plants by hand generally does not provide them with enough water. Sprinklers, soaker hoses, and drip irrigation systems are effective devices for delivering water slowly over time for thorough watering.

Plants in the landscape growing in containers need much more frequent watering, sometimes every day during hot weather. When watering container plants, water generously until water flows from the drainage holes. Water again when the soil feels dry to the touch but before the plants wilt.

WHAT DOES "WINTER HARDY" REALLY MEAN?

You'd think that worrying about cold protection would not be necessary during our relatively mild winters. And it wouldn't be if we used only hardy plants in our landscapes. But tender tropicals are, and probably always will be, part of most Louisiana gardens; container plants in the landscape are often tender tropicals as well.

The gardening term "hardy" refers to plants that can withstand temperatures below freezing (32 degrees Fahrenheit) with little or no damage. There are degrees of hardiness. A plant that can tolerate 10 degrees is hardier than one that is hardy only to 20 degrees. In zone 9 areas of the state, plants hardy to 15 degrees are considered winter hardy because the likelihood of lower temperatures is rare. In zone 8, plants hardy to 5 degrees are considered winter hardy.

The term "tender" indicates plants that will be severely damaged or killed by temperatures below freezing. Factors such as how long the temperature stays below freezing, how far below freezing it goes, and how protected is the plant's location in the landscape will all affect the amount of damage that occurs. Cold protection is needed by tender tropicals whenever temperatures are predicted to go into the low 30s or upper 20s. Do not be concerned about wind-chill factors—look at the actual temperatures that are predicted.

INTRODUCTION

HOW TO OVERWINTER PLANTS

One benefit of our mild winters is that the ground here never freezes. Tropicals growing in the ground that produce fleshy underground parts, such as bulbs or rhizomes, are generally very reliable about coming back even if the tops are killed by freezing temperatures. Cannas, agapanthus, elephant ears, gingers, callas, achimenes, philodendrons, bird-of-paradise, crinums, hymenocallis, clivia, and amaryllis fall into this category.

You can ensure the survival of these below-ground parts by placing 4 to 6 inches of mulch over the soil around the base of these plants for additional protection. Pine straw is one of the best mulches. It stays loose and does not pack, a quality which improves the insulating qualities. Remember that mulches protect only what they cover. They are most useful in protecting below-ground parts or covering low-growing plants. Mulch may help keep the lower stems, crown, and roots of a tropical alive, but it won't protect the uncovered upper part of the plant. To protect the upper parts of tropicals you must cover them.

Plastic, canvas, or fabric may all be used as covers. There must be enough material to extend all the way to the ground when the plant is covered. If possible, find two or three posts or stakes that are taller than the plant. Drive them into the ground around the plant and they will hold the cover off the foliage. This is particularly important if the weight of the cover might damage the plant or if plastic is used—leaves will freeze where they come into contact with a plastic cover.

Covering plants works particularly well when temperatures dip into the mid-20s overnight and rise again the following day. Providing a heat source under the cover improves protection when there are more severe freezes or prolonged temperatures below freezing. One of the safest and easiest methods I've seen is to wrap or drape the plant with miniature Christmas lights. Not enough heat is generated to damage the plant, but the heat that is given off by the small bulbs can make a big difference in the plant's survival. Be sure to use outdoor extension cords.

BRINGING PLANTS INDOORS

You must also decide what to do with tender plants growing in containers outside. You have three choices. One, leave them out and let them take their chances (at least gather them together under some protection such as a carport or patio cover). This could be an option with low-value, easily replaced plants. Two, bring them inside and keep them in through the winter. Make sure you put them in a good location that receives plenty of light. Or three, move them inside on those nights when a freeze is predicted and back out again when the freezing episode is over.

Good: Sheets or quilts

Better: Cloth cover or row cover

Stakes

Light Bulbs

USDA Cold Hardiness Zones

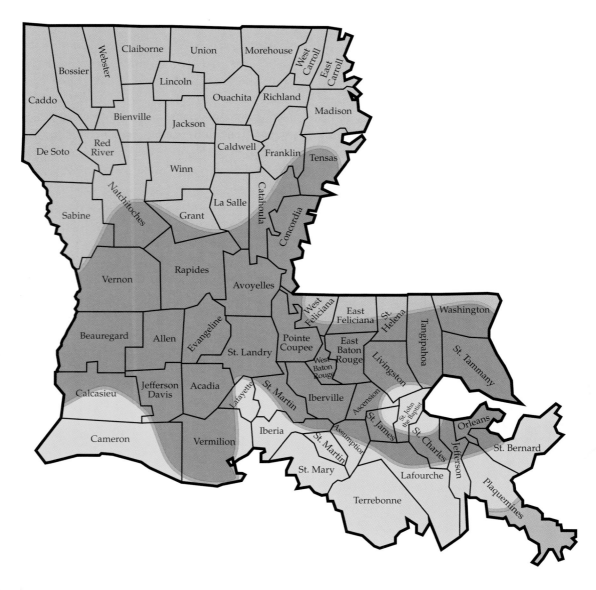

ZONE	Average Annual Minimum Temperature °F)
8a	15 to 10
8b	20 to 15
9a	25 to 20
9b	30 to 25

ANNUALS

Annuals are plants that sprout from seeds, grow, mature, flower, set seed, and die in a single growing season. The group is divided into warm-season annuals and cool-season annuals, with classification depending on cold hardiness and heat tolerance.

WARM-SEASON ANNUALS

Warm-season annuals are killed or severely damaged by freezing temperatures and therefore grow best during the warm to hot months of April to early November. Seeds or transplants may be planted into the garden from late March through August. They thrive during the long, hot months, although the performance of some will diminish during the hottest weather in late summer.

Since we have a growing season that is seven months long, it is unusual for true annuals to last from April to November. There is a group of plants called tender perennials that does have the stamina to last the entire season. Since they are often killed during winter freezes and so last for just one season, these plants are grown as warm-season annuals and are generally

grouped with them even though they are perennials. Unlike true annuals, tender perennials are not programmed by their genes to die after flowering and setting seed. Beds planted with tender perennial bedding plants will not have to be replanted in July or August as is typical for true annuals. This makes them a good choice for lower-maintenance landscapes. As a bonus, some tender perennials can survive mild winters and may live to bloom another year. Tender perennials on the Warm-Season Annuals chart (page 256) are marked with single asterisks.

COOL-SEASON ANNUALS

Flower beds can remain colorful through the winter when planted with cool-season annuals, a wonderful group that will grow and bloom from November to May. Seeds for most may be planted in flats or direct-seeded from August through January. Transplants should be planted from October through February.

Cool-season bedding plants will generally tolerate freezing temperatures into the low 20s and even teens without protection (nasturtiums are the exception, as they are damaged by temperatures below 30 degrees Fahrenheit). Many will bloom all winter during mild weather, peaking in March and April. With the onset of hot weather in May, most cool-season annuals are quick to decline.

There are several hardy perennials that are commonly used as cool-season annuals in Louisiana. Although foxglove, delphinium, and hollyhock are reliable perennials in cooler zones, they have a hard time surviving our summers. Transplants are set into the garden from October through February for blooms in April through early June.

GROW ANNUALS SUCCESSFULLY

Successful annual growth is dependent on good bed preparation, planting each type of annual in the growing conditions it prefers, and attention to proper care after planting.

Don't scrimp on bed preparation, as this is essential for plants to perform their best.

1. First remove any weeds or other unwanted plants from the bed. Growing weeds may be killed with a systemic, non-selective herbicide that does not leave residues in the soil, such as glyphosate. Be sure to follow label directions carefully.

2. Turn the soil to a depth of at least 8 inches.

3. Spread a 2- to 4-inch layer of compost, rotted leaves, aged manure, finely ground pine bark, or peat moss over the bed, and then evenly sprinkle with a light application of a granular all-purpose fertilizer. Blend the organic matter and fertilizer into the bed thoroughly, rake smooth, and then plant.

PLANNING THE ANNUAL FLOWER GARDEN

Before you go to the nursery to buy annuals, look carefully at the growing conditions in the area to be planted. Most annuals do best with six to eight hours of sun a day (partial to full sun). Several will do well with two to four hours of direct sun (shade to partial shade). Make sure you select plants that will thrive in the light conditions they will receive. Annuals generally need good drainage, so plant them in a raised bed if the area tends to stay damp. Look at the size of the bed and calculate how many plants it will hold. Although spacing varies depending on the type of annual, about 8 inches is average and can be used for estimating.

It is also a good idea to make some decisions on the color or colors that will be used in the flower bed, as well as desirable heights (taller plants in the back of beds, shorter in front) and general layout. You can always change things or make adjustments if necessary, but it is best to have developed your ideas as completely as possible before heading out to buy plants.

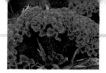

PLANTING ANNUALS

When planting annual transplants, make sure you space them properly. Too close, and the plants will crowd one another and be less healthy. If planted too far apart, the plants will not grow together to completely fill the bed. Plant transplants so that the top of the rootball is level with the soil in the bed. If the roots are in a dense mass, tear open the mass slightly to encourage the roots to grow into the surrounding soil.

Many annuals are easy to direct-seed into the garden—but in this day of instant gratification, many gardeners don't have the patience for this and rely on transplants instead. If you have the patience, plant seeds at the proper depth in a well-prepared bed and water frequently until they come up. When direct-seeding, it is important to thin seedlings so that they are spaced properly. Check the seed package for recommendations.

GENERAL CARE

Proper care of annuals will keep them attractive for a long time. Annual beds are relatively high maintenance, and this should be remembered when deciding how many beds you want and how large the beds will be. Regular watering and weeding are necessary, although both of these jobs can be reduced with the use of a mulch. A 2-inch layer of pine straw, leaves, or pine bark will work well.

Thorough watering during dry weather, especially when it's hot, is important to keep annuals growing vigorously and blooming. Soaker hoses, where suitable, are a great way to water without getting the flowers or foliage wet. This can reduce disease problems and damage to open flowers.

Whenever it is practical, remove the old flowers to keep the plants looking attractive and to encourage continued flowering.

Insect and disease problems are fairly common, especially with warm-season annuals. Keep a watchful eye out for symptoms and act promptly before a lot of damage occurs. Most annuals will not recover well if badly damaged. Remember, it is important to properly identify the cause of a problem before taking action, especially if you're going to use a pesticide.

JANUARY
ANNUALS

PLANNING

Make a New Year's resolution to start a gardening journal.

An important part of planning for the future is remembering what was done in the past.

A favorite pastime of gardeners is to look through the many seed catalogs that arrive in December and January. There is still plenty of time to decide what to plant when the cool-season annuals finish, but it won't hurt to start coming up with some ideas. Look for new cultivars of reliable plants that you'd like to try. Nurseries may or may not carry the newest cultivars, but it is fun to know what's on the cutting edge. You can also consider growing the plants yourself from seed. Note the All-America Selections winners for the new year, as well as past winners. These cultivars have proven themselves in trials all across the country and are usually a good choice.

PLANTING

There is still time to order and plant seeds of fast-growing cool-season annuals such as **alyssum, annual phlox, calendula, forget-me-not,** and **nasturtium.** Although the selection in nurseries may be somewhat skimpy now, you can continue to plant cool-season transplants in January during periods of pleasant weather.

CARE

Keep beds well mulched to suppress weed growth, retain soil warmth, and conserve water.

Our coldest weather usually occurs in January and February. Most bedding plants will not need protection. Cover **nasturtiums** if temperatures below 30 degrees Fahrenheit are predicted. **Pansies, dianthus, ornamental kale** and **cabbage, viola,** and **snapdragons** are among the most hardy. They survive temperatures below 20 degrees with no problem, so they are especially reliable for north Louisiana. Protect **sweet peas** if temperatures in the low 20s are predicted.

WATERING

Cool temperatures and normal rainfall generally make watering unnecessary this month. Do watch the rainfall amounts, and if it seems dry, water thoroughly. Annuals in container plantings will need to be watered regularly.

FERTILIZING

Cold temperatures often slow the growth of cool-season bedding plants in January. If the weather has been mild and plants are in active growth, you may decide to fertilize them, if fertilizer has not been applied in a long time. Before deciding to fertilize, check the type of fertilizer you are using to see how long it will last, and evaluate the appearance and condition of the plants:

• If plants are deep green: don't fertilize.

• If plants are pale or yellow-green: fertilize.

All-purpose granular fertilizers such as 8-8-8 or 15-5-10 will generally feed for about six to eight weeks. If you used a slow-release fertilizer at the time of planting, it will generally last the entire growing season. Soluble fertilizers (those dissolved in water) must be applied every two weeks during active growth.

PESTS

Pest problems are relatively mild this time of year. Watch for aphids if the weather is mild, and control with insecticidal soap or Ultra-Fine® Oil. Follow the label directions carefully.

FEBRUARY

ANNUALS

 PLANNING

Order seeds of warm-season annuals this month.

Many seeds can be planted in flats outside or directly in beds in March.

Seed packets often contain more seeds than needed to produce enough plants for a garden. Get together with a gardening friend and agree to share packets of seeds (and cost) for those plants you both want to grow. Or you can each grow more transplants than you need of different plants and trade the extras. Draw simple sketches of your flower beds and begin to plan what will go into them for the warm season. Decide on a color scheme.

 PLANTING

If you are just getting around to planting cool-season bedding plants or have decided to plant more, it is best to choose transplants in 4-inch pots this late in the season. Do not plant transplants too deeply, especially those that tend to form a crown (rosette of leaves on a short stem) such as **pansy, viola, dusty miller, delphinium, hollyhock, foxglove, English daisy,** and **statice.** Planting too deeply encourages stem rot.

 CARE

Spring is here. Flowering trees and spring bulbs are blooming, but February can still produce bitterly cold weather. Keep an eye out for extreme cold, but rest assured that most cool-season bedding plants can recover from whatever comes along. If severe weather is predicted, it doesn't hurt to throw some old blankets, sheets, tarps, or plastic over a bed if you are concerned about cold damage. Low-growing bedding plants can be covered with several inches of leaves or pine straw for protection.

 WATERING

Rain is usually generous in February, so watering chores are minimal. There may be too much rain this time of year, but because of the low temperatures, rot is generally not as much of a problem as would be expected. Still, if beds seem to be staying too wet, pull back the mulch to allow water to evaporate.

 FERTILIZING

If you haven't fertilized since you planted several months ago, you might need to now. Peak flowering on cool-season bedding plants generally occurs in March and April. Encouraging strong, robust growth now is important, especially if the plants do not appear vigorous. At this time it is best to use soluble or granular fertilizer formulations, as slow-release fertilizers will continue to fertilize longer than the plants will be in the garden.

Pansies are especially heavy feeders, so keep a close watch on them.

 PESTS

Weeds do not take the winter off. Oxalis, henbit, chickweed, and annual bluegrass are just a few of the weeds that plague cool-season flower beds. Oxalis must be lifted with the roots and bulbs attached, using a trowel or weeding tool. Systemic herbicides such as glyphosate are effective if you are persistent and make several applications as the weed reappears. You must apply these herbicides only to the foliage of the weeds you want to control. Do not allow any herbicide to contact the foliage of desirable plants nearby.

MARCH

ANNUALS

PLANNING

March is a transitional month, especially in south Louisiana. The possibility of frost diminishes greatly, and gardeners begin to think about planting warm-season bedding plants.

At the same time, the cool-season bedding plants are gearing up for their finale, which should last until May. Sit back and enjoy. Now is a good time to begin to evaluate the performance of the cool-season bedding plants in your garden.

- How well are they blooming?
- Were there any problems?
- What are the good points or bad points?

Keeping good records helps us avoid repeating mistakes and continue our successes. Look at other plantings in private landscapes and public gardens and note plants that you might want to try the next cool season.

Some gardeners who did not plant in the fall notice the amazing display of **pansies, dianthus,** and **alyssum** in other gardens and just have to go out and buy some for their gardens. If you want to plant cool-season plants, choose well-established plants in 4-inch pots. At this point, it is probably better for most gardeners to leave beds unplanted and focus on planting warm-season bedding plants later this month or in April. It is time for you to seriously begin planning your warm-season flower beds.

PLANTING

The weather may still be chilly, but some warm-season bedding plants may be direct-seeded into the garden now, including **cleome, cosmos, Dahlberg daisy, marigold,** and **rudbeckia.** Once the shoots come up, remember to cover them if nighttime lows are predicted to go below the low 30s.

Think about starting some warm-season annual seeds in flats or pots for transplants to be set out in May. Seeds may be started indoors, but light inside is generally insufficient to produce healthy transplants—windowsill seedlings usually end up stretched, weak-stemmed, and floppy.

1. Plant the seeds in containers filled with a damp potting soil or seed-starting mix, following directions on the seed package.

2. As soon as the seeds germinate, move the containers to a location outside where they will receive the light they need.

Seedlings of plants that like full sun should receive direct sun for about six hours, those that prefer shady beds should be placed in a spot that receives sun for about three to four hours.

3. Watch the weather carefully.

As long as daytime highs are in the 60s and 70s and nighttime lows in the 40s or higher, you may leave the seedlings outside. Bring them in whenever temperatures will be in the 30s, or during windy, chilly weather.

CARE

As the days lengthen and grow warmer, cool-season annuals respond by growing faster and blooming more. Deadhead

Many plants can be started easily from seed; follow directions on the seed packets.

(remove spent flowers) as often as possible to keep plants looking neat and encourage continued flowering. This is particularly effective with **annual phlox, bachelor's button, calendula, dianthus, pansy, snapdragon,** and **sweet pea.** Do this as the flowers fade, but before a seedpod develops.

WATERING

Adequate rain generally falls in March, but dry conditions can occur. With warmer temperatures (we occasionally get above 80 degrees Fahrenheit in March), plants use water faster. Although cool-season annuals planted in the fall should be well established at this point, water deeply and thoroughly whenever we are without rain for ten days or more. Newly planted bedding plants should receive water twice a week if conditions are dry.

If you have started seeds in pots or flats for transplants, watch them carefully. Those in sunny locations, in particular, will dry out rapidly. Plan on watering once a day, maybe even twice. Do not allow the seedlings to wilt.

FERTILIZING

If it has been over six weeks since your last application of granular fertilizer, or over two weeks since you last used a soluble fertilizer, consider fertilizing cool-season annuals now. Those that were previously fed with a slow-release fertilizer should be fine, but if they seem pale or sluggish, an application of your favorite soluble fertilizer will give them a push. If your plants are dark green and growing vigorously but not blooming much, do not fertilize. You may have overdone the nitrogen, and it's best to leave them alone.

PESTS

Weeds, insects, and diseases will take advantage of the warmer weather to attack flower beds with surprising swiftness.

Stay on top of the weeds! Keep beds well mulched. Many gardeners either do not use mulches or do not apply them deep enough. Mulches should be at least 2 inches thick. Pine straw, chopped pine straw, pine bark, leaves, and dry grass clippings are just some of the suitable, commonly used mulches.

Snails and slugs can be a major problem, chewing holes in leaves and flowers, particularly those of low-growing plants like **pansies.**

Use commercial baits per label directions to reduce snail and slug populations. Trapping also works if you are persistent, and it is a good way to monitor population levels. A trap is easily constructed using a small, disposable bowl and some beer. In the early evening, place several bowls around the garden where snails and slugs have been a problem. Sink the bowls in the soil or mulch up to their rims, and fill half full with fresh beer. Snails and slugs are powerfully attracted by the smell of the beer. They crawl into the bowl, and once the beer washes off the slime from their undersides, they cannot crawl out again. Empty the traps every morning, noting how many pests you caught. Continue to put out traps every evening until very few of the pesky critters show up in the beer. Toads are an excellent ally in this fight, and you should welcome them in the garden, even if you are squeamish about them.

APRIL

ANNUALS

PLANNING

This is the month that cool-season annuals really shine, **azaleas** and other spring-flowering shrubs put on a spectacular show, and the last of the spring-flowering bulbs and trees chime in for good measure. But with temperatures in the 70s and 80s, April can definitely feel like summer.

Most of the warm-season bedding plants can be planted this month (late April in north Louisiana), but many gardeners are too busy enjoying flower beds full of blooming cool-season annuals to start planting yet. This is a great time to make notes on color schemes you liked (or didn't like) and how all your cool-season annuals performed.

Even if you are not ready to plant your warm-season flower garden, you will notice that nurseries begin to carry a good selection of warm-season annual transplants this month. You might want to stop by and get ideas on what to plant later. Don't forget to take a notepad and pen to jot down the names of plants that catch your eye. Then you will able to look up information on those plants and learn more about them before you decide to purchase.

PLANTING

Tempting as it may be, resist buying the cool-season annual transplants that nurseries continue to carry. Their season is nearing its end. In particular, be aware that the **petunias** sold by the truckload in April and May will not bloom through the heat of the summer.

If you started warm-season annual seeds last month in flats, the seedlings of many types may be large enough to separate into individual cell-packs or small pots. Tease them apart gently, primarily handling them by their leaves to avoid damaging the delicate stems. Pot them up in the same mix you used to start them. Give them extra shade for a few days after separation. Make sure you keep them well watered.

CARE

Many cool-season annuals are achieving full size now. Make sure larger plants are not crowd-

Tall plants such as hollyhock often need staking.

ing smaller plants around them. Stake or otherwise support plants that need it. **Hollyhocks, snapdragons, foxgloves,** and **larkspur** are among the taller-growing plants that may need support.

 WATERING

As the weather warms and the plants grow larger, cool-season annuals growing in containers will need more frequent watering. Apply water until it runs from the drainage hole. This will ensure that the entire rootball has been moistened. However, a large part of the water moving quickly through the drainage hole(s) may sugest that the soil has been a bit too dry too long and has shrunk away from the pot's walls. This condition allows the water to bypass the rootball without wetting it. Make sure this is not the case before your satisfied that the soil mass has been sufficiently moistened. Smaller containers and those planted with a combination of several plants will dry out the fastest.

April is typically one of our drier months. Continue to water beds as needed. Soaker hoses are good to use where practical. They apply water slowly to allow

deep penetration of water into the soil. The foliage and flowers stay dry, however, preventing damage to open blossoms and reducing disease problems.

 FERTILIZING

Fertilize growing transplants once a week with your favorite soluble fertilizer at half the recommended rate.

Annuals growing in containers need regular fertilization, as constant watering leaches available nutrients quickly. Use a soluble fertilizer regularly, or apply a slow-release fertilizer according to label directions, as needed.

HELPFUL HINTS

The flowers of many cool-season annuals that are blooming so beautifully now are edible. They make colorful garnishes or an attractive addition to fresh salads. See if you have some of the following in your garden: **pansy, viola, dianthus, nasturtium, calendula,** and **ornamental cabbage** and **kale** (flowers and foliage). Do not use flowers that have been sprayed with pesticides.

We in Louisiana grow two species of **cosmos,** *Cosmos bipinnatus* and *C. sulphureus.* For summer planting, choose the gold-to-orange-red-flowering *C. sulphureus,* which is more heat tolerant.

Collect seed of such cool-season annuals as **annual phlox, bachelor's button, sweet pea, larkspur, poppies, nasturtium, calendula,** and **viola** when seedpods begin to turn yellow or tan.

 PESTS

Hungry caterpillars are on the prowl. Look for their droppings, which can be the size of a BB or pencil eraser and dark green to black. Look for holes in the leaves as well.

An excellent biological pesticide to control them is based on the bacteria *Bacillus thuringiensis*—usually abbreviated Bt. Apply at dusk since most caterpillars feed at night and the bacteria can be killed by ultraviolet rays. Many other pesticides will control caterpillars. Follow label directions carefully.

MAY

ANNUALS

 PLANNING

In May we see a transition from warm weather into intense heat. Many cool-season annuals are in decline. Daytime highs begin to reach 90 degrees Fahrenheit, and by the end of the month cool weather is but a memory. Still, the weather is pleasant compared to how hot it will be next month . . . so take advantage of it.

May is one of the busiest months in the flower garden. As cool-season annuals become unattractive, the beds should be cleaned out and replanted with warm-season annuals. By this time you have probably developed a working plan of how you want your summer gardens to look and what you want to plant. Don't forget that summer heat makes the care of flower beds uncomfortable to say the least. Keep this in mind when deciding on how many beds you can practically maintain and how large they can be. Remember, tender perennials are excellent choices (see Warm-Season Annuals chart on page 256).

 PLANTING

After removing finished cool-season annuals, put some effort into getting the bed ready for the next crop of flowers. Careful attention to bed preparation is very important to successful gardening.

1. First completely remove any weeds or other unwanted plants from the bed.

2. Herbicides such as glyphosate can be used to kill any weeds that may have sneaked in while the cool-season annuals were growing (follow the label directions carefully).

3. Turn the soil to a depth of at least 8 inches. Spread a 2- to 4-inch layer of compost, rotted leaves, aged manure, soil conditioner, or peat moss over the bed, and then evenly sprinkle with a light application of a granular all-purpose fertilizer.

4. Blend the organic matter and fertilizer thoroughly into the bed, rake smooth, and you're ready to plant.

It is best to plant transplants in staggered rows. Plant the first row at the recommended spacing. Plant the next row at the recommended spacing from the first row, but the plants should be positioned so that they form triangles with the plants of the first row (see diagram). Continue in

this way until the bed is planted. This arrangement is more visually pleasing.

If the rootball of a transplant is a solid mass of roots, slightly loosen the roots prior to planting to encourage them to spread into the surrounding soil. Do not plant transplants too deep and make sure they are spaced properly. If anything, annuals have a tendency to grow larger in our

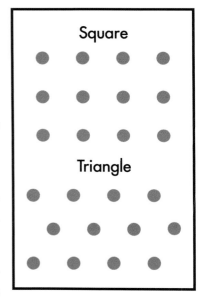

It's more pleasing to
the eye if annuals are planted
in staggered rows.

climate than their tags predict. Water-in the transplants with your favorite soluble fertilizer to get the young plants off to a good start.

WATERING

Newly planted flower beds will need regular, thorough watering if the weather is dry. (Do not water lightly every day.) A deep watering twice a week should be sufficient if you do a good job with a sprinkler or soaker hose. It is generally best to water early in the day so that plants have the water they need when heading into the hot afternoon.

HELPFUL HINTS

If your cool-season annuals are way past their prime and you are not ready or able to replace them, pull them up anyway and heavily mulch the bed until you can plant. An empty, mulched bed looks much better that one full of dying cool-season annuals.

If you have had problems with **periwinkles** wilting and dying, the problem is most likely aerial blight caused by the Phytophthora fungus. Research indicates that the Pacifica and Nirvana groups of periwinkles are the most blight-resistant, and you should wait until May to plant them.

Don't forget to put all of those dead cool-season annuals in your compost pile.

FERTILIZING

Some gardeners use a slow-release fertilizer when planting bedding plants. About 1 teaspoon can be placed in each planting hole and nutrients will be provided for the entire growing season. This is a rather expensive (slow-release fertilizers cost more than granular) and tedious way to fertilize, but it does save time and labor throughout the summer. You must choose one method to use, however. It is never a good idea, for example, to add a granular fertilizer during bed preparation, use a slow-release during planting, and then follow up with repeated applications of a soluble fertilizer.

PESTS

Get ready: here they come. Crawling, hopping, flying, and walking, there are lots of bugs out there ready to damage your annuals. Fortunately, most of us get by with only occasional major outbreaks of pests. Do keep a constant eye out and regularly inspect your plants for early signs of problems. This practice is perhaps the most important part of pest control. Some damage is inevitable—just don't let it get out of hand.

Note which annuals tend to have the worst problems from year to year, and consider avoiding them in the future. **Celosia,** for instance, are highly susceptible to caterpillars. **Marigolds** have problems with spider mites. **Periwinkles** plantings are more and more often devastated by *Phytophthora* fungus. Record this type of invaluable information in your journal.

Small pale specks all over leaves are commonly seen this time of year. This damage is the result of sucking pests such as spider mites, lace bugs, leaf hoppers, and plant bugs. Regular applications of Ultra-Fine Oil, insecticidal soap, or acephate (Orthene®) will minimize the damage. Damage to cool-season annuals is generally not worth treating now. Just pull them up and replace with warm-season plants.

JUNE
ANNUALS

 PLANNING

Think of ways to deal with the intense heat of the next three or four months. Try to work on days that are overcast, or work in shady areas of the landscape, moving as the shade moves from one location to another.

Evaluate flower plantings and decide if more plants or beds need to be added. Make sure you have included colorful plants around outdoor living areas like patios were you can enjoy them. Don't overlook the use of containers and hanging baskets planted with warm-season annuals.

 PLANTING

Most planting should have been done last month, but our growing season is long enough to continue planting warm-season annuals if you need to. You can also continue to direct-seed warm-season annuals in well-prepared beds, or plant seeds in flats or pots to grow your own transplants.

 WATERING

Drought stress will be a constant concern over the next few months. Pay careful attention to the weather and rainfall amounts. We tend to be either very dry or very soggy—you just have to deal with whatever situation arises. Drought-stressed plants may be more susceptible to pests like spider mites. Keep in mind that light, frequent irrigation promotes a shallow root system, making plants even more drought-susceptible and possibly increasing disease problems.

Vacation plans this summer mean deciding how plants will be watered while you are away. Here are some ideas:

A soaker hose, mulch, and a rain guage could be your best allies against drought.

1. Place all of your outdoor container plants, including any hanging baskets, in a shady location near the northern side of a building or within the protective cover of a large shade tree or covered patio. Group your plants fairly close together, as this will help slow water loss. Water thoroughly just before you leave.

2. Container plants outside should be watered almost every day. If you'll be gone for more than two or three days and you can't find a friend to water regularly for you, small inexpensive water timers are available at local nurseries and building supply or hardware stores. They can be hooked up to a sprinkler or drip irrigation system to periodically water your plants while you are gone.

3. Water your home grounds very well prior to leaving, especially if there has been little rainfall. A slow, thorough soaking will provide a lasting supply of moisture. Make sure that you have mulched all flower beds with a 2- to 3-inch layer of leaves, pine straw, or other material to conserve moisture and hold down weeds.

4. To water automatically, attach either soaker hoses or sprinklers to cover various beds with a timer attached to each faucet close to your garden

beds. Set the timers to come on twice a week and stay on long enough to thoroughly soak an area. Set the times so that each water timer comes on at a different hour so you won't lose water pressure while irrigating. Morning irrigation is preferred.

FERTILIZING

Monitor the growth, foliage color, and vigor of your annuals. If plants are pale and low in vigor, try an application of soluble fertilizer (use a hose end applicator for faster, easier application). If the plants respond within about a week, either continue to apply a soluble fertilizer regularly or sprinkle the bed with a general-purpose fertilizer appropriate for your area. Follow package directions carefully. Continue to regularly fertilize annuals in containers and hanging baskets.

Overfertilization can lead to lush growth with fewer flowers, runoff which contributes to the pollution of lakes and rivers, or even damage to your plants. Always use fertilizer in moderation. A little goes a long way.

HELPFUL HINTS

Plants that you know will grow tall may need some sort of support. Plan for this and decide what method would be best in different situations. Have the materials on hand and use them before tall plants lay over. Left alone they may damage or kill nearby plants. Stakes, cages, and bricks pushed against the base of a plant are some of the more common supports.

PESTS

It is to be hoped that your early efforts have prevented any major pest outbreaks.

Hot, dry weather favors the outbreak of spider mites. These very tiny spider relatives are almost too small to be seen with the naked eye. Damage starts as tiny pale or white speckles on the upper surface of foliage. The foliage may eventually turn faded tan and the infested plants appear very sick. Fine webbing may be seen on plants that have very heavy infestations.

Insecticidal soap and light oil sprays like Ultra-Fine Oil (spray early in the morning when temperatures are somewhat cooler) are effective. They must be sprayed under the leaves and several applications will be necessary. Miticides such as Kelthane and insecticides such as Malathion and acephate are also effective.

All of the effort you put into making your annuals grow well will make weeds in the bed grow even faster. Deal with weed problems promptly while weeds are still young and small. They can ruin an annual planting with just a few weeks of inattention.

Hand weeding, mulches, and herbicides are the primary methods of weed control. Use them regularly and use them all.

PRUNING

Gardeners rarely think about pruning annuals, but they may need to be shaped or controlled like any other plant in the landscape. Feel free to pinch or snip back plants in flower beds so that everything has enough room to grow. Trimmings from tender perennials generally root easily.

JULY
ANNUALS

 PLANNING

Plan on doing most of your gardening during the early morning or early evening when temperatures are more bearable. True annuals planted back in March or early April may be winding down toward the end of this month or in early August. Evaluate them and make plans for their replacements as they finish. New plants should do well until cool-season annuals are planted in October or November.

When it's too hot to be outside, spend some time indoors reading a good gardening book. I find it especially interesting to choose a book by a Northern gardener and read about what they go through during the winter. It somehow makes the summer easier to bear. Make a point of reading one gardening book each summer.

Decide on cool-season annuals you might like to grow from seeds. It's not too early to send off an order for seeds to plant next month or in September to raise your own transplants.

 PLANTING

If you need to add color to your landscape, you will find that most nurseries carry a decent selection of warm-season bedding plants through the summer. You can also direct-seed some of the quick, easy annuals such as **amaranthus, balsam, cosmos, gaillardia, marigold, portulaca, sunflower,** and **zinnia.**

Since there are still three or four months left of the growing season, you can purchase smaller transplants available in cell-packs, or those in 4-inch pots if you want larger plants.

Cosmos sulphureus

WATERING

High temperatures place great stress on annual flower beds, and this time of the year can be either soggy or dry. Watch the weather and water appropriately. Newly planted transplants will need more frequent irrigation than plants that are established. Seedbeds will need to be watered lightly every day until the seeds sprout. Annuals in containers may need to be watered twice a day.

FERTILIZING

July is probably the month we are least likely to fertilize our warm-season annuals. There are generally enough nutrients left in the soil from earlier fertilizer applications to keep plants vigorous. High temperatures can also lower the vigor and slow the growth of many plants, making them less needful of additional nutrients. Continue to fertilize container plants.

PESTS

Over the next three months, be sure to evaluate and record the performance of your annuals. You will note striking differences in the amount of pest damage from one type of plant to the next. If you are trying to minimize the use of pesticides in your landscape, plan to plant more of the relatively pest-free types next time, avoiding those that were more frequently attacked.

HELPFUL HINTS

Working outside in especially hot weather places extra stresses on the body. Gardeners working outside may lose up to two quarts of water each hour. To prevent dehydration, drink water before, during, and after working outside. Drink before you're thirsty, and drink cold liquids because they are absorbed by the body faster. Drink water if you can; if you choose other liquids, make sure they contain only a small amount of sugar, as it slows down liquid absorption by the body. Avoid beverages containing alcohol and caffeine.

Work in your garden in the early morning or late afternoon when it is cooler, and stay in shady areas as much as possible. Follow the shade in your landscape as the sun moves across the sky; leave areas as they become sunny and move into areas as they become more shaded.

Wear a hat and loose, comfortable clothing, and use sun screen and mosquito repellent. Take frequent breaks and try not to stay outside in the heat for extended periods.

Planting the same annual in the same bed year after year can lead to a buildup of disease organisms that like that particular plant. Nematodes (microscopic roundworms, some types of which attack and damage plant roots) and fungus organisms (root rot, stem rot) are the leading culprits. If you have planted a bed with a particular annual successfully for several years and then you notice the plants are not doing as well as before, it may be time to rotate. It is best to plant different bedding plants in beds every few years, if not more often. This will also keep you from getting in a rut.

AUGUST
ANNUALS

PLANNING

August is a month of evaluation. True annuals planted earlier will often need to be replaced. Hanging baskets of annuals may also be past their prime, and they need to be redone.

Although milder weather is still about two months off, we should begin to think about the next transition, which will occur in late September or early October. What needs to be done now to make our flower beds look their best until cool-season annuals are planted in late October and November? This may include cutting back or trimming, deadheading, staking or supporting, replacing plants, pest control, and fertilization.

PLANTING

Plant replacements for annuals that are no longer attractive. Check local nurseries for colorful, heat-tolerant bedding plants. Don't overlook colorful foliage plants such as **ornamental sweet potatoes, copper leaf, Joseph's coat, coleus, dusty miller, perilla, amaranthus, alternathera, graptophyllum,** and **purple leaf basil.**

Scaevola takes the heat and looks great lining a walkway.

34

EXCELLENT HEAT-TOLERANT ANNUALS AND TENDER PERENNIALS

UNDER 2 FEET:
Abelmoschus+
Ageratum
Angelonia
Balsam+
Blue Daze
Coleus
Dahlberg Daisy+
Dusty Miller
Dwarf Cosmos+
Dwarf Gomphrena
Dwarf Melampodium
Dwarf Pentas
Gaillardia
Celosia
Gerbera Daisy
Impatiens
Lantana
Scaevola
Mexican Heather
Narrow-leaf Zinnia
Ornamental Peppers
Perennial Verbena
Periwinkle
Portulaca+
Purslane
Salvia 'Victoria'

Marigold+
'Wave' Petunias
Wax Begonia
Wishbone Flower

OVER 2 FEET:
Angelonia
Butterfly Weed
Canna
Cigar Flower
Cleome+
Coleus
Cosmos+
Four o'Clock+
Hardy Hibiscus (Mallow)
Melampodium+
Mexican Sunflower (Tithonia)+
Perilla
Rudbeckia
Salvias
Shrimp Plant
Sunflower+

+Seeds may be planted in flats or direct-seeded this month where the plants are to grow.

 CARE

Larger-growing annuals often lean, sprawl, fall over, or simply grow too large for the plants around them to tolerate. This is especially common in mixed beds where a variety of annuals are planted together. Stake, support, trim back, or even remove those that are "overly enthusiastic" to make sure everybody has enough room.

 PRUNING

Tender perennials grown as annuals are expected to look good until late October, but they may be looking overgrown and a little "tired" now. Many will look better over the next two or three months if they are cut back now when warm temperatures will encourage rapid regrowth. Even though they are in bloom, trim them back $1/3$ to $1/2$ their height. It is worth the temporary loss of flowers to have more shapely, attractive plants for the late summer to fall period. Don't put this off.

 FERTILIZING

Fertilize those annuals that you have pruned back to encourage regrowth. A light sprinkling of an all-purpose granular will carry them through to the end of the season. If you used a slow-release early in the season, no granular is needed now. It would still be good, however, to give the plants an application of your favorite soluble fertilizer to give them a little "kick."

 PESTS

To minimize the impact on beneficial insects, spray only infested plants. Effective low-toxicity insecticides include:
- Bt or spinosad to control caterpillars
- Sevin or spinosad to control chewing insects
- Insecticidal soaps to control soft-bodied sucking insects such as aphids
- Ultra-Fine Oil to control white flies, scale, soft-bodied insects, and insect eggs

It is not unusual to experience almost daily afternoon showers, particularly in the southern part of the state. These may wash off and reduce the effectiveness of many pesticides. Repeat applications as needed. Damp weather also favors snails and slugs.

Continue to use baits, traps, and barriers as needed. Choose baits containing iron phosphates as they are less toxic and safer around pets.

Disease problems are difficult to deal with. While not as common as insect pests, diseases such as root rot or stem rot can be devastating. Avoid root rot by making sure beds are well drained and incorporate generous amounts of organic matter, preferably compost, into the bed during preparation. Don't plant transplants too deep or too close together and rotate plantings from year to year. Water deeply and occasionally, not lightly and frequently.

To avoid foliar diseases, avoid wetting the foliage when watering, if possible, and water when the foliage will dry quickly. Good air circulation and proper spacing when planting also help. A broad-spectrum fungicide such as thiophanate methyl can be used if warranted.

HELPFUL HINTS

Order seeds for cool-season annuals this month, particularly those that you want to grow as transplants.

SEPTEMBER

ANNUALS

PLANNING

Can it be that the hot season is almost over? Often, especially in north Louisiana, a cool front will make through sometime in September, relieving the intense heat of the last four months. We can begin to look forward to the upcoming mild weather and the cool season that will follow. Cool-season annual seed can be sown this month . . . if you have not begun to think about plans for the cool-season garden yet, perhaps you should.

PLANTING

It is too late to plant warm-season and too early to plant cool-season annual transplants. Not much should be added to the flower garden now unless it is really necessary. You can still plant transplants of warm-season annuals, but we are getting toward the end of their season. Even a bare area is probably best mulched and held until next month when cool-season annuals can be planted. You can plant seeds of cool-season annuals in flats or small pots to raise for transplants which will be planted in the garden in November and December. Note temperature requirements for

germination; some cool-season annual seeds need cool temperatures to germinate.

Use a peat-based potting soil or seed-starting mix to start the seeds.

1. Pre-moisten the mix by blending it with some water in a bucket.

2. When moist, but not soggy, place it into the seed-starting container and gently firm it with your hand.

3. Plant the seeds thickly and cover to the depth recommended on the package.

4. Keep the container in a completely shaded area outside and make sure the mix stays moist (the container may be covered with clear plastic wrap to retain moisture).

5. When the seeds come up, remove any cover and place the container in a part-shady or part-sunny location, depending on the type of annual.

6. When seedlings are large enough to handle, gently separate them into small individual pots or cell-packs filled with pre-moistened potting soil.

7. Plant when transplants are large enough to plant and when there is space for them in the garden.

Keep the seedlings moist and cover the tray with plastic wrap.

WATERING

We aren't out of the hot season yet. Continue to monitor rainfall, and water thoroughly when necessary.

After months of growth, annuals in containers will have filled those containers with roots. Frequent watering is critical to plantings in this condition since the roots will deplete water in the soil rapidly. Consider repotting into a larger pot if watering once or twice a day is insufficient.

FERTILIZING

Other than making sure that container plantings are receiving adequate nutrients, little or no fertilization chores are needed this month.

HELPFUL HINTS

Continue to make entries in your garden records about the performance of your annual plantings. Sketches of bed layouts, lists of varieties used, and comments are all helpful to include in your notes. Photographs are priceless in recording how a garden turned out and are far more effective than words alone. Take pictures of your garden regularly and include them with your records.

PESTS

White flies are often a major pest on **lantana, hibiscus, abelmoscus,** and a variety of other ornamentals. Control is difficult once they get out of hand. The adults are snow-white, gnat-sized flies that fly up from the plant when disturbed. The larvae are attached to the underside of the foliage and look like pale green or whitish disks. Oil sprays are generally effective, but they can damage plants when applied during hot weather. Choose a light, highly refined paraffinic type of oil such as Ultra-Fine Oil, and spray during the early morning when it is cool. Bifenthrin (Talstar) is also effective.

When using pesticides, always carefully read the label and use the product in strict accordance with the directions. Whenever possible, use the least toxic pesticide that will do the job, and only spray infested plants.

Continue to deal with weed problems before they get out of control. The intense heat makes it easy to just let the garden go this time of year. Even if only for ten or fifteen minutes in the early morning or evening, spend a little time two or three times a week on weed control.

OCTOBER

ANNUALS

PLANNING

October is another transitional month when reliably milder weather relieves the heat of summer. Along with April, October is considered one of the most pleasant months of the year. Once again it becomes a pleasure to get out into the garden . . . and there's lots to do.

It is time to think about your cool-season annual garden:

• What color schemes will you use in various beds?

• What types of plants will you select?

Look at your notes from the last cool season as you begin to make these plans and decisions.

PLANTING

Most flower beds are still full of attractive warm-season annuals. If you have some empty spots, some of the more heat-tolerant cool-season annuals may be planted. Select from **snapdragons, alyssum, annual phlox, calendula, dianthus, petunia,** and **nicotiana** (to name a few). Prepare the beds properly prior to planting.

We can have hot, muggy weather in October, particularly in the southern part of the state. If we do, early plantings of the popular **pansy** will often rot and need to be replaced. If you want to play it safe, wait until November to plant pansies and **violas.**

If you started seeds for transplants in community pots, it may be time to separate them into cell-packs or individual pots. Do not allow the seedlings to become too large and overly crowded before separating them.

You can direct-seed **poppies, larkspur, sweet pea, Virginia stock, calendula, alyssum,** and **bachelor's button** now.

Chrysanthemums are often planted in flower beds this month to provide an added punch of color. **Marigolds** are becoming a popular substitute—they provide some of the same yellow, gold, orange, and mahogany colors, but bloom longer than mums. Look for marigold transplants in local nurseries.

WATERING

October tends to be a relatively dry month. Water plantings as needed. Pay special attention to any newly planted areas. It is generally best to water direct-seeded beds lightly every day to make sure the seeds do not dry out.

FERTILIZING

When raising your own transplants, it is sometimes necessary to fertilize them. The soilless mixes used to grow transplants contain only enough nutrients for a few weeks. After transplants have been in new pots for about three weeks, begin to fertilize them once a week with your favorite soluble fertilizer at half the recommended rate.

PESTS

Caterpillars can be a major problem on annuals now as moths have had all summer to build up populations. Treat promptly with Bt, spinosad, or another approved insecticide.

Butterfly gardening has now become very popular. Never use insecticides around those plants you have planted to attract adult butterflies (nectar plants) or caterpillars (larval food plants).

NOVEMBER

ANNUALS

PLANNING

Finalize your plans for beds of cool-season bedding plants. Now is the time for serious planting.

Have a good idea of the colors and heights and amounts needed, as well as the growing conditions in the areas to be planted, before you go to the nursery.

PLANTING

Along with May, November is the most active month for planting beds of annuals. Some will bloom well from now through next April (depending on the mildness of the winter), while others will save their best for the spring.

The hard decision now is what to do with the tender perennials in our flower gardens that may still be looking attractive. Tempting as it may be to leave them in the bed, they must eventually make way for cool-season plants.

In northern Louisiana, go ahead and remove the tender perennials this month, and plant the new plants. If you want to pot some of the removed plants, they will usually transplant successfully if they are not too large. In southern Louisiana, leave them in the ground for a few more weeks

if you like, but remove them and plant your cool-season annual transplants by early December at the latest.

CARE

You generally don't need to replace the potting mixture in containers when changing plantings. If the mix seems to be dense and compacted, blend it with some sifted compost or peat moss along with some vermiculite or perlite. If you decide to replace the mix, throw the old potting mix in your compost pile or a garden bed.

WATERING

If you used soaker hoses to water warm-season annual beds, the hoses can be easily removed from the bed while your prepare it for the next planting. Once the bed is prepared and replanted, lay the soaker hose back, snaking it throughout the bed area. Cover the soaker hose with mulch for a more attractive appearance.

Rain in November is usually adequate, but water as needed—especially your new plantings, containers, and transplants.

FERTILIZING

Make sure you add some fertilizer along with organic matter during bed preparation. Don't be too generous with the fertilizer, as you can always add more later. For example, in a 3-by-10-foot bed (30 square feet), only 1 cup of 8-8-8 or $^1\!/_2$ cup of 15-5-10 is needed during bed preparation.

PESTS

With the onset of cooler weather, many insect and disease problems are reduced. Snails and slugs always seem to be waiting in the wings for an opportunity—control as needed with baits, traps, and barriers. Some gardeners find that some plants can be protected to some degree by a ring of diatomaceous earth placed around the plant. Snails and slugs do not like to crawl across the tiny sharp particles, and they tend to leave those plants alone.

Wet weather can promote root rot. Make sure beds are well drained. If necessary, build up raised beds during bed preparation and add generous amounts of compost if you have had problems in the past.

DECEMBER

ANNUALS

 PLANNING

Things should be coming together for your cool-season flower beds in early December. Try to get most plantings done well before the holidays. You know you won't have time later.

 PLANTING

Continue to plant cool-season annual seeds or transplants. Should temperatures below freezing be predicted, bring flats or pots of transplants that have not been planted yet into a protected location for the night. Direct-seeded annuals will probably be fine, but if they are newly germinated and temperatures will drop into the mid- to low 20s Fahrenheit, cover them.

In beds where direct-seeding was done, remember to thin out the seedlings to the proper spacing before they get too crowded.

 CARE

Annual beds should be mulched. Weeds do not take the winter off, and oxalis, henbit, chickweed, and bedstraw along with many others are growing now. Mulches prevent weed seeds from germinating and can save tremendous amounts of effort and time. Mulches also help retain a considerable amount of the warmth stored in soil from summer. This encourages strong root systems to form on annuals over the cool season before their explosive growth in March.

 WATERING

Cool temperatures and adequate rainfall generally make watering this month less important. Keep an eye on newly planted or seeded beds and plants growing in containers. Make sure beds are well watered whenever a freeze threatens. Drought-stressed plants are less able to deal with sub-freezing temperatures.

 FERTILIZING

Fertilize only if plants show definite deficiency symptoms such as

Bring flats or pots into a protected location, such as a cold frame, if temperatures fall toward freezing.

pale leaves, stunted growth, and yellow lower leaves.

 PESTS

It is a relief to see insect and disease problems diminish. Weeds, however, are not so kind. Oxalis, a weed that looks like clover but has a sour taste when you bite a stem, is a persistent perennial weed that plagues many gardeners, particularly in southern Louisiana where winters are milder. If you handweed, you must dig down and get the fleshy root or bulb from the ground. Where you can, spray the foliage of the oxalis with glyphosate. More than one application is needed, and you must not get these herbicides on the foliage of nearby desirable plants.

HELPFUL HINTS

We're always looking for nice gifts for the hosts of the parties and gatherings that come with the holiday season. Think about a basket filled with blooming cool-season annuals growing in 4-inch pots, the pots hidden by sphagnum moss or greenery. They can be enjoyed this way inside for a few days and then planted into the garden where they will continue to bloom for months.

BULBS, CORMS, RHIZOMES, & TUBERS

Gardeners tend to use the term "bulb" for any fleshy, underground organ produced by a plant, and I'll conform to that tradition in this chapter. But the term actually refers to several botanically distinct structures including true bulbs, corms, rhizomes, tubers, and tuberous roots.

A **true bulb** consists of a compressed stem and a growing point or flower bud enclosed with thick, fleshy, modified leaves. In some bulbs, the fleshy leaves form concentric rings (onions), and in others they look like thickened, overlapping scales (lilies). Examples of plants that produce true bulbs are allium, amaryllis, crinum, clivia, garlic chives, hyacinth, hymenocallis, spring starflower (*Ipheion*), lilies, narcissus, oxalis, rain lily (*Zephyranthes*), shell flower (*Tigridia*), snowflake (*Leucojum*), society garlic, spider lilies (*Lycoris*), tuberose, and tulip.

A **corm** is a compressed, fleshy stem with a growing point on top. Roots grow only from the base. Corms can develop small buds around their base called cormels, which are useful in propagation. Examples of corms are brodiaea, crocus, crocosmia, freesia, gladiolus, lapeirousia, and sparaxis.

Rhizomes are fleshy, horizontal, underground stems. Shoots occur along the top and roots grow from the bottom. Plants that produce rhizomes include canna, dietes, calla lily, agapanthus, bird-of-paradise, gingers (*Alpinia, Hedychium, Zingiber, Curcuma, Costus, Kaempferia*), iris (Louisiana, bearded, Siberian, Japanese), and walking iris *(Neomarica)*.

Tubers are similar to corms but tend to be more irregular in shape and have more growing points. Both shoots and roots arise from these growing points. Examples of tubers are tuberous begonias

(very difficult to grow in Louisiana summers), caladium, Chinese ground orchid (*Bletilla*), and Jack-in-the-pulpit (*Arisaema*).

Tuberous roots are thickened, fleshy roots. Often, as with dahlias, a portion of the crown or stem containing buds must be attached to the tuberous root in order for it to grow. Others, such as sweet potatoes, are able to grow shoots directly from the tuberous root. Some plants grown from tuberous roots are alstroemeria, dahlia, gloriosa lily, ornamental sweet potato, and ranunculus.

Bulbs are divided into two groups according to their season of growth and bloom: spring or summer. Spring bulbs are planted between October and early December (tulips and hyacinths in late December and early January) and bloom from January through April. Summer bulbs, usually planted between March and May, are in active growth from March through November and bloom at some time during that period.

PLANNING THE SPRING BULB GARDEN

Unfortunately, most spring-flowering bulbs originate in climates cooler than ours and do not rebloom well in our state, especially in the southern areas.

Determine where spring bulbs would make a nice addition to the landscape. Since most provide only one season of bloom, it makes better sense economically to use them to embellish rather than to produce lavish displays. Plant groups or drifts of bulbs among existing shrubs, flower beds, and ground covers, especially in areas where they can be appreciated up close.

Mail-order spring bulbs in time for them to arrive by October or November. Bulbs become available in local nurseries as early as September. You can go ahead and purchase them, but there is no hurry to plant them.

SELECTING SPRING BULBS

Buy the largest bulbs of the best quality your budget will allow. With bulbs, you definitely get what you pay for. When choosing loose bulbs at a nursery or garden center, pick the plumpest bulbs in the bin. They should be firm with no obvious cuts, soft spots, insects, or disease damage. When purchasing daffodils, look for double-nosed bulbs, which look like two bulbs joined together at the base.

PLANTING SPRING BULBS

Avoid low, wet areas, or use raised beds as necessary since most spring-flowering bulbs need excellent drainage. Prepare the area for planting:
- Remove any weeds.
- Turn the soil 8 to 10 inches deep.
- Spread 2 to 4 inches of organic matter (compost, rotted manure, peat moss) over the area and sprinkle with $1/2$ to 1 cup of general-purpose fertilizer per 30 square feet.
- Thororoughly incorporate everything together. Rake the area smooth, and plant.

It is important to plant bulbs at the proper depth. Dig individual holes or excavate the entire area to be planted to the recommended depth, and plant all the bulbs at once.

Bulbs that are expected to rebloom reliably should be planted in areas that receive at least four to six hours of direct sunlight. This allows them to build up food reserves for next year's bloom. Bulbs that will be grown for just one season may be planted in shadier locations since they are discarded after blooming, although the same amount of direct sunlight is still preferred.

CARE FOR YOUR SPRING BULBS

Keep areas planted with spring bulbs mulched and weed-free. Little supplemental watering is needed during our usually rainy winters.

Bulbs grown as annuals may be removed from the bed anytime after they finish flowering. Repeat-blooming bulbs may simply be left in the ground from year to year. This works best in settled situations such as in front of shrubs, at the base of deciduous trees, or in areas of low-growing ground covers. If the bulbs are growing in a location where you intend to plant something else to bloom during the summer, they may be lifted, stored, and replanted in the fall.

In order for repeat-blooming bulbs to bloom the following year, you must allow the foliage to persist after flowering. Do not cut back the leaves until they have turned mostly yellow.

PLANNING YOUR SUMMER BULB GARDEN

Most summer-flowering bulbs are native to tropical or subtropical climates and will reliably bloom here for many years. Indeed, for some of these plants the trick is not getting them to grow but keeping them under control.

These plants offer a wide variety of uses in the landscape, providing valuable additions to flower beds, perennial borders, ground covers, and containers. Think carefully about the characteristics of each type of bulb and the growing conditions it needs. Then determine where they will grow and look best, before you plant.

PLANTING YOUR SUMMER BULBS

Generally, dig 2 to 4 inches of organic matter (such as compost, finely ground pine bark, rotted manure, or peat moss) into the area before you plant your bulbs. Raise beds to improve drainage if necessary. A light sprinkling of general-purpose fertilizer appropriate for your area ($1/2$ to 1 cup per 30 square feet) added during bed preparation and every six to eight weeks during active growth (beginning in March and ending in August) is sufficient for most summer bulbs.

CARE FOR YOUR SUMMER BULBS

No matter what situation you have—from shady to sunny and from dry to wet conditions—at least a few kinds of bulbs will thrive there. Most summer bulbs prefer good drainage. Calla, canna, spider lily (*Hymenocallis*), Louisiana iris, blue flag, crinum, yellow flag, and some gingers are a few exceptions. Full to partial sun (six or more hours of direct sunlight) is needed by most of these plants for healthy growth and flowering, although many, such as achimenes, caladium, gingers, and bletilla, do fine in shadier spots.

Many summer bulbs have a dormancy period when foliage dies off and the bulb rests. This period generally occurs during winter. At that time, yellow or brown foliage may be trimmed back to the ground. Place markers where the dormant bulbs are located so you won't accidentally dig into them later. Avoid removing any of a bulb's foliage when it is healthy and green.

Most summer bulbs are best propagated by dividing the clumps in early March. Some bulbs, such as crocosmia, do best when divided every year or two, while others, like agapanthus, prefer to be left alone.

The following lists include many of the best summer-flowering bulbs for Louisiana. Those marked with an (+) may be better suited to the southern part of the state but could be grown successfully farther north with a thick winter mulch.

Summer bulbs for full to partial sun are: agapanthus, belamcanda, canna, crinum, crocosmia, dahlia, dietes, eucomis+, garlic chives (*Allium tuberosum*), gladiolus, gloriosa lily+, habranthus, hymenocallis, iris (bearded, Siberian), lilies, oxalis, tigridia, society garlic (*Tulbaghia violacea*), zephyranthes.

Summer bulbs for partial shade to shade are: *Arum italicum*, achimenes, alpinia, bletilla, hedychium, caladium, clivia+, crinum, costus, curcuma, globba, hymenocallis, kaempferia, oxalis, walking iris+.

JANUARY
BULBS, CORMS, RHIZOMES, & TUBERS

PLANNING

Start keeping simple records or a journal of your bulb-gardening efforts. This information is invaluable for future projects. Keep track of where you obtain your bulbs, when they are planted, when they bloom, and their overall performance. Include helpful information such as major pest problems, where the bulbs were planted, height and spread of growth, and weather conditions. Look through catalogs and choose summer bulbs to add to your landscape. Most can be planted in March and April, so make sure you get your order off in time for timely delivery. Try something different like **blackberry lily, gloriosa lily, crinum, crocosmia,** or one of the **gingers.**

It's time to get those **tulips** and **hyacinths** out of the refrigerator and plant them. This needs to be finished by mid-month. Take an inventory of what you have (in case you've forgotten since storing them), and decide where everything is to be planted. A little planning before you get the bulbs out will make planting go faster.

Decide if you want to grow some bulbs in containers. It's not hard to do, and nothing beats a pot of tulips or hyacinths blooming indoors.

PLANTING

Plant prechilled tulips and **hyacinths** into the garden now. Both are planted at about 4 inches deep in well-prepared beds. In north Louisiana, where tulips and hyacinths are more likely to rebloom, plant in an area that receives at least six hours of direct sunlight if you want to use the same bulbs next year. In south Louisiana, poor-quality blooms, if any, will be produced the following year. Since bulbs will be discarded after blooming, you can plant in shadier areas.

Tulips, hyacinths, and other bulbs you have kept refrigerated

for growing in containers should be potted now:

1. Fill a container that has drainage holes about 2/3 with potting soil.

2. Place enough bulbs, pointed end up, on the soil surface to fill the container without the bulbs touching. Plant tulip bulbs with the flat sides facing the rim of the pot. The first leaf of each bulb will grow facing the outside, creating a more attractive planting.

3. Add soil until just the tips of the bulbs show, and water thoroughly.

4. Place the containers outside in shade and keep the soil evenly moist.

5. When the sprouts are about 1 inch high, move the pots into a sunny location. Continue to water the pots regularly. If temperatures below 28 degrees Fahrenheit are predicted, move

Crinum

the pots to a cool location that will not freeze.

6. Move the pots back outside as soon as possible.

7. When the flower buds begin to show color, move them indoors and enjoy.

Keep the plants as cool as possible and the flowers will last longer.

Hyacinths may also be planted in bowls filled with pebbles. Bury the bulbs 2/3 deep in the pebbles and add enough water to touch the bottoms of the bulbs. Maintain water at that level. Next, follow the above directions, starting with step 4. Individual hyacinth bulbs may also be grown in a special hyacinth vase shaped like an hourglass. Hyacinths are incredibly fragrant and wonderful to have indoors.

CARE

Spring bulbs planted in fall are up and growing. Do not be concerned about freezing temperatures damaging the leaves. Some early bulbs, such as **paperwhite narcissus**, may already be blooming. Indeed, narcissus in

> ## HELPFUL HINTS
> During the rooting and sprouting phase, water potted bulbs, allow them to drain thoroughly, and place them in plastic bags. That way you don't have to water them. Check occasionally, and if the pots are too wet, leave the bag open for a day. When the sprouts of the bulbs are about 1 inch tall, remove the pot from the bag and place in a sunny location.

the garden will often bloom in December, though the flowers and flower buds are susceptible to cold injury. If a severe freeze threatens blooming bulbs, cut the flowers and put them in vases to enjoy indoors.

No additional water or fertilizer is needed by bulbs growing in the landscape. Be sure to keep beds weeded and mulched.

If the foliage of summer bulbs is frost-damaged and unattractive, cut it to the ground. Make sure tender bulbs have a 4- to 6-inch layer of mulch over them for protection, especially in north Louisiana. Pine straw is ideal; it does not pack down and provides excellent insulation.

Our ground never freezes in south Louisiana, and most gardeners leave tender summer bulbs in the ground during the winter. North Louisiana garden-

ers might choose to dig and store bulbs in frost-free conditions over the winter, but it is generally not necessary. Bulbs commonly lifted and stored include **caladium** and **gladiolus** because they are prone to rot in wet, cool soil. Check stored bulbs occasionally to make sure they are doing fine.

WATERING

Pots of spring bulbs should be watered as needed to keep the soil moist. Don't overdo it. Until the bulbs produce roots and begin to grow, the pots will dry out slowly. Soil that is constantly wet will promote rot.

FEBRUARY
BULBS, CORMS, RHIZOMES, & TUBERS

 PLANNING

If you are still drooling over catalogs offering colorful summer bulbs, make your decisions soon and send in your order. Make sure you have appropriate locations in your landscape to grow the bulbs you order. Although we all do it, wandering around your yard with a bag of bulbs looking for a place to plant them is not the best idea.

If you are unfamiliar with a bulb, get as much information as you can. Order just a few to see how well they grow for you before making a major investment.

Next month is a good time to divide most summer bulbs (excluding **Louisiana irises** and **calla lilies,** which are in active growth). It's not too soon to decide which bulbs you want to divide. Plan on what will be done with the extra bulbs, whether they'll be planted in other areas of the landscape, given to friends, or traded for other plants.

Early spring bulbs such as **crocus** and **early narcissus** generally bloom this month. Note the times when bulbs bloom in your yard for future reference.

 PLANTING

Resist spring-flowering bulbs that are put on clearance sale. They are unlikely to do well if planted this late. Exceptions are **amaryllis** and **paperwhite narcissus**. If you find bulbs in good shape that haven't started to sprout yet, they will usually bloom if they are planted now.

Most crocus are up by now.

Plant **gladiolus** bulbs starting in February, especially in the southern part of the state. For blooms in May and June, continue to plant groups of gladiolus at two-week intervals through early April. It is best for gladiolus to bloom before the intense heat arrives and thrips are a major problem, damaging flowers later in the summer.

Procrastinator's alert: Shame on you if you haven't planted your refrigerated bulbs by now. They may still do fine (as I have found from experience, shame on me!). Either plant the bulbs now or throw them away. You cannot hold them until next season for planting.

In mid- to late February, plant **caladium** bulbs in flats of sifted compost or potting soil to get a head start. Individual bulbs may also be planted in 4-inch pots.

1. Plant the bulbs about 1 inch deep and keep the soil moist.

2. Place the flats in a warm location.

3. When the bulbs sprout, move the flats to a sunny windowsill, greenhouse, or hotbed where they will receive plenty of light. Plant growing bulbs into the garden in April.

 CARE

A light application of an all-purpose granular fertilizer is appropriate for **Louisiana iris, calla lily,** and fall-planted spring-flowering bulbs that are in active growth. About 1 cup per 30 square feet of bed area is generally fine, but check the label and follow the manufacturer's recommendations for the product you choose.

If a severe freeze threatens, cut any open flowers from blooming bulbs and put them in vases inside, as they are likely to be damaged.

Continue to care for spring bulbs growing in containers outside. Bring them in on nights when temperatures below 28 degrees Fahrenheit are predicted.

Watch spring bulbs that have been overplanted with cool-season annuals. Make sure the bulbs are growing well, and trim the annuals slightly if needed to allow the bulbs room to grow.

Check summer bulbs you have dug up and stored. If any are sprouting, pot them and provide a bright, warm location for growth.

 WATERING

Natural rainfall is generally plentiful this month. If it is unusually dry, however, thoroughly water bulbs that are actively growing in beds, as needed. Water bulbs growing in containers regularly.

 PESTS

Stored **caladiums** occasionally become infested with mealybugs, which appear on bulbs and look like a white, cottony substance. Dip or spray the bulbs with Malathion or insecticidal soap for control. Another alternative is to plant them as directed under Planting. Mealybugs cannot survive underground.

Pest problems are unlikely at this time on bulbs that are growing outside. If the weather is mild, snails and slugs may be a problem. Control with baits or traps.

MARCH
BULBS, CORMS, RHIZOMES, & TUBERS

 PLANNING

The coldest weather has passed, and spring bulbs really begin to "wow" us this month. Don't forget to take notes on the performance of bulbs in your landscape. Take photos and/or videotape for an excellent record of how things looked. Do this about once a week during the prime blooming season.

Make decisions on where to plant summer-flowering bulbs. The location should provide the growing conditions needed for best performance. Decide if established plantings have grown beyond their designated spot. Plan to lift and divide them this month, or in early April at the latest.

Order summer-flowering bulbs from catalogs now so you will have them to plant in April (at the latest, early May). Don't let your enthusiasm lead you to order more bulbs than you have room to plant, and try to have a definite purpose and location in mind for the bulbs you order. Keep records of what you order and the name of the company. Check with your local nursery to find out what kind of summer bulbs they intend to carry and when they will be in.

Bearded iris benefit from being divided, and you get more plants too!

 PLANTING

Plant summer-flowering bulbs into the garden beginning this month.

- Plant at the proper depth and spacing (see chart on page 258) into beds or areas where 2 to 4 inches of organic matter and a general-purpose fertilizer have been incorporated into the soil.
- Water-in thoroughly and apply about 1 inch of mulch.
- Add more mulch to create a layer 2 or 3 inches thick as the bulbs grow. Don't be alarmed if they don't take off and grow rapidly right away. Most bulbs will wait until April or even early May to produce vigorous growth.

This is also the time to dig, divide, and transplant summer bulbs you already have in your garden. Most bulbs benefit from being divided every two to three years. If you noticed last year that the plants were growing but flower production was not what it had been, consider dividing the clump. Division is an excellent way to create new plants. Plant the extras in new areas of the landscape or share them with friends. Consider donating bulbs (especially if they are rare or unusual) to local public gardens, church fundraisers, or schools.

CARE

Remove faded flowers and developing seedpods from spring-flowering bulbs that are to be kept for bloom next year. Do not remove any of the green foliage, and fertilize them if you did not do so last month. Spring-flowering bulbs being grown as annuals can be pulled up and discarded any time after flowering. Chop them up and put them in your compost pile.

Remove any dead or cold-damaged foliage from summer bulbs before new shoots have grown substantially. This makes the job much easier.

Bring spring-flowering bulbs grown in pots indoors when buds show color. As wonderful as they are in the garden, spring bulbs enliven the indoors with their beauty and fragrance as few other flowers do.

WATERING

It is seldom necessary to do much watering of spring-flowering bulbs, but warm, dry weather occasionally makes it necessary. Pay attention to rainfall, and water plants if needed. Newly

planted or transplanted summer bulbs will need more attention. Their root systems are not yet well developed, and they will benefit from irrigation once or twice a week if rain does not occur. Continue to regularly water spring bulbs in containers as well as any summer bulbs you've started in pots or flats.

PESTS

Do not let weed problems get ahead of you. Mild temperatures will encourage weeds to grow. Many cool-season annual weeds like henbit, chickweed, and annual bluegrass are beginning to bloom and set seed now.

Don't let that happen! Remove weeds promptly and keep beds mulched.

Snails, slugs, and caterpillars may chew holes in leaves or flowers, but damage is generally minor. Control caterpillars with Bt or other pesticides. Use baits or traps for snails and slugs. If you see toads while working in the garden, remember that they are excellent predators of slugs.

APRIL
BULBS, CORMS, RHIZOMES, & TUBERS

 PLANNING

What a beautiful time of year! Louisianans often consider April and October two of our finest months. Mild temperatures and abundant flowers create a gardener's paradise.

Spring-flowering bulbs continue to grace flower beds with their charming beauty. Don't let the season pass without at least making some notes about the performance of the different bulbs you planted. Take pictures of or videotape your garden for a visual record words could never capture.

It is getting late for ordering summer bulbs, so get your order in as soon as possible. Don't rule out sites on the Internet when selecting and ordering bulbs. Many companies that send out catalogs also have a website where you can order bulbs directly, which can speed things up considerably. There is usually growing information as well as lists of other resources available at these sites. Local nurseries also have bulbs available. Many summer bulbs grow vigorously and make large plants, even during their first year. Keep in mind how tall the plants will grow, along with their projected spread, when planning on where to plant them.

Louisiana irises reach their peak this month. Now is a good time to assess color combinations and how crowded the plantings are becoming. Write down what you see, and this will help guide you when it is time to divide and transplant these irises in August and September.

 PLANTING

Check local nurseries and garden centers for summer-flowing bulbs. **Tuberous begonias** tempt many gardeners every year.

Unfortunately, they are poorly adapted to our hot summer conditions and performance is disappointing. Otherwise, as the summer bulb chart (page 258) indicates, there are lots of great bulbs to choose from.

It's time to plant bulbs you started in pots or flats. Bulbs such as **achimenes, arum, alpinia, bletilla, caladium, clivia, crinum, costus, curcuma, globba, hedychium, hymenocallis, kaempferia, oxalis,** and **walking iris** may be planted into shady beds that receive two to four hours of direct sunlight.

Good choices for sunnier areas (six to eight hours of direct sunlight) are **agapanthus, belamcanda, canna, crinum, crocosmia, dietes, eucomis, garlic chives, dahlia, gladiolus, gloriosa lily, habranthus, hymenocallis, iris, lilies, oxalis, tigridia, society garlic,** and **zephyranthes.**

Plant bulbs into well-prepared beds. If you are creating a new bed, follow these steps:

1. Remove any unwanted weeds or turf.

2. Turn the soil 8 to 10 inches deep.

3. Spread 2 to 4 inches of organic matter (compost, rotted manure, peat moss) over the area and sprinkle with 1/2 to 1 cup of general-purpose fertilizer per 30 square feet.

Caladium

4. Combine everything thoroughly, rake smooth, and plant.

When planting into established beds, it's generally sufficient to simply dig in organic matter and a little fertilizer prior to planting. Most summer bulbs are planted close to the soil surface (see summer bulb chart on page 258).

Now is the time to plant **amaryllis** bulbs that were purchased in the fall and potted for bloom over the winter. Choose a location that receives partial sun (four to six hours) and afternoon shade. They will bloom beautifully each April. You may also continue to grow them in a container.

HELPFUL HINTS

Summer bulbs make great candidates for container growing. A bronze-leaf **canna** surrounded by white **caladiums** in a large container is a real show-stopper. **Achimenes** are ideal in hanging baskets. Place containers on decks and patios and at entrances. An added benefit of growing summer bulbs in containers is the ability to move plants around to suit your changing needs or impulses.

Salvage potted **Easter lilies:**

1. As soon as the flowers fade, trim them off. Do not remove any of the green foliage.

2. Plant the **lilies** in a well-drained, prepared spot outside that receives morning sun and afternoon shade.

3. The bulbs will go dormant in mid- to late summer, and at that time the yellow foliage may be removed. Mark where the bulbs are located. Each year they will begin growth some time in October or November, grow very little over the winter, put on a burst of growth in spring, and bloom again in late April or early May.

They may skip the first year but should eventually begin to bloom again.

 CARE

Do not remove the foliage of repeat-blooming spring-flowering bulbs until it is mostly yellow.

 WATERING

April can be somewhat dry. It is especially important to keep newly planted summer-flowering bulbs watered as they grow and establish their root systems. Mulch beds to conserve moisture and reduce drying.

 PESTS

Warmer weather increases pest problems. Continue to keep bulb beds well mulched to prevent weed problems.

Caterpillars may be a problem, especially the highly destructive canna leaf roller. Treat with acephate, Sevin, or Bt as needed. Follow label directions carefully.

Cats are attracted to freshly turned soil and will use beds as litter boxes. Avoid this by mulching immediately, especially with pine straw. Use commercially available animal repellants in problem areas.

MAY

BULBS, CORMS, RHIZOMES, & TUBERS

PLANNING

The foliage of spring-flowering bulbs may be cut back, and most gardeners are quite ready to do so after watching it gradually flop over and turn yellow. Decide which repeat-blooming spring-flowering bulbs will be left in place and which will be lifted and stored. Lift bulbs from spots where you want to dig the bed and plant colorful summer bedding plants.

Do you need more summer bulbs? Continue to look at your landscape and flower beds for possible planting sites. Anticipate the abundant growth summer bulbs such as **canna, gingers,** and **crinum** can produce, and avoid overplanting. Procrastinator's alert: last chance to order summer bulbs from catalogs to plant no later than June.

PLANTING

Continue to add summer bulbs to the landscape. **Agapanthus** is in bloom this month, and the nurseries will have container-grown plants available. When planting summer bulbs that are growing in containers, follow these steps:

1. Remove the plant from the container.
2. Slightly loosen or untangle the roots if tightly packed.
3. Plant so that the top of the rootball is even with the soil in the bed.
4. Firm the soil around the roots with your hands.
5. Water-in to finish settling the soil around the roots and mulch.

I wish **dahlias** would flourish for us. I see the pictures in catalogs and I'm always impressed. Unfortunately, the fierce heat of typical Louisiana summers seems to be more than they can handle. Don't expect them to live up to their descriptions, but give them a try if you like. Your best success might be with the smaller-flowered types.

CARE

Summer bulbs are in vigorous growth now, and many have begun to bloom. In bloom this month are **shell gingers, hidden lily gingers, canna, crinum, clivia, dietes, agapanthus, gladiolus, gloriosa lily, Siberian iris, walking iris, peacock ginger, oxalis, sprekelia, society garlic,** and **rain lilies,** among others. The severity of the previous win-

ter has a substantial influence on how early summer bulbs begin to bloom. The colder the winter, the later flowers will appear.

As flowers fade, trim them off to keep the plant looking neat. With plantings such as **crinum** and **agapanthus,** flowers are produced on a thick stalk. When a stalk finishes flowering, cut it back to where it emerges from the leaves. Others, such as **gingers** and **canna,** produce flowers at the top of leafy shoots. Each shoot blooms only once. When the flowers have faded you can just cut off the dead flowers, leaving foliage, or cut the entire shoot back down to the ground.

Store spring-flowering bulbs in something that will "breathe." The net bags that onions are purchased in are ideal. Paper bags or cardboard boxes with ventilation holes also work well. Do not use plastic bags. Label the bulbs carefully to prevent confusion when it comes time to plant them next fall. Store the bulbs inside your house, where temperatures and humidity are lower. Avoid garages and sheds. Their high temperatures and humidity during the summer make for poor storage conditions.

 WATERING

As the weather gets hotter, bulbs will require regular watering if there is not enough rain. It is better to water thoroughly and occasionally than to water lightly and frequently. Use sprinklers or soaker hoses for proper watering. I like to stick my thumb over the end of the hose and wet everything down as much as the next gardener. But watering by hand, except for in the case of container-grown bulbs, does not provide adequate water when the garden is really dry.

 FERTILIZING

Fertilize bulbs growing in containers with your favorite soluble fertilizer, dissolved in water and applied as a solution, or use a slow-release fertilizer. Regularly fertilize bulbs in containers, as the constant watering they require rapidly washes out available nutrients. Bulbs growing in the ground can be fertilized regularly to encourage vigorous growth. It is easiest to use a slow-release fertilizer once in spring. You can also use a general-purpose granular fertilizer once every six to eight weeks. Follow package directions carefully.

 PESTS

One of the great things about growing summer bulbs is that they are not particularly afflicted by major pest problems. Aphids occasionally infest new growth and flowers buds. Spray as needed with insecticidal soap, SunSpray Ultra-Fine Oil (spray in early morning when temperatures are in the upper 70s or low 80s), or malathion. **Cannas** are affected the most, as they are prone to the dreaded canna leaf roller. This pest can be so invasive that some gardeners give up trying to grow cannas. Regular treatment with acephate (Orthene) can help. Acephate will also help control leaf miners that attack **irises.** Caterpillars will chew holes in the leaves. They are generally a minor problem on other summer bulbs and can be controlled by acephate, Sevin, or Bt. When using pesticides, always read the label carefully and follow directions concerning rates of application and safety precautions.

Agapanthus

JUNE
BULBS, CORMS, RHIZOMES, & TUBERS

 PLANNING

Catalogs for spring-flowering bulbs are arriving in the mail. There is no hurry to order, but it is impossible to resist looking through them as soon as they come in. As you flip through the catalogs, it wouldn't hurt to begin to make some notes on who has what on sale or what new bulbs you might want to try.

Bulbs in the landscape have pretty much filled in their spaces by now, and you can assess the need for any additional planting. Avoid overcrowding beds. Don't overlook the use of bulbs in containers on patios, decks, porches, and other outdoor areas.

 PLANTING

Most planting now should be done using actively growing bulbs in containers. This is the last month I would recommend planting unsprouted bulbs. Exceptions are fall-flowering bulbs such as **spider lily** (*Lycoris*)—also known as **hurricane lily** or **naked ladies**—and **fall crocus** (*Colchicum*).

Try one of the **ornamental sweet potatoes**. Three commonly available cultivars are 'Blackie,' 'Margarita,' and 'Tricolor,' also known as 'Pink Frost'. 'Blackie' produces very dark purple foliage on a vigorous vine suitable for hanging baskets, containers, ground cover, weaving among other plants in a bed, or training up a support. 'Margarita' has leaves that are a bright yellow-green and can be used in the same manner as 'Blackie.' 'Tricolor' is colorful but subtle, with light-green leaves generously splashed with white and pale pink. It is less vigorous than the other two and looks smashing in hanging baskets or around the edge of a large pot. All do well in full to partial sun, and thrive on summer heat.

 CARE

Seedpods will sometimes form after a summer bulb has bloomed. Unless you are breeding the plants or want to grow some from seeds, allowing the seedpods to develop is a waste of the plant's energy. Remove the old flower spikes or developing seedpods as soon as you notice them. Growing most summer bulbs from seed is not especially difficult, but it requires patience, as most will

not bloom until they are at least two to three years old.

There are very few summer bulbs that climb. Of those that do, most notable is the **gloriosa lily** and its relatives. Provide a support for them to climb on, such as strings, netting, lattice work, or a trellis. Many gardeners simply allow their gloriosa lilies to ramble and weave themselves among shrubs or other plants. They are not rampant growers, so this generally does not bother the other plants—and it looks great.

If needed, stake or otherwise support taller-growing summer bulbs such as the larger **gingers (alpinia, hedychium, curcuma), gladiolus, lilies,** and **dahlias.**

 WATERING

Typical summer weather patterns emerge in June. That means hot days, warm nights, and frequent afternoon rains interspersed with dry periods. Rainfall can be very unreliable. It is not unusual for heavy rain to occur in one location and not at all a few miles away. Watch the rainfall your garden receives and water as needed.

Bulbs growing in containers and hanging baskets generally need to be watered every day.

Do not allow them to wilt before watering. This can lead to scorched leaf edges and bud drop.

FERTILIZING

Continue to apply soluble fertilizers regularly to container plantings, unless you used a slow-release fertilizer earlier.

Fertilize actively growing bulbs in garden beds with a general-purpose granular fertilizer every six to eight weeks. If the bulbs are growing well, additional fertilizer is optional.

PESTS

Continue to watch for signs of damage from chewing insects such as caterpillars. Generally, damage is slight and control is not necessary. Otherwise, treat with Sevin, Bt, or acephate (Orthene). Acephate will also control sucking insects such as aphids and leaf hoppers. Thrips may be a problem on **gladiolus.** Spray once a week with acephate as spikes begin to appear.

Weeds grow like crazy this time of year, especially while frequent afternoon showers are occurring. Here are some tips for controlling them:

• Keep beds well mulched and pull weeds promptly when they appear.

• Dig up the roots, bulbs, or rhizomes of tough perennial weeds such as torpedograss, bermudagrass, and nutgrass.

• If you are careful to spray only the foliage of the weeds without getting any on the foliage of nearby desirable plants, you can use systemic herbicides such as glyphosate.

Aphids and leaf hoppers may be a threat this month; keep your eyes open.

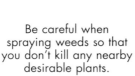

Be careful when spraying weeds so that you don't kill any nearby desirable plants.

JULY
BULBS, CORMS, RHIZOMES, & TUBERS

PLANNING

Heat and humidity make gardening uncomfortable, to say the least. Plan on doing most of your garden chores early in the morning or late in the afternoon.

Continue to take notes and keep records on the growth and performance of your bulbs. It is especially important to note when bulbs bloomed, how long they stayed in bloom, major insect or disease problems, and comments on their overall appearance. Perhaps you will decide to move them to a different location next year or divide them. Comments jotted down now can help with those decisions later on. It is just as—or perhaps even more—important to record failures. Those who don't remember mistakes are bound to repeat them.

An easy record-keeping technique is to have a calendar on hand dedicated to the garden. It should have large squares for writing comments. It's easy to flip to the appropriate day and make an entry such as "**Philippine lily** showing buds today," or "slug damage bad on **peacock ginger**."

PLANTING

You can still purchase and plant summer bulbs growing in containers. Check local nurseries for new types of **ginger**. **Peacock ginger** is gaining in popularity as a substitute for **hostas** in shady areas. The large leaves lie close to the ground and are richly patterned in green, dark green, silver, and bronze. There are some with creamy-white variegation as well. Lavender flowers the size of a quarter or larger nestle among the foliage all summer. Plant gingers in beds generously amended with organic matter, and keep them well watered and mulched during the summer.

CARE

Tropical bulbs like **achimenes, crinum, ginger, gloriosa lily, oxalis, caladium,** and **society garlic** live it up in the midsummer heat. They certainly enjoy it more than we do. Perhaps you can look out a window from your air-conditioned house and appreciate the show.

Continue to deadhead and groom bulbs. Diseased, insect-damaged, brown, or yellow leaves do not contribute to the appearance of the plant and should be regularly removed. Avoid cutting off any healthy foliage unless absolutely necessary (to relieve a crowded situation, for instance).

Caladiums are grown for their attractive foliage but do send up unusual looking flowers. These contribute little to the overall appearance of the plants and should be removed promptly to encourage the bulbs to put more effort into producing leaves.

Bulbs growing in containers may have outgrown their pots by midsummer. Repot into larger containers if necessary. Since the roots will be disturbed, keep the newly repotted bulbs in a shady area for several days to recover before moving them back into the sun.

When **gladiolus** foliage has turned mostly brown, lift the bulbs and lay them in an out-of-the-way area to dry. Cut off foliage when it is completely dry, and break off the shriveled old bulb from the base. Store in paper bags, cardboard boxes, or net bags. Try cutting back the foliage, marking the spot, and leaving them in place if you like. They will often return if the bed is well drained.

 ## WATERING

Typically, summer weather tends to be too wet or too dry. Near-daily afternoon showers are not unusual, especially in coastal areas. North Louisiana often bakes in hot, dry conditions. Under the circumstances, the best we can do is watch the weather and water as needed. If weather conditions are very wet, consider pulling back mulch from plants to allow the soil to dry out. Water thoroughly and deeply twice a week if weather conditions are very dry.

Check bulbs growing in containers daily since they dry out rapidly in the heat.

 ## FERTILIZING

In particular, watch the fertilizer needs of container bulbs. If the constant need to apply soluble fertilizer every two weeks is too much of a bother, apply a slow-release fertilizer. Such a fertilizer releases nutrients slowly over the entire growing season with one application. Follow label directions concerning the amount to use per pot.

 ## PESTS

Leaf spots caused by fungus diseases are an occasional problem on a variety of bulbs when the weather turns wet. Broad-spectrum fungicides such as chlorothalonil (Daconil) or thiophanate methyl will help control these problems should they occur, but it's rarely necessary to apply them.

Get ready for snails and slugs if the weather turns rainy. They just love to eat low-growing plants in shady areas. Apply iron phosphate baits according to label directions. Beer traps are an effective way to catch these slimy critters that chew holes in leaves and flowers. Here's how to do it:

• In the early evening, sink small plastic bowls up to their rim in areas of the garden where snails and slugs are a problem.

• Fill the bowls halfway with fresh beer. The brand does not matter. Snails and slugs are attracted by the yeasty smell of

Be prepared to spray a fungicide if needed.

the beer and crawl down into the bowl. Once in the bowl, the beer washes off their slimy coating and they can't crawl back out.

• Dump out the trap the next morning.

• Continue to set out traps until you catch few or no snails and slugs.

AUGUST
BULBS, CORMS, RHIZOMES, & TUBERS

PLANNING

Since it's too hot to enjoy working in the garden, get out those spring bulb catalogs. Now is the time to start looking through them for what you want to order. Just looking at those pictures of tulip fields and beds of daffodils can almost convince you that it's not 95 or 100 degrees outside.

Here is where those notes, pictures, and videos you took last spring will be useful. Review what worked and what didn't. Don't get stuck in a rut and do exactly the same thing every year. But on the other hand, if it ain't broke, don't fix it.

If you are wishing you had taken more careful notes in the spring, let that inspire you to do a good job now while the summer bulbs are growing in the garden.

PLANTING

Finish planting container-grown summer bulbs this month, or early next month at the latest. Most summer bulbs are left in the ground over winter and need time to become well established before cold weather arrives.

Last chance to plant dormant bulbs of late summer- and fall-blooming **lycoris** and **fall crocus** (*Colchicum*). They begin to bloom next month.

CARE

Thin out the shoots of **cannas** and **gingers (hedychium, costus, globba, zingiber)** if the clumps are becoming overly thick. Each shoot produces only one spike of flowers, so you can cut any shoots that have already bloomed to the ground. This will make room for fresh, new shoots to grow and bloom. These plants will continue to grow new shoots and bloom until October or November.

One of the most magnificent and stately of the summer bulbs is the **Philippine** or **Formosa lily** (*Lilium formosanum*). Blooming sometime between July and early September, the plants grow 4 to 6 feet tall and produce clusters of large, white trumpets at the top. An established clump produces several flowering stems. Be ready to stake them as the heavy load of buds and flowers form. Also blooming in late summer is the brown-spotted orange **tiger lily** (*Lilum lancifolium*), which grows to about 4 feet.

Dig up, divide, and transplant **Louisiana iris, Easter lily,** and **calla lily** this month.

WATERING

Typically, summer weather tends to be too wet or too dry. Almost daily afternoon showers are not unusual, especially in coastal areas. North Louisiana often bakes in hot, dry conditions. Under the circumstances, the best we can do is watch the weather and water as needed. If weather conditions are very wet, consider pulling back mulch from plants to allow the soil to dry out. If weather conditions are very dry, water thoroughly and deeply twice a week.

Remember to check bulbs growing in containers daily since they dry out rapidly in the heat.

FERTILIZING

Make your last application of granular fertilizer to actively growing bulbs in the ground this month. These fertilizers will continue to feed plantings until the end of October when it is time for bulbs to start slowing down.

spray the plants with SunSpray Ultra-Fine Oil, insecticidal soap, or Malathion. Get under the leaves with the spray.

Continue to watch for and control caterpillars with Sevin, Bt, or acephate (Orthene). Prune off badly damaged foliage.

Don't let the summer heat keep you from controlling weeds. Work in shady areas during the day, or work during early morning or late evening. If you have maintained a good layer of mulch in beds, weed problems should be minimal. Weedy vines such as **bindweed, cayratia, cat's claw, poison ivy,** and **Virginia creeper** can cover a planting in no time. Be very aggressive and persistent when you encounter these weedy vines. When possible, use systemic herbicides such as glyphosate (Roundup) or Finale. Dig out the vine, root and all, when herbicide use is impractical.

There are many types of weeding tools; having several will be helpful.

PESTS

Spider mites cause **oxalis** foliage to look faded and unhealthy, eventually leading to brown edges. If the condition of the foliage is already bad, cut all of the leaves back to ground level. The new growth will come out healthy, and the bulbs don't mind regrowing new foliage. If symptoms begin to appear again,

September
BULBS, CORMS, RHIZOMES, & TUBERS

 PLANNING

Okay, it's time to finalize those spring bulb ideas and send off your orders. Bulbs should arrive for planting in October or November. Don't let Northern information confuse you. September days frequently go above 90 degrees Fahrenheit, and no one with good sense goes out to plant bulbs this month. Bulbs are often available at local nurseries now. You can go ahead and purchase them, but there is no hurry to plant them.

Decide on the kind, color, quantity, and location of the spring bulbs you want to plant. Since most provide only one season of bloom, it makes better sense economically to use them to embellish, rather than to produce lavish displays.

It's generally better not to buy bulbs in mixed colors, as the colors included often clash. Buy individual colors of your choice, then combine them in groups or masses. I have noticed, however, that bulb suppliers are starting to create special blends of bulbs with colors carefully chosen to look good together. These might be more acceptable than mixes sold in the past.

Tulips and **hyacinths** must be stored in paper or net bags (clearly labeled!) in the lower drawers of a refrigerator for at least six to eight weeks before planting in late December through early January. Make sure you will have enough refrigerator room for the number of bulbs you purchase.

 PLANTING

Not much is going on this month. It's too late to plant most summer bulbs unless you really have to, and it's too early to plant spring bulbs.

It is time to divide and transplant **Louisiana iris, Easter lily,** and **calla lily,** as they are dormant at this time. Louisiana irises generally do best when divided every three years or so. Here's how to do it:

1. Lift out the iris clumps and set aside.

2. While the irises are out of the ground, rework the bed, adding generous amounts of organic matter and a sprinkling of general-purpose fertilizer.

3. Shake off the soil and study the rhizomes. Cut off 6- to 8-inch sections of rhizomes with a fan of leaves at the end. These will be planted. The older back rhizomes with no growing points can be discarded.

4. Plant the rhizomes just below the soil surface with the fan of leaves pointed in the direction you want the plant to grow. Space rhizomes at least one foot apart. Mulch the bed and water thoroughly.

WATERING

Cool fronts may begin to make their way into the state sometime this month. The relief from the heat is incredibly welcome. Along with the fronts, we often receive good, drenching rains. None of this is guaranteed, however. Water as needed, especially if the weather is hot. Water newly divided and transplanted **Louisiana irises** generously and often.

Achimenes in containers and in the garden may begin to lose steam this month. When this occurs, those in containers should be given less water. As we move into late October, dry them out, cut off the brown foliage, and store them for the winter. Mark the location of those growing in the ground.

PESTS

Pests that have been a problem all summer are still around, often in greater numbers after a summer of breeding. Don't let your guard down now. Continue to watch for and control pests as they appear.

A display of Louisiana iris.

OCTOBER
BULBS, CORMS, RHIZOMES, & TUBERS

 PLANNING

Visions of spring bulbs should be dancing in your head. This is absolutely, positively the last opportunity to mail-order spring bulbs, and you should do it early this month. Check with the supplier and make sure they can deliver the bulbs by mid-November. This is particularly important for **tulips** and **hyacinths**. Other bulbs can be planted as late as early December with good results. Since tulips and hyacinths need to be refrigerated for at least six to eight weeks before planting in late December to early January, they must go into the refrigerator no later than late November.

It is best to have a specific purpose and location in mind when ordering each kind of bulb you choose. The size of an area to be planted with a particular type of bulb, for example, will determine how many bulbs you need. Choose colors and heights carefully based on where they will be planted and what will be blooming alongside them. There will always be a few "I've-just-got-to-try-this" bulbs in your order. That's fine, just don't base all of your plans on sentiments like: "Oh, I'll find some place in the garden for the bulbs when the time comes to plant them."

It helps to wander about the garden and carefully consider where bulbs would make an effective display in the landscape. Take the catalogs outside with you, and as you walk through the landscape, try to imagine where the bulbs that have caught your eye would look perfect. Make sketches, notes, and diagrams of your ideas so that when it is time to plant you will remember what you had in mind when you sent off the order.

Local nurseries and garden centers can also be a good source for spring bulbs, and you should take advantage of whatever they have available. Mail-order sources, however, will provide you with a far greater selection.

 PLANTING

If patience is a virtue, gardeners must be a particularly praiseworthy group. Those who demand instant gratification will find themselves often frustrated. Indeed, gardeners frequently play the role of time travelers in their minds—imagining some glorious future when a planting bursts into flowers or a young tree provides needed shade.

Nothing illustrates this better than planting spring-flowering bulbs. Here, the impatient gardener has no choice. The bulbs we purchase and plant in October and November will not bloom until spring. But it is worth the wait.

All bulbs except **tulips** and **hyacinths** may be planted into the garden this month. Planting depth and spacing are important. Check the Spring Bulb Chart (on page 257) for recommendations. Generally, we plant bulbs shallower than is recommended for the North, so don't

Magic lily (*Lycoris*)

be confused if the recommended depths do not agree with other information you may have seen.

CARE

Caladiums may be dug up in early to mid-October. Don't wait until all of the foliage is dead. When many of the leaves have fallen over and the plants are looking decidedly "tired," it's time to lift them. Leave the foliage attached and lay them in an out-of-the-way area to dry. When the foliage is dry and papery, it will detach from the bulb with a gentle tug. Brush off any dirt clods clinging to the bulbs, and store them in a frost-free location in cardboard boxes, paper bags, or net bags. You may also choose to leave the bulbs in place if the bed space will not be needed for other plantings. If the bed is well drained and the bulbs are mulched, many gardeners find that they return reliably.

Daytime highs can still reach 90 degrees Fahrenheit this month, though 80s and 70s are typical. The nights are cooler, but many summer bulbs are still going strong. Watch for the foliage on **spider lilies** to appear after they finish blooming. It is important not to cut the foliage once it appears.

WATERING

October is often one of our drier months, so even though the weather may be cooler, watch the rainfall and water as necessary. **Louisiana irises, Easter lilies,** and **calla lilies** are waking up and would appreciate some water if the weather is dry.

FERTILIZING

Add some fertilizer when preparing areas for planting bulbs. Summer bulbs may still be growing, but colder weather is in the not-too-distant future. None of them should be fertilized now. Bulbs that are beginning active growth, such as **Louisiana iris, calla,** and **spider lily** (*Lycoris*), can be fertilized lightly now.

PESTS

Less stressful weather conditions contribute to a general reduction in pest problems. Fortunately, bulbs are not particularly susceptible to major insect or disease problems when grown properly.

Weeds, on the other hand, will flourish in any cultivated situation, no matter what type of plants are being grown. In October, the summer weeds are still growing and the cool-season weeds begin to show up. The use of preemergence herbicides is beneficial this month. These herbicides are applied to weed-free beds in order to prevent the growth of new weeds from seeds. Applied this month, they can reduce or prevent the appearance of such cool-season annual weeds as henbit, chickweed, annual bluegrass, and others. Make sure the product you choose is safe to use around your ornamentals, and follow label directions carefully.

NOVEMBER
BULBS, CORMS, RHIZOMES, & TUBERS

PLANNING

As the warm weather subsides, keep up with notes and records on the performance of the summer bulbs in your garden. I hope you took lots of pictures of your garden and videotaped it. Sometimes we forget just how great a bed or area of the landscape looked.

Decide now if you would like to grow some of your spring bulbs in containers. Most spring bulbs are readily grown in containers, and it is not that difficult. This practice is not the same as "forcing bulbs," which is inducing them to bloom earlier than their normal season. Spring bulbs bloom relatively early in Louisiana anyway, and bulbs that are prepared and potted bloom concurrently with the same bulbs that were planted in the ground.

PLANTING

You should finish planting your spring bulbs this month. Wrap up by early December at the latest. You can plant low-growing cool-season annuals such as **alyssum, violas,** or **pansies** over the bulbs. They will provide flowers before, during, and after the bulbs bloom.

Remember that **tulips** and **hyacinths** go into paper or net bags in the lower drawers of your refrigerator. (Be sure to label them: NOT TO BE EATEN.) This seemingly odd practice is necessary because our winters are not cold enough long enough to satisfy the chilling requirements of the bulbs. Without this cold treatment, the bulbs will not bloom properly. Do not place apples, pears, or other fruit in the same drawer with the bulbs. Ripening fruit gives off ethylene gas, which can cause the bulbs to bloom abnormally (too short, blasted buds, etc.). Plant in late December or early January. Any spring bulb you would like to grow in containers should be handled in the same way.

Dormant **amaryllis** bulbs become available in the fall, but they should not be planted into the garden now as the flowers could be damaged by cold weather.

1. Plant amaryllis bulbs into pots using a well-drained potting soil. The bulb's neck should be above the soil's surface. Use a pot that is large enough so that there is a 1-inch clearance between the pot rim and the bulb. Clay or plastic pots may be used, but since a blooming amaryllis can be somewhat top-heavy, clay pots provide a little more stability. You can also buy amaryllis bulbs pre-planted.

2. Place the pot in a sunny window (the more sun, the better) and keep the soil evenly moist.

3. When the flower stalk begins to emerge (some bulbs will produce two), rotate the pot $1/2$ turn every few days so it will grow straight. If you provide your amaryllis with too little light, the flower stalk will grow excessively tall and may even fall over. Flowering generally occurs in December or early January from bulbs planted now.

Narcissus 'Soleil d'Or'

garden in April so they will get into the normal cycle of blooming in April each year.

Paperwhite narcissus (and other Tazetta narcissus, such as 'Soleil d'Or') may be planted in pots this month and are easily grown for winter bloom as well.

 CARE

Some summer bulbs have gone dormant, some are winding down, and some are still growing, especially in south Louisiana. In north Louisiana, the first freezes often occur in November, putting an end to the summer bulb season. Cut back the foliage that has browned, and mark the locations of dormant summer bulbs to avoid digging into them later on. After you cut them back, mulch tropical bulbs with 4 to 6 inches of leaves or pine straw to protect them from winter cold.

Spring bulbs require no special care now.

Sometime after the flower stalk has emerged, strap-shaped leaves will grow from the top of the bulb. After the flowers have faded, cut the stalk at the point where it emerges from the bulb, but do not cut any foliage. Keep the plant inside and continue to provide plenty of light or the leaves will be weak. Water regularly when the soil begins to feel dry. It is not really necessary to fertilize your **amaryllis** during this time. Plant bulbs into the

DECEMBER
BULBS, CORMS, RHIZOMES, & TUBERS

 PLANNING

Go over your notes on your spring bulb plantings. Make sure everything has gone according to plan. (You did have a plan, didn't you?) If you simply have to, you may still make some final additions to your bulb plantings early this month. This is a busy time of year, so it's best to have most of the work done by now.

Is it already time to think about summer bulb planting for next spring? There is no hurry, but catalogs do start arriving this month. Put them where you can find them later. When the holiday frenzy is over in January, pull them out and start to dream.

Check on stored bulbs periodically; if you find any signs of rot, cut it out.

HELPFUL HINTS

Review the list of summer bulbs at the beginning of this chapter. I'll bet you aren't familiar with all of them. During a quiet winter day when the weather is too rough to go out and work in the garden, try to find out more about the bulbs by looking them up in one of your references (or check one out at the library). Talk to some friends to see if they have grown any of them successfully. You are sure to discover some wonderful new plants to excite you and your garden next summer.

 PLANTING

Begin planting **tulips** and **hyacinths** into the garden in the later part of this month, or early January. You may also begin potting up bulbs to grow in containers at that time. See January (page 44) for how to do it.

Continue to plant **amaryllis** bulbs. **Paperwhite narcissus** can also be planted in pots and easily grown for winter bloom. Plant the bulbs with their pointed ends exposed, in pots of well-drained potting soil. Keep the pots in a sunny, cool location (outside if the weather is mild). If grown in a warm location or one with too little light, the leaves and flower stalks will be tall and tend flop over. Paperwhites may also

be grown in bowls of pebbles and water. Amaryllis and paperwhites in bloom make wonderful holiday gifts.

 CARE

There is not much to do for bulbs planted in the garden. Keep beds mulched and weed free. Provide proper light and water to bulbs growing in containers indoors. Do not allow the soil to dry out in pots of **tulips, hyacinths,** and other spring-flowering bulbs that are outside forming roots.

Check on any stored summer bulbs occasionally to make sure they are fine.

HERBS & VEGETABLES

There is something satisfying about putting fresh homegrown vegetables on the table—food that you actually grew yourself. Gardening, after all, was orignally done in response to needs for food, seasonings, and medicines.

People decide to grow vegetables for various reasons. For many, it is a way to have the freshest possible produce. Other gardeners crave types of vegetables or varieties that are not available at the local supermarket. Some want control over what pesticides, if any, are used on the produce they eat. And, although economy is usually not the main reason these days, the harvest from the home garden can save money.

Thanks to the mild winters of our region, Louisiana gardeners can harvest something from their vegetable and herb gardens 365 days of the year. All that is needed is some planning, along with awareness of the many different types of vegetables and herbs we can grow throughout the year.

Vegetable and herb gardening seasons can be divided roughly into the cool season and the warm season, but the intensely hot summer presents its own challenges. Most vegetables grow, produce, and die within their particular season. There are several herbs that live for one season and finish, but there are also many perennial herbs. There are a few perennial vegetables that are year-round residents of the garden, including asparagus, horseradish, and, in the southern part of the state, mirlitons.

Vegetable gardeners must be attuned to the seasons and observe the proper planting times for

vegetables. Planting times relate to a variety of factors, temperature being a major one. Cool-season vegetables are grown from August to May. They need cooler temperatures to perform their best and are able to tolerate the below-freezing temperatures of the winter season.

Warm-season vegetables cannot experience frost without significant injury or death. They are grown from a period that covers March through November, divided up into the spring planting season, the summer planting season, and the fall planting season. Only certain heat-tolerant vegetables such as okra, Southern peas, hot pepper, and eggplant remain productive in the extremely hot months of June, July, and August. Most spring-planted vegetables can be planted again in August and September for fall production.

Planting dates can vary by two to four weeks from northern Louisiana to southern Louisiana. When reading the Vegetable information on pages 359–360, you will notice that specific planting dates are not given. Instead, an appropriate planting period indicates when a vegetable is best planted. North Louisiana gardeners will generally want to avoid the earliest dates given for spring planting and plant earlier than the latest dates given for fall planting. South Louisiana gardeners would plant earlier in the spring and later in the fall. For average first and last frost dates, see page 8 of the Introduction.

Although herb gardens also have their seasons, planting times are not as critical as they are for vegetables. Herbs are a far more diverse group that includes trees, shrubs, herbaceous perennials, bulbs, warm-season annuals and cool-season annuals. Several that are easily grown, reliable perennials in the northern United States have difficulty with our hot, humid, and often wet summers. Included in this group are sage, the thymes, French tarragon, and the lavenders.

PLANNING THE VEGETABLE GARDEN

Choose a sunny, well-drained spot. Most vegetables, particularly those grown for their fruit or seeds (tomato, corn, cucumber, beans) need at least eight hours of direct sun for best production. Vegetables grown for their roots (carrot, turnip, radish) can do well with about six hours of direct sun. Most leafy crops (mustard, lettuce, chard, cabbage) can be productive with as little as four hours of direct sun. Still, all vegetables do their best with full sun.

Convenience in relation to the house is nice, but a nearby source of water is a much more important consideration, since irrigation will be necessary. Vegetable gardens can be beautiful at certain times, but the appearance is variable with the seasons and harvesting. I've known gardeners who were reluctant to harvest vegetables because they did not want to ruin the appearance of the garden! For that reason, these gardens are generally not located in a prominent spot in the landscape, if such is possible.

Think carefully about the size of the garden. If you are new to vegetable gardening, start off small and gradually enlarge the garden as you become more familiar with the amount of work involved. Consider the size of your family and the space you have available, too. Whether to plant in traditional raised rows or raised beds is another decision to be made.

Next, decide on the vegetables you want to grow. Make a list of your family's favorites. The size of the garden is also a factor. Some large-growing vegetables such as corn, okra, pumpkins, and brussels sprouts occupy a lot of room and would not be as suitable for smaller gardens.

Choose vegetable varieties recommended for growing in Louisiana. Check with your local parish office of the Louisiana Cooperative Extension Service, a branch of the Louisiana State University Agricultural Center. Free copies of the *Louisiana*

Vegetable Planting Guide are available. The *Guide* lists the current variety recommendations based on trials done here in Louisiana. There are tons of available varieties not on the lists which may do very well here but have never been tested. Be as adventurous as you like, but rely on tested varieties for your main plantings.

At this point it helps to draw up a diagram of the garden you're planning. Use graph paper and draw to scale if possible. Make several photocopies of the original and use them to draw in the vegetables you intend to grow—where they will be located in the garden and how much space will be devoted to each crop.

SOIL PREPARATION

Soil preparation is critical to successful vegetable gardening.

Remove any unwanted weeds that may have grown up between crops, or lawn grass in a new bed. The plants may be physically removed by pulling or digging them out. Make sure you get the roots. You may also use glyphosate to kill the weeds or lawn grass, and remove or turn under the dead weeds. Do not turn under living weeds or lawn grass.

Use a shovel or garden fork to turn the soil 8 to 10 inches deep.

Spread a layer of organic matter such as compost, rotted leaves, rotted manure, or peat moss 2 to 4 inches thick over the bed. If a soil test indicates the need for lime, sprinkle the appropriate amount over the organic matter. Sprinkle a general-purpose fertilizer over the bed, such as 8-8-8 (1 cup per 30 square feet), or if your soil is high in phosphorus, 15-5-10 ($^1/_2$ cup per 30 square feet).

Thoroughly incorporate the amendments into the upper 8 to 10 inches of soil. Rake the bed smooth and you are ready to shape the raised rows.

Using a hoe or shovel, push soil out of the walkways and up onto the area where the vegetables will be grown. Form a raised row about 3 feet across and 8 to 12 inches high.

Vegetables can also be grown in raised beds. Form the bed's edges with pressure-treated 1-by-8-inch or 1-by-12-inch boards, landscape timbers, molded plastic, cinder blocks, or any other material you feel is suitable. Turn over the soil in the bottom, fill with a high-quality garden soil mix, and then plant.

PLANTING

Vegetables are usually planted using transplants, or by direct-seeding into the garden. Transplants are used for those vegetables that are not easily direct-seeded or for those that need to be started early in a protected environment before planting later into the garden. Most vegetable gardeners purchase their transplants from local nurseries, but you can start your own. They should be planted into the garden according to their recommended spacing.

In direct-seeding vegetables, seeds are planted two to three times thicker than necessary for the number of plants needed. This ensures a good stand of seedlings. Once the seedlings are up and growing, the extras are pinched off with the thumb and forefinger, leaving behind seedlings at the proper spacing.

PEST CONTROL

Pest control is an absolute necessity when it comes to vegetable gardening, especially during the late spring, summer, and fall growing seasons. Even organic gardeners may occasionally need to resort to pesticides that meet the standards of organic farming.

Before using any pesticide, make sure you have properly identified the pest (insect, mite, fungus, bacteria). Help is available from your parish office of the Louisiana Cooperative Extension Service, a branch of the Louisiana State University Agricultural Center, or from your local nursery staff.

CHAPTER THREE

WEEDS

The best defense against weeds is to take care of any problems promptly and keep your beds well mulched.

Glyphosate may be used to kill weeds in a bed prior to planting and is particularly useful in controlling perennial weeds such as bermudagrass, Johnsongrass, nutgrass, torpedograss, buttonweed, and oxalis. Glyphosate is not intended for use in beds where vegetables are growing.

Preemergence herbicides are applied to weed-free soil for suppressing the growth of weed seeds. Some are labeled for use around vegetables and can be helpful in weed control. Read labels carefully before use, and remember that most cannot be used in an area that is to be or has been direct-seeded.

Keep beds mulched with 2 to 4 inches of leaves, dry grass clippings, or pine straw. Black plastic, newspaper, and other materials are also useful as mulch. Promptly pull or hoe any weeds that appear.

INSECTS

There are lots of bugs that would just love to eat your vegetables before you get a chance to harvest them. The judicious use of insecticides, along with cultural techniques (such as planting early in the season, and handpicking), will generally prevent major outbreaks. When choosing to use pesticides, always read the label carefully and follow directions exactly.

Major categories of insect pests include:

Caterpillars: control with Bt, carbaryl (Sevin), or a variety of other insecticides.

Aphids: control with insecticidal soap, strong spray of water, oil sprays (UltraFine Oil), or insecticides such as Malathion.

Spider mites: though not technically insects, they are generally grouped with them for pest control purposes. Control is the same as for aphids, with the addition of miticides such as Kelthane and sulfur.

Stinkbugs: control with carbaryl (Sevin), endosulfan (Thiodan), or rotonone plus pyrethrins.

Whiteflies: control with oil sprays (UltraFine Oil), Malathion, or pyrethrins plus insecticidal soap.

Beetles: control with carbaryl (Sevin), endosulfan (Thiodan), or rotonone plus pyrethrins.

OTHER PESTS

Control nematodes by rotating crops, adding organic matter whenever beds are being prepared, and planting nematode-resistant vegetable cultivars when available.

Snails and slugs chew holes in the leaves of many vegetables, especially leafy crops grown during the cool season. Baits containing iron phosphate are labeled for use around food crops. Various traps and barriers can also be helpful.

DISEASES

Fungi cause the majority of vegetable diseases, although viruses and bacteria are also problems in the vegetable garden. Rotate crops as much as possible, plant at the appropriate times, space plants properly for air circulation and keep beds mulched to keep soil-borne diseases from splashing up onto vegetables.

Broad-spectrum fungicides used in the vegetable garden include chlorothalonil (Daconil), benomyl, sulfur, maneb, mancozeb, and copper fungicides (tribasic copper sulfate, liquid copper). Controlling diseases is different from controlling insects. To be effective, fungicides must be used earlier, before much damage occurs, and then regularly after.

There is no cure for viral infections. Since most are spread by insects, insect control can help. Weeds may serve as alternate hosts, so keep surrounding areas weed free. Pull up and dispose of infected plants promptly to prevent spread to healthy plants.

CHAPTER THREE

PLANNING THE HERB GARDEN

Most gardeners grow herbs for culinary uses—these are the herbs I will emphasize. Unlike vegetables, which require relatively large plantings in order to produce sufficient harvest, a single herb plant will often provide enough for a gardener's needs. Herbs may be grown in the vegetable garden, in their own area, or even among landscape plantings. Since few plants are needed, herbs are also excellent when grown in containers.

Most herbs require direct sun at least four to six hours a day (six to eight hours is best) and excellent drainage. Use raised beds or containers if drainage in your yard is questionable. Locate your herb-growing area as close to the kitchen as possible so the herbs are convenient to use while you are cooking. Those you choose to grow should initially be those you are familiar with and like to use in cooking.

PLANTING

Prepare the planting area as for vegetables. Containers are also excellent for growing herbs. Because relatively few plants are needed, most herb gardeners buy transplants of the herbs they intend to grow. You may also plant seeds or raise your own transplants.

For growing purposes, herbs can be loosely grouped into cool- and warm-season annuals that live for one season and then die, and perennials, which live for several years.

Cool-season annuals should be seeded or transplanted between September and February and include borage, celery, chervil, cilantro/coriander, dill, fennel, and parsley.

Warm-season annuals should be seeded or transplanted in March through August and include basil, perilla, sesame, and summer savory.

Perennial herbs that grow well in Louisiana include bay, lemongrass, scented geraniums, beebalm, burnet, catnip, chives, garlic chives, horseradish, Mexican tarragon, mints, lemon balm, oregano, pennyroyal, rosemary, sage, sorrel, marjoram, thyme, and winter savory.

Thyme, sage, catnip, and scented geraniums need good drainage and are often more successful when grown in containers. Even then, they may succumb to root and stem rots in the hot, wet, late-summer season. Several perennial herbs cannot tolerate our summers at all, including French tarragon, feverfew, lavender, and chamomile. They are generally grown as cool-season annuals, planted in fall, and harvested in spring and early summer, although a few gardeners have some success with lavenders.

HARVESTING HERBS

Harvest herbs frequently and regularly, being careful not to deplete all of the plant's foliage. Generally, take no more than 1/3 of the total foliage at any one time. Herbs are more attractive and compact in size when harvested regularly.

PEST CONTROL

Although they have a reputation for being resistant to attack from insects, herbs are occasionally damaged by various bugs. Diseases can be a problem during the hot summer months, especially during rainy periods.

Few pesticides have been labeled for use on herbs. Insecticidal soaps and UltraFine Oil will control mites and most sucking insects such as aphids and leaf hoppers. Use Bt for caterpillars. Remember, herbs are generally chopped and added to dishes before cooking. No one will know if there were a few holes in the leaves. For disease control, make sure herbs are planted in well-drained beds, and space them properly for good air circulation. Plant herbs according to the proper season and choose those that grow well in Louisiana. A mulch of light pebbles or marble chips seems to help herbs such as rosemary, thyme, sage, oregano, and catnip avoid stem and crown rots.

JANUARY
HERBS & VEGETABLES

 PLANNING

Dreaming about juicy vine-ripened **tomatoes**? Transplants will not become available in local nurseries until March. But if you want to grow your own transplants, plan on getting seeds planted this month. Look through seed catalogs and you will see a huge number of tomato varieties available. Try a few new types, but plan on using tried-and-true varieties such as 'Celebrity', 'Mountain Pride', 'Better Boy', 'Super Fantastic', and 'Cherry Grande' for your main crop.

While looking through the seed catalogs, think about other vegetables you want to plant in the late winter and spring garden. It is not too early to plan the spring garden. Review your records of last year's garden, choose the vegetables and varieties you want to grow this year, and order your seeds. Your local office of the Louisiana Cooperative Extension Service can provide you with a list of recommended varieties.

Order seeds for such cool-season vegetables as **radish, beets, broccoli, cabbage, spinach, lettuce,** and others. There is still time to get them in for planting. Or buy seeds at local stores.

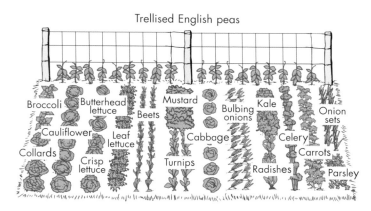
Trellised English peas

Plan your spring garden.

Some vegetables to plant in January: **beets, broccoli, cabbage, carrots, cauliflower, celery⁺, Chinese cabbage, collards, eggplant⁺⁺, English and snow peas, Irish potatoes⁺⁺⁺, kale, kohlrabi, leeks⁺, lettuce, mustard, onions⁺, peppers⁺⁺, radish, rutabaga, snow peas, shallots⁺, spinach, Swiss chard, tomatoes⁺⁺,** and **turnips.**

⁺Use sets, or transplants.
⁺⁺Plant seeds in hotbeds or greenhouses. ⁺⁺⁺Plant seed pieces.

 PLANTING

Many vegetables can be direct-seeded in the garden this month. January weather is frequently rainy. Do not work vegetable beds when the soil is wet, as it will destroy the structure of the soil. Remember to incorporate generous amounts of organic matter into beds before planting. Use transplants of **celery** and **leeks,** as it is too late to seed these long-growing crops. Transplants and sets (small bulbs) of **bulbing onions, bunching onions,** and **shallots** may still be planted. **Irish potatoes** are planted from tubers cut into egg-sized pieces, each containing at least one "eye." These are allowed to air-dry for a few days after cutting but before planting and are known as "seed pieces."

Producing your own transplants of **tomatoes, peppers,** and **eggplants** is a bit tricky, so it's good to know that nurseries will have them available in spring. If you want to grow your own, providing sufficient light is the biggest challenge. If you have a greenhouse or a hotbed, the situation is not so hard. Trying to raise transplants on a sunny windowsill, however, generally produces leggy, stretched, poor-quality transplants. Indoor light setups can work quite well.

1. Suspend a 48-inch fluorescent light fixture by adjustable chains on hooks over a table in an area where temperatures can be maintained above 55 degrees Fahrenheit. Use light tubes made for growing plants.

2. Sow seeds in peat pots filled with a damp potting soil or seed-starting mix.

3. When the seeds begin to germinate, adjust the light fixture so that the tubes are about 2 inches over the seedlings. As the seedlings grow, gradually raise the light fixture so that it remains at 2 inches above the tops of the seedlings.

4. Water regularly.

5. Use a water-soluble fertilizer at half the recommended strength once a week. In about six to eight weeks, the transplants will be ready for the garden.

CARE

Cool-season vegetables and herbs must be able to tolerate freezing temperatures in order to grow at this time of year. Still, newly emerged seedlings and some vegetables can be more susceptible to cold. Throw a sheet or tarp over young and newly germinated vegetable seedlings growing in the garden if temperatures lower than the

HELPFUL HINTS

Don't forget to record how vegetables in the garden are doing. These records are invaluable when making future decisions. Note the variety, when it was planted, when harvest began and ended, major problems, and overall performance. Also record information on seed orders you submit.

upper 20s are predicted. Harvest any **broccoli, cauliflower, snow peas,** and **lettuce** that are ready if temperatures in the mid-20s are predicted.

WATERING

Dry weather is possible but unlikely this time of the year. Keep beds mulched. Other than watering newly planted transplants and seeded beds, little additional irrigation is necessary.

FERTILIZING

Depending on when you last fertilized garden vegetables, you may need to sidedress some of them. Many of the cool-season crops such as **broccoli, cabbage, cauliflower, collards,** and other greens are heavy feeders and need a constant supply of nutrients to do their best. Sidedressing means fertilizing vegetables while they are growing.

Nitrogen is the most important nutrient to apply. Use any high-nitrogen fertilizer, such as ammonium nitrate, ammonium sulfate, or bloodmeal.

PESTS

Caterpillars, aphids, snails, and slugs may be active if the weather is mild. Control caterpillars with Bt or Sevin; aphids with insecticidal soap, UltraFine Oil, or Malathion; and snails and slugs with baits (check the label and make sure the one you use is okay around vegetables) or traps. Winter weeds will grow on warm, sunny days. Pull them up promptly and keep gardens well mulched.

FEBRUARY

HERBS & VEGETABLES

 PLANNING

Spring planting is almost upon us, and it's time to decide what to grow, how much to plant, and where everything will go. Remember last year? Did you have so many **cucumbers** you couldn't give them away? Plant fewer this year. Unless your memory is a lot better than most folks', it's important to keep at least a few simple notes each season to refer to.

When deciding on the quantity and location of cool-season vegetables, don't forget that lots of warm-season vegetables will be going in next month. Some of the cool-season vegetables, such as **carrots, cabbage,** and **Irish potatoes** will not mature until late April or May. Keep this in mind, and don't use up too many beds or you will have little or no room to plant next month.

Vegetables to plant in February include **beets, broccoli+, cabbage+, carrots, cauliflower+, collards, corn++, Swiss chard, eggplant+++, Irish potatoes+, kohlrabi, lettuce, mustard, peppers+++, radish, rutabagas, snap beans++, shallots, tomatoes+++,** and **turnips.**

+Plant transplants or seed pieces.
++Plant in late February in south Louisiana.
+++Sow seeds in hotbeds or greenhouses

 PLANTING

February can be intensely cold or remarkably mild. This month separates the gamblers from the more conservative gardeners. In southern Louisiana, a few brave souls will set out early **tomato** transplants in late February, preparing to protect them should a frost threaten.

Early planting of vegetables has more benefits than just beating out everybody else on the block with the first harvest. Early plantings often have fewer insect and disease problems. **Corn** planted in late February and early March will have very few earworms, even without the use of pesticides. April-planted corn, on the other hand, will require vigorous control efforts.

Finish planting most cool-season vegetables this month. A few gardeners may choose to plant fast-maturing vegetables such as **radish** or **lettuce** into early March, but the relatively hot weather of May is not that far off. When it comes to planting lettuces, leaf and semi-heading varieties are much more reliable that head types. Some varieties are less likely to turn bitter as the weather heats up. Try romaines, 'Red Sails', and 'Salad Bowl', to name a few.

 CARE

Clumps of **shallots** and **bunching onions** planted in fall can be dug up and divided for harvest one last time this month. Lift out the entire clump and divide it in half. Replant one half, and keep the other for harvest. The replanted part will grow until early June, when it will be lifted and dried, and the small bulbs stored for planting next fall.

When **cauliflower** heads are about the size of a silver dollar, pull the leaves over the center of the plant and fasten them together with a clothespin. This process is called *blanching*. Shading the head from light will cause it to come out creamy white. Check every few day to see if it is ready to harvest. Several of the newer cultivars are self-blanching and do not require the use of this technique.

 WATERING

Don't forget that newly seeded beds should be watered just about every day until the seeds come up. It is easy to forget that cool weather can be dry. Newly planted transplants need some extra coddling the first couple of weeks after planting. It is generally a good idea to water them

HARVESTING HERBS AND VEGETABLES

Many herbs produce in winter. Harvest individual lower leaves from **parsley, cilantro, arugula, chervil,** and **dill.** Herbs such as **bay, rosemary, thyme, sage, oregano,** and various **mints** can also be harvested, especially if the winter has been mild.

When just the lower leaves of leafy vegetables are regularly harvested, this is called "cropping." The method allows a regular harvest while allowing the plant to continue to produce. Cropping works great on **collards, Swiss chard, leaf lettuce, mustard, turnip greens,** non-heading **Chinese cabbage, spinach,** and **kale.** Harvest **snow peas** frequently, while the pods are still flat and the seeds have not yet developed; mid-February is your last chance to plant them. Try planting some edible podded peas such as 'Sugar Snaps' as well.

in initially with a water-soluble fertilizer. Use a watering can for individual plants or a hose-end applicator for larger areas. Most cool-season vegetables need a regular, even supply of water for best production. Make sure they do not become drought-stressed between rains.

FERTILIZING

Tender, succulent foliage is what we want from greens such as **mustard, Chinese cabbage, kale, collards, turnips,** and **spinach.** Regular applications of fertilizers containing nitrogen will encourage lush, tender growth that is best for eating.

PESTS

Holes in vegetable leaves may mean caterpillar or snail and slug activity. If you see small, dark green, or black pellets on the foliage, the culprits are likely to be caterpillars. Silvery trails on the leaves indicate snails or slugs have been there. If in doubt, put out a beer trap. Place a plastic bowl in the soil up to its rim near the plants and fill it half full with beer. Snails and slugs will crawl into the beer and not be able to crawl out. They are not after the alcohol—it is the smell of the yeast that attracts them. If you catch a lot of snails and slugs in the trap, you have a problem. (Continue to put out traps, or apply bait to the area.) If you don't catch any or catch just a few, your problem is probably caterpillars (treat your plants with Bt or Sevin).

Newly planted transplants may need to be watered by hand.

MARCH
HERBS & VEGETABLES

PLANNING

The time for procrastination is over—decisions need to be made. Over the next six weeks, all of the many vegetables that we rely on for early- to midsummer production must be planted either by direct-seeding or transplanting into the garden. If you have been meaning to order this year's All-America Selections winners or some unusual or delicious new variety, send it off immediately. Remember, it is too late to start seeds for **tomatoes** and **bell peppers.** Check at local nurseries to see what transplants they are carrying. Feed-and-seed stores often sell vegetable seeds in bulk. The price is lower than purchasing seeds in packets, which is especially good for larger gardens. The varieties carried are generally based on Louisiana Cooperative Extension Service recommendations.

Live oaks around the state drop lots of leaves in February and March. Gather them up, store them in bags or bins, and use them to mulch the garden.

Vegetables to plant in March include **cantaloupe, collards, corn, cucumbers, cucuzzi, eggplant+, kohlrabi+, lima beans, mirliton++, mustard, peppers+, pumpkin, radish, snap beans, Southern peas, summer squash,** **Swiss chard, tomatoes+, watermelons,** and **winter squash.**

+Plant transplants.
++Plant the entire fruit with the sprouted end in the soil about 3 inches deep.

PLANTING

There are three ways to plant seeds directly into the garden (this is called "direct-seeding").

Drilling: Seeds are planted in straight lines at the proper depth, but two to three times closer than the plants will ultimately be spaced. If more than one row will be planted in a bed, space the rows at least twice as far apart as the recommended spacing (if the vegetables will be spaced 12 inches apart in the rows, the rows should be at least 24 inches apart). When the seeds come up, thin (pinch off at ground level) the extras, leaving behind seedlings at the proper spacing. This technique is good if you don't know what the seedlings of the vegetable you are planting look like. The vegetables are in the drills—the weeds are in between.

Broadcasting: Seeds are scattered evenly over a bed area and covered to the proper depth. Two to three times as many seeds are planted as actual plants that will be needed. When the seedlings come up, the extras are thinned out so that the remaining plants are at the proper spacing. This technique is popular with smaller-growing vegetables such as **carrots, radishes,** and **beets,** and greens such as **lettuce** and **mustard.**

Hills: A few vegetables are sometimes planted in hills—raised mounds planted with several seeds per hill. **Watermelons, cucumbers, pumpkins,** and **squash** are some of the vegetables gardeners may plant in hills.

CARE

If you plant super-sweet **corn** varieties (noted on the seed package or in the vegetable description), they must be isolated from any regular sweet corn you plant. Cross-pollination will reduce the quality of the super-sweet variety. Corn is wind-pollinated. To improve pollination, plant corn seeds in several side-by-side short rows rather than one long row.

Transplants purchased in nurseries have been grown in greenhouses and have led a very sheltered, pampered life. Planting them into the real world of the vegetable garden can be a bit traumatic. Hardening off transplants prior to planting helps them deal with the change. It takes about a week. Place the transplants in a partial-sun location for a few days. Allow them to wilt very slightly before watering. Move into full sun for a few days and continue to water regularly, then plant into the garden.

Here's an alternative: When planting transplants, my Papa Oden used to break off a leafy twig from a nearby tree or shrub, and stick it into the ground on the south side of the transplant in order to shade it. The twig should be slightly larger than the transplant. Over the next few days, the leaves on the twig would gradually wilt and wither away, slowly exposing the transplant to more sun. Try to plant transplants on a cloudy day when rain is predicted.

 WATERING

Newly seeded beds and planted transplants need regular watering if the weather is sunny and dry. Seedbeds should be watered lightly every day. Established vegetables need thorough, deep watering about twice a week during dry weather. Mulch around vegetable plants to conserve moisture in the soil.

Water-in new transplants with a fertilizer solution at half strength.

HARVESTING ROOT CROPS

Harvest root crops before the roots become large and tough. Harvest the following vegetables when the top of the root is the appropriate diameter: **radish**—1"; **carrot**—1"; **turnip**—2"; **beet**—3"; **rutabaga**—3" to 4". Brush away the soil on top of the root if necessary to see the size. Harvest **broccoli** when the largest flower buds in the head are the size of the head of a kitchen match. Crop leafy vegetables regularly.

 FERTILIZING

Plan to dig fertilizer into garden beds, along with organic matter, when preparing them for planting. Water-in newly planted transplants with a fertilizer solution mixed at half strength with water.

Sidedress established vegetables to keep them growing vigorously.

 PESTS

As the weather warms up, so does the activity of various pests. Newly-set transplants may be cut off at ground level by a caterpillar called (appropriately enough) the cutworm. Place a 2- to 3-inch piece of cardboard tubing from a paper towel or bathroom tissue roll around the base of the transplant to prevent damage. Spray **onions, garlic, shallots,** and **leeks** with Malathion to control thrips.

APRIL
HERBS & VEGETABLES

 PLANNING

Even the best laid plans leave room for spontaneity and change. All of the warm-season vegetables can continue to be planted this month. Cool-season vegetables still growing in the garden should be finished in April or May. Make plans now for which warm-season vegetables you will plant in those areas.

Vegetables to plant in April include **cantaloupe, collards, corn, cucumber, cucuzzi, cushaw, eggplant+, honeydew, lima beans, luffa, Malabar spinach, mirliton** (plant sprouted fruit), **okra, peppers+, pumpkin, snap beans, Southern peas, squashes, sweet potato** (rooted cuttings known as "slips"), **Swiss chard, tomato+,** and **watermelon.**

+Plant transplants.

 PLANTING

Nurseries sell transplants of **cucumbers** and **squash** in cell-packs. The plants are often rootbound by the time you purchase and plant them, resulting in stunted, unproductive plants. It is easier and more productive to direct-seed these plants into the garden. Grow cucumbers on sturdy trellises that are about 4 feet tall for increased production, better-quality fruit, and saved space in the garden.

Do not delay planting many of the warm-season vegetables beyond this month. **Tomatoes, snap beans, lima beans,** and **bell peppers** all set fruit poorly when temperatures are hot. **Squashes** and **corn** are both far more likely to have major insect and disease problems when planted later. Herbs to plant include **basil, perilla, sesame, lemon balm, mints,** and **rosemary.**

 CARE

Tomatoes are staked to keep the plants from sprawling on the ground, where the fruit would be more likely to rot. Wait for the first cluster of flowers to appear, and place the stake on the opposite side of the plant's stem. All of the flower clusters will grow from the same side of the stem, and this will keep developing fruit from getting caught between the stake and the stem. Train tomatoes to one or two main shoots by pinching off the side shoots or "suckers" that appear where leaves join the stem. Do not desucker bush-type tomatoes such as 'Patio', 'Celebrity', and 'Better Bush'.

Tomatoes may also be grown in cages. The plants can grow quite large (5 to 6 feet is not unusual), and the small commercially available tomato cages are woefully inadequate. Here's a better solution:

• Purchase concrete reinforcing wire available at building supply stores—you'll need about 5 feet for each tomato plant.

• Cut into sections about 5 feet long, using heavy wire cutters.

• Form the pieces into cylinders and fasten them with wire.

• Place the cages over the tomato plants, pushing them into the ground.

Tomatoes grown in cages are generally not desuckered.

 WATERING

Vegetable and herb gardeners who grow plants in containers need to pay careful attention to proper watering. Containers dry out faster than you may realize, and the results of even one severe wilting can be disastrous. The need to water daily is not unusual, especially as the season progresses, when temperatures are higher and plant roots fill the container.

Watering plants in containers by hand is common and effective, but for plants growing in the ground this is largely ineffective during very dry weather. When watering by hand, water is applied rapidly over a short period of time—the result is shallow water penetration and shallow roots. Water thoroughly and deeply using soaker hoses or sprinklers, which apply water slowly over a relatively long period of time. Vegetable gardens need about 1 to 2 inches of water per week.

HARVESTING COOL-SEASON HERBS AND LEAFY VEGETABLES

Cool-season herbs and those that thrive during mild weather (such as **parsley, dill, tarragon, thyme, sage, cilantro, borage, lavender, chamomile, chervil,** and **arugula**) are at their peak this month. They will begin to decline toward late May and finish in early June. Harvest them generously over the next six to eight weeks. Any extra can be dried or frozen for use during the summer.

When leafy vegetables such as **mustard, lettuce, spinach, kale, Chinese cabbage,** or **celery** send up a flower stalk, it is referred to as "bolting." This generally signals a decrease in quality and the end of the productive season. Harvest promptly and either discard (in your compost pile, of course) or consume.

FERTILIZING

Vegetables planted last month and this month have a good supply of nutrients from the fertilizer incorporated into the bed during preparation. Sidedress cool-season vegetables about six weeks after transplanting, and every six weeks thereafter. Generally, a high-nitrogen fertilizer such as ammonium nitrate, ammonium sulfate, or bloodmeal is used. An all-purpose complete fertilizer such as 8-8-8 or 15-5-10 would also work.

PESTS

Mild winters in Louisiana do little to curb the populations of insect pests. Inspect vegetables regularly for signs of damage, and monitor population levels carefully. For those of you trying to minimize pesticide use, it's generally not necessary to spray at the first sign of damage. If populations begin to rapidly increase, however, or if the damage reaches unacceptable levels, prompt action may be necessary in order to save the crop.

It is important to identify the insect causing the damage so that the proper insecticide can be used. Gardeners sometimes spray their plants after seeing insects only to discover later that these were beneficial predators.

If you have had disease problems in the past, you may choose to spray some vegetables once a week with a fungicide to prevent devastating outbreaks. **Squash, cucumbers, tomatoes,** and **beans** are susceptible to a wide variety of fungal diseases. See the chapter introduction (page 70) for a list of appropriate vegetable fungicides.

Keep vegetable beds weeded and mulched. The mulch should be at least 2 inches thick.

MAY

HERBS & VEGETABLES

PLANNING

Most of the cool-season vegetables still lingering in the garden will be cleared out this month. If you haven't thought about what you'll want to plant in their place, now is the time to decide. Focus on planting those vegetables that will thrive and produce in the intense heat of June, July, and August.

May is one of the most productive months in the Louisiana vegetable garden. If you haven't started keeping records, make it a point to get a tablet or spiral notebook and jot down some observations. It is hard to get into the habit of keeping records, but you will be glad you did later on.

Vegetables to plant in May include **collards, cucuzzi, eggplant, hot pepper, luffa, mirliton** (plant the sprouted fruit), **okra, peanut, pumpkin, Southern peas, squash, sweet potato** (use slips), heat-tolerant **tomatoes** (seed for transplants), **cantaloupe,** and **watermelon.** Due to heat and pest problems, **corn, cucumber, lima bean, snap bean,** and **Swiss chard** are generally not as productive when planted this late. Plant in early May in south Louisiana and by mid-May in north Louisiana.

PLANTING

As cool-season crops go out of production and are removed, rework beds and plant heat-tolerant vegetables for production during the summer.

Luffa is an edible gourd that I highly recommend for home gardeners. I first encountered it under the name **"climbing okra,"** and it does require a trellis to climb on. It is related to **cucumbers** and **squash,** but the fruit, when sliced, breaded, and fried, tastes remarkably like fried okra. The vine stays healthy all summer with no spraying and produces quantities of large, attractive yellow flowers. The fruit should be harvested for eating when about 1 inch in diameter and about 8 inches long. Leave some of the gourds on the vines until they turn brown and rattle when shaken. When the outer skin is pulled off, the inner fibrous "sponge" is revealed. Beautiful flowers, edible fruit, and useful luffa sponges—what more could you ask from a vine?

WATERING

Dry, hot weather is not unusual in May. Drought-stressed vegetables may drop flowers and young fruit and are more suscep-

tible to pest damage. Vegetable gardens need 1 to 2 inches of water per week, and when rain is insufficient you must make up the difference. To calculate the time it takes your sprinkler to apply 1 inch of water, place several cans in open areas of the garden. Check the time and turn on the sprinkler. When 1 inch of water has accumulated in the cans, check the time again. That's how long it takes your sprinkler to apply 1 inch of water.

Soaker hoses are excellent to use because they keep water off the foliage. This is helpful both in preventing diseases and in slowing their spread. Leave the soaker hose on long enough for it to water the bed thoroughly. After it has been on for 30 minutes, dig into the area several inches out from the hose and see how far the water has penetrated. Continue to apply water until the soil is moist down to 6 to 8 inches.

FERTILIZING

It is time to sidedress vegetables planted in March if you haven't already done so. As a rule of thumb, **tomatoes, peppers, eggplant,** and **squash** are sidedressed when they set their first fruit. **Cucumbers, watermelons,** cantaloupes, and **winter squash** are sidedressed when they begin to run. **Beans, peas,** and other legumes are not commonly sidedressed. Choose a fertilizer rich in nitrogen such as ammonium nitrate or bloodmeal, and follow package directions.

PESTS

Pest problems become worse this month. When using any pesticides, read and follow label directions.

Look for beetles such as bean beetles, cucumber beetles, and flea beetles. All of them chew the leaves of a wide variety of vegetables. Control with Sevin or rotenone.

Caterpillars will feed on both the foliage and fruit of vegetables. The tomato fruitworm eats holes in fruit. Sevin and Bt regularly applied will keep them in check. Birds peck holes in **tomatoes** just when they become ripe enough to harvest. If birds are a problem, cover your plants with bird netting, or harvest the fruit in the pink stage and ripen them inside.

Another caterpillar, the squash vine borer, is very destructive to **squash** and **pumpkins** planted in the summer. Apply Sevin or *Bt* to the vines every few days to prevent this pest from getting into the stem and killing the plant.

HARVEST YOUR VEGETABLES

Harvest **bell peppers** when they reach full size but are still green. You may leave them on the plant until they turn red, but this runs the risk of fruit rot. Harvest **tomatoes** any time after they begin to turn pink to get them out of harm's way. Ripen at room temperature. They do not need light to ripen, so there is no need to put them in a window. Harvest **snap beans** when pods are the diameter of a pencil. Pick frequently. **Squash** and **cucumber** produce prolifically and need to be harvested regularly. Their fruit is harvested immature, so don't let them get too big before you pick them. To see if **sweet corn** is ready to harvest, pull back the shuck partway. Puncture a kernel with your thumbnail. If the juice is clear, leave it for a few more days; if the juice is milky, it's time to harvest; and if there is no juice, it is too old. Dig up **Irish potatoes** in late May when the tops have turned mostly yellow. Save the smallest potatoes to use in planting a fall crop.

Stinkbugs damage **tomatoes** and **okra,** causing spotted tomatoes and curled okra pods. Sevin and thiodan may help, but controlling these green or brown shovel-blade-shaped insects is difficult.

Diseases really take off, especially when weather is rainy. Prompt and regular (every five to seven days) use of fungicides such as mancozeb, Daconil, benomyl, or maneb will help control common diseases such as powdery mildew on **squash** and **cucumbers,** rust on **beans,** fruit rot on **tomatoes, eggplant,** and **squash,** and the many leaf diseases that attack tomatoes.

To see if corn is ready to harvest, pull the shuck back partway and puncture a kernel to see if the juice is milky.

JUNE
HERBS & VEGETABLES

 PLANNING

Vegetables such as **snap beans, corn, cucumbers,** and **squash** that were planted back in March will generally finish up this month. Plan on planting heat-tolerant vegetables to take their place. If you don't need the space right away or prefer to reduce the size of the garden in the summer heat, mulch empty beds heavily with 6 inches of leaves, grass clippings, pine straw, or other available materials.

Vegetables to plant in June include **cantaloupe, collards, cucuzzi, eggplant, luffa, okra, peanuts, hot peppers, pumpkin, Southern peas, sweet potato** (slips), **Swiss chard,** and **watermelons.** Although **squash** and **cucumbers** can be planted in June and July, production is difficult in midsummer due to pest problems. In late June you can plant seeds of **tomatoes, bell peppers,** and **eggplant** for producing fall transplants.

Continue to keep records and make notes on the performance of your vegetables. This is a good month to evaluate whether or not early summer crops lived up to your expectations. Note which varieties did best, which pests were a problem, and what you did to correct the situation. It

is also a good idea to add comments on how your friends' or neighbors' gardens did. They might have grown a vegetable or variety that you want to try next year.

 PLANTING

Transplants of **eggplants** and **hot peppers** may be planted this month. Oriental-type eggplants, which produce a long, narrow fruit, are often more productive during high temperatures. Many gardeners consider green-fruited eggplants less bitter during mid- to late-summer heat. Though **bell peppers** may be less productive due to high temperatures, some small-fruited **sweet peppers** such as 'Banana' or 'Gypsy' are quite productive now.

You can also plant seeds for fall transplants in late June. It is easier to raise your own transplants of **tomatoes, peppers,** and **eggplants** for fall planting because the transplants can be grown outside. Spring transplants must be started in January in a protected location such as a greenhouse or hotbed, or indoors under lights. Plant seeds in cell-packs, peat pots, or any small container, using a potting soil or seed-starting mix. Keep evenly moist until the seeds come up; then make sure the seedlings

receive sun for most of the day (some afternoon shade is beneficial). Transplants will be ready to go into the garden about six weeks after seeds are planted.

 CARE

Mulches are especially important in midsummer. They shade the soil and keep it cooler, in addition to controlling weeds and conserving moisture. A cooler soil is healthier for vegetable roots.

By now most **tomatoes** have already set their main crop. High temperatures interfere with pollination, so don't be surprised if most of the flowers fall off without setting fruit—it's just that time of year.

Herbs that do not like the heat are suffering now. Do your best, but there is not much you can do to moderate the effects of heat. Herbs in containers can be moved into slightly shadier locations. Keep herbs somewhat on the dry side to minimize root rot. Regularly harvest herbs such as **basil, perilla, sesame, rosemary, lemon balm, bay, lemon grass, Mexican tarragon, Mexican oregano, garlic chives,** and **mints,** along with others that stay productive during the summer.

WATERING

Continue to monitor rainfall amounts. Summer weather patterns in June, July, and August often bring frequent afternoon rains, especially in coastal areas. Do not be fooled by quick light showers that do little to thoroughly water the garden. On the other hand, several inches of rain can fall in a day or two. That's when the wisdom of growing vegetables on raised beds or raised rows becomes clear.

FERTILIZING

It does little good to fertilize vegetables toward the end of their productive season. Sidedress only vigorously growing vegetables that will continue to produce for a long period of time.

Vegetables and herbs growing heartily in containers should be fertilized regularly with a water-soluble fertilizer. You can choose a slow-release product instead, and apply it once at the beginning of the growing season.

HELPFUL HINTS

Try to do most of your vegetable gardening in the early morning or late afternoon to avoid the worst of the heat. Since vegetable gardens must be located in a sunny area, there will be no shade to help. Don't forget—you need generous amounts of water in the heat, just like your vegetables.

Hurricane season runs from June to the end of October. Should a hurricane head your way, harvest all the vegetables that are even close to the right stage and get them out of harm's way. Floodwaters could contaminate any vegetables left in the garden, or high winds may blow them away. Put away anything that might blow around in high winds, such as tomato cages, tools, and other loose items. They become deadly projectiles when winds reach 70 to 100 miles per hour.

PESTS

Populations of leaf miners have gotten to high levels by this time. These tiny insect larvae feed inside vegetable leaves, leaving behind white, meandering lines. A few lines in a leaf are not too damaging, but when most of the leaves have numerous lines, the damage can affect the harvest. Control is difficult since the pest dwells inside the leaf. Regular applications of spinosad will help reduce the number of larvae in the leaves.

Aphids are a particular problem on **Southern peas** but may also attack **eggplants, tomatoes, peppers,** and other vegetables. Insecticidal soap and UltraFine Oil are the least-toxic insecticides for controlling them. Malathion is also very effective. Watch for and welcome ladybugs, one of our best predators of aphids.

HERBS & VEGETABLES

PLANNING

"Dreaming" might be a better term for this month than planning. We are all dreaming of cooler weather, but it's still a long way off. In the meantime, our thoughts can begin to turn to fall gardens and, believe it or not, to cool-season vegetables. Seeds for cole crops such as **cabbage, broccoli,** and **cauliflower** can be planted this month to produce transplants. Check over the garden and decide if there will be room to plant them in late August when they are ready. If not, decide when space will become available and plan on growing transplants for planting at that time. There will be about six weeks between planting seeds and finished transplants.

Start looking through seed catalogs and make decisions about what to grow in the fall garden. Try some new varieties of **lettuce.** Get your orders off this month and in August so seeds will arrive in plenty of time for the fall planting season.

Vegetables to plant in July include **broccoli+, cabbage+, cantaloupe, brussels sprouts+, cauliflower+, Chinese cabbage+, collards, cucumbers, luffa, okra, peppers+, pumpkins, shallots, squash, Southern peas, tomatoes+,** and **watermelons.**

+Plant seeds for transplants.

PLANTING

Most Louisiana gardeners don't plant much in the vegetable garden in July. It's hard enough to get out in the heat to take care of and harvest what we already have. If you can brave the heat, however, there is always something that can be planted.

Plant **pumpkin** seeds this month for Halloween jack-o-lanterns. The squash vine borer can be very destructive to pumpkins and squash planted at this time of the year. The borer is a grublike caterpillar that burrows into the stem and hollows it out, causing the plant to wilt and die. If you have had major problems with these insects in the past, treat plants regularly with Sevin or Bt.

This is the last month to plant such heat-loving vegetables as **okra, peanuts, luffa,** and, in southern Louisiana, **sweet potato** slips. They should all be planted within the first week of the month.

Shallot and **bunching onion** sets may also be planted. Southern Louisiana gardeners tend to call everything shallots, even bunching onions and green onions (more properly called scallions). Shallots are actually a different plant altogether, but in the green stage they all pretty much look and taste the same. Plant the sets that you saved from your spring crop. You may be able to harvest some as early as October and then continue to harvest regularly through the winter.

Plant seeds to produce transplants of fall **tomatoes, peppers, broccoli, cauliflower,** and others in cell-packs, peat pots, or any small container, using a seed-starting mix. Keep evenly moist until the seeds germinate, and provide the seedlings with direct sun about six hours a day. Fertilize once a week with an all-purpose soluble fertilizer mixed at half strength. These vegetables may also be direct-seeded into the garden, but transplants tend to be more reliable. If you don't want to fool with growing transplants yourself, local nurseries will have transplants of these vegetables available in August.

CARE

Continue to harvest vegetables in the garden frequently and regularly. Hot weather causes vegetables to mature rapidly, and it's not unusual to find a giant **zucchini** lurking under the foliage. Remove and discard overly large vegetables to keep the plants productive. **Okra** should be checked every day as pods rapidly become overmature and tough.

Never leave rotten or diseased vegetables in the vegetable garden. They can serve as a continuing source of infection.

WATERING

Provide at least 1 inch of water for the garden each week if rainfall is scarce. A 2- to 4-inch layer of mulch will reduce the wide variations in moisture content that may occur. Drought-stressed vegetables are more susceptible to such pests as spider mites and whiteflies.

FERTILIZING

Peppers and **eggplants** planted in early summer will revive and produce well in the fall if kept in vigorous growth. Sidedress them every six weeks and you will be amazed at how productive they can be in September, October, and early November.

Add fertilizer to beds whenever preparing them for planting. If you haven't had your soil tested in several years (or have never had it tested), consider contacting your parish office of the Louisiana Cooperative Extension Service. You can get a soil test done by the Louisiana Soil Testing Laboratory for a modest fee.

PESTS

Keep up with weeds. Weeding in 95-degree-Fahrenheit weather is no fun, so keep beds well mulched to minimize problems. Maintaining weed-free beds is one of the greatest labor demands of the vegetable garden, and it is not uncommon to see weedy, overgrown gardens this time of year. This is the main reason for not creating a vegetable garden larger than you can practically handle. Next March, when you are contemplating enlarging the garden during the delightfully cool weather, remember what it was like weeding the garden in July and August.

Hopefully your vegetables did not have any disastrous pest outbreaks. Know that sooner or later, every gardener has gardening catastrophes. Don't let them get you down—there is always the next season.

Maintain regular surveillance of your garden for signs of insect or disease problems. Get help diagnosing problems from knowledgeable gardening friends, references, local County Agents, Master Gardeners, the Extension Service, or the staff at your local nursery. Whenever a pesticide is recommended, ask if a pesticide you have on hand will do the trick. We all have so many bottles of stuff as it is; we shouldn't buy more needlessly. Always ask for the least toxic pesticide that is still effective.

AUGUST

HERBS & VEGETABLES

PLANNING

Even though it is still hot, we need to make plans for the fall garden when weather will, at last, be cooler. Cool-season vegetables can begin to be planted into gardens. Visit area nurseries to find out what vegetable transplants they have or will have. Check out available seeds while you're at it. Send off orders from seed catalogs so the shipment will arrive in plenty of time for the right planting date. Cool-season planting begins in earnest next month.

The days are becoming noticeably shorter, and the fewer hours of sun relieve a little of the stress on plants in the garden. Take time to jot down some observations on how your garden did during the summer. Gardening is a learning experience, and the more you remember and learn from past efforts, the more successful you will be in the future.

Vegetables to plant in August include **bell pepper**[+], **broccoli, brussels sprouts, bunching onions**[++], **cabbage, cauliflower, Swiss chard, Chinese cabbage, collards, cucumbers, lima beans, mustard, snap beans, Southern peas, peppers**[+], **Irish potatoes**[+++], **rutabagas, shallots**[++], **squashes, tomatoes**[+], and **turnips.**

[+]Plant transplants.
[++]Plant sets.
[+++]Plant small, whole potatoes saved from the spring crop.

PLANTING

Irish potatoes can be planted using small, whole potatoes saved from the spring crop. Warm soils in late summer are full of active fungi, and cut seed pieces are likely to rot if used. Some gardeners have success direct-seeding cole crops such as **broccoli, brussels sprouts, cabbage,** and **cauliflower.** Many gardeners either raise their own transplants or purchase them, finding this method is more reliable than direct-seeding.

Choose bush varieties of **snap beans** ('Provider', 'Top Crop', 'Derby') and **lima beans** ('Henderson Bush', 'Jackson Wonder', 'Baby Fordhook'), as they tend to be more productive in the fall garden. Snap beans are so easy and productive that every gardener should plant a few rows.

Transplant **tomatoes** and **peppers** by mid-August. Tomatoes, peppers, and **eggplants** from the spring planting can be left for fall production if they are healthy. Most tomatoes are not worth keeping, but peppers and eggplants can stay remarkably productive.

CARE

When a crop is finished, pull it up promptly and throw it in your compost pile. If you don't have anything to plant in the area, mulch with 4 to 6 inches of leaves, grass clipping, pine straw, or other materials you have on hand. Old crops left in place look untidy, allow weeds to grow, and may harbor insects or diseases since they tend to be ignored.

Don't forget to harvest your herbs regularly. If you get too high a yield, you can easily dry the extras for later use. Here's how:

• Harvest so that stems are long enough to tie together easily.

• Rinse the herbs and blot them dry.

• Make small bundles of 3 to 5 stems, held together with rubber bands, and insert an unbent paper clip or S-shaped piece of wire for a hook.

• Hang the bundles in a cool, dry location indoors with good air circulation.

In about two weeks, when the leaves are crispy-dry, crumble the herbs and store them in a tightly sealed, labeled container.

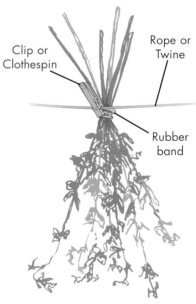

Clip or Clothespin

Rope or Twine

Rubber band

Herbs can be dried for later use.

WATERING

Will it rain today? Gardeners often delay watering if there is a chance it will rain. Days can go by with no rain, and significant damage can occur while the garden waits. If plants need water, don't wait for possible rain. If you water and it rains later, no harm is done, other than wasting some water and effort. Continue to water regularly as needed.

Water newly planted seeds and transplants more frequently than you do established vegetable plants.

FERTILIZING

Incorporate fertilizer when preparing beds for new plantings. Use a general-purpose fertilizer and follow package directions. Continue to sidedress vegetables that have been growing in the garden longer than six to eight weeks.

PESTS

Insects have had all summer to build up their populations and can be especially damaging in the late-summer and early-fall garden. Many gardeners put vegetable gardens on a regular weekly spray schedule at this time of the year instead of spraying as needed. Use your best judgment, based on past experience. Stinkbugs, leaf miners, caterpillars, aphids, whiteflies, beetles, and spider mites are all active. Broad- spectrum insecticides will handle most of these, although stinkbugs, leafminers, and whiteflies can be difficult to deal with. The key is to not let these pests get completely out of hand before you implement control.

September

HERBS & VEGETABLES

 PLANNING

Cool fronts may begin to make their way into the state, bringing welcome relief from the heat toward the second half of this month. Still, daytime highs regularly reach the 90s well into October. During this transition period, warm- and cool-season vegetables rub elbows in the garden. Most of the warm-season vegetables, such as **snap beans, okra, cucumbers, tomatoes, peppers,** and **eggplants,** will finish up in November or early December around the state as weather becomes colder. It is not too soon, however, to plan the cool-season vegetables that will take their place. This advance planning will allow you to purchase seeds that you will need to have on hand for growing your own transplants timed to be ready to go into the garden as the warm-season vegetables finish.

Vegetables to plant in September include **beets, broccoli+, cabbage, carrots, cauliflower+, Chinese cabbage, collards, English** and **snow peas, Irish potatoes+++, kale, kohlrabi, leek, lettuce, mustard, onion, radish, rutabagas, shallots++,** **snap beans** (plant in early September), **Swiss chard,** and **turnips.**

+Plant seeds early; use transplants only in northern Louisiana.

++Plant sets.

+++Plant small, whole potatoes saved from the spring crop.

 PLANTING

As we move into the cool season, root crops such as **carrot, radish,** and **turnip** become a prominent part of the garden. Root crops are always direct-seeded—never transplanted. A tiny root first produced by the seed eventually develops into the edible root. It is easily damaged when the seedling is young, and this damage can cause a deformed final product of poor quality. When thinning root crops, do not be tempted to transplant extra seedlings to other spots. You will be disappointed with the results.

Plant **bush snap beans** early in the month so they will have time to produce a good crop before cold weather. Bush varieties produce faster and concentrate their harvest in a shorter period of time than do **pole beans,** making them preferred for fall planting.

Plant seeds of **bulbing onions, bunching onions,** and **leeks** this month. Sets of bunching onions may also be planted this month, but do not plant sets of bulbing onions until early December. Onion seeds are slow to germinate and need a constant supply of water during the process. The seedlings grow slowly at first, so be patient. **Onions, shallots, leeks,** and **garlic** (planted next month) are long-term residents of the cool-season vegetable garden. Bulbing onions, shallot bulbs, leeks, and garlic will not be ready to harvest until late May or early June of next year.

 CARE

Regularly remove the flower spikes of **basil** to encourage plants to continue producing leaves. Ultimately, the plants will begin to lose steam. Basil transplants should be planted into the garden no later than early September for a late crop. If herbs such as **sage, lavender, thyme,** and **catnip** managed to make it through the summer, they should begin to revive as the weather gets cooler. Remove any dead parts and fertilize lightly to encourage new growth. Many herbs will have grown vigorously during the summer if not regularly harvested. Cut them back about halfway to get them into shape. Dry or freeze the extra harvest, or share it with friends. Here's how to freeze herbs:

- Harvest, rinse, and blot dry.
- Remove leaves from woody stems and chop finely.
- Place the chopped herbs in a freezer bag, spreading them out in a ¹/₂-inch layer.

This makes it easier to break off usable pieces later on when the herbs are frozen solid.

- Force out as much air as possible, seal and freeze.

Label the bag with the name of the herb, since chopped and frozen herbs tend to look the same.

 WATERING

This month can be hot and dry, and with new plantings going in, you should pay careful attention to the water needs of the garden. Newly planted transplants and seedbeds are especially vulnerable to drought conditions and may need frequent irrigation. As seeds come up and transplants become established, water deeply and less frequently to encourage a deep root system.

 FERTILIZING

Add fertilizer to beds when preparing them for new plantings. If appropriate, sidedress vegetables that have been growing long enough to need it. Sidedress transplants of cole crops such as **cabbage, broccoli,** and **cauliflower** four to six weeks after they are planted into the garden, and every four to six weeks until harvest.

Fertilize transplants you are growing yourself once a week with a water-soluble fertilizer mixed at half strength.

 PESTS

Population levels of insects are high, so be vigilant and treat problems promptly. If a crop is about to finish up, as **okra** is now, you should generally not be as concerned about controlling pests on it as on a vegetable crop that has been planted more recently.

White Grub

Caterpillars can be particularly troublesome in the fall garden. Regular applications of Bt or Sevin will keep their damage down to a minimum.

When turning the soil to plant crops you may encounter white, C-shaped beetle larvae called grubs. They are very common and feed on the roots of vegetables. Simply picking them out and disposing of them is generally all the control that is necessary.

OCTOBER
HERBS & VEGETABLES

PLANNING

October is often one of the nicest months of the year. Working and planting in the garden is a joy when temperatures and humidity are lower. Fall is an excellent time to plant many perennial herbs in the garden. Plan the location of the herbs and think of how many you would like to plant. A few herb plants provide a lot of harvest, so don't plant more than you can use.

Many shade trees drop their leaves in November. Now is a good time to plan on saving them for use in the vegetable garden. Leaves may be stored in plastic bags in an out-of-the-way location for use later on as mulch. Decide now if you have a suitable location. Leaves are also an important source of organic material for our compost piles. If you are not yet composting, what a shame! You are missing out on creating an outstanding free source of the organic matter that is so critical to proper bed preparation. Excellent free information on home composting is available from your local Extension office of the LSU AgCenter.

As warm-season plantings such as **okra, sweet potatoes, watermelons, Southern peas, cantaloupes,** and **pumpkins** are removed, decide on the cool-season vegetables that can be planted in their place.

Vegetables to plant in October include **beets, broccoli+, cabbage, carrots, celery, Chinese cabbage, cauliflower+, collards, garlic++, kale, kohlrabi, lettuce+++, leeks, mustard, onions, radishes, shallots,** and **Swiss chard.**

+Plant transplants by mid-month.
++Plant individual toes.
+++Leaf and semi-heading varieties are more reliable than heading types.

PLANTING

Beds that you do not intend to plant with vegetables may be planted with a cool-season green manure crop. These are seeded into the beds, allowed to grow for a few months, and then turned under to provide organic matter to the soil. Good choices are rye, vetch, crimson clover, and oats. Do not allow cover crops to set seed. They should be turned under when they begin to bloom, if not before.

Intercropping is a way of maximizing production from vegetable beds. Vegetables that are spaced relatively far apart such as **broccoli, cauliflower, cabbage,** and **brussels sprouts** do not fully occupy the bed early in their season. Use the space between the plants to grow a quick-maturing crop such as

Have some type of compost pile; it doesn't have to be elaborate.

radishes or **lettuce.** If planted at the same time, they will be harvested and gone by the time larger plants begin to cover those spaces.

With winter on the way, new gardeners sometimes wonder if now is the time to plant **winter squash.** The answer is *No.* Winter squash, such as **acorn, hubbard,** and **butternut,** is grown during the warm season along with **summer squash,** so it should have been planted long before now. The difference is that the fruit of winter squash is harvested when the rind is hard, so they are kept in the garden much longer than summer squash, which is harvested while still tender. Winter squash stores well and may be kept and used during the winter. Hence the name.

Plant **garlic** by separating bulbs into individual cloves and pressing the cloves big end down into well-prepared beds. The tip of the clove should be about 1/4 inch below the soil surface. Space the cloves 4 to 6 inches apart.

CARE

Fall is an excellent time to have soil tests done. Many soils around the state require lime to raise the pH and provide calcium. A soil test will indicate if you need to apply lime and how

much is recommended. If you do not intend to grow a winter vegetable garden, lime applied in the fall will have plenty of time to do its work before the spring planting season.

If you notice large knobs, knots, and bumps on the roots of vegetables (such as **okra**), it is a sign that your soil is infested with nematodes. These microscopic roundworms attack and damage the roots of a wide variety of vegetables. You can have your soil evaluated for the presence of nematodes through your parish Extension office of the LSU AgCenter.

Mulch heavily any beds that will stay empty for the winter. Winter weeds will grow vigorously in unmulched beds, creating problems when the beds are planted next spring.

WATERING

October is typically relatively dry. Water established vegetables thoroughly and deeply as needed. Newly planted seeds and transplants will need more-frequent irrigation.

FERTILIZING

Add some fertilizer to all of those leaves going into your compost pile to make them decompose

faster. Sidedress vegetables such as **broccoli, cabbage, peppers, tomatoes, cauliflower,** and **collards** to keep them growing vigorously. Legume crops, which include **English peas, snow peas,** and edible **podded peas,** are usually not sidedressed.

PESTS

With cooler weather, pest problems don't seem as bad. Diseases are much less common in the cool-season garden.

Watch for aphids and control with insecticidal soap, UltraFine Oil, or Malathion. Follow label directions carefully.

Caterpillars continue to damage vegetables. When they infest leafy greens such as **collards, kale, turnips, mustard,** and **lettuce,** they can eat your produce in no time. Control them with regular weekly applications of Bt or Sevin.

Snail and slug populations may be high, and they eat foliage just as caterpillars do. They especially love **cabbage, turnips, mustard,** and **lettuce.** Control with traps, barriers, and baits before the damage gets out of hand.

NOVEMBER
HERBS & VEGETABLES

PLANNING

Freezing temperatures become a possibility in northern Louisiana later this month. As things slow down some, take the time to record how well fall plantings of warm-season vegetables did for you. In particular, note the cultivars that seemed to do the best, along with any pest problems.

If you still haven't decided whether or not to plant a cool-season vegetable garden, there is still time. At least put in a few easy crops such as **shallot** sets, **mustard greens,** and **lettuce.** Many of the most delicious and nutritious vegetables can only be grown here during the cool season.

Additional plantings of cool-season vegetables can continue into late winter and early spring. Continue to look through arriving seed catalogs and order vegetable seeds for planting then. Vegetables to plant in November include **beets, cabbage, carrots, celery, collards, garlic, kohlrabi, leeks, kale, lettuce, radishes, mustard, onions, Swiss chard, rutabagas, shallots, spinach,** and **turnips.**

PLANTING

Direct-seed root crops such as **beets, carrots, radishes,** and **turnips.** Transplants of **broccoli** and **cauliflower** may still be available at local nurseries, but the possibility of freezing temperatures damaging the heads makes planting them risky, especially in northern Louisiana. Transplants of **cabbage, celery, kale, kohlrabi, lettuce, spinach,** and **Swiss chard** can all be purchased and planted this month, or you can plant seeds in the garden. In north Louisiana, plant in the first half of the month.

CARE

Lettuces, especially the leaf and semi-heading varieties, are very productive in the cool-season garden. Fall is the best time to plant lettuces, as they mature during progressively cooler temperatures. Problems with bitterness that often affect spring-grown lettuce do not occur in the fall. Keep lettuce growing vigorously with regular watering and

Vegetables such these colorful lettuces can also be ornamental.

occasional sidedressing with a nitrogen-containing fertilizer such as ammonium sulfate or blood-meal. There are so many different colors and leaf shapes available now; lettuce patches can rival ornamental plantings.

Don't overlook the ornamental qualities of many of the cool-season vegetables and herbs. **Curly parsley** makes a great edging plant for flower beds. **Curly leaf mustard** and **red leaf mustard** are outstanding when mixed with cool-season bedding plants. **Bronze fennel** is used as often in flower beds and perennial borders as it is in the herb and vegetable garden. Watch your use of pesticides on vegetables in ornamental beds. The pesticides used on ornamentals may not be labeled for use on food crops, which means you should not harvest and eat vegetables sprayed with them.

HARVESTING MIRLITONS

Mirlitons are ready for harvest this month. This vining relative of squash and cucumber is popular in southern Louisiana but virtually unknown to gardeners in the northern part of the state. Popular for use in Cajun dishes, mirlitons are light-green pear-shaped vegetables that have a mild squashlike flavor. The mirliton vine grows vigorously all summer but generally does not begin to bloom and produce fruit until October and November (an early-summer lagniappe crop sometimes occurs). Harvest continues until the first killing frost. At that time, remove the dead vine and mulch the perennial roots heavily. The vine will return in the spring.

 WATERING

Cooler temperatures and more-frequent rains make watering the vegetable and herb gardens less of a chore during the winter growing season. Watch rainfall amounts and water when necessary.

 FERTILIZING

Even though many plants are going dormant for the winter, cool-season vegetables and herbs remain in active growth. Fertilize as needed to keep them healthy and productive.

DECEMBER
HERBS & VEGETABLES

 PLANNING

As seed catalogs begin to arrive, I know you'll find a moment to look at new offerings of vegetables and herbs. There is plenty of time to make decisions and order warm-season vegetable seeds (except **tomatoes, peppers,** and **eggplants,** which must be started from seed in January), but you should order cool-season vegetable seeds this month or in January.

Vegetables to plant in December include **beets, brussels sprouts+, cabbage, carrots, celery+, Chinese cabbage, collards, garlic++, kale, kohlrabi, leeks++, lettuce, rutabaga, Swiss chard, mustard, onions++, radishes, shallots++, spinach,** and **turnips.**

+Plant transplants.
++Plant sets or transplants.

 PLANTING

Planting continues. Although exceptionally cold severe weather can cause problems, winter weather is mostly mild. Watch the weather and avoid setting out transplants when a major freeze is predicted.

 CARE

Any vegetable started in winter will be subject to freeze damage while young. The following lists are quick guides to the ability of some vegetables to endure freezes. Factors such as the age of the plant, prior weather conditions, and the location of the garden will also influence the amount of freeze damage.

Less Hardy: (protect if temperatures are to go below 28 degrees): **broccoli** (heads); **cauliflower** (heads); **lettuce; English, snow,** and edible podded **pea** (flowers).

Moderately Hardy: (will tolerate temperatures down to the mid to low 20s with little or no damage): **Swiss chard; Chinese cabbage; kohlrabi; mustard greens; radish** (will resprout from roots); **turnip** (will resprout from roots); **spinach.**

Very Hardy: (will survive temperatures in the low 20s and teens): **beets; brussels sprouts; carrots; celery; collards; garlic; kale; onions; leeks; shallots.**

 WATERING

Monitor the needs of your vegetables and water. Winter is usually relatively rainy, and irrigation will seldom be necessary.

 FERTILIZING

Long stretches of cold weather will slow the growth of vegetables and lessen the need for additional fertilizer. On the other hand, an unusually mild winter may encourage vigorous growth, requiring additional fertilizer. Watch the weather and use your best judgement.

 PESTS

One of my favorite parts of cool-season gardening (other than the mild temperatures) is reduced problems with insects and diseases. Diseases are a minor problem, if they occur at all.

Aphids and caterpillars will be active depending on the weather. During mild periods, watch carefully for their appearance and control if necessary.

Snails and slugs may show up, especially early in the month. Beer traps or baits approved for use around food crops will help keep their numbers down.

Do not slack off on weed control. Maintain mulches and deal with growing weeds promptly. Mulches can also be useful in protecting vegetables during freezes.

LAWNS

Almost every landscape includes a lawn. These areas of mowed grass provide important spaces for outdoor activities and a restful contrast to beds of flowers and shrubs. For some, the lawn is a source of pride and is lavished with as much attention as a prized rose garden. For others, the lawn is just something that has to be mowed—as long as it's mostly green, they're happy. Most of us fall somewhere in between.

Lawn care does not have to be complicated, but there are certain necessary elements. Knowing how to select the right grass, providing the right care at the right time, and dealing appropriately with problems that may arise are all important to success.

Our mild climate and long, hot summers dictate the types of lawngrasses that will grow here. The warm-season grasses we use grow vigorously at 80 to 95 degrees Fahrenheit in spring, summer, and fall. They typically go dormant and turn brown with the first frost, greening up again as the weather warms in March and April. Properly maintained, they are long-lived and rarely need to be replaced. The primary warm-season turfgrasses include common bermudagrass, hybrid bermudagrass, centipedegrass, St. Augustinegrass, and zoysiagrasses.

Cool-season grasses are also planted, but not to create permanent lawns as they are in the northern United States. They are used to overseed warm-season lawns in the fall, maintaining a green lawn during the winter when those grasses are brown and dormant. The cool-season grasses are temporary residents in the lawn and die during the early-summer heat. The cool-season grasses generally used for overseeding are annual ryegrass and perennial ryegrass. Fine fescues, creeping bentgrass, rough bluegrass, and Kentucky bluegrass may also be used in blends with perennial ryegrass.

CHAPTER FOUR

SELECTING THE RIGHT GRASS

New homeowners rarely change the type of grass in an existing lawn but occasionally will if sufficient reasons arise. New construction generally allows you to decide which type of grass you want to plant. The choice of grass and how it is planted is a matter of taste, available labor, growing conditions, predicted use, and economics.

Historically, St. Augustine has been the most popular lawngrass, and it is still the most commonly seen in yards around the state. Centipede has become popular for new lawn installation, owing primarily to its lower maintenance needs. It requires less mowing and fertilization and has fewer insect and disease problems than does St. Augustine. The chart on page 97 will briefly acquaint you with the warm-season grasses appropriate for planting in Louisiana.

PLANTING A LAWN

Have a soil test done through your local LSU AgCenter Extension office to determine the fertilizer, lime, sulfur, etc., that is needed. Remove any debris (especially important around newly constructed homes). Kill weeds growing in the area with glyphosate, following label directions. Till the soil 4 to 6 inches deep. Apply soil amendments recommended by the soil test and work into the soil. Establish the grade and rake smooth. Use the planting method of your choice. The methods below are most common:

Seeding: Broadcast half the seed walking east to west, the other half north to south, to ensure even coverage. Drag a rake over the area to lightly cover the seeds. Water lightly every day until seeds come up, then regularly until the plants are established.

Plant bermuda April through August and centipede April through July.

Plugging: Plant 2- to 4-inch-diameter plugs 6 to 12 inches apart (greater spacing may be used, but coverage will take longer). Once planted, step on them to firm them in place. Water lightly every day for one week, every other day for another week, then less frequently but more thoroughly, especially if weather is dry.

Plugging is best done April through August.

Sodding: Lay the sod in a brick pattern (alternate ends and middles) with the seams pressed together. Roll the area to firm the sod into the soil. Water lightly every day for a week, every other day for another week, then less frequently but more thoroughly, especially if weather is dry.

Sodding is best done April through September.

CARING FOR A LAWN

Regular mowing is important during the growing season. This may mean mowing every five to seven days during hot and rainy summer weather. Mow often enough so that no more than $1/3$ of the grass blade is removed each time. Mowing height is very important and your mower blades must be sharp. Set your mower to the following recommended heights:

Common bermuda: 1 to $1^{1}/2$ inches (reel mower recommended); hybrid Bermuda: $1/2$ to 1 inch (reel mower recommended); centipede: 1 to 2 inches (rotary or reel mower); St. Augustine: 2 to 3 inches (rotary or reel mower); zoysia: $1/2$ to $1^{1}/2$ inches (reel mower recommended).

Irrigation is generally needed only during hot, dry weather, but when necessary it is important. Water deeply and thoroughly, applying $1/2$ to 1 inch of water. Lawns are generally fertilized in April, June, and August for maximum growth and quality. Fertilize centipede lightly in April and July. Insect and disease problems are most common during the summer growing season (although brown patch fungus attacks in spring and fall). Watch carefully for damage, get an accurate diagnosis, and treat appropriately. Practice good weed control when necessary.

LAWNGRASSES

Common bermuda

Characteristics: Fine texture, dark green color; used on athletic fields; coarser texture than hybrids; new, improved named cultivars becoming available. Plant seed, sod, or plugs.

Strengths: Rapid establishment rate; excellent wear tolerance; good ability to recover from damage; excellent drought tolerance; excellent salt tolerance; can be seeded.

Weaknesses: Poor shade tolerance; high to medium maintenance.

Hybrid bermuda

Characteristics: Very fine texture; dark green; excellent quality; used extensively on golf courses and athletic fields; high fertility requirements. Plant sod or plugs.

Strengths: Rapid establishment rate; excellent wear tolerance; good ability to recover from damage; excellent drought tolerance; excellent salt tolerance.

Weaknesses: Very poor shade tolerance; very high maintenance; should use reel mower.

Centipede

Characteristics: Medium texture; slow growth; low fertility requirements; requires acid soils; popular for home lawns. Plant sod, plugs, or seed.

Strengths: Good disease and insect resistance; low maintenance; fair tolerance to part shade. Advantages over St. Augustine: finer leaf texture, better cold tolerance, better resistance to chinch bugs and brown patch, can be seeded.

Weaknesses: Poor wear tolerance; quality can decline if overfertilized; lighter green leaf color; poor drought tolerance; poor salt tolerance; seed is slow to establish; for acidic soils only.

St. Augustine

Characteristics: Coarse texture; rich green color; popular for home lawns. Generally, plant sod or plugs; seed occasionally available, but not best quality.

Strengths: Best grass for part-shade; excellent salt tolerance; medium maintenance; establishes fairly quickly.

Weaknesses: Poor cold tolerance; very susceptible to chinch bugs, brown patch; coarse texture.

Zoysia

Characteristics: Several species and cultivars; medium fine to fine texture; dark green color; very dense growth; used on golf courses and home lawns. Plant sod or plugs.

Strengths: Excellent wear tolerance; good tolerance to part shade ('Emerald' and 'El Toro' cultivars); excellent cold tolerance.

Weaknesses: Slow establishment rate; accumulates thatch readily requiring removal; medium to high maintenance.

JANUARY
LAWNS

PLANNING

Relax while there is not much to do. Plan on repairing any damage that may have occurred during the late summer (chinch bugs) or fall (brown patch) to your **St. Augustine** lawn. The grass may return from brown patch, but chinch bugs kill the grass outright and those areas will need to be replaced in spring.

Consider hiring a lawn care service to care for your lawn if it is getting to be a bit too much for you. Now is a good time to look into this so that a decision can be made by the time mowing season arrives. Interview several companies and compare prices and services. Find out the type of equipment used and how often they will mow. Do they fertilize or treat for pests? (The use of pesticides requires a Certified Pesticide Applicators License in Ornamentals and Turf issued by the Louisiana Department of Agriculture and Forestry; ask to see a copy.)

PLANTING

Gardeners in the southern part of the state can still overseed dor-

mant lawns with **ryegrass** or a blend this month, but it is risky if severe cold weather occurs before the grass has had a chance to establish. If you haven't done it by now, it's probably not worth it. More seed may be spread over lawns overseeded earlier to thicken sparse areas. Overseeding with a cool-season grass means, of course, you will have to continue to mow through the winter.

CARE

Mow overseeded lawns as needed. If the weather is moist and mild, this could be every week. If the weather is cold, the grass will grow more slowly. **Ryegrass** is mowed to a height of 1 to 2 inches, so it should be cut when it has grown to $1\frac{1}{2}$ to 3 inches tall. Clippings may be bagged or not. Put bagged clippings in your compost pile. Do not bag if you use a mulching mower.

WATERING

Cool, moist weather generally makes irrigation unnecessary this month. Water as needed.

FERTILIZING

In south Louisiana, cool-season grasses should have been fertilized last month and can be fertilized again in early February. In north Louisiana, fertilizer may be applied in late November (once the warm-season grass goes dormant) and again around the middle of this month.

PESTS

Winter weeds may be growing in the lawn now. Mow them back if you like.

Mow overseeded lawns as needed.

FEBRUARY

LAWNS

 PLANNING

The weather is cold and lawn care is easy. Review the notes you made last year on the performance of the lawn, and make decisions on what will need to be done this spring. If you don't have any notes from last year, don't you wish you did? Plan to keep at least a few simple records this year for future reference.

 PLANTING

Save all that energy for later. Now is not the time to plant either cool-season grass seed or worry about planting warm-season grasses. Dormant sodding is occasionally done. If you have new construction and need to lay sod to stabilize the bare ground, some companies will lay dormant sod for you. The turf will be brown when planted, but should green up nicely in March or April. There is a risk that severe freezing temperatures can damage vulnerable, newly laid sod. Cool, moist weather and a dormant condition mean you don't have to fuss over watering the new sod.

 CARE

Overseeded lawns are a rich emerald green and provide a beautiful setting for the spring flowers beginning to bloom. Mow overseeded lawns as needed. If the weather is moist and mild, this could be every week. If the weather is cold, the grass will grow more slowly. **Ryegrass** falls over, matts, and looks unattractive if allowed to grow too tall.

 WATERING

Cool, moist weather this month and the fact that warm–season grasses are dormant make the need to water unlikely. Still, if the weather does turn dry and you have **ryegrass** growing, irrigation may be necessary.

 FERTILIZING

In northern Louisiana, overseeded lawns may be fertilized early this month. A light application of a brand-name lawn fertilizer, a balanced fertilizer such as 8-8-8 (8 to 12 pounds per 1000 square feet), or a 3:1:2 ratio fertilizer such as 15-5-10 (6 pounds per 1000 square feet) will do the trick. Water-in fertilizer immediately after application.

 PESTS

Mild weather will encourage enthusiastic growth from cool-season weeds in the lawn. Since the lawngrass is dormant and you are not mowing, green weeds are really noticeable against the tan-colored turf. Do not reach for a bag of weed-and-feed (fertilizer combined with a weedkiller). It is far too early to fertilize warm-season grasses. After all, they're dormant. Use a broadleaf herbicide labeled for use on the type of grass you have, following label directions carefully. You may also just mow them back occasionally. During warm, moist weather, Pythium blight may attack **ryegrass**, causing areas to "melt." Treat with captan or mancozeb, following label directions carefully.

Broadleaf Weed
(dandelion)

MARCH

LAWNS

 PLANNING

Regular mowing is just around the corner, and you may need to begin mowing occasionally any time now. Plan on getting your lawn mower in good repair for the coming season. If you are handy with small engines, service your mower according to the manufacture's directions. Otherwise, take your mower to a local shop that can do it for you. It is very important to have them sharpen the blades while they have the mower. All that mowing last summer dulled the blades, and dull blades produce a poor-quality cut, leaving the grass blade tips brown. As the lawn greens up, begin to evaluate the condition of the grass.

- Note bare areas, areas that are not greening up, and areas of thin grass.
- Plan to renovate (where necessary) by seeding, plugging, or sodding.
- Try to identify what caused the problem and take steps to correct it if necessary. Don't be too hasty in this early evaluation as grass will continue to recover into April. **St. Augustine** damaged by brown patch last fall, for instance, will green up more slowly, but it often recovers by late April.

 PLANTING

This transitional period is not a particularly good time to plant warm-season grasses. The weather is still cool and unsettled, with the possibility of freezes lingering in the northern part of the state. Planting warm-season grasses should be delayed until at least next month.

 CARE

During late winter and early spring, the root systems of warm-season grasses actually decline, and as spring progresses, new vigorous roots grow. This month is a particularly critical time in this process, and care needs to be taken not to do anything to interfere with the re-establishment of a strong root system. The performance of the turf through the coming summer depends a great deal on what you do now. Do not disturb or stress the grass this month. This would not be a good time to aerate, fill over, or dethatch the lawn.

 WATERING

Warm days and dry weather may make watering necessary as turf wakes up from winter dormancy. If needed, water thoroughly. This encourages roots to grow deep into the soil, increasing drought tolerance this summer. Irrigating this month is generally not required, though, as sufficient rain usually falls.

 FERTILIZING

As the grass begins to grow, some gardeners are just itching to fertilize. Generally, it is better to wait. Warm-season turfgrasses are just waking up this month and re-establishing a strong root system. They tend to perform better when the first fertilizer application is made in early to mid-April. Early fertilization stimulates leafy vegetative growth at the expense of a strong root system. Brown patch disease is also more likely to occur on **St. Augustine** that has been fertilized early.

 PESTS

Cool-season weeds such as henbit, chickweed, annual blue grass, and cranesbill continue to flourish in the mild weather. The use of broadleaf weedkillers may be questionable at this time. The warm-season grasses are more vulnerable while waking up from winter dormancy. Use weedkillers early this month, if needed.

On the other hand, warm-season weeds are not apparent at this time, but the seeds will soon start germinating. To prevent a problem with summer weeds, apply a preemergence herbicide. These herbicides are applied before weeds become a problem and prevent the seeds from growing. This month is the ideal time for applications of preemergence herbicides such as oxadiazon, simazine, benefin, or bensulide for summer annual weed control. Do not apply to areas where you intend to later plant seeds of a warm-season grass.

Brown patch thrives in the cool, moist weather this month. **St. Augustine** is particularly vulnerable, although **centipede** is occasionally damaged by this fungal disease. Look for areas of green grass turning tan with a slight orange cast. These areas may rapidly enlarge if the weather is moist. Brown patch will often show up in low, moist areas of the lawn. Treat with an approved fungicide labeled to control brown patch in lawns.

 MOWING

After a winter of not mowing, many of us are reluctant to get out the lawn mower and start. Watch the lawn, and if sufficient growth occurs, you should mow. It is

HELPFUL HINTS

One of the most popular shade trees around the state is the **live oak.** It drops lots of leaves in late February and early March, and you should rake or mow (with a bag attached) these from the lawn promptly. If left on the lawn, they will cover the turfgrass as it begins to grow, and this could cause problems. Those leaves make a great addition to the compost pile.

unhealthy to let the grass get too tall before mowing. Some people have the mistaken idea that they should mow grass especially short the first few times. Scalping the lawn is not recommended and can actually lead to a weakened root system that will affect the turf negatively all summer.

St. Augustine is the most shade tolerant of the warm-season turfgrasses.

APRIL

LAWNS

 PLANNING

It's finally time to get up and get busy. April is full of lawn care activities that require some planning for best results. Do you want or need to fertilize? How much lawn renovation is necessary, and why did the grass die? Are there signs of diseases that need to be controlled? How about weeds? If you are planting a new lawn, what kind of grass will you plant and how will you establish it?

There's plenty of excellent free information available at your local parish LSU AgCenter Extension office. County agents or LSU AgCenter Master Gardeners can talk to you about lawn decisions you need to make and provide you with free literature on lawn maintenance, grass selection, and pest control specifically for our state.

 PLANTING

This month begins the prime planting season for warm-season grasses, which runs until August or September. With the exception of **common bermuda,** I recommend solid sodding as the preferred method of establishing a lawn whenever possible.

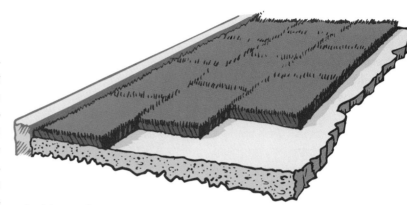

Sodding is the most reliable method of establishing warm-season grasses.

Although more expensive and labor intensive at the beginning, solid sodding more than makes up for it in advantages:

• It provides an instant lawn.

In this age of instant gratification, that is no small thing. Other methods may take an entire growing season or more before solid coverage is achieved. Traffic on the lawn area must be minimized during this entire period.

• Weed problems are minimal.

When seeding, plugging, or sprigging, weeds grow easily in the bare-soil areas and compete with the establishing grass. Hand-weeding is often the only way to deal with the situation, as herbicides are generally not used on young, establishing grass.

• Solid sodding is the most reliable method of establishing most warm-season grasses.

Plugs are the next most reliable. Runners, or stolons, and seeds must be carefully watered

and nurtured as they establish. Seeds are also subject to loss from birds, washing away by rain, and other factors that can reduce a stand. Common **bermudagrass,** on the other hand, establishes readily and easily from seeds. Birds and washing away are still possible problems and careful watering is needed, but bermudagrass seedlings grow vigorously and can cover a lawn area in six to eight weeks.

 CARE

Ideally, wait until next month to do filling, aerification, or dethatching, when the grass is growing more vigorously.

 WATERING

April can be one of our drier months, though mild weather

generally keeps the grass from getting too stressed. Watch the weather, and if things get too dry, water thoroughly and deeply as needed.

FERTILIZING

I always think about fertilizing the lawn around tax time. Fertilization is critical to producing optimal growth in the lawn. Without it, the lawn will not be as lush, vigorous, or dark green. On the other hand, fertilization is not a matter of life and death, and many lawns get along well enough to satisfy the owner without it. Lawns that have been damaged or are in low vigor certainly should be considered for fertilization.

• Choose a commercial lawn fertilizer that has much of its nitrogen in a slow-release form. This will provide nitrogen to the grass over a longer period, prevent excessive early growth, and reduce runoff into drains . . . and ultimately, into streams, lakes or rivers.

• If your soil is low in phosphorus, you may choose to use a balanced fertilizer such as 8-8-8 or 13-13-13. For soils medium to high in phosphorus, select fertilizers that have about a 4:1:2 or 3:1:2 ratio. Determine the ratio of a fertilizer analysis by dividing each number by the smallest number in the analysis. A fertilizer with an analysis of 16-4-8, for instance, has a ratio of 4:1:2.

• Do not apply lawn fertilizer by hand. The results will be uneven and can damage the grass if you aren't careful. Use a drop or centrifuge-type spreader to evenly distribute the fertilizer at the recommended rate.

• Do not guess. Follow the label directions carefully.

• Ideally, apply fertilizer to a freshly mowed lawn, as this allows the granules to fall to the soil more easily.

• The grass blades should not be wet, so wait for the dew to dry.

• Water the lawn immediately after application to wash the fertilizer down to the soil and off the blades of grass.

• If weeds are a problem, you may choose to use a fertilizer with a herbicide added, the so-called "weed-and-feeds." They are handy and can be very effective, but it is especially critical that you read and follow label directions carefully.

These products contain a toxic pesticide that may damage the lawn, trees growing in the lawn, and other ornamental plants if applied improperly.

PESTS

Apply broadleaf weedkillers now and next month. Summer weeds are young and vulnerable, and mild temperatures make using herbicides easier on the grass. Choose a product that is labeled as safe to use on the type of grass you have. Products suitable for **bermuda** and **zoysia** may damage or kill **St. Augustine** and **centipede.** Be sure to read the label for tolerant grasses and application rates. There are a number of products that combine several different herbicides in one formulation which makes them effective in controlling a wide variety of weeds.

Brown patch disease is still active. Treat with a lawn fungicide labeled to control brown patch promptly, before extensive damage occurs.

MOWING

Mowing becomes a regular job this month, though not as often as will be needed during midsummer. One of the consequences of fertilization is increased growth, which means more frequent mowing will be needed. Make sure your mower blades are sharp, and mow as needed.

MAY
LAWNS

PLANNING

Plan on doing any needed filling this month. You may also begin topdressing, dethatching, or aerification. Continue to apply herbicides, and fertilize if you didn't do so last month. Evaluate your lawn now. Are there areas that did not green up or recover well from the winter that need to be renovated? Talk to your local county agent and try to decide what may be the cause or causes before you begin work. Decide what needs to be done and correct any problems.

PLANTING

Planting warm-season grasses may be done through August or September. Planting lawns now allows the grass to grow and establish over the long summer months. This is especially important when choosing seeding, sprigging, or plugging to establish your lawn. Grass planted in early summer will also better endure the cold of its first winter, should the weather become severe.

Here are the steps to lawn planting:

1. Have a soil test done through your local LSU AgCenter Extension office to determine needed fertilizer, lime, sulfur, etc.

2. Remove any debris, especially around newly constructed homes.

3. Kill weeds growing in the area with glyphosate. Follow label directions.

4. Till soil 4 to 6 inches deep.

5. Apply soil amendments recommended by the soil test and work into the soil.

6. Establish the grade and rake smooth.

7. Use the planting method of your choice. The following are most commonly used:

• **Seeding:** Broadcast half the seed walking east to west, the other half walking north to south to ensure even coverage. Drag a rake over the area to lightly cover the seeds. Water lightly every day until sprouts come up, then regularly until the young plants are established. Plant **bermuda** May through August, **centipede** May through July.

• **Plugging:** Plant 2- to 4-inch diameter plugs 6 to 12 inches apart (greater spacing may be used, but coverage will take longer). Once planted, step on them to firm them in place. Water lightly every day for one week, every other day for another week, then less frequently but more thoroughly, especially if weather is dry.

• **Sodding:** Lay the sod in a brick pattern (alternate ends and middles) with the seams pressed tightly together. Roll the area to firm the sod into the soil. Water lightly every day for a week, every other day for another week, then less frequently but more thoroughly, especially if weather is dry. This is best done by September.

CARE

In some areas of the state it is necessary occasionally to spread fill over the lawn area to maintain the soil. This is especially common in the New Orleans area. This can be done now through August.

1. Choose a light, sandy soil for filling. If you intend to fertilize, do so before applying the fill.

2. Mow the lawn immediately before spreading the fill.

3. Spread the fill no deeper than 2 inches where you expect the grass to survive.

4. Where fill must be applied deeper, remove the sod, spread the fill, and replace the sod on top. Or, spread the fill and if the original grass does not grow through, plant new plugs or sod to replace it.

WATERING

Temperatures in the 90s generally make their debut this month. Calibrate your sprinkler system to apply $\frac{1}{2}$ to 1 inch when irrigation becomes necessary. Here's how:

1. Set out several cans in the spray pattern of the sprinkler you use to water the lawn.

2. Turn on the water and check the time.

3. Check cans at fifteen-minute intervals.

4. When 1 inch of water has accumulated in most of the cans, check the time. That is how long it takes your sprinkler to apply 1 inch of water to your lawn ($\frac{1}{2}$ inch would take half as long).

Water in the morning or early enough in the day so that the lawn does not go into the evening wet. Late watering can encourage fungal diseases.

FERTILIZING

This should have been done last month, but if you didn't, you may still do so. Do not be in a hurry to fertilize newly planted sod. There is not much root system left when the sod is harvested, so there are few roots with which the sod can absorb nutrients. Generally, wait about six to eight weeks after the sod is laid before fertilizing it.

HELPFUL HINTS

Button weed is particularly troublesome around the state. This low, mat-forming weed has 1-inch pointed leaves and small 4-petaled white flowers. Most people don't notice it until July, but it is beginning to grow now. When using a weed killer to eliminate it, herbicides containing more than one active ingredient are more effective when the weeds are young.

PESTS

This month is the last chance to apply broadleaf weedkillers before the weather gets too hot. Button weed is particularly troublesome around the state. This low, mat-forming weed has 1-inch pointed leaves and small 4-petaled white flowers. Most people don't notice it until July, but it is beginning to grow now. A combination herbicide is more effective on the weed when it is young.

MOWING

Mowing is one of the most critical parts of proper lawn care. It must be done regularly before the grass gets too high. Ideally, no more than the top $\frac{1}{3}$ of the grass blades should be cut each time you mow. Do not wait too long before mowing, especially as the rate of growth speeds up during summer.

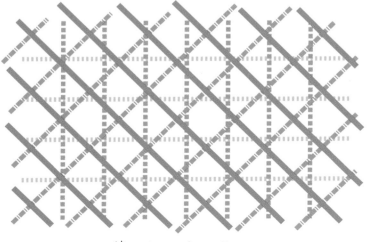

Alternate mowing patterns.

JUNE

LAWNS

PLANNING

Lawns that feel too spongy when you walk on them may have developed a thick layer of thatch. Thatch is dead grass that accumulates between the green leaf blades and the soil, and some is present and desirable in every lawn. But excess thatch reduces water penetration, creates shallow-rooted turf, encourages insect and disease infestations, and makes mowing difficult. Excessive fertilization, mowing infrequently, and mowing too high encourage this problem. Plan on topdressing, dethatching with a vertical mower, or core aerification this summer if your lawn has this problem.

PLANTING

Continue to plant warm-season grasses throughout the summer. The earlier you get them in, the longer they have to grow and get established before winter. Choose the type of grass for your lawn carefully. The chart on page 97 is a good start. Talk to friends and neighbors about their experiences with different types of grass, and contact your local LSU AgCenter Extension office for free literature on lawn

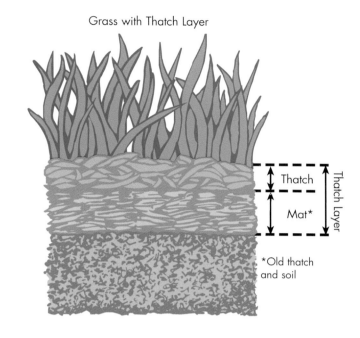

Grass with Thatch Layer

Thatch

Mat*

Thatch Layer

*Old thatch and soil

If you have a thatch problem, use a vertical mower or core aerification.

selection. Repair small bare spots by digging plugs from thick, healthy parts of the lawn and planting them where needed (or purchase plugs). Loosen the soil in the area and rake it smooth before planting the plugs. Water frequently until the plugs begin to run.

CARE

Deal with excessive thatch buildup during the summer. The least traumatic method for dealing with excessive thatch is topdressing. Apply $1/4$ to $1/2$ inch of sand or a sandy soil evenly over the lawn. The topdressing will settle over the thatch, creat-

ing a moist environment that will encourage fungi and bacteria to naturally decay the organic material.

Core aerification is also effective and is especially recommended if there is also a problem with soil compaction. The machine used for this process creates small holes in the turf and upper layer of soil with hollow tines, and deposits soil on the surface. Raked in, this soil acts like a topdressing, and the holes reduce compaction and improve air content in the soil.

Heavy thatch buildup may need to be corrected by vertical mowing. Vertical mowers, or dethatchers, have numerous blades mounted vertically on a rod and pull out the thatch when run over the lawn. This is the most traumatic method. Core aerification and dethatching with a vertical mower are best handled by a professional lawn care company.

WATERING

Water newly laid sod for fifteen to twenty minutes every day for a week. The roots are mostly lost when sod is harvested, and the sod easily dries and will die if not kept moist. During the next seven to ten days, water the sod every other day if it does not rain. Finally, apply $1/2$ inch of water to the lawn twice a week for several weeks if the weather is dry while the sod finishes establishing.

Do not continue to water the lawn every day for more than a week or you will increase the risk of fungus diseases damaging the new turf. Water established turf only as needed during hot, dry weather. Drought-stressed turf will look pale or slightly grayish, the leaves will roll lengthwise, and footprints will show on the grass for several minutes after you walk across the lawn. Water thoroughly if you observe these symptoms.

FERTILIZING

Lawns (other than **centipede**) that were fertilized in April may be fertilized again this month. This is more important in those situations where a high degree of quality and vigorous growth are desired. Also, fertilize lawns that were sodded in April or early May. Many gardeners find it acceptable to fertilize once in April to get the grass off to a good start and leave it at that.

PESTS

Be cautious before using weed-killers for the rest of the summer. Many will damage the lawn if temperatures are high.

Insect problems like chinch bugs and mole crickets may need to be dealt with this month. Chinch bugs suck the sap out of grass and are especially damaging during periods of hot, dry weather. Look for areas of dead, straw-like grass starting in sunny, hot areas of the lawn. Treat with insecticides labeled to control chinch bugs in lawns.

Mole crickets are more of a problem in south Louisiana. They tunnel through the turf, and the tawny mole cricket eats the roots. At this time, the adults die off and the young nymphs are most susceptible to insecticides. Make several applications in late June and early July with insecticides labeled for control of mole crickets in lawns. When using any pesticide, always read the label carefully and follow the directions exactly.

MOWING

Given our long growing season, it is not a bad idea to sharpen mower blades again in midsummer. Dull mower blades tear the grass blades, leaving ragged, brown tips that make the lawn look less attractive. Set your mower to the following recommended heights:

Common Bermuda: 1 to
  $1^1/2$ inches
  (reel mower recommended)
Hybrid Bermuda: $1/2$ to 1 inch
  (reel mower recommended)
Centipede: 1 to 2 inches
  (rotary or reel mower)
St. Augustine: 2 to 3 inches
  (rotary or reel mower)
Zoysia: $1/2$ to $1^1/2$ inches
  (reel mower recommended).

JULY
LAWNS

PLANNING

Mow, edge, and deal with pest problems before you go on vacation. Plan on having your lawn mowed if you will be on vacation longer than seven days. Lawngrass grows rapidly and, if left uncut, will show that no one is home. The heat index in Louisiana will top 100 most days in July and August. Do yard work in the early morning or late evening when temperatures are not so hot. Drink plenty of water and take frequent breaks.

PLANTING

You may continue to plant lawns despite the heat. Watering newly plugged, sprigged, or sodded lawns is especially critical when it is this hot. Check sod carefully before laying it. Ask the nursery or dealer how long it has been since it was harvested. Ideally, sod should be planted within a day or two of being harvested. It is very perishable in summer heat. This is the last month to seed **centipede** and allow it ample time to establish before winter.

CARE

As landscapes mature, shade trees begin to do what they were planted to do—shade the yard. Lawngrasses eventually receive more shade than they can tolerate and will begin to thin and disappear when that happens.

Increase the amount of sunlight reaching the turf by selectively pruning the trees in your landscape. Prune the lower branches and some of the inner branches to allow more light to reach the lawn below (often best done by a professional arborist). This is a temporary solution, as the trees will continue to grow.

St. Augustine (cultivars such as 'Palmetto') will tolerate the most shade. **Centipede** and **zoysia** varieties 'Emerald', 'Meyers', and 'El Toro' are also considered fairly shade tolerant.

Grass growing in shady areas needs less fertilizer and should be mowed at the highest recommended mowing height.

Don't expect any of them to grow in heavy shade. Set your mower at the highest recommended mowing height. St. Augustine can be mowed at a height of 3 inches, centipede can be allowed to grow to 2¹/₂ inches, and zoysia mowed at 1¹/₂ inches. Avoid excessive fertilization; grass in the shade does not grow as fast. If after these efforts you still can't get grass to grow under your tree, it's time to accept the situation (as we gardeners often must do) and stop wasting your effort and money trying to make grass grow where it can't. Unless cutting down the tree is an option, your next step is to plant shade-loving ground covers such as **ferns, monkey grass, liriope, Asiatic jasmine,** or **cast-iron plants (aspidistra).**

WATERING

Do not water needlessly. Overwatering your lawn wastes water and promotes disease problems. Wait at least seven to ten days after the last good rain before you consider irrigation. Even then, look at the grass and dig into the soil. If the grass is not showing drought stress and there is still some moisture in the soil, wait a while longer to water. Do not water lightly every day, a practice which encourages diseases and creates a shallow root system.

FERTILIZING

If you last fertilized in April you might fertilize again this month, especially if the grass is not growing fast enough and you would like to mow more often. Fertilizer will create a deeper green color along with faster growth. For most lawns, two fertilizer applications, one in April and another this month, produce acceptable color and growth. A second light application of lawn fertilizer could be applied to **centipede** now as well. This grass will actually decline in vigor and fade away if you fertilize it too much. A slight yellow tint to the green color of the blades is normal for this grass.

PESTS

Continue to treat with insecticides if you have had problems with mole crickets. They tend to be worst on **bermuda** lawns, but also damage **zoysia** and **centipede.** This is prime chinch bug season for **St. Augustine,** especially if the weather turns dry. Watch for tan strawlike dead areas that enlarge over several days. Do not delay controlling this pest. It kills the grass outright, and extensive damage means a lot of turf replacement.

The most effective weed control should have taken place in late spring and early summer. Handpull and spot-treat weeds now. Wait until the weather is not so hot to use most broadleaf weedkillers. Common summer weed problems include button weed, dallisgrass, goosegrass, and nutgrass. Spot-treat button weed, dallisgrass, and goosegrass with glyphosate. Spray directly on the weed, minimizing contact with the lawngrass (it will kill it). Control nutgrass with imazaquin (Image), which may be used on all warm-season turfgrasses.

MOWING

Mow regularly at recommended heights. Mulching mowers prevent the need to bag clippings. The clippings return nutrients to the lawn, lowering the need for fertilizers. If you don't have a mulching mower, mow frequently so that the clippings are small—that works just about as well. If you do bag clippings, make sure you compost them for use in garden beds.

AUGUST
LAWNS

 PLANNING

This is a good month to evaluate your lawn. If it's in poor shape, try to identify the problems and plan on how to do a better job preventing them. Make some notes of what you would do differently next year. Earlier and better weed control is a good example. Learn from your experiences and record them for future reference.

 PLANTING

Finish up seeding common **bermudagrass** this month. As fast as it grows, expect good coverage before cool fall temperatures slow it down. Lay sod and plant plugs if possible. Every week of delay now is one less week of growing season for the turf to establish. This is particularly true for plugs.

 CARE

Areas of your lawn that still need to be renovated should also be handled now. Kill any weeds, loosen the soil, and sprig, plug, or sod new turf into the area. Keep the grass adequately watered and keep pets and people away until it has established.

 WATERING

These long, hot days coming at the end of a long, hot summer are especially stressful. Watering continues to be important. There is no way to predict the amount of rainfall that will occur. It could be very dry, or we could see almost daily rain. Do not be fooled by quick thundershowers. Unless at least $1/2$ inch of rain falls, it should not be considered a "good rain." Water early in the day if possible. Avoid watering in the early evening, which does not give the grass time to dry before nightfall, encouraging disease problems.

 FERTILIZING

Those who want maximum quality and growth should make their third and last fertilizer application this month. Use fertilizers with an approximate 4:1:2 or 3:1:2 ratio analysis. Basically, look for a fertilizer that has a high first number, a low second number, and a third number somewhere in between. Apply fertilizer evenly with a drop or centrifuge-type spreader and water it in immediately after application.

 PESTS

Fleas are insects that infest lawns. Although they don't damage the grass, they sure pester the people and pets. Treat the lawn with an approved insecticide. Several applications will be necessary, and don't forget to treat any pets according to your vet's advice.

Fire ants are other lawn pests that don't damage the grass but bother us. Treat individual mounds with any of the available insecticides labeled for fire ant control. Baits are more effective than individual mounds when spread over the entire yard, though they are slower acting. Fire ants are excellent predators of other insects (like fleas and ticks), and if they aren't in a spot where they are causing a problem, you may choose to leave them alone.

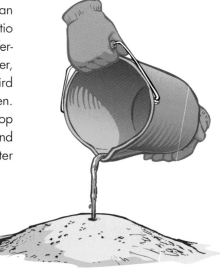

Control fire ants by applying an appropriate pesticide to the mound.

SEPTEMBER

LAWNS

 PLANNING

This month, relief from the heat is possible, but not guaranteed. Still, the heat is generally not so intense. Lawns are in active growth, but cooler weather in October and November will finally begin to slow them down. With that in mind, plan to finish up filling, sodding, dethatching, and aerification early this month.

 PLANTING

It's late for planting plugs or sprigs, and really too late to plant seeds of **centipede** or even fast-growing **bermuda.** You may continue to lay sod this month. Don't forget that newly laid sod must be watered regularly to keep it from drying out while the roots establish. In north Louisiana, **ryegrass** seed may be planted later this month. There is no hurry, and if the weather is hot the ryegrass will not appreciate it. Warm-season lawns are still nice and green, and there is really no need to plant seed this early.

 CARE

You may as well repair dead areas caused by chinch bugs this month:

1. Remove any dead grass plaguing your lawn.

2. Turn the soil and rake it smooth.

3. Lay sod, or at least plant some plugs in the area.

4. Keep well watered during establishment. You will feel better next spring not seeing the dead spots in an otherwise green lawn, and your lawn will be more attractive this fall.

September is a prime month for hurricanes (the season runs from June to October). Should a hurricane threaten your area, pick up and store all loose objects in the lawn, including sprinklers, tools, lawn ornaments (yes, your pink flamingos), and anything else that could be picked up by 100-mile-per-hour winds. Should a hurricane hit your area, rake and hose off debris and mud from your lawn-grass as soon as possible after the storm. If it stays covered for several days, significant damage can occur. If the area was covered by salt or brackish water, **St. Augustine** and **bermuda** have good tolerance. Rinse the salt water away with fresh water as soon as possible.

 WATERING

Water as needed, especially newly laid lawns or lawns that are recovering from dethatching or aerification.

 FERTILIZING

Put up the bags and spreaders, we're through for the year.

 PESTS

Watch for caterpillars such as armyworms or sod webworms. They chew grass blades and can make the lawn look terrible. Control with Bt or other insecticides labeled to control lawn insects. The grass will generally recover well from the damage.

 MOWING

You may not have to mow quite as often as the weather turns cooler, but don't let your grass get overgrown before mowing.

OCTOBER

LAWNS

 **PLANNING**

As we move into the cool dormant season for our warm-season grasses, plan on whether or not you want to overseed with a cool-season grass. Remember, you will have to continue to mow throughout the winter if you do.

 **PLANTING**

Plant **ryegrass** seed this month and in November. Annual ryegrass is the least expensive, most readily available, and most commonly used.

1. Spread the seeds evenly over a freshly mown lawn using a spreader.

2. Apply $1/2$ the seeds walking east to west, $1/2$ walking north to south. Use about 10 pounds per 1000 square feet.

3. Water the seeds lightly every day for the seven to ten days it takes them to germinate. Ryegrass usually fills in nicely in about four to five weeks after it comes up. For higher quality, use perennial ryegrass or a perennial ryegrass blend. The color will be darker, the texture finer, and it will last longer into the spring. It is, of course, more expensive.

 **CARE**

Some gardeners are afraid that overseeding existing warm-season turf will damage it. Don't worry. Overseeding will not harm any of the commonly used warm-season grasses. In fact, overseeding tends to reduce competition from cool-season weeds since the lawn is mowed and maintained throughout the winter.

 **WATERING**

The weather now makes this one of the most enjoyable months of the year. It is, however, usually dry. Do not allow turfgrass to go into dormancy when it is drought stressed. Water deeply and thoroughly if a good rain does not occur for ten to fourteen days. Overseeded lawns will need more frequent watering while the **ryegrass** establishes.

 **FERTILIZING**

You will be encouraged by nurseries and garden centers to "winterize" your lawn with a high-potassium fertilizer (the analysis will have a high third number). This is meant to pre-

pare the grass for the winter and increase its hardiness. There is adequate potassium in the 3:1:2 ratio fertilizers you used this summer, and there is absolutely no need to add more now.

Caution: The winterizers available at some national chain stores are high in nitrogen (over 20 percent) and should NOT be used. They are meant for winterizing Northern lawns, not ours.

 **PESTS**

If the weather is unusually wet, brown patch may appear on **St. Augustine.** Watch for it and treat if necessary. Apply preemergence herbicides to the lawn this month to control cool-season annual weeds such as henbit, chickweed, and annual blue grass. These herbicides that prevent weeds from growing must be applied before the weeds show up in the lawn.

 **MOWING**

Do not mow an overseeded lawn until the **ryegrass** seed germinates and you see the green blades. Mowing newly overseeded lawns can suck up the seeds into the bag or damage them.

Closeup view of perennial ryegrass

NOVEMBER

LAWNS

 PLANNING

In the northern part of the state, warm-season grasses are going dormant with the first freeze. Down south, mowing is greatly reduced as the weather cools. Cool fronts bring rain. This is a good time to review successes and failures of the past season. What would you do differently? Write brief entries on your gardening calendar for next year at the proper times when lawn maintenance jobs will need to be done. The calendar will provide you with a handy guide and remind you when things like fertilization, herbicide applications, and planting need to be completed.

 PLANTING

Continue to overseed **ryegrass** if you have not already done so. The look of ryegrass is outstandingly beautiful throughout the winter. The rich green is nicer than any of the warm-season grasses. You will need to continue mowing throughout the winter, but many people think it is worth it. If you have bare areas where soil might wash away during the winter, use ryegrass seed to stabilize the soil until spring. Ryegrass can also be planted around newly constructed homes to stabilize the soil until it is time to lay sod next April. Turn ryegrass under before laying sod. It will enrich and add organic matter to the soil.

 CARE

After a long growing season, it's nice to be able to slow down. Little needs to be done to warm-season grasses other than watch them slow down and go dormant. **Zoysia, bermuda,** and **centipede** go off color (turn tan) relatively early. This increases their hardiness, as they are quite dormant if and when severe freezes occur. **St. Augustine** is not so inclined to go dormant, especially in south Louisiana, and may stay fairly green well into December, and even into January if no freezes occur. This may make it more likely to sustain freeze injury during a sudden drop to the low 20s or teens. A new cultivar, 'Palmetto,' apparently combines the ability to stay green with increased cold hardiness.

 WATERING

Cool, moist weather and a dormant condition make the need for irrigating warm-season grasses unlikely for the rest of the cool season.

 FERTILIZING

In north Louisiana, **ryegrass** planted in October should be fertilized in late November or early December, after the warm-season grass in your lawn has gone dormant.

 PESTS

Apply a preemergence herbicide early this month if you did not do so in October. In south Louisiana, watch for brown patch on **St. Augustine** and treat promptly with an appropriate lawn fungicide.

 MOWING

Mow **ryegrass** regularly at a mower height of 1 to 2 inches.

DECEMBER

LAWNS

PLANNING

Unless you overseeded with ryegrass, lawns are wonderfully care-free this time of the year. Review your notes and make sure you have recorded everything you need to do before you forget. Before you store your lawn mower, be sure to service it properly (check the manufacturer's instruction booklet), or take it to your local lawn mower shop for servicing.

PLANTING

In the warmest parts of the state, **ryegrass** is often planted successfully through the winter. If the winter is mild, there is no problem. If temperatures in the teens occur while the grass is getting established, however, the grass can be damaged. If there are some areas of the lawn where the ryegrass seems a little thin, feel free to scatter some seed to thicken those spots a bit. Dormant sodding of warm-season grasses is done during the winter but is not very popular. The grass goes in dormant and brown, which is a bit disconcert-

ing, and there is some risk involved during particularly cold winters since the turf is more susceptible to freeze injury. Laying sod during the winter has no real advantage other than to stabilize soil around new construction. The grass will not begin to grow and establish until the weather warms up next March.

CARE

Honestly . . . you really can ignore the lawn this time of the year and devote more time to other gardening activities such as planting trees and shrubs.

WATERING

Cool to cold weather and a dormant condition make watering warm-season grasses unnecessary during this month. Continue to irrigate lawns overseeded with **ryegrass** as needed if the weather is mild and dry. Mixed in with the freezes, temperatures in the 70s are not unusual in December.

FERTILIZING

In south Louisiana, fertilize **ryegrass** around the middle of this month after warm-season grasses go dormant. This will make the ryegrass darker green and encourage vigorous growth.

PESTS

As with other aspects of lawn care, pest control is minimal this time of the year. Cool-season weeds should not be a problem if you applied a preemergence herbicide in October or early November.

MOWING

Mow **ryegrass** regularly. A height of 1 inch is used for ryegrass overseeded on **bermuda** or **zoysia**. Mow ryegrass at a height of 2 inches if it was used to overseed **centipede** or **St. Augustine**.

PERENNIALS

Perennials are the delight of the flower gardener. Though showy and colorful like annuals, their longer lives make them a less transient part of the garden. Their ability to live for years allows them to become old friends that can provide you with beauty for many seasons. As with annuals, though, perennial beds and borders are a high-maintenance part of the landscape.

Perennials are plants that live for three years or longer. Unlike annuals and biennials, perennials do not die after flowering and setting seed. Techni-cally, trees, shrubs, lawngrasses, and bulbs are all perennials, but gardeners use the term "peren-nial" as an abbreviation for "hardy, herbaceous perennial"—a group of non-woody, hardy plants grown for their attractive flowers or foliage. Some herbaceous perennials are evergreen and never go completely dormant, while others go dormant, lose their leaves, and essentially disappear at cer-tain times of the year, usually winter.

Success with perennials in Louisiana depends largely on proper selection, beginning with a

rejection of perennials that only grow well north of zone 8. To survive here, perennials must be able to endure the heat, humidity, and rain of summer, along with the diseases that season brings. Stop planting perennials recommended in books written for the rest of the country and focus on those that will thrive in our climate. You will discover that not only is perennial gardening possible here, but we can plant beds that rival those in the Northeast and in England.

PLANNING THE PERENNIAL GARDEN

Gardening with perennials is something that gardeners often develop an interest in as they become more experienced. When you finally reach that "been there, done that" stage with annuals, perennials offer exciting challenges and great fun. Utilizing perennials effectively does, however, require learning and careful planning.

Different perennials have different seasons of bloom—some over a long period, some for just a few weeks. Utilizing a variety of perennials that bloom at different times can keep your perennial garden blooming throughout much of the year. Some other important questions you need to answer about the perennials you want to use:

• What species or cultivars are best for Louisiana?

• How tall will the plant grow?

• What colors are the flowers?

• What light conditions does the plant prefer—full or part sun, part shade or shady?

• Does it need excellent drainage?

• Is it evergreen? If it goes dormant—when?

• How fast will it spread?

With some thoughtful planning, perennials can serve many purposes and attractively embellish the landscape in a variety of ways. They are impressive in perennial borders or mixed borders (which could include annuals, bulbs, shrubs, and even small trees). Tucked in pockets among shrubs, they can brighten up an area when the shrubs are not in bloom. Some, such as monkey

Dwarf Monkey Grass

grass (*Ophiopogon japonicus*), are useful as ground covers. Many perennials make outstanding specimens in containers.

PLANTING

The first step in planting perennials is excellent bed preparation. It is important to do a good job at each of the following stages:

1. Remove weeds and other unwanted plants from the bed. Growing weeds may be killed with a systemic, nonselective herbicide such as glyphosate that does not leave residue in the soil.

2. Turn the soil to a depth of at least 8 to 12 inches.

3. Spread a 4-inch layer of compost, rotted leaves, aged manure, finely ground pine bark, or sphagnum peat moss over the bed, then evenly sprinkle a light application of a granular all-purpose fertilizer. If needed, add sand, lime, or sulfur at this stage. Have your soil tested through your parish LSU AgCenter Extension office to learn more about what might improve your soil.

4. Thoroughly blend the amendments into the bed, rake smooth, and you're ready to plant.

Perennials are most often planted using purchased transplants or divisions. Transplants may be purchased in 4-inch to gallon-sized pots. Spring- and early summer-flowering perennials are generally planted in October through early December, and late summer- or fall-flowering perennials are planted from February through early April (they may also be planted in fall). Many gardeners plant perennials throughout the winter when weather is mild, especially in the southern part of the state.

PLANTING TRANSPLANTS

1. Space plants according to label information, references, or local advice. Most perennials will grow considerably larger than the size of the transplant. Do not crowd them.

2. Plant transplants with the top of the rootball even with or slightly above the soil. Many perennials will rot if planted too deeply. If the roots are in a tightly packed mass, pull them apart and spread them when planting. A small amount of slow-release fertilizer may be placed in the planting hole. Firm the soil around the plant once you are finished planting.

3. Water newly planted transplants thoroughly. A fertilizer solution that is half-strength may be used.

4. Mulch the bed to control weeds, but do not cover the perennial plants.

Some perennials are relatively easy to grow from seed. Seeds are generally planted directly into garden beds or in containers outside to raise transplants. This is best done after the danger of frost is past, and early enough for the plants to become established before winter (April through August).

CARE FOR YOUR PERENNIALS

Perennial beds require regular watering, fertilizing, grooming, staking, cutting back, dividing, transplanting, weeding, and mulching. Do not plant more beds of perennials than your time will allow you to properly care for.

Supporting tall-growing perennials is important and often neglected by gardeners. Sprawling perennials are unattractive and can damage the plants around them. Plan to stake, cage, tie up, or otherwise support perennials that need it early, before they fall over.

WATERING

Watering is most critical for newly planted perennials, especially during hot, dry summer weather. Water deeply and thoroughly by applying water slowly over a period of time. Sprinklers may be used, but water can damage flowers and encourage leaf diseases. Soaker hoses provide an excellent alternative. The use of mulches in peren-

nial gardens will conserve moisture and reduce the need for irrigation.

FERTILIZATION

Fertilizer should be dug into the soil during bed preparation. A small amount of slow-release fertilizer such as Osmocote or Nutricote can be added to the planting hole at planting. During the growing season, fertilize established perennials beginning in March or early April. If you don't use slow-release fertilizer, you may apply fertilizer every six to eight weeks using a general-purpose fertilizer appropriate for your area. Follow package directions. Scatter the fertilizer granules evenly throughout the bed, and water-in to wash the fertilizer off the foliage and into the soil.

PEST CONTROL

Pest control is certainly going to be a part of perennial gardening, but the use of tough, well-adapted perennials will minimize the need for pesticides. When using pesticides, always read the label thoroughly before you purchase and use them.

Caterpillars are common and damage plants by chewing holes in leaves. Treat with Bt, spinosad, or other insecticides labeled to control caterpillars on ornamentals. The whitefly can be a difficult insect to control, especially in mid- to late summer when populations can get way out of hand. The adults are small, snow-white flies; the larvae appear as small disks under the leaves. Spray with acephate (Orthene), SunSpray Ultra-Fine Oil, or Talstar. Aphids cluster on new growth and flower buds, sucking the sap from the plant. They are relatively easy to kill but may return, requiring additional applications of pesticide. Spray with insecticidal soap, Ultra-Fine oil, or acephate. Various sucking insects, such as leaf hoppers, thrips, and plant bugs, cause small white flecks to appear on the foliage of many perennials. The damage is generally little more than cosmetic but can weaken the plant if extensive. Spray with SunSpray Ultra-Fine Oil, Malathion, Talstar, or acephate.

Spider mites can be devastating, especially during hot, dry weather. Spray with Ultra-Fine Oil, Malathion, insecticidal soap, or Kelthane.

Snails and slugs love hostas and other plants that have succulent leaves and grow in shady areas. Control with handpicking, traps, or iron phosphate according to label directions.

Perennials that are well adapted and planted in the right location generally have minor problems with diseases. Leaf spots caused by various fungi and powdery mildew will sometimes occur and can be treated with a fungicide such as chlorothalonil or thiophanate methyl. Root and crown rot may occur if drainage is inadequate, during periods of excessive rain, or if perennials not well-adapted to Louisiana are planted.

JANUARY
PERENNIALS

 PLANNING

Look through mail-order catalogs that offer perennials, or check out gardening sites on the Internet to develop a list of perennials you might want to plant. Note the recommended hardiness zones indicated for any perennial you are interested in. You are looking for plants for zones 8 and 9. It doesn't hurt to experiment (in fact, I expect you to), but do so on a small scale and be prepared for disappointment. When ordering, specify that you would like to receive your order as soon as possible. Our mild winters allow us to plant hardy perennials virtually any time during the cool season.

 PLANTING

Gardeners frequently move perennials around, trying to find a location where they will look and grow their best, or just to try out a different combination. Often we are unfamiliar with exactly what a perennial will do for us until we have grown it in our own garden. After a year or two, a gardener may realize that another location for the plant would be better. Now would be a good time to do this.

 CARE

Apply mulch over the crowns and roots of some of the less hardy perennials during the coldest part of winter. This will help prevent cold damage. Pine straw works well, as it tends to stay looser. Mulch perennials such as **acanthus, asparagus fern, spider plant, cigar plant, ruellia,** and **salvias.**

 WATERING

Cool to cold temperatures, typical rainy weather, and the dormant condition of many perennials generally make watering unnecessary. If the weather turns mild and dry, water beds containing evergreen perennials as needed.

 FERTILIZING

Few herbaceous perennials are in active growth during the winter, and January is not the best time to fertilize them. Dormant perennials do not need fertilizer.

 PESTS

Insect and disease problems are at a minimum this time of year. Cool-season weeds, however, will be in active growth any time a stretch of mild weather occurs. Keep beds well mulched and promptly pull up any weeds as they appear. If the temperatures will go above 65 degrees Fahrenheit, spray tough weeds, like oxalis, with glyphosate. Since you have to be careful not to get any on the foliage of desirable plants, it is easier to use when the perennials are mostly dormant and there is little or no foliage present on them.

 PRUNING

Cut back and remove old, dead upper portions of dormant perennials. This will keep the garden looking more attractive. Chop up the material and put it in your compost pile. Some perennials don't go dormant until the first freezes hit, and in the southern part of the state, freezes may not occur until late December or January (or sometimes not at all in the southeast corner).

FEBRUARY

PERENNIALS

 PLANNING

Part of the fun of using perennials is planning. It's like choreographing a dance, each member of the troupe with a role to play. There are supporting cast members, soloists that enliven the dance at various times, and even prima donnas. Throw a bunch of dancers on the stage without a carefully thought out plan, and the result will be chaos that may even lead to injuries. Purchase and plant perennials without carefully designing the composition, and the result may be chaos in the garden and disappointing results.

Planning begins with the site, not the perennials themselves. Just as a choreographer looks at the size of the stage, where the audience will be, the lighting available, and the backdrops, you must study the site where the planting will be located. How large is the bed? From which direction will it be viewed? How much light does the area receive? Is the drainage good? What existing trees, shrubs, or other features will contribute to the composition?

Next, develop your ideas on what characteristics the perennials must have to create the composition you imagine.

• Is the bed location sunny or shady? Dry or damp? Choose perennials that will thrive in the growing conditions of the area.

• Flower colors are important—they must blend, harmonize, or contrast attractively with one another. Decide on a visual scheme and which colors you will use to achieve it.

• Time of bloom should be considered. Select perennials that bloom at various times.

• Height must be decided. How tall do you want the tallest perennials to be? They should be placed toward the back of a bed from the direction it will be viewed, or toward the middle of a bed to be viewed from all sides. The tallest perennials will guide the height of shorter perennials to be used in the bed.

• Choose perennials with a variety of textures (coarse-textured plants have large leaves, fine-textured plants have small or thin leaves, and medium-textured plants fall somewhere in-between) and growth habits (upright, bushy, mounding) to create interest and contrast.

Make a sketch of the bed and section it off into areas indicating where the tall, intermediate, and short plants will go.

Begin to make lists of perennials that have the characteristics for which you are searching. Beside each name, indicate briefly the major features of the plant (height, bloom time, color). Use the lists to make your final perennial choices, and place the names and number of plants needed into areas on your sketch. Depending on the size of the bed and how large a peren-

Beds may be prepared now; remove turf as your first step.

nial will grow, it is generally best to plant perennials in groups, masses, or drifts of the same type rather than a lot of different individual plants. Do not fall into the "I'll take one of each" blunder. This is to be a garden, after all, not a botanical display.

Order or purchase the selected plants, plant them into the garden, and watch the magic of the dance that careful planning creates.

PLANTING

It's time to gear up for major planting this month and in March. Although a fall planting is preferred, it is especially important to get spring and early-summer perennials planted. Perennials such as **acanthus, blue star, false indigo, daylily, blue phlox,** and **Indian pink** are in this group.

Work on getting beds ready and in shape for planting. Kill and remove any weeds in existing beds, or remove turf from new beds. Turn the soil, add generous amounts of organic matter and a light application of all-purpose fertilizer, and dig everything in. Beds may be prepared several weeks prior to planting. Mulch newly prepared beds heavily until you are ready to plant them.

If you need to dig up and move or divide perennials, get started now. This needs to be finished by late March (southern Louisiana) or early April (northern Louisiana).

CARE

Watch for new growth on dormant perennials, and be careful. They are easily damaged by hoeing or digging. Hostas are late sleepers and often do not wake up until April. Note where dormant perennials are located (it is hoped that you marked them with small stakes in the fall as they went dormant), and do not damage them while digging.

WATERING

Cool, moist weather means little watering will need to be done. Water-in newly planted perennials thoroughly, and continue watering regularly if needed. Perennials growing in containers will need regular watering, especially if they are in a location where they do not receive rain, such as on a covered patio.

FERTILIZING

In south Louisiana, perennials that are in active growth may be fertilized in late February. It's generally best to wait a few weeks until mid-March to fertilize perennials still dormant or just waking up. North Louisiana gardeners should certainly wait.

Incorporate fertilizer into the soil during bed preparation, and a little slow-release fertilizer may be placed in the planting hole when planting perennial transplants.

PESTS

There are generally no major insect or disease problems in February. If winter has been mild, aphids may be seen on new growth. Spray with insecticidal soap or Malathion for control as needed. Continue to weed.

PRUNING

Remove old, dead growth on perennials as soon as possible if you have not already done so. It will become increasingly difficult to remove dead stalks without damaging the new growth as it grows taller.

MARCH

PERENNIALS

PLANNING

Get your orders off as soon as possible if you are planning to buy mail-order perennials from catalogs or over the Internet. Mail-order plants are often shipped bare root or are fairly small (a 4-inch pot size is common), and they will need as much time as possible to become established before the heat of summer.

Before ordering perennials, plan where they will be planted based on the growing conditions they need and how they grow. Avoid perennials that have little chance of thriving in the growing conditions you are able to provide. It is a wise, experienced gardener who can say, "I'd really love to grow that, but I just don't have the right spot."

Avoid the temptation of buying more new perennials than you have room to plant, or dig up and give away perennials you've grown for some time to make way for the new ones.

PLANTING

Finish transplanting and dividing perennials as soon as possible. Transplanted now, most perennials will barely miss a beat if moved with most of their roots. Later on, warmer weather makes it more likely that perennials will suffer increased transplant shock.

Divide clumps of perennials that need it. Some are best divided every year or two, but most can be left alone for two to three years, or even longer. Dividing helps control the size of the plant and the space it occupies, as well as rejuvenating it. Dividing perennials is also a good way to propagate many of them.

To divide perennials:

1. Lift the entire clump.
2. Study the clump carefully. Note the crowns or shoots present.
3. Decide how many pieces to divide the clump into. Generally, each division should have several crowns or shoots.
4. Decide where to make the cuts. Avoid cutting through crowns or damaging shoots.
5. Cut apart the clump with a large, sharp knife. Be careful. Wear leather gloves.
6. Replant or pot up the divisions immediately.

Perennials may not look like much when you purchase them this month. This is a reason newer gardeners, accustomed to buying annuals in full bloom, are slow to appreciate perennials. You must be able to imagine how they will look when they bloom in two or three months—or even at the end of the summer—to value them in March.

Growers have overcome this to some extent by producing perennials in gallon containers. These can be planted later since the perennials have more room to develop a strong root system. This allows gardeners to purchase plants in bloom, but they pay a premium price for it. Buy and plant perennials in smaller containers now, and it is likely that the plants in your garden will be as attractive as the gallon-sized perennials available later.

Plant perennials into beds so that the top of the rootballs are level with or slightly above the soil of the bed. Many perennials are more likely to suffer crown

March is a good month to divide perennials; give away the extra ones or expand your beds.

rot if planted too deeply. If you see that the rootball is tightly packed when you remove the perennial from the container, pull it apart and spread out the roots a little when planting

CARE

Watch the weather carefully. March is an unsettled month, and periods of warm temperatures can be followed by a sudden freeze, particularly in the northern part of the state. It is unlikely that you will need to protect hardy perennials. Tender new growth, however, is more susceptible to sudden freezes. Mulch, fabric sheets, or plastic may be thrown over perennials you think might be vulnerable. Promptly remove coverings when freezing temperatures have ended.

WATERING

Warmer temperatures and active growth make watering increasingly important if regular rainfall does not occur. Apply water slowly over time with a sprinkler or soaker hose to ensure a deep, thorough watering. It is far better for the health of the perennials to water them thoroughly and occasionally rather than lightly and frequently.

Newly planted perennial beds will need special attention. Until new perennials have a chance to grow a strong root system into the surrounding soil, they are vulnerable to drying out. Water new plantings once or twice a week as needed.

FERTILIZING

Established perennials should be fertilized this month. This is most efficiently and economically done using a granular fertilizer scattered evenly throughout the bed. If your soil has adequate phosphorus, choose a general-purpose fertilizer with about a 3:1:2 ratio, such as 15-5-10. For soils that test low in phosphorus, select a balanced fertilizer with a 1:1:1 ratio, such as 8-8-8. Follow label directions, but use a light to moderate amount. Use about $1/2$ cup of 15-5-10 in a 30-square-foot bed, or about 1 cup of 8-8-8. You may use slow-release or organic fertilizers instead. Follow package directions.

After the fertilizer has been applied, water the bed by hand to wash any fertilizer granules off the foliage and down to the soil. Some gardeners pull out the mulch, fertilize, water, and replace the mulch to allow the fertilizer granules to reach the soil more efficiently. I'm too lazy

for this, however, and generally find that the fertilizer eventually reaches the soil without the trouble of moving the mulch.

PESTS

Make notes of pest problems in your perennials records.

Snails and slugs will be active during mild weather. Get an early start on control and do not let their populations build. Various baits and traps, or hand-picking, will help reduce populations. **Hostas,** which generally begin to grow in late March or April, are particularly vulnerable. Control aphids with insecticidal soap, Ultra-Fine Oil, or Malathion. Control caterpillars with Sevin, acephate (Orthene), or Bt. Keep these pesticides away from your butterfly garden area.

Whoever said, "A job well done doesn't have to be done again," never weeded a flower bed. Apply preemergence herbicides such as Preen, Eptam, or Amaze to weeded beds to prevent the growth of new weeds from seeds. Check the label carefully, and make sure the herbicide is appropriate to use around the ornamental plants growing in the bed.

APRIL
PERENNIALS

PLANNING

The nurseries are full of plants, and if you never quite got around to sending off that mail order for perennials, at least you can find out what's new at the nursery. Choose larger plants in larger containers for planting this late, if possible. Send off your mail order if you simply have to. When your plants come in, be ready to give them extra care, and don't expect too much from them this first year unless they are fall bloomers.

No one said that a plan cannot allow for some spontaneity or change. "I saw it and just had to have it" is often reason enough for a purchase. But, it is difficult to create a planting that really comes together effectively if you make that the primary way you choose your plants.

PLANTING

Pay careful attention to spacing when planting perennials. If you are accustomed to planting annuals, you may be tempted to plant the perennials too close. Most perennials grow considerably larger than the small transplants you set out. Remember as well that these plants will grow in that location for sev-

eral years, getting larger every year. The full look you see in beautiful photographs of perennial borders happens after the perennials have been growing for some time—don't expect your bed to look like that a couple of months after planting. Despite our long growing season, it will take most perennials more than one season to reach full size.

If you would like to try your hand at growing perennials from seed, now is a good month to start. Since many perennials will not bloom until their second year, most gardeners plant seeds in containers to raise transplants which are planted into the garden in the fall or early the next spring.

1. Fill a flat or pot with moistened seed-starting mix.

2. Plant seeds thickly at the recommended depth, and gently water the flat to settle them in.

3. Cover the flat with clear plastic wrap and place it in full shade.

4. Check the mix frequently and do not allow it to dry out or stay too wet. With the plastic cover, you may not need to add more water. If the mix stays too wet, vent or remove the plastic for a few hours.

5. When the seeds begin to germinate, remove the plastic and immediately move the flat to

a location that receives about six hours of sun early in the day, for sun-loving perennials. Place the flat in part shade to shade if you are growing perennials that prefer shadier conditions. Water regularly!

6. When the seedlings begin to look crowded, gently separate them (try to handle them by their leaves rather than their stems) and plant into cell-packs, or individually in 4-inch pots using moistened soilless mix or potting soil.

7. Water the growing transplants daily, if necessary, to prevent the soil from drying out. Fertilize weekly with half-strength, soluble fertilizer.

8. Repot into larger containers as needed.

9. Plant out in October or November, or even during the summer if the plants get big enough.

CARE

Some perennials, such as **acanthus, blue star, butterfly weed, Shasta daisy, blue phlox,** and **Indian pink** are in bloom this month, especially in the southern part of the state. **Blue phlox** (also known as **Louisiana phlox**) is particularly beautiful. Deadhead (remove the faded flowers) regularly to keep plants attractive and, in some cases, encourage more flowers. Indian pink will generally send up a few more blooms if the faded flower cluster at the shoot tips is pinched off.

As perennials grow, make sure your layer of mulch is about 2 inches thick. Add more mulch to beds if necessary. A proper layer of mulch will keep soil cooler as the weather heats up, conserve soil moisture, and prevent weeds, as well as make perennial plantings look more attractive.

 WATERING

Deep watering is especially important this time of year if sufficient rain does not fall. It will encourage your perennials to develop a deep root system that will make them stronger and more drought resistant later in the summer.

 FERTILIZING

Fertilize perennial plantings if you have not done so. Finish up this month. Don't overlook perennials growing in containers. The easiest way to fertilize them is to apply a slow-release fertilizer, such as Osmocote or Nutricote, in the container according to

HELPFUL HINTS

Perennials easily grown from seed include **yarrow, butterfly weed** (A. curassavica), **asparagus fern, aster, coreopsis, purple coneflower, daylily, mallow, monarda, rudbeckia, wild petunia, salvia, goldenrod,** and **spiderwort.** Many of these perennials will bloom the first year if seeds are started early.

label directions. You won't have to fertilize again all summer. This also works for plants growing in beds.

 PESTS

Pest problems will likely become more numerous from now on.

Watch out for caterpillars and beetles, which chew holes in the leaves (treat with Sevin), and aphids (treat with insecticidal soap or Malathion).

Look for a white, powdery coating on the leaves of perennials in your garden. Powdery mildew is a common disease that attacks a variety of ornamentals. Treat with chlorothalosil, sulfur, or thiophanate methyl. Gray mold (Botrytis) will attack flowers and foliage during cool, wet weather, causing tissue to brown and rot with a gray fuzzy growth on it. Except for sulfur, the fungicides mentioned above will also control this disease.

Powdery mildew is a common fungus that attacks many different plants.

Cool-season weeds are still around, but warm-season weeds are beginning to grow. Do not let them get out of hand.

MAY
PERENNIALS

PLANNING

Summer arrives this month as we move into the hot season and daytime highs in the 90s begin (unfortunately) to occur. Perennials are growing vigorously and happily.

Vigorous growth of many perennials leads to plants that need support. Some supports are less noticeable and more effective when used earlier rather than later. Short tomato cages are useful and effective. I find them less conspicuous if I spray-paint them dark green prior to use. Commercial plant supports in many designs are available, and many will work well only if the plant grows through them early in the season. Keep in mind that excessive fertilization can cause overly vigorous, weak growth and increase the need for supports.

As the growth and development of your perennials accelerate, make sure you keep up with entries in your garden journal. Evaluate and enter comments on the spring-blooming perennials as they finish.

PLANTING

If you're just getting around to planting a perennial garden with transplants, you're late. If you are willing to put in extra effort to get them established in the heat, however, you should be successful. If you just want to add a few more perennials to existing beds, choose transplants in larger containers for best results. Perennials in small pots are often rootbound and stunted this late in the planting season.

It is very risky to dig and transplant or divide perennials this late. If you absolutely must transplant a perennial, lift it with as much of a rootball as you can and replant it immediately in its new location. Water it in and keep it well watered until it recovers from the shock. There is a high probability that the plant will be stunted and sulk the rest of the season, but you never know—it may not miss a beat.

CARE

Continue to care for the perennial seeds you planted. Although not a lot of work, they do require daily monitoring for water. As soon as they are large enough to handle, begin transplanting seedlings into cell-packs or 4-inch pots. Their stems are delicate and easily broken. A broken stem kills the seedling. Handle seedlings by leaf to avoid damaging stems. Provide newly transplanted seedlings with shadier conditions for several days, then move them back into their original location.

Cut back **blue phlox** about halfway after it finishes flowering.

WATERING

Soaker hoses are an effective way to water perennial beds without getting water on the flowers and foliage. Flowers are sometimes damaged by water spraying on them, and foliage that stays dry is less likely to develop disease problems. Snake the soaker hose through the bed to cover the entire area. Water does not move a great distance from the hose, so it is important to make sure all the plants in the bed are receiving water. Mulch may be placed over the soaker hose so no one even knows it's there. To determine how long to leave it on in order to thoroughly water the bed:

1. Turn on the soaker hose and check the time.

2. After 30 minutes, turn off the hose and go check the bed. Dig in several places with a trowel to determine how deep the water has penetrated, and how far out from the hose. Note any dry areas and readjust the hose if necessary.

3. If sufficient water was applied to soak most of the bed 4 to 6 inches down, you know to leave it on 30 minutes. If not, leave the hose on for another 20 to 30 minutes, and check the soil. Continue to water and check until the bed is properly watered. Note the time it takes.

It's a bit of a bother, but you only have to do it once.

HELPFUL HINTS

Take some time to notice the wildflowers blooming along the highways in late spring and early summer. Many are the ancestors of perennials growing in your garden. **Blue phlox, stokesia, Mexican primrose** (*Oenothera speciosa*), **obedient plant,** and **mallow** are just a few garden perennials that are derived from plants native to this state.

Mexican primrose

 FERTILIZING

Most of your fertilizer applications should be finished by now. If for some reason you haven't fertilized yet, better late than never. Apply a general-purpose granular fertilizer appropriate for your area at the rate recommended on the label. Spread the fertilizer evenly and water-in immediately by hand to wash the granules off the foliage and down to the soil.

 PESTS

Most perennial plantings are not constantly plagued by pests. Carefully chosen, well-adapted perennials generally need only occasional help with pest problems. Watch your plants and try to eliminate pests before they do too much damage. On the other hand, don't reach for the spray bottle every time you see a hole in a leaf.

JUNE
PERENNIALS

 **PLANNING**

Most activity in the perennial garden now centers on care and maintenance and recording notes in your journal. Take some pictures throughout the summer as the garden grows and develops. Video is also a great way to record your gardens throughout the season. Digital cameras allow you to store pictures in your computer, and photo processors will also put pictures taken with regular film on diskettes these days. If you're not inclined to write in a journal, dated pictures are an invaluable way to record how things looked at particular times, when plants bloomed, problems with color schemes, the performance of plants, and a myriad of other details—and you don't have to write a word.

 **PLANTING**

Perennial transplants growing in containers can be planted now, but it's harder for them to become established when it is this hot. Container-grown perennials are liable to be potbound and of poor quality this time of the year. Check the roots before you purchase the plants, slipping them out of the pot. If the plant does not look vigorous and the root system is a tightly packed solid mass, put it back. Generally, avoid planting during the hottest months of the year.

Vigorously growing, healthy transplants you raised yourself from seed, however, can be planted now if they are large enough. Disturb the roots as little as possible and keep them well watered for the first several weeks while they become established.

Do not transplant perennials growing in the ground until the weather cools in October.

 **WATERING**

These next three or four months are the most stressful of the year. The weather is bound to be too wet or too dry at various times. Excessive rain will rot perennials, especially those not well-adapted to the Deep South.

In a surprisingly short time, 95-degree Fahrenheit days and 75-degree nights can dry out the soil. Water deeply and thoroughly once or twice a week when rain has not occurred for seven to ten days.

Perennials grown as container specimens may need daily watering. Transplants you have grown from seed will also need regular attention to watering.

 **FERTILIZING**

Another application of fertilizer may be applied to beds last fertilized with granular fertilizers in March or April. Evaluate the plants before you do. If they are growing vigorously (or too vigorously) and have a rich green color and plenty of flowers, fertilization is optional at best.

Check the roots of container-grown plants to see if it's rootbound.

If your soil has adequate phosphorus, choose a general-purpose fertilizer with about a 3:1:2 ratio, such as 15-5-10. For soils that test low in phosphorus, select a balanced fertilizer with a 1:1:1 ratio, such as 8-8-8. Follow label directions, but make a light to moderate application. Use about 1/2 cup of 15-5-10 in a 30-square-foot bed, or about 1 cup of 8-8-8.

After the fertilizer is applied, water the bed by hand to wash any fertilizer granules off the foliage and down to the soil.

PESTS

Pest problems abound at this time of the year, but we hope that not too many have found your gardens.

Caterpillars are common and damage plants by chewing holes in leaves.

Treat with Bt, spinosad, or Sevin.

The whitefly can be a difficult insect to control, especially in mid- to late summer if populations get way out of hand. The adults are small, snow-white flies; the larvae appear as small disks under the leaves.

Spray with acephate (Orthene), SunSpray Ultra-Fine Oil (early morning, when it's cooler), or Talstar.

Aphids cluster on new growth and flower buds, sucking the sap from the plant. They are relatively easy to kill but may return, requiring additional applications of pesticide.

Spray with insecticidal soap, Malathion, or acephate.

Various sucking insects, such as leaf hoppers, thrips, and plant bugs, cause small white flecks to appear on the foliage of many perennials. The damage is generally little more than cosmetic, but it can weaken the plant if extensive.

Spray with SunSpray Ultra-Fine Oil (early morning when it's cooler), Malathion, Talstar, or acephate.

Spider mites can be devastating, especially during hot, dry weather.

Spray with Ultra-Fine Oil (early morning, when it's cooler), Malathion, insecticidal soap, or Kelthane.

Snails and slugs love **hostas** and other plants that have succulent leaves and grow in shady areas.

Control with iron phosphate baits using the label directions, by handpicking, or with traps. Check under pots where they like to hide during the day. Collect and dispose of them.

Perennials that are well adapted and planted in the right location generally have minor problems with diseases. Leaf spots caused by various fungi and powdery mildew will sometimes occur and can be treated with a fungicide such as chlorothalonil or thiophanate methyl. Root and crown rot may occur if drainage is inadequate, especially during periods of excessive rain, or if perennials not well adapted to Louisiana are planted. Remove the affected plant and drench the soil with thiophanate methyl to prevent the fungus from spreading to other adjacent plants of the same type.

If using pesticides, always read the labels thoroughly before you purchase and use them. Make sure the problem has been properly identified. Check with your local LSU AgCenter Extension office for help with diagnosing a problem.

JULY
PERENNIALS

 PLANNING

Plan on getting most of your gardening work done during the cooler morning and evening hours. The heat this time of year is brutal. Perennials that aren't going to make it should be showing signs of stress by now. Excessive rain combined with high temperatures can be deadly to all but the best-adapted perennials. Don't forget to record failures as well as successes in your garden journal.

 PLANTING

I certainly wouldn't want to go out and dig up a bed to plant perennials this time of year, so I'm glad it's not a good time to plant anyway. If the perennial transplants you started from seed have outgrown their containers, shift them into larger containers that will hold them until the fall. It is important for the plants not to become rootbound so they will continue to grow vigorously. If you would like to plant them into the garden, plant them with as little root disturbance as possible and keep them well watered until they get established.

 CARE

Take some time now to wander around the yard. It seems pointless, but the fact is, the more you do it, the better. During these walks you can mark gaps and note which plants are doing poorly. Make plans and decide which plants might need to be transplanted or replaced this fall. You can see the beginnings of pest and disease attacks, the onset of weed problems, the need for water, the overgrown plants that might need to be pruned back or supported, and the faded flowers that need to be removed. If you catch these problems early, you will have a much easier time correcting them, and the plants will be better off as a result.

Most importantly, I think it gives you a chance to savor and appreciate what your efforts have accomplished. Don't let life's hectic pace keep you from enjoying what you have worked so hard to create. Take the time.

The gardener's most valuable tools are these moments of undivided attention given to the garden. I think you will find they benefit you as much as they do the garden.

 WATERING

Proper watering is critical during this stressful time of year. Do not think that watering perennial beds by hand is adequate. We apply water by hand too fast and over too short a period for it to deeply penetrate the soil. As relaxing and therapeutic as it is for the gardener, it is not good

Use soaker hoses or sprinklers, and leave them on long enough for the water to moisten the soil about 4 to 6 inches down.

for your plants. Use soaker hoses or sprinklers, and leave them on long enough for the water to moisten the soil about 4 to 6 inches down. Morning is the preferred time to water so that plants are well supplied with water going into the hottest time of the day. Late afternoon or early evening watering with sprinklers is less desirable. The foliage goes into the night wet, which can encourage fungal diseases on some plants.

Create some sort of barrier to protect desirable plants when you spot treat weeds.

FERTILIZING

Only perennials in active growth should be fertilized, and only if needed. Those that have already bloomed or are finishing should be left alone. High temperatures stress plants and can actually slow down the growth of many perennials. If you're not sure, or you fertilized last month, don't fertilize.

PESTS

"Melting out" means that a herbaceous plant suddenly collapses, withers up, and dies. Sometimes the dead tissue is slimy to the touch. This condition is common in perennials poorly suited to our growing conditions. There is little you can do other than record what happened in your journal. Check with gardening friends and references. If other people have had success, try the plant again in another location with better drainage, and perhaps some afternoon shade. You will likely find, however, that everybody else has had the same problem with the plant. You might have even known that, but just had to find out for yourself.

The judicious use of a nonselective systemic herbicide such as glyphosate can be helpful in controlling tough weeds such as torpedograss, bermudagrass button weed, and nutgrass.

The spray must be applied to the foliage of the weeds only. If any gets on the foliage of a desirable plant, wash it off immediately. Use a piece of cardboard as a shield, along with a hand-held sprayer, when spraying close to desirable plants.

AUGUST

PERENNIALS

PLANNING

The fall perennial planting season is still a couple of months off, but it's not too early to get out catalogs and start checking them and Internet sites for perennials you would like to grow. I have already covered the proper way to plan a perennial garden and select the plants for it (February, pages 120-121). This is highly recommended if you are just getting into perennial gardening.

Experienced gardeners should also use the planning and perennial selection process, especially when designing new beds or extensively redesigning old ones. There is, however, a less formal way of choosing perennials that all of us succumb to sooner or later. It's called the "I gotta have this and I'll worry about where to plant it later" technique of garden design. I can't begin to count the times I've wandered around the garden holding a plant purchased on a whim or given to me by a friend, looking for some place to plant it. Gardening should be fun, or why bother? These plants, however, often end up planted in some random, empty spot where the growing conditions are not suitable or where they do not combine well with adjacent plants. Try to keep this type of planting to a minimum.

PLANTING

You can continue to plant perennial seeds throughout the summer to raise your own transplants, but you should finish up this month. Planted now, seeds should still have time to germinate and grow into reasonably-sized transplants before winter. If they are still too small to plant in the garden by November, they can be grown outside in containers over the winter. Bring them indoors only on those nights when temperatures below the upper 20s Fahrenheit are predicted.

Buy and plant salvias now if you can find plants in the nurseries and you have some open spots in the garden. Most salvias put on a wonderful display of flowers in the fall and early winter—well into December if the weather stays mild. Since the weather is still so hot, disturb the roots of the salvias as little as possible when planting them, and keep them well watered for the first few weeks to help them get established. A few of the more reliable and outstanding **perennial salvias** for Louisiana gardens include:

- *Salvia coccinea* (**Texas sage** or **red sage,** especially 'Lady in Red')
- *S. farinacea* (**mealycup sage,** especially 'Victoria')
- *S. gregii* (**autumn sage**)
- *S. leucantha* (**Mexican bush sage**)
- *S. madrensis* (**forsythia sage**—yellow, an unusual color for **salvias**)
- *S.* 'Indigo Spires'
- *S. guaranitica* (**anise sage**—'Argentine Skies' is pale sky-blue)
- *S. miniata* (**Belize sage**)

Keep the base of these plants well mulched during the winter.

Autumn Sage

 CARE

Our long growing season combined with plentiful rainfall can produce abundant and even rampant growth during the summer. Now would be a good time to look over your perennial beds and evaluate how things are growing. A gardener must often play the role of referee.

Tall plants can shade out, or fall over onto, smaller plants. Plants will spread into areas where they were not intended to grow. Note these observations and make decisions about what to remove, divide, or transplant this fall. In the meantime:

• Prune back perennials that are overgrown, especially those that bloom over a long period and well into the fall (*Artemisia ludoviciana, Asclepias curassavica,* **cigar plant, wild ageratum, purple loosestrife, ruellia, salvias**).

• Stake or otherwise support larger perennials that need it. If young children will be playing around the garden, the stakes should be taller to avoid injury.

• Straighten a leaning plant and wedge a piece of brick or stone at the base. This will support the plant more without being visible.

• Many perennials spread by underground stems, some fast, some slow. Promptly dig out unwanted growth outside the area allotted to the plant, pot it up, replant it somewhere else, or throw it away. Barriers extending 8 to 12 inches down in the ground around aggressive spreaders can help keep them under control.

 WATERING

Even one week without a good rain will create dry conditions in August heat. Perennials are well established by this time, but may still need to be watered deeply once or twice a week during dry periods. If you notice plants wilting, you are waiting too long before watering your garden.

 FERTILIZING

Salvias are heavy feeders, and as they gear up for their outstanding fall blooming season, a light fertilizer application will encourage vigorous growth and abundant October flowers. Other fall-blooming perennials, such as **chrysanthemums,** may also be fertilized now. Generally, however, it should not be necessary to fertilize most other perennials.

 PESTS

Whiteflies can be a major problem in late summer.

Acephate (Orthene), Ultra-Fine Oil, and Talstar are recommended controls. You will need repeated applications of whatever you use, and spray under the foliage thoroughly. Consider cutting back heavily infested plants.

Spider mites thrive in hot, dry late-summer conditions.

Insecticidal soap, Malathion, and Ultra-Fine Oil are effective pesticides. It is important to spray under the foliage where the spider mites live. A strong spray of water under the leaves every day for a week is often effective in controlling spider mites.

 PRUNING

Continue to cut back and remove dead flower stalks and unattractive growth on perennials. Look for vigorous new growth at the base of many perennials, and when you see it, cut back the plant hard.

Deadhead regularly.

SEPTEMBER

PERENNIALS

 PLANNING

Make lists of perennials you would like to plant this fall. Local nurseries, unfortunately, generally do not offer as large a selection of perennials in the fall as they do in spring. Now is a good time to check with your nurseries to see what, if any, perennials they will have available. There are always plenty of mail-order companies that handle perennials.

Evaluate the performance of your perennials this summer and record information in your garden journal before you forget it.

Cut back iris foliage to prepare for dividing.

This is also a good time to think about the amount of care your perennial gardens required. Did they become a burden? Were you able to keep up with the weeding and general maintenance? Look at ways to reduce maintenance if you need to. Plant part or all of a bed with low-maintenance shrubs and ground covers. Eliminate some beds altogether and replant the spaces with lawngrass. Do not allow your landscape to demand more time than you have to give it— redesign it to fit your needs.

 PLANTING

It is still too hot to transplant or divide most perennials. **Daylilies** and **acanthus** may be divided now. This is also a good time to divide your **Louisiana irises** (included in the Bulbs chapter but often thought of as perennial).

Perennial transplants started from seeds earlier this summer are probably large enough to go into the garden now, if there is room. You should have already decided where they will be planted. If you raised more than you can use (and we almost always do), share some with

friends, donate some to a fundraiser like a church fair, or sell them at a garage sale.

 CARE

Most of the summer-blooming perennials are finished or are finishing up their floral display for the year. Cut back the flower stalks and old faded flowers to keep the plants looking attractive.

It's a good idea to carry a pair of garden scissors or hand pruners whenever you walk through the garden. Grooming plants is an important part of flower gardening. These colorful beds are meant to draw attention, and must be kept as attractive as possible at all times. Make sure the setting is just as nice for the late-blooming perennials as it was for the ones that bloomed earlier. No matter how stunning a perennial in bloom may be, if it is surrounded by plants with brown stalks, faded leaves, and dead flowers, the effect is diminished.

Mulches may have decayed and thinned out over the summer. Replenish mulch layers with fresh material to maintain about a 2-inch thickness. Ideally, use what you can get for free. Stockpile leaves in bags when you rake them up this fall. Pine straw is an excellent material for mulching and is readily available at no charge if you have pine trees in your yard. It is also available in bales at local nurseries and is one of the least expensive of the commercially available mulches. You can also find chopped or shredded pine straw available in bags. Other popular materials for mulches are chopped leaves, finely ground pine bark, and other agricultural by-products.

Check specimen perennials growing in containers. If they have become rootbound, transplant them into larger containers now. This will give them time to get established in their new pots before winter.

WATERING

We often get some relief from the heat this month, especially in the northern part of the state. Cool fronts are so very welcome after the long, hot summer and often bring needed rain. Daytime highs in the 90s Fahrenheit still occur in September, and the month can be dry. Continue to water as needed using sprinklers or soaker hoses.

FERTILIZING

Be cautious fertilizing this late. Few perennials grow actively throughout the winter, nor should they be encouraged to do so with late fertilizer applications. Perennials that have finished blooming for the year and those that are slowing down should not be fertilized. Perennials showing nutrient deficiencies may be fertilized, but use a soluble fertilizer to deliver available nutrients immediately. Soluble fertilizers feed for a short time and will not continue to stimulate growth into fall and winter.

PESTS

Pests have had all summer to build up population levels.

Inspect plants frequently. Spray only infested plants to minimize the impact on beneficial insects.

Effective low-toxicity insecticides include Bt (to control caterpillars), Sevin (to control chewing insects such as caterpillars and beetles), insecticidal soaps (to control soft-bodied sucking insects such as aphids), and Ultra-Fine Oil (to control whiteflies, scale, soft-bodied insects, and insect eggs).

Use Ultra-Fine Oil in the very early morning hours to minimize the possibility of burning the foliage. Rain that falls soon after controls are applied may wash off and reduce the effectiveness of many pesticides. Repeat applications as needed.

Damp weather favors snails and slugs. Continue to use baits, traps, and barriers as needed. Beer traps are effective and popular.

Disease problems are difficult to deal with. While usually not as common as insect pests, diseases such as root rot or stem rot can be devastating.

Avoid root rot by making sure beds are well drained. Incorporate generous amounts of organic matter, preferably compost, into the bed during preparation; don't plant transplants too deep or too close together; and water deeply and occasionally, rather than lightly and frequently.

For foliar diseases, avoid wetting the foliage when watering (if practical) and water at a time when the foliage will dry quickly.

Good air circulation and proper spacing when planting also helps. A broad-spectrum fungicide such as thiophanate methyl can be used if warranted.

OCTOBER

PERENNIALS

PLANNING

The prime fall planting season for perennials runs from October through early December. Get your perennial orders in to mail-order companies as soon as possible. If you have access to the Internet, it is quick and easy to place your orders online. Specify that you want fall delivery. Make sure you have appropriate locations in your garden for the perennials you order. Check your local nurseries to see what they have available. In areas of the state with milder winters, planting can continue throughout the winter months.

PLANTING

Now is the time to begin putting all of that summer planning to work. Dig and prepare new beds for fall planting. Before you do, decide if you have the additional time that the maintenance of more beds will require. For information on bed preparation, see the Planting section in the introduction to this chapter.

Many perennials can be dug and transplanted over the next couple of months. Now you can correct problems with plants in the wrong location you noticed this summer. Do not move perennials that are in bloom now or will be later on this fall.

Most perennials can be dug and divided over the next couple of months as well. This is especially important for fast-growing or rampant perennials in order to keep them under control. Do not divide perennials that are in bloom now or will be later on this fall. For information on dividing perennials see the Planting section of November (page 138).

Plant perennial transplants in the garden now. These could be transplants you grew yourself, divisions from friends, or transplants purchased from local nurseries or mail-order companies.

1. Space plants according to information on the label, references, or local advice. Most perennials will grow considerably larger than the size of the transplant. Do not crowd them, even if the bed looks relatively empty when you finish.

2. Set transplants so that the top if the rootball is even with or slightly above the soil of the bed. Many perennials will rot if planted too deeply. If the roots are in a tightly packed mass, pull apart and spread the roots when planting. A small amount of slow-release fertilizer may be placed in the planting hole. Firm the soil around the plant once you have finished planting.

3. Water newly planted transplants thoroughly. A half-strength solution of a soluble fertilizer may be used.

4. Mulch the bed to control weeds, but do not cover the perennial plants.

Blooming **chrysanthemums** are available now. Plant a few if you need to "punch up" the color in some of your flower beds.

CARE

As perennials finish and are cut back, remove stakes, cages, and other supports when they are no longer needed. Clean them up and store them out of the way. How well did they work? Can you think of a better way to support the plants? Note in your journal which perennials needed support so you can be prepared to provide it next year.

Enjoy the flowers of such late-season bloomers as **wild ageratum, narrow-leaf sunflower, butterfly weed, salvias, chrysanthemum, cigar plant, ligularia, toad lily** (*Tricyrtis*), **ruellia**, and **goldenrod**. Deadhead these plants as needed to keep them looking attractive.

# WATERING

October is typically one of our driest months. Cooler weather relieves the stress on perennials to some degree, but watering is still needed if it does not rain. In particular, pay careful attention to watering newly planted, moved, or divided perennials, and those that are blooming or in active growth.

# FERTILIZING

Sprinkle an all-purpose granular fertilizer appropriate for your area over beds being prepared for planting. Thoroughly work it in along with the organic matter. Slow-release fertilizer is not added to the planting hole of fall-planted perennials that will be dormant over the winter. It is sufficient to water-in newly planted perennials with a soluble fertilizer mixed half strength.

# PESTS

Cooler, drier weather greatly reduces the incidence of diseases. They should not be a worry until next summer.

HELPFUL HINTS

If you are growing **butterfly weed,** watch for the appearance of monarch butterflies. They migrate through Louisiana on their way back to Mexico each fall and will stop to feed on nectar and lay eggs on your butterfly weed. The monarch caterpillars are large and striped black, white, and yellow. Do not spray with insecticides. They should be allowed to feed on your butterfly weed to their heart's content. The plants will recover, and everyone will enjoy the beautiful butterflies they grow up to be.

Take a few photographs of your fall garden for your journal, and make sure you have updated your entries for the summer.

Butterfly weed

Cool-season weed seeds will be germinating soon.

Keep beds mulched. Preemergence herbicides may be applied now to help prevent the weeds from appearing. Dacthal, Eptam, Amaze, and Preen are commonly available materials. Check the label carefully. Make sure they are appropriate to use around the types of plants you have in the bed.

Armyworms are large, dark caterpillars that can chew up a perennial planting in no time. Common in September and October, they feed during the day and are easily seen if you look carefully.

Control with Bt or spinosad.

NOVEMBER
PERENNIALS

 PLANNING

Fall-blooming perennials continue to put on a show. November weather can run from delightful to downright chilly. If freezes threaten in north Louisiana, plan on covering some of the blooming perennials that could be damaged. The plants will survive without protection, but it would be a shame to lose out on some of the flowers. Perennials you might consider covering include **butterfly weed, cigar plant, ruellia,** and the **salvias.** If the weather stays mild, these plants can bloom well into December.

 PLANTING

Continue to plant and transplant perennials in the garden.

1. When digging up and transplanting a perennial, get as much of the root system as possible.

2. If the soil falls away, immediately wet the roots and wrap them with plastic to keep them from drying out. Replant the plant immediately.

3. If the plant will stay out of the ground for an extended period, pot it up in a container large enough to hold the rootball. Add some potting soil if necessary. Place the potted plant in a shady area and keep it well watered. Plant as soon as possible.

Mums are still available at local nurseries. Buy plants that have few open flowers and mostly buds. The plant will be attractive longer. Do not buy mums if all the flowers are fully open, especially if some of them have begun to fade. Plant in a sunny to partially sunny location and keep well watered. Deadhead regularly, and when all of the flowers have faded, cut the plant back by about one-third. Sometimes we get a few more flowers. Cut them back hard in late January and they will bloom again next fall, or pull the plants up and put them in the compost pile if they were planted for temporary color.

 CARE

Continue to keep things neat. Tall-growing, fall-blooming perennials, like **narrow-leaf sunflower, goldenrod,** and **cigar plant,** may need to be staked. Remember how windy some of those cold fronts can be. Deadhead perennials that are in bloom as needed. After they finish flowering, most should be cut back hard (except **ligularia,** which is evergreen). Cut back and remove dead flower stalks and unattractive foliage from perennials winding down for the year. Mark each spot where perennials are growing that go totally dormant and disappear. This will keep you from accidentally digging into the plant later.

 WATERING

Cool to cold weather and regular rainfall generally allow us to ease up on this chore. Other than for newly planted, transplanted, and divided perennials, little or no irrigation should be necessary. Water these plants two or three times a week if weather is dry.

 FERTILIZING

Fertilizer is not needed at this time of year.

 PESTS

Few, if any, pests bother perennials in November. Watch for caterpillars, aphids, snails, and slugs, and treat if necessary. Weed gardens regularly and maintain a good layer of mulch to keep weeds under control.

DECEMBER

PERENNIALS

 PLANNING

Although gardening does not stop in winter, it does slow down. This is a good time to take inventory of your gardening tools. How many were broken or lost last summer? In what condition are the rest? What needs to be replaced? Are there tools you need that you don't have? Now, with gift-giving season right around the corner, would be a good time to pick out some new tools and let those gift-givers know what you want. While you're at it, ask for a copy of *Perennial Garden Color* by William Welch. It is an outstanding reference on designing with, selecting, and growing perennials adapted to our state.

 PLANTING

Try to finish things up early this month. You know how hectic it gets around the holidays.

 CARE

Cut back fall-blooming perennials that have finished blooming. If freezes have killed the foliage of **salvias, cigar plant,** or **ruellia,** cut them back and mulch over the roots and base of the plant.

HELPFUL HINTS

Collect, clean, and store stakes, cages, and other supports used in the perennial garden. Make a note in your journal if you think you will need more next year. While you're at it, update your journal with what happened in the fall perennial garden.

 WATERING

Water-in newly planted, transplanted, or divided perennials as soon as they are in the ground. Cool weather and regular rainfall make the need for additional irrigation unlikely. If mild, dry weather does occur, give them a good soaking. Established perennials need little or no additional irrigation beyond natural rainfall.

 FERTILIZING

No fertilizer is required by perennials this month. Even if the weather has been mild and late-flowering perennials like **salvias** are still in bloom, don't fertilize them. Winter is on its way and little of the fertilizer would be used effectively. Later fertilizer applications may also decrease the hardiness of perennials by stimulating growth.

 PESTS

Most perennials go dormant in the winter, so there is little that pests can do to them. A few evergreen perennials, like **strawberry begonia, spider plant,** and **ligularia,** may have problems with snails and slugs eating holes in their leaves.

Sink a plastic bowl up to its rim in the soil, fill it half-full of beer, and you will trap lots of the critters. Dump out the bowl every morning and continue to set out traps until you catch very few in a night. Baits are also effective.

Ruellia

ROSES

People have been cultivating roses for several thousand years. It's even possible that very early humans appreciated the edible and medicinal qualities of the hips and delighted in the color and fragrance of the flowers. This long history (as well as the flower's extraordinary beauty) has created a special relationship between gardeners and roses. Indeed, it would be difficult to find a more universally loved flower.

The original garden roses were tough, resilient plants that could pretty much take care of themselves. A strong focus on perfecting flower form and color in the late 1800s and early 1900s led to the modern roses that are so popular today. The use of pesticides that became available in the early to mid-1900s allowed breeders to over-

look disease resistance in their pursuit of the perfect flower. As a result, many of the modern roses, such as the hybrid teas, grandifloras, and floribundas, are not very resistant to diseases. With their outstanding beauty, however, these types have dominated the rose scene since they were introduced.

In the late 1900s, gardeners began to rediscover the beauty, fragrance, and durability of the old garden roses. Although modern roses are still the most commonly planted and grown, the popularity of old garden roses is steadily increasing. Today's rose breeders have been strongly influenced by current trends. New cultivars such as David Austin's English roses, landscape roses (such as the outstanding 'Knock

Out' rose), and other shrub roses share many traits with the old garden roses, including flower form, fragrance, attractive growth habit, and increased disease resistance.

PLANNING

First decide how you want to use roses in the landscape and why you intend to grow them. The trend these days is to incorporate roses into landscape plantings just like any other shrub. This works particularly well with the old garden roses, shrub roses, polyanthas, and floribundas.

If you want to grow roses with perfect flowers on long stems for cutting, you will probably choose the hybrid teas and grandifloras. These rosebushes often have rather awkward shapes that do not combine easily with other plants. That, along with their exacting cultural requirements, is why they are often grown in separate beds.

If you want to train roses on a trellis, arbor, or fence, you'll want to grow rose cultivars from the climbers, ramblers, and old garden roses that produce long vigorous canes.

Hybrid teas, grandifloras, and floribundas, the most popular and widely available groups of roses, are also relatively high-maintenance plants. Keep this in mind when planning how many roses you want to include in your landscape and where you want to plant them.

When purchasing roses from nurseries or mail-order firms, note whether the bushes you are buying are grafted (budded) or growing on their own roots. Most roses are grafted onto a rootstock to increase their vigor. This part of the plant is located below the large knob on the lower part of the bush. Never allow shoots from below the graft union to grow—prune them off as soon as they're discovered. Old garden roses are sold growing on their own roots, and miniatures almost always are. Low sprouts may be allowed to grow if roses are on their own roots.

PLANTING

Do not plant roses in shady areas. They must have at least six to eight hours of sun daily to perform up to your expectations. Any shade they receive should ideally come in the afternoon. Morning sun helps dry the foliage early, reducing disease problems. Roses need excellent drainage; avoid low areas that stay wet.

Bed preparation is important:

1. Remove unwanted vegetation from the area. If this is a new bed, remove the sod or kill it with glyphosate. In an existing bed, remove weeds or kill them with glyphosate.

2. Turn the soil at least 8 to 10 inches deep.

3. Spread amendments over the turned soil. Add at least 4 inches of organic matter such as compost, sphagnum peat moss, rotted manure, or composted, finely ground pine bark. Sprinkle a general-purpose fertilizer appropriate for your area over the bed according to label directions. Sulfur should be applied if the soil's pH is over 7. Lime is needed if the pH is lower than 5.5 and calcium levels are low. To find out what your soil needs, have it tested through your local parish LSU AgCenter Extension office.

4. Thoroughly blend the amendments into the existing soil and rake smooth. A tiller is great for this step.

Note: If your soil is heavy clay, blend 3 to 4 inches of builder's sand into the bed first. Then, spread 4 inches of composted, finely ground pine bark and other needed amendments and incorporate them into the soil. Or, build a raised bed 8 to 12 inches deep and fill with a commercial garden soil or topsoil.

Roses are sold in containers or bare root and generally become available at nurseries around January or February. Buy the highest-quality bushes available, preferably 1 or $1\frac{1}{2}$ grade. It is well worth the extra cost for a healthy, vigorous plant that will produce lots of flowers. Purchase

and plant roses in late winter or early spring so they can get established before beginning to bloom. Do not purchase bare-root roses after February. Container roses can be planted as late as May with acceptable results, but an earlier planting is much better.

To plant roses:

1. Dig a hole in a well-prepared bed as deep and wide as the roots or rootball.

2. For bare-root roses, place a cone of soil in the hole, remove the roots from the wrapper, position the plant over the cone, and spread the roots out over it. Hold the plant in place so the graft union (large knob on lower part of plant) is about 2 inches higher than the soil of the bed. Use your other hand to push and firm soil into the hole to cover the roots. Make sure the graft union remains 2 inches above soil level.

3. For container roses, slide the plant out of the container. Put the rootball in the hole. Its top should be level with the soil of the bed. Make sure the graft union is 2 inches above soil level. Fill in around the rootball and firm with your hand.

4. Water plants in thoroughly to finish settling the soil, and mulch.

WATERING

Irrigation will be necessary when rain does not occur regularly , especially in the warm to hot months of April through November. An occasional, thorough soaking is preferred to light, frequent irrigation. If done properly, irrigation should not be necessary more than once or twice a week during dry periods. Use soaker hoses if practical. They apply water without wetting the foliage, which helps reduce disease problems.

A 2- to 3-inch layer of mulch, such as pine straw, leaves, or pine bark, will help retain soil moisture and reduce the need for irrigation by preventing surface evaporation.

FERTILIZATION

Roses require an adequate supply of available nutrients to produce vigorous bushes and high-quality flowers. Begin to fertilize in mid- to late February or early March. In areas where the phosphorus levels in the soil are high, choose an all-purpose granular fertilizer with about a 3:1:2 ratio, such as 15-5-10. Where phosphorus levels are low, use an all-purpose 1:1:1 ratio granular fertilizer, such as 8-8-8 or 13-13-13. Follow label directions. Apply granular fertilizers every six to eight weeks throughout the growing season until late August or early September. Two level tablespoons of ammonium nitrate per plant every six weeks is an alternative.

You may also use your favorite rose food, organic fertilizers, or slow-release fertilizers, following label directions.

PEST CONTROL

If you want to minimize the use of pesticides in your landscape, roses are probably not your best choice. Louisiana's hot, humid climate creates perfect conditions for a variety of insects and diseases that attack roses.

For roses in general, hybrid teas, grandifloras, and floribundas in particular, controlling the fungal disease blackspot requires weekly spraying from late March to November. Other fungus diseases you are likely to see include powdery mildew and stem canker, while downy mildew and rust are less common. To control these diseases, it is critical that a spray program be started early and continued on a regular basis. Fungicides that contain benomyl, mancozeb, triforine, thiophanate methyl, thiophanate methyl plus mancozeb, or chlorothalonil are effective for control.

Insects are not generally as destructive, and spraying can be done on an as-needed basis. Thrips damage flowers in April and May. Control with Acephate (Orthene) or Mavrik. Aphids attack new growth and flower buds primarily in spring and early summer. Control with insecticidal soap, Ultra-Fine Oil, or Malathion. Leaf-cutter bees cut neat, round holes from the edges of rose leaves to line their nests. Control with Sevin. Beetles and caterpillars are occasional problems. Control with Sevin, Malathion, Acephate, or, for caterpillars only, Bt.

Spider mites attack rose foliage and are generally worse during hot, dry weather. Control with insecticidal soap, Ultra-Fine Oil, or Kelthane.

PRUNING

In Louisiana, roses are generally pruned twice a year—in late January to mid-February and again in mid-August to early September. The classic pruning technique for hybrid teas and grandifloras is designed to encourage the production of high-quality flowers with long stems for cutting. This involves rather hard pruning, back to 18 to 24 inches in the late winter and 24 to 30 inches in the late summer. Current recommendations are more relaxed and involve less severe pruning. Floribundas, shrub roses, miniatures, and old garden roses require only moderate pruning to shape them.

Roses are pruned primarily to:
- remove dead wood.
- stimulate new growth.
- control size and shape.

Cut the bush back to the desired height (usually 2 to 3 feet for hybrid teas and grandifloras). Remove all dead wood, diseased canes, and twiggy growth. Cut each remaining cane back to just above a bud (preferably one facing away from the middle of the bush).

Some rose cultivars (ramblers, some climbers, and old garden roses) bloom prolifically in the spring and early summer, and then stop. These roses bloom on growth they made the summer before and generally are not as popular as repeat-blooming roses that bloom all summer. They should be pruned as needed in early to mid-summer soon after they finish their bloom season.

Most roses look and bloom better if they are regularly deadheaded. Prune faded flowers back to the first five-leaflet leaf on the stem. The exception is roses that produce attractive "hips" or fruit after flowering. Gardeners may allow these bright orange or red structures to develop for their ornamental qualities and for wildlife food.

JANUARY
ROSES

PLANNING

Rose catalogs are wonderful to look through, and it's fun to dream about all the roses growing to perfection in your garden. Order catalogs from the numerous sites on the Internet. Local nurseries should be getting in their roses sometime this month. Call around or stop by and see what types they will carry.

Make decisions on where, how many, and which types and cultivars you want to add to your landscape. Early planting, this month or next month, is especially important for bare-root roses.

Keep records on your efforts to grow roses. Notes jotted in a spiral notebook on a regular basis create an important tool to help you grow roses better. Record the cultivar names and types of roses you're growing, where you bought them, and where they are located in the landscape. Note times of bloom, best bloom periods, pest problems, and overall performance. Try to make an entry at least once a month.

PLANTING

Late January through early February is the best time to transplant roses. To move a bush to a new location, prune it back

appropriately, dig it with as much of the roots as possible, and plant immediately. It is critical for the roots not to dry out. If the bush cannot be planted immediately, wrap the roots with plastic or temporarily pot up the plant. This is also an excellent time to plant roses.

CARE

Roses may continue to bloom during mild winters. Still, very little is done to them this time of the year other than enjoying the flowers, if any, and deadheading. Even if they are not dormant, you do not have to be concerned about freezes.

WATERING

It is extremely unlikely that you will need to water your roses this month. They are probably dormant, but even if they are still blooming, natural rainfall this time of the year is generally adequate.

FERTILIZING

No fertilizer should be applied to roses this month.

PESTS

Blackspot may be active if the weather is mild and the roses have not gone dormant. Most gardeners take a break from spraying this time of the year. Defoliation is not as debilitating to the roses now as it would be during the summer.

PRUNING

Repeat-blooming roses should be pruned in late January or early February even if they are blooming. Do not prune **climbers, ramblers,** or **bush roses** that bloom heavily in the spring and early summer and then stop. These roses bloom on last year's growth. Pruning them now will remove much or all of the flowering wood, and the roses will bloom very little this spring.

FEBRUARY

ROSES

 **PLANNING**

When planning the location of roses in the landscape, keep in mind the extraordinary fragrance many cultivars possess. Plantings of fragrant roses are especially nice around porches and patios and at entrances. Some fragrant cultivars are 'Blush Noisette' (light-pink **noisette**), 'Chrysler Imperial' (deep-red **hybrid tea**), 'Double Delight' (bicolor **hybrid tea**), 'Fragrant Cloud' (coral hybrid tea), 'Sombreuil' (creamy-white tea), 'Mrs. B. R. Cant' (silvery, dark-pink tea), 'Summer Fashion' (yellow **floribunda**), and 'Don Juan' (dark-red **climber**).

 **PLANTING**

This is a good month both for planting and transplanting roses. Finish transplanting in the early part of the month, especially in the southern part of the state.

Plant rosebushes in well-prepared beds with good drainage and plenty of sun. It is important for the graft union to be 2 inches above the soil of the bed. If you are planting container roses, this was taken care of when the nursery planted the rose in the container. Just plant the bush so the top of the rootball is level with the soil of the bed. In the case of bare-root roses, you must see to this yourself during the planting. See pages 141-142 for complete directions on bed preparation and planting roses.

 **CARE**

Roses generally do better with good air circulation. Make sure they are not crowded. When they are used in mixed plantings, nearby shrubs, vines, and even large perennials should not be allowed to crowd the rosebushes. While pruning your rosebushes, trim or snip back shoots or branches from nearby plants that are growing into the roses' space.

 **WATERING**

It's unlikely you will need to water established roses. Newly planted roses should be watered-in thoroughly. If there is no rain and the soil in the bed becomes dry, soak the soil of the rose bed.

 **FERTILIZING**

It is important to incorporate fertilizer into the soil during bed preparation for new rose plantings. Established roses can be fertilized in the latter part of this month, but there is no hurry.

 **PESTS**

If your roses have blackspot, collect and dispose of leaves as they yellow and fall.

 **PRUNING**

Finish pruning during the early to middle part of this month. Cut **hybrid teas, grandifloras,** and **floribundas** back to a height of 2 to 3 feet, or at least cut the bush back to about 1/3 its height. Some gardeners even favor more severe pruning, back to 18 inches. This produces fewer but larger flowers on long stems for cutting.

Old garden roses, shrub roses, miniatures, and **repeat-blooming climbers** are pruned more to the preferences of the gardener. They generally are not pruned so severely unless to control their size. Prune out any dead wood or canes infected with canker, and shorten excessively long shoots and anything else needed to produce a pleasing, balanced shape.

Rosebushes should be pruned even if they have blooms on them.

MARCH

ROSES

 PLANNING

If you plan to spray your roses regularly, check out your supply of pesticides this month. Spraying should begin soon, and you will need materials on hand when the time comes.

 PLANTING

Continue to plant roses purchased in containers. If you are still expecting a mail-order shipment of bare-root roses, hope they will arrive soon and plant them immediately.

You might still give unsprouted bare-root bushes a try—but it is a little late.

 CARE

Evaluate your roses carefully. They will begin active growth this month. Any bushes that are dead, sprouting poorly, or have only a few weak living canes may need to be replaced. Evaluate the location to make sure it is good for roses.

HELPFUL HINTS

Organic gardeners also need to feed their roses this month. According to Liz Druitt in her book *The Organic Rose Garden*, each bush can be fed with alfalfa pellets or meal (about 1/2 cup per bush), bloodmeal (a few tablespoons per bush), bonemeal (about 1/2 cup per bush), and compost (a few cups per bush). Other fertilizers for organic gardeners to consider are Epsom salts, fish emulsion, granite dust, greensand, guano, gypsum, manure, seaweed, soybean meal, and sulfur.

 WATERING

Watering should not be a major concern this month. Warmer weather and new growth, however, make it important for you to watch the rainfall and water if beds begin to dry too much. Newly planted roses need particular attention.

 FERTILIZING

Roses throughout the state should be fertilized this month. In areas where the phosphorus levels in the soil are high, choose an all-purpose fertilizer with about a 3:1:2 ratio, such as 15-5-10. Where phosphorus levels are low, use an all-purpose 1:1:1 ratio fertilizer such as 8-8-8 or 13-13-13. Follow label directions. If you have a favorite rose fertilizer that has worked well for you in the past, by all means continue to use it.

 PESTS

Regular spray programs for blackspot should begin as soon as **hybrid teas, floribundas,** and **grandifloras** have new leaves beginning to open. Other types of roses will also get blackspot to some degree, sometimes just as bad. If you want to keep those roses free from blackspot, you will also have to spray any of them that have problems with this disease.

 PRUNING

Prune immediately if you have not already done so. Pruning this late will not hurt your bushes, but your roses will bloom later.

APRIL

ROSES

PLANNING

Take a few moments to make some notes in your records about when various roses started blooming. Note how many weeks since you pruned. You can manipulate, to some degree, when your roses bloom by pruning earlier or later within the recommended period.

PLANTING

Blooming roses are available in containers at local nurseries. You can pick out the color, shape, fragrance, and size of the flowers you want. There is a price, however. Planting roses now means they have to establish themselves while blooming.

CARE

The grafted roses we grow are composed of two genetically different roses joined together at the graft union to form a single, functioning plant. The part that provides the roots is called the stock. It makes a great root system but should never be allowed to sprout and grow. The upper part that produces beautiful flowers is the scion. It is nurtured and

trained into the ornamental part of the plant. The graft union is the large knob at the base of the plant.

WATERING

Supplemental water is usually needed this month. Water until the soil is moistened at least 5 to 6 inches down. Leave sprinklers on long enough to provide 1 inch of water. Ideally, use a watering method that does not wet the foliage. Soaker hoses work very well and are inexpensive and easy to use. Place them so that a hose lies about 6 inches from each bush.

FERTILIZING

Since you fertilized last month when you were supposed to, no additional fertilizer is needed at this time. (If not, fertilize now . . .)

PESTS

You should not wait for blackspot to occur before you start spraying. Begin spraying as soon as possible, and spray every seven to ten days through November. Powdery mildew appears as a white powdery coating on

flower buds, new growth, and leaves. Both diseases can be controlled with triforine (Fungi-nex), thiophanate methyl (Ferti-lome Halt), sulfur (Natural Guard Wettable Dusting Sulfur), or copper oleate (Ferti-lome Blackspot and Powdery Mildew Spray, Natural Guard Liquid Copper Fungicide).

Orthene or Mavrik are effective on thrips when used weekly from now until June. These insecticides will also control aphids, relatively small insects that congregate in large numbers on flower buds and new growth.

Many rose gardeners use products that combine two or three pesticides for effective control of diseases, insects, and mites. These are great, and I recommend them. Several combination products available are specially labeled for roses.

Keep rose beds well mulched to control weeds.

PRUNING

Roses are in bloom now and should not be cut back. Deadhead faded flowers regularly by cutting the stems back to the first or second five-leaflet leaf.

MAY

ROSES

PLANNING

Stop and smell the roses. Forgive the cliché, but this is another of our best rose-blooming months. Record comments on each type of rose you are growing. In particular, note which cultivars seem to be susceptible to disease and which do not seem to be affected much. Careful records will help tremendously when, at the end of the growing season, you are deciding which roses to keep and which just did not live up to expectations or were highly susceptible to pest problems.

Climbing roses must be trained to their support by tying.

PLANTING

This is the very last month I would plant roses from containers. Do not disturb the roots of container-grown roses when you plant them, even if the root system looks potbound. They will not tolerate any root damage when in active growth and when temperatures are hot. It is much better to plant rosebushes earlier in the year.

Do not transplant any roses now.

CARE

Ramblers and **climbers** are in full bloom. Pay attention to training and tying these roses to the arbor, fence, trellis, or other structure they are to grow on. Climbing roses are not like most vines and generally cannot climb or hold on to structures well on their own. New growth will continue throughout the summer, and these types of roses can easily get out of control. Regular efforts to train them produce far better results than letting them go and dealing with an overgrown mess.

WATERING

More heat means that the need for water is more likely. Watch the weather closely. From now on, a week or ten days without a good rain means turning on the irrigation. If dry weather continues, water thoroughly once or twice a week. Avoid wetting the foliage, or plan to water when the foliage will dry rapidly.

FERTILIZING

You can fertilize again this month (six to eight weeks after your spring fertilizer applica-

HELPFUL HINTS

When cutting roses for indoor arrangements, avoid cutting stems too long from roses just planted this spring. New roses need their foliage to get well established. Have a container of water in the garden with you when cutting roses, and place the stems in water immediately after cutting. For the longest-lasting cut flowers, harvest blossoms just as the buds begin to open.

Place rose stems in water immediately after cutting.

tion). Use your favorite rose fertilizer according to label directions, or a general-purpose fertilizer appropriate for your area. Be moderate. Overfertilization can damage plant roots or lead to lush, rapid growth that makes a plant more susceptible to pest problems.

 PESTS

Are you spraying regularly? If not, expect to see blackspot on virtually every type of rose.

Many old garden roses will lose some to most of their leaves, look weak, then recover without spraying. This may happen several times during the summer. Notice which roses seem to be more disease resistant. **Lady Banks' rose** and many of the **Chinas, teas, polyanthas, swamp roses, landscape roses** (such as 'Knock Out'), and **noisettes** are less susceptible to blackspot, even if not sprayed.

Spider mites may occur if the weather is hot and dry.

Spray with Ultra-Fine Oil, insecticidal soap, Kelthane, or Malathion.

Continue a regular spray program with a combination product to keep pests under control.

 PRUNING

Other than deadheading and pruning off suckers from below the graft union, no pruning is required this month for ever-blooming roses. Prune once-blooming roses, if needed, after they finish blooming.

JUNE
ROSES

 PLANNING

Roses are entering the most stressful time of the year this month. Plan for the efforts you will make to help them come through in the best shape possible. Regular watering, mulching, deadheading, and insect, weed, and disease control will all continue to be important in caring for your roses.

The outstanding spring and early-summer bloom season draws to a close. Don't despair. With good care throughout the summer, the fall bloom season can be just as (or even more) spectacular for repeat-blooming roses.

 PLANTING

The intense heat this time of the year stresses roses too much to make this a good time to plant them. To transplant a rose in this heat would almost certainly kill it or set it back significantly.

 CARE

Despite your best efforts, do not expect to get the same high-quality flowers during mid- to late summer as you did earlier. The problem is the heat, and there is nothing you can do to make it go away. It is still important to take proper care of your roses. Without a regular spray program, rose cultivars that are susceptible to blackspot will yellow and drop their leaves almost as fast as they can grow them. By the end of the summer, the bushes will be too weak to produce the outstanding flowers we expect in the fall.

 WATERING

The intense heat this time of year can dry out beds surprisingly fast. Roses planted this year need a regular deep watering whenever we go five to seven days without a good rain (a "good" rain means receiving $1/2$ to 1 inch of rain—do not count brief showers). Older, more established plants should be watered seven to ten days after the last good rain. During exceptionally dry periods when rain has not fallen for two weeks or more, water roses in the landscape once or twice a week as needed.

As always, avoid wetting the foliage if possible by using a bubbler hose attachment, drip irrigation, soaker hoses, or another irrigation system that sprays water below the foliage. If you must wet the foliage, irrigate during the morning or whenever the foliage will dry rapidly.

 FERTILIZING

If you did not fertilize last month, you may this month. Use your favorite rose fertilizer according to label directions, or a general-purpose fertilizer appropriate for your area.

 PESTS

Although it will seem as if your hybrid tea roses have pest problems no matter what you do, you must not give up.

A regular weekly spraying with a combination product that includes a fungicide for blackspot control and an insecticide for insect control is important. Frequent rains can make this job difficult, but stick with it.

Blackspot may still occur on very susceptible cultivars, but less than if you were not spraying.

More disease-resistant roses, on the other hand, will have few serious problems even without fungicides. Keep this in mind when deciding which cultivars to plant in your landscape.

Keep weeds under control by regular handpulling or mulching, or by spot-treating with glyphosate. Follow label directions carefully.

Do NOT get these herbicides on the stems or leaves of the roses.

 PRUNING

This is a good month to prune roses that are not repeat-blooming types. These roses, which bloom heavily in the spring and early summer and then not at all or very little the rest of the year, will bloom next year on growth they produce this summer. Prune appropriately now.

Climbers and **ramblers** may need excessively long shoots shortened, old, low-vigor canes pruned back hard, and growth in areas where it is not wanted removed. The structure on which you are training these roses and the effect you are trying to achieve will have a great influence on how you prune them. Non-repeat-blooming bush roses are simply pruned to shape them and remove dead or weak growth.

If your rose is not a repeat-blooming type, go ahead and prune now.

151

JULY
ROSES

PLANNING

Plan on gardening during the cooler early-morning and late-afternoon hours. Heat is brutal this time of year for gardens and gardeners alike.

Before you forget, make sure you have made entries in your garden journal on the performance of roses during the early bloom season. Note which roses have the most difficult time with the heat and pest problems this summer.

PLANTING

The intense heat of midsummer stresses roses too much to make this a good time to plant them. To transplant a rose in this heat would almost certainly kill it or set it back significantly.

CARE

Daytime highs in the mid-90s and nighttime lows in the mid- to upper 70s actually lower the vigor of roses. Despite your best efforts at proper care, you will notice that the flowers your rosebushes produce now are often smaller with less-vivid colors. The flowers seem to fade almost as soon as they open. Don't give up! Continue regular care. It is

important to get your roses through the summer in the best shape possible so they will be able to produce a wonderful crop of flowers during the fall blooming season.

WATERING

Keep your roses regularly watered. Soil in beds can dry out surprisingly fast when weather is this hot. Do not allow your roses to wilt before you water them. Water thoroughly to moisten the soil at least 4 to 6 inches down, and avoid wetting the foliage if possible.

FERTILIZING

July is generally not a good month to fertilize roses. High temperatures reduce vigor, and roses may actually grow less than they did earlier. If you fertilized in May or early June, no fertilizer is required now.

No maintenance pruning is needed, but do prune out dead or diseased branches.

PESTS

Blackspot, spider mites, leaf-cutter bees, caterpillars, beetles, and weeds are the most common problems this time of the year.

See the introduction in this chapter (pages 142-143) for information on controlling these pests.

PRUNING

Other than deadheading and pruning out diseased or dead growth, no pruning is required this month.

AUGUST
ROSES

PLANNING

We are almost through the worst part of the summer, and it's time to focus on the fall blooming season and the beautiful flowers it will bring. With that in mind, plan on fertilizing and pruning this month.

This is also a good time to evaluate how your roses did over the summer. By now, roses will show how well they endured the heat, drought, rain, and humidity of a Louisiana summer. Make some notes in your garden journal. A rose that performs poorly for two seasons should probably be replaced with another cultivar.

PLANTING

Don't even think about planting or transplanting roses this month. Cooler weather may be on the horizon, but it's not here yet.

CARE

Tell your roses to hold on for just a few more weeks. Cool fronts often make their way through the state in late September, particularly in north Louisiana. In the meantime, care this time of the year is focused on the fall bloom-ing period. Roses need to be fertilized, pruned, and otherwise groomed.

FERTILIZING

Fertilizing in August is second in importance only to the spring fertilization. Extra nutrients provided now will encourage vigorous growth and flowering over the next three months.

- Use a rose fertilizer, a general-purpose fertilizer suitable for your area, or any of the various organic fertilizers.
- Fertilizer should be applied immediately after you prune your roses.
- If using organic fertilizers, apply them in early August so they will have begun to break down and release nutrients when pruning is done in late August.

PRUNING

It is important to prune roses now to get them in shape for the fall blooming season. After a long summer of growth, most roses are rather overgrown. Top the bush back to the desired height (usually 2 to 3 feet for **hybrid teas** and **grandifloras**). Remove all dead wood, diseased canes, and twiggy growth. Cut each remaining cane back to just above a bud (preferably facing away from the center of the bush).

The **ramblers,** many **climbers,** and some of the **old garden roses** bloom prolifically in spring and early summer and then stop. These roses bloom on growth they made the summer before. They should have been pruned, as needed, in early to midsummer soon after they finished their bloom season. Prune now if absolutely necessary, but do so right away.

PESTS

Blackspot continues to be the number one problem.

Keep yellow, fallen leaves raked or picked up from rose beds. These fallen, infected leaves often serve as a continuing source of disease. As new growth begins to emerge on newly pruned roses, continue a regular spray program to control blackspot for those types that need it.

Leaf-cutter bees may chew round holes from the edges of rose leaves. The damage is generally little more than cosmetic but can be rather extensive. Control with Sevin if necessary.

SEPTEMBER

ROSES

PLANNING

When a bed of hybrid tea roses is planted, it often functions as a collection of different cultivars. Flower color is chosen for individual beauty—little consideration is given to how well the different colors will complement one another.

If you are using roses in the landscape, however, the colors should be thought out carefully. Many of the modern **hybrid teas** and **floribundas** have brilliantly colored flowers that may overpower some of the pastel shades common in **old garden roses.** Take a critical look at the colors you have combined and make sure they work.

PLANTING

Have you identified a rose that is having problems with its growing conditions? Perhaps the spot is shadier than you thought and the rose is languishing. You will want to move it, but it is still too soon to transplant roses. Wait at least until early December.

It is also too hot to plant roses. Plant no sooner than late October when the weather is cooler.

CARE

It has been a long growing season, and well-grown roses have certainly needed their share of your gardening time. Don't slow down yet! Continue to keep your roses well watered and keep pest problems from getting out of control. Over the next two months some of the finest flowers of the year will be produced in great abundance from healthy rosebushes.

WATERING

Summer rainfall is unpredictable. By this time, we might be cursing a drought or dreading the next downpour. Although roses need excellent drainage, they are not drought tolerant. During this growing period before their fall bloom, pay careful attention to rainfall amounts; water roses if an inch of rain has not fallen for about a week. Water deeply and thoroughly once or twice a week as needed.

FERTILIZING

You may fertilize in early September if you did not fertilize last month. This is the last fertilization required for this season.

PESTS

Most common pests of roses stay active through the fall. An exception is thrips. These insects, so destructive to the spring and early-summer flowers, are rarely a problem in the fall. Blackspot, powdery mildew, spider mites, aphids, and various other pests may still occur.

PRUNING

Roses that were not cut back in late August should be cut back in early September. Pruning roses later generally means they will come into bloom a little later.

HELPFUL HINTS

Rose hips make great wildlife food, and various types are used to make jelly. Rose hips are very high in vitamin C. Rose petals are also edible. Use petals only from flowers that have not been sprayed with pesticides.

OCTOBER

ROSES

PLANNING

Plan to enjoy all the beautiful roses blooming this month. Pleasant weather makes it a delight to be outside. Fall planting is certainly possible in Louisiana. Roses are hardy and will not mind winter's cold. Look around the landscape and determine if and where you want to plant more roses. If you don't have room for standard-size roses, think about **miniatures.** A row of miniature roses in matching containers looks great on a low wall, bench, or small outside table.

PLANTING

Container-grown roses that may be available at local nurseries can be planted into the ground from late October through winter. These roses have likely been growing in their pots for some time and may have become pot-bound.

1. Remove the rosebush from its pot.

2. Use your fingers to pull apart the rootball a little. This will help the roots grow and spread into the surrounding soil.

3. Plant the rosebush in a well-prepared spot amended with organic matter. The top of the rootball should be level with the soil of the bed, and the graft union should be about 2 inches above ground.

4. Firm the soil around the rose's roots with your hands, and water thoroughly to finish settling the soil.

The weather must be cool for the plant to tolerate the pulling apart of its rootball. If October is warm, wait for the more reliably cool month of November to plant.

CARE

Now that flower production has resumed, it's time to start dead-heading. Some rose cultivars reliably produce attractive fruit called "hips." They turn red or red-orange when mature and can add color to the winter landscape. If you grow rose cultivars that produce hips, do not deadhead.

WATERING

Although the weather is mild to cool, October is one of our driest months. Water roses deeply once or twice a week as needed, based on rainfall. Avoid wetting the foliage as this encourages blackspot. If you must wet the foliage, water in the morning when the leaves will dry quickly.

You can still enjoy roses if you don't have a lot of space. Plant miniatures in ground or in containers.

FERTILIZING

No fertilizer is needed for the rest of the growing season.

PESTS

Cooler, drier weather will reduce blackspot.

If the weather cooperates, reduce spray frequency to once every ten days. If the weather is warm and wet, spray weekly for those types that need it.

Cool-season weeds start to show up next month.

Prevent them with 2 to 4 inches of mulch, such as pine straw placed over the soil of the bed. A pre-emergenct herbicide, labeled for roses, may also be used on the soil prior to mulching.

NOVEMBER

ROSES

PLANNING

Roses continue in full bloom. Many rose gardeners consider these fall flowers the finest of the year. Roses will continue to bloom well into December.

Little has to be done to prepare roses for the coming winter. Mild winters in south Louisiana often prevent roses from going dormant at all, and they may still be blooming when it is time to cut them back in February. Full dormancy is more likely in north Louisiana, but it is not a certainty.

Planning for winter primarily means refraining from fertilizing this late. Late fertilization would make the roses even less likely to go dormant.

PLANTING

Planting roses in fall is a good idea because it allows a plant to grow roots and become established during the cool season. Fall-planted shrubs are more likely to be stronger and more vigorous during their first summer. The container roses available at local nurseries may be left over from last spring. See October page 155 for proper planting techniques.

If you need to move a rosebush, wait until December. They could be moved in late November, but since they may still be in full bloom, it would be a shame to disturb them. Roses may be transplanted at any time from early December through late February.

CARE

Rose flowers provide a great deal of pleasure when cut and brought indoors.

• Cut roses just as the buds start to open with stems long enough for arranging.

Feel free to take longer stems, 8 to 12 inches, from the more vigorous bushes. Limit stem length to 6 to 8 inches on less vigorous cultivars.

• Make your cut just above a five-leaflet leaf with sharp hand pruners or scissors.

Immediately after cutting, place the rose stems in a bucket of warm water.

November is ideal rose planting time.

• When you have gathered enough roses, bring them inside to arrange them. Strip off any foliage that would be underwater in the vase, and recut the stem of the rose while holding it under water.

Arrange in a container filled with water or with wet florist foam.

WATERING

Cool to chilly weather and normal rainfall make it unlikely that you will have to water much this month. Dry, mild weather can occur, and irrigation during those periods is important. Try to use a watering method that applies water directly to the roots, such as soaker hoses or irrigation systems that spray the water onto the soil below the foliage.

FERTILIZING

No fertilizer is needed for the rest of the growing season.

PESTS

You may finally begin to relax. Most gardeners do not continue to spray their roses after this month, but for now, spray roses as you have done throughout the growing season. Blackspot is still active, and aphids may show up on flower buds or new growth. Overall, pest problems are diminishing.

PRUNING

Avoid heavy pruning that would stimulate new growth. Other than deadheading (see October information on rose hips, page 155), no pruning is needed now.

Tie up and otherwise train **ramblers** and **climbers.** Only limited pruning should be done, if absolutely necessary, as you tie them to their supports.

Blackspot is a common rose malady that can be treated with an appropriate fungicide.

DECEMBER

ROSES

 PLANNING

Need more roses? Check out Internet sites and the new catalogs to see what new roses are being offered. Rose breeders are always coming up with beautiful new cultivars. Look for roses that offer attractively shaped plants and disease resistance as well as beautiful flowers. These are excellent to use in the landscape as you would any flowering shrub.

When you order roses, specify that you need to receive them for planting in January (south Louisiana) or February (north Louisiana).

 PLANTING

Early to mid-December is a good time to transplant roses to a new location. If you aren't in a hurry and the bushes are still blooming, this can be done any time from now to late February. To move a bush to a new location, dig it up with as much of the root system as possible and plant immediately. It is crucial to keep roots from drying out in the process. If the bush cannot be planted immediately, wrap the roots with plastic or temporarily pot up the plant. Do not prune it back hard until late January or early February. Many gardeners wait to transplant roses until then since the pruned roses are smaller and easier to handle in the move.

Continue to plant container-grown rosebushes purchased from local nurseries.

 WATERING

Slower growth, cool to cold temperatures, and abundant rainfall generally make watering unnecessary this month. Newly planted or transplanted roses, however, should be watered regularly if sufficient rain does not occur.

 FERTILIZING

No fertilizer is needed this month.

 PESTS

Most gardeners have put away the sprayers by now. Although roses may continue to grow and bloom and blackspot can occur during the winter, it does not hurt the rosebushes enough to merit continued spraying. Keep beds mulched and weeded.

 PRUNING

No pruning will be needed until next month.

SHRUBS

Shrubs are woody perennial plants that produce multiple stems from the soil or multiple branching close to the ground, and grow no larger than 10 to 15 feet. They may be evergreen or deciduous. (In Louisiana, mild winters allow us to grow a wide variety of evergreen shrubs—few deciduous shrubs are really popular). Shrubs are generally grown for their colorful flowers or attractive foliage, but they may also provide fragrance and ornamental or edible fruit.

PLANNING

Shrubs are a fundamental and essential part of most landscape designs. They are the primary plant material used to shape spaces, create structure in the landscape, enhance the home and other buildings, provide privacy, screen views, and guide traffic patterns. See the Introduction (pages 10–11) for information on how to develop a landscape design.

Planting the right shrub in the right location is critical to the plant's health and your happiness with the planting. Every gardener has favorite shrubs he or she wants to plant in the landscape. By all means, choose shrubs you like, but it is also important that you consider the growing conditions of the area, size limitations, the purpose of the planting, and the characteristics you want the shrubs to have.

First evaluate the site. Is it shady or sunny? Well drained or damp? Is the soil acid or alkaline? You must choose shrubs that will thrive in the growing conditions in which they will be planted.

Next consider the purpose of the planting. Is it to beautify the house, screen a view, provide colorful flowers, create privacy, or another of the many reasons for which shrubs are planted?

List the characteristics the shrubs must have in order to satisfy your taste and the purpose they will serve. Decide on the mature size needed, between evergreen or deciduous, whether or not you want

flowers (and if so, what color and when), and any other features you feel are important.

Finally, choose the shrubs that will most closely fit the growing conditions, purpose, and desired characteristics. Choose your favorite shrub if it's the best choice, but if not, plant another shrub.

Planting a shrub that will grow too large for its location is the most common mistake gardeners make. Always ask about or find out the mature size of the shrubs you intend to plant. If someone says, "You can always keep it pruned to whatever size you want," walk away and choose a smaller growing shrub.

PLANTING SHRUBS

The ideal planting season for shrubs in Louisiana is October through March. Fall planting in November and early December is especially good. Roots grow readily at that time of year. Shrubs then have until May to make root growth and get established before hot weather. Shrubs are almost always sold as container-grown plants. On occasion, larger specimens are available balled and burlapped. Shrubs are generally planted into well-prepared beds.

BED PREPARATION

1. Remove unwanted vegetation from the bed area. Weeds or turfgrass may be removed physically, or killed with a herbicide such as glyphosate (follow label directions carefully) and turned under.

2. Turn the soil to a depth of at least 8 to 10 inches with a shovel, spade, garden fork, or tiller.

3. Spread any desired amendments over the turned soil. Have your soil tested through your local Extension Service office to find out what it needs. You should always add about 4 inches of organic matter, such as compost, sphagnum peat moss, rotted manure, or finely ground pine bark. Sprinkle a general-purpose granular fertilizer over the area next. Use a 1:1:1 ratio fertilizer (such as

8-8-8 or 13-13-13) if your soil is low in phosphorus, or a 3:1:2 ratio fertilizer (such as 15-5-10) if your soil is high in phosphorus. Depending on your soil and the type of shrubs that will be planted, additional materials might include sand, lime, sulfur, or gypsum.

4. Thoroughly blend the amendments into the soil, rake the bed smooth, and shape the edges. The level of the soil in the bed will be higher than it was before. This is good, as it will improve drainage.

See Planting steps on page 165.

CARING FOR SHRUBS

Carefully chosen shrubs that are well adapted to Louisiana's climate are relatively easy to take care of. Which shrubs you choose and where you plant them will greatly influence the amount of maintenance required. Pruning is sometimes needed to control the shape or size of shrubs. Fertilization is required to stimulate growth or provide needed nutrients. Well-established shrubs can thrive with irrigation only during the hottest, driest periods. Pest problems do occur, but most shrubs are only occasionally bothered with outbreaks that would require treatment. In south Louisiana, the use of less hardy shrubs such as yesterday-today-and-tomorrow, or daisy shrub, may require efforts at cold protection. Overall, shrub beds require far less maintenance than lawns or beds of annuals or perennials.

WATERING

Newly planted shrubs will need careful attention to watering the first year after planting. Watering once or twice a week during hot summer weather will be needed if adequate rain does not occur. Established shrubs will need supplemental irrigation only during the hottest, driest weather. It is important to water thoroughly enough to moisten the soil 4 to 6 inches down. This is best accomplished with sprinklers or soaker hoses.

FERTILIZING

Shrubs are best fertilized in March and, where rapid growth is desired, again in June or July. Granular fertilizers will feed for about six to eight weeks. Applied in early spring, they supply nutrients to shrubs during their primary growth period from spring to early summer. This is adequate in most circumstances. Young shrubs that are being encouraged to grow rapidly, or shrubs in low vigor, may be fertilized again in midsummer.

A general-purpose granular fertilizer is fine for most situations. Use a 1:1:1 ratio fertilizer, such as 8-8-8 or 13-13-13, if the soil is low in phosphorus. Use a fertilizer with about a 3:1:2 ratio, such as 15-5-10, if your soil tests high in phosphorus.

Acid-loving shrubs, such as azaleas, camellias, and gardenias, will occasionally have problems with iron deficiencies and may require fertilizers rich in available or chelated (KEY lay ted) iron.

PEST CONTROL

Insects are an occasional problem on most shrubs. A few popular shrubs have fairly common pest problems, lacebugs on azaleas and whiteflies on gardenias, for instance, but most of the time we simply monitor shrubs and deal with pest problems as they occur. Common insect pests on shrubs are lacebugs, scale, whiteflies, caterpillars, and aphids. Insecticides commonly used to control insect problems are acephate (Orthene), Malathion, oil sprays (such as Ultra-Fine Oil), insecticidal soap, Talstar, and Mavrik.

Spider mites are an occasional problem during hot, dry weather. Control with insecticidal soap, Kelthane, Malathion, or oil sprays.

Diseases can be very destructive, particularly root rots. The best defense against root rot is choosing well-adapted plants and providing good drainage. Leaf spots are not uncommon but generally are not severe enough for you to worry about spraying if shrubs are vigorous and otherwise healthy. Powdery mildew creates a thin, white, powdery film on the foliage of certain shrubs, such as Chinese mahonia and hydrangea. It can be fairly easily controlled with sprays of benomyl, chlorothalonil, thiophanate methyl, sulfur, or any fungicide labeled for controlling powdery mildew.

Weeds must be dealt with in any garden situation, including shrub beds. The use of mulches will minimize weed problems. Preemergence herbicides can be used in certain situations. When weeds do occur, deal with them regularly and quickly to prevent major problems. Handweeding and spot treatment with a nonselective systemic herbicide, such as glyphosate, will take care of weeds that do crop up.

PRUNING

Pruning is a regular part of shrub care. Done primarily to keep shrubs attractively shaped, make them bushier and fuller, rejuvenate old, overgrown specimens, or control size, pruning can be minimized with careful plant selection.

Specially shaped shrubs, such as topiary and clipped hedges, require the most pruning. Shrubs that grow too large for their location may require almost constant pruning to keep the right size. Do not plant shrubs that will grow significantly larger than needed for a location.

Hedges, topiaries, and shrubs not grown for flowers can be pruned anytime between mid-December and August. Prune hedges so that the base is slightly wider than the top.

Shrubs that bloom from January through April should be pruned after they finish flowering, but before late June. Shrubs that bloom from May through September should be pruned January through March (except hydrangeas and gardenias, which are pruned right after they finish flowering in June or July).

Prune flowering shrubs at the wrong time and you may prevent them from flowering during the ensuing growing season.

JANUARY

SHRUBS

 **PLANNING**

Many gardeners focus on spring to do major planting in the landscape, but the best season for planting shrubs is October through March. You still have time to make decisions and choices before the end of the ideal planting season, but do not put it off. Decide where and what kind of shrubs you want to plant. When choosing a shrub, consider the following questions:

• What are the growing conditions where the shrubs will be planted?

• What purpose will the shrubs serve—decorative, screen, hedge, privacy?

• What mature size would be desirable for the shrubs?

• What characteristics do you want the shrub to have—evergreen or deciduous, flowers (color, season of bloom, fragrance), decorative fruit, freedom from pests, growth rate, shape (low, mounding, upright)?

Draw simple sketches of the areas you intend to plant. How many of each type of shrub should you plant? You need to know before you go to the nursery. Here's how to find out.

Measure the space to be planted, and draw it out on a piece of graph paper, allowing one square (or more if you like) to equal a foot.

When you have selected the shrub you want to plant in that area, look at the Shrub Chart (pages 269-271) or another reference to see how wide it spreads. I recommend *Southern Plants* by Odenwald and Turner. This excellent reference includes the height and spread of most plants that can be grown in Louisiana.

Draw circles, representing the shrubs, on the graph paper. The diameter of each circle should be the number of squares needed to equal the spread of the shrub in feet: if one square equals a foot in your sketch, a shrub that spreads three feet would be represented by a circle three squares in diameter.

See how many circles you can fit into the area, allowing them to overlap only slightly. Remember to locate shrubs an appropriate distance from the house, patios, walks, and driveways.

 **PLANTING**

This is an excellent month for planting and transplanting shrubs.

• Do not plant immediately after rainy weather. Soil is difficult to dig and will compact if worked while wet.

• If possible, do not plant immediately before a freeze in the teens. This cannot always be predicted, and the shrubs you are planting will take the cold, but keep it in mind.

• Shrubs are as dormant as they will get this month, and the weather is cool to cold and moist. That makes it an ideal time to transplant.

• Don't fight a shrub that has grown too large for where it is planted. Move it to a new location where its size is more appropriate, and plant a smaller-growing shrub in its place. Lift the shrub with as many roots as possible and replant it in its new location immediately. Do not allow the roots to dry before planting.

 **CARE**

Extremely cold weather is stressful to shrubs, especially when following a spell of mild weather. The hardy shrubs we use in our landscapes, however, usually seem to make it through. If temperatures reach the low teens, some shrubs (such as **azaleas** and **pittosporum**) may experience bark splitting. Check your shrubs a week or two after a severe freeze for splits in the branch bark. Spray those plants with thiophanate methyl (Ferti-lome Halt) to prevent the wounds from becoming infected.

 WATERING

There is generally no need to water shrubs in January. Newly planted shrubs should be watered-in thoroughly but may not need to be watered there-after if rainfall is regular. Should the weather be dry and mild, water newly planted shrubs once or twice a week.

 FERTILIZING

No shrubs should be fertilized this month.

 PESTS

Winter is an excellent time to apply horticultural oil sprays to shrubs that are prone to scale. These include **camellias, hollies, magnolias, euonymus, privets,** and **cleyera.** Spray **gardenias** with oil for whiteflies. Check over these and other shrubs in your landscape and treat if necessary. Do not spray with oil if the night-time low is predicted below 40 degrees Fahrenheit.

 PRUNING

Not much pruning is done this month, although you may prune just about anything except spring-flowering shrubs if you like. Some of the earliest flower-ing shrubs, such as **flowering quince,** may bloom in January. Cut a few branches and place them in a vase in your home to be enjoyed and to help herald the coming of spring.

Flowering Quince 'Nicoline'

FEBRUARY

SHRUBS

PLANNING

Continue to develop your ideas for shrub planting. Remember that all parts of a landscape must work together. Shrub plantings should also take into consideration flower beds, areas of ground covers, outdoor living areas, and structures in the landscape.

Descriptions of plants in books rarely do them justice. Pay a visit to nurseries or public gardens, where the plants are labeled. Look at the shrubs you are thinking about planting. Once you see them, you might like them even better, or you may decide not to plant them (do not wait to find this out the day you go the nursery to purchase the shrubs).

Talk to local nursery staffs and your parish agent about your choices. They can provide additional information based on experience and observation to make sure you are selecting appropriate shrubs.

PLANTING

It would be great to finish up planting shrubs this month, giving them even more time to get established before hot weather arrives. Remember: next month ends the ideal planting season.

Shrubs should be planted into well-prepared beds. Have your soil tested through the local parish LSU AgCenter Extension office. The cost is nominal, and the information it provides is very helpful when it comes time to prepare beds for planting.

If your soil is heavy clay, the addition of several inches of sharp sand is recommended. If your soil has a pH below 5.5 and is low in calcium, dig lime into the bed (if the soil is also low in magnesium, use dolomitic lime). If your soil test shows a pH above 7 and you are planting acid-loving shrubs, add sulfur, copperas, or aluminum sulfate during bed preparation to make the soil more acid. It is more effective to make these additions during bed preparation than after the shrubs have been planted.

Depending on the results of your soil test, you may choose to use any one of a number of amendments or soil conditioners.

Follow the steps below for bed preparation:

1. Remove unwanted vegetation from the bed area. Weeds or turfgrass may be removed physically, or killed with a herbicide such as glyphosate (follow label directions carefully) and turned under.

2. Turn the soil to a depth of at least 8 to 10 inches with a shovel, spade, garden fork, or tiller.

3. Spread any desired amendments over the turned soil. You should always add about 4 inches of organic matter such as compost, sphagnum peat moss, rotted manure, or composted finely ground pine bark. Sprinkle a general-purpose granular fertilizer over the area next. Use a 1:1:1 ratio fertilizer (such as 8-8-8 or 13-13-13) if your soil is low in phosphorus, or a 3:1:2 ratio fertilizer (such as 15-5-10) if your soil is high in phosphorus.

4. Thoroughly blend the amendments into the soil, rake the bed smooth, and shape the edges. The level of the soil in the bed will be higher than it was before. This is good as it will improve drainage.

Bed preparation may be done several weeks prior to planting; it's great to have the bed already completed when you are ready to plant. Mulch the bed about 4 inches deep to keep rain from packing the soil back down and also to prevent weed growth. Plant through the mulch, or move it off the bed, plant, and replace it.

CARE

February can have spells of bitter cold. Make sure shrubs are well watered prior to a freeze if the ground is dry. Should you have tender shrubs, such as **brunfelsia, hibiscus, tibouchina, Mexican heather,** or **thryallis,** planted in your landscape, cover and protect them during temperatures in the mid- to low 20s. See the section on cold protection in the Introduction for more information (pages 16-17).

WATERING

Little additional water is needed by shrubs this time of year. Shrubs are mostly dormant, and the weather is cool with adequate rain.

FERTILIZING

It is still a little early for fertilizing most shrubs. Although shrubs like **camellias, star magnolia,** and **flowering quince** may be blooming, encouraging new growth with fertilizer may cause plants to be damaged by a late freeze. If you use organic fertilizers, go ahead and apply them later this month so the nutrients can begin to break down and become available to shrubs when they start growing later.

PESTS

Diseases are rarely a problem during the winter.

Continue to apply oil sprays to shrubs to control scale and whiteflies.

Winter weeds will take advantage of moist, mild weather and grow . . . like weeds!

Keep beds well mulched, pull weeds promptly, and spot-treat with glyphosate or Finale.

PRUNING

Prune summer-flowering shrubs now if you need to (do not prune **gardenias** or **hydrangeas** now). The fact that it is time to prune does not mean you must. Prune with a definite purpose in mind. Study the shrub carefully, decide specifically what needs to be done, and prune accordingly. Take your time. Until you build your confidence, do a little, wait a few days, and do some more until you are satisfied.

MARCH

SHRUBS

PLANNING

Plan on getting your shrub planting finished up this month. Don't panic. Shrubs may be planted from containers throughout the year, but they like it so much better when they have a chance to make some root growth before the hot weather arrives. From March on, the later you plant, the more you will have to pamper new plantings, increasing the chance that some of the shrubs will not survive.

Evaluate your established landscape for areas where shrubs are needed. The unattractive view you have always wanted to screen, for instance, would be such a spot.

PLANTING

Proper planting will get your container-grown shrubs off to a good start. Here is how to plant in a well prepared bed.

1. Place shrubs in their containers on top of the soil where they will be planted. Make sure the spacing and arrangement are proper before going on to the next step.

2. Push down slightly on a pot to make a shallow depression, then set the shrub—in its container—aside.

3. Dig a hole into the depression deep enough to accommodate, and a little wider than, the rootball.

4. Remove the shrub from the container. If the roots are tightly packed in a solid mass, cut into the ball in several places or pull apart the root system somewhat. This will encourage the roots to grow into the surrounding soil.

5. Place the shrub's rootball into the hole. It is critical for the top of the rootball to be level with or slightly above the soil surface of the bed.

6. Use your hands to push and firm soil into the space between the rootball and the sides of the hole.

7. After planting all the shrubs in the bed, water them in thoroughly by hand to finish settling the soil around their roots.

8. Finally, mulch the bed.

You can follow the same procedure for balled-and-burlapped shrubs. Larger sizes are sometimes sold that way. After you set the rootball into the hole, remove any twine, nails, or wire securing the burlap. Pull down or remove the burlap (use a knife or scissors), being careful not to break the rootball.

CARE

Many shrubs begin to wake up and grow this month. Watch out for insect and disease problems. Late freezes may nip back new growth, but hardy shrubs will recover.

Check the mulch situation in your shrub beds. If it has broken down and become thin over time, now is a good time to replenish it. There is no need to remove the old mulch; just add new mulch on top of it—a 3-inch layer is recommended.

Remove the container by cutting it away.

WATERING

Established shrubs rarely need water except in hot, dry weather. Water newly planted shrubs thoroughly if the weather is dry and warm this month. The advantage of planting shrubs during the cool season is not having to fuss over them as much.

FERTILIZING

This is the month to fertilize shrubs in your landscape. Granular fertilizers provide an easy and economical way to feed shrubs. You usually will not need a separate fertilizer for the different types of shrubs you are growing. Acid-loving plants may be fed with a fertilizer formulated for them, especially where soils are alkaline. But, otherwise don't make fertilizing too complicated.

If your soil is low in phosphorus, choose a granular fertilizer with a 1:1:1 ratio such as 8-8-8; where soils are high in phosphorus, use a fertilizer with a 3:1:2 ratio such as 15-5-10. Do not apply too much fertilizer! If using 8-8-8, 1 cup per 30 square feet of bed area is sufficient. Apply 15-5-10 at only 1/2 cup per 30 square feet.

Scatter the fertilizer evenly over the bed and water it in. Fertilizers can be applied directly over the mulch, or you can pull back the mulch, apply the fertilizer and replace the mulch.

Apply aluminum sulfate around the roots of **hydrangeas** now if they are pink and you want them to be blue. It may take a couple of years for the color change to occur.

PESTS

With mild weather comes pest problems.

Aphids are fairly common on the new growth of a variety of shrubs. Fortunately, they are easy to control.

Spray as needed with insecticidal soap, Ultra-Fine Oil, or any insecticide labeled to control aphids on ornamentals.

Leaf spot diseases may attack new growth on some shrubs. Watch carefully for the first signs and treat with a fungicide if necessary. Leaf spots generally do not warrant treatment unless the shrubs have a history of serious problems.

PRUNING

Finish pruning summer-flowering shrubs such as **althea, olean- der, and dwarf crape myrtle** by the end of this month. Oleanders and dwarf crape myrtles are often cut back to stimulate bushy new growth. Have a definite purpose in mind when pruning.

Do not be too hasty to prune growth that has been damaged by winter freezes. Wait until the shrub has begun to grow and look at which branches are sprouting. Some branches that look dead may have only lost their leaves to the cold and will resprout.

APRIL

SHRUBS

PLANNING

Take some time to appreciate the abundant flowers produced by spring-flowering shrubs this month. **Azaleas** in particular really put on a show. This would be a good time to check out the combinations of colors you have created. Sometimes colors we thought would look good together, don't. Make notes to move or replace shrubs in November if you need to change or refine color combinations in your landscape.

When you go to nurseries and see the crowds this month, you'll be glad you bought and planted your shrubs months ago when the staff had more time to help you with questions.

PLANTING

You may continue planting shrubs from containers. If you choose to plant balled-and-burlapped shrubs, do so in early April. Hot weather is just around the corner, and there is little time for them to make root growth before the heat arrives. When shrubs are planted this late, you should pay very careful attention to their water needs in the coming summer.

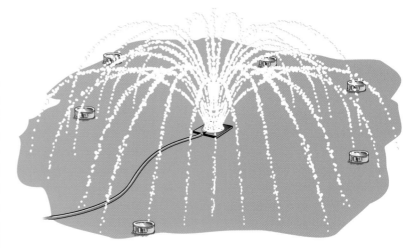

Measure the amount of water you're actually applying by timing how long it takes to accumulate 1 inch of water.

It is too late to transplant shrubs unless absolutely necessary. Even then you are taking a substantial risk. Transplant as soon as possible with as many roots as you can dig, keep the plants well watered, and cross your fingers.

CARE

In order to do well, shrubs must be planted in the growing conditions they prefer. The wrong location can mean constant problems:

• Too much shade produces leggy, low-vigor shrubs that bloom poorly or not at all and are more susceptible to disease problems.

• Too much sun can cause a shrub to appear stunted, with bleached-out, burned foliage.

• Poor drainage leads to root rot.

• Soil that stays too dry can cause excessive wilting and scorched leaves.

Observe your shrubs carefully throughout the year. Those that are not thriving may be in the wrong location.

WATERING

Newly planted shrub beds need to be watered once or twice a week if five to seven days pass without a good rain ($1/2$ to 1 inch). These plants do not have well-established root systems growing out into the soil and are very susceptible to drought stress. Plantings that are two or more years old will not need as much attention. The first summer after planting is always the most critical time for newly planted shrubs.

When you water, water thoroughly so that the soil is moistened 4 to 6 inches down. Apply an inch of water with a sprinkler or use a soaker hose. To calibrate your sprinkler to apply 1 inch of water, place several cans in the area the sprinkler covers. Turn on the sprinkler and check the time. When 1 inch of water has accumulated in most of the cans, check the time again. That's how long it takes your sprinkler to apply an inch of water.

If you use a soaker hose, make sure it passes within several inches of the base of each shrub in the bed. Water does not move a great distance from the soaker hose, and it needs to be fairly close to a plant in order to properly water its roots.

FERTILIZING

Fertilize now if you did not do so last month. Your shrubs will need the extra nutrients during the next six to eight weeks when they do much of their growing for the year. If you are fighting with a shrub that wants to be bigger than you want it to be, don't fertilize it—you will just be encouraging it to grow faster. Generally, if a shrub is growing well and has good color and vigor, fertilization is optional.

Slow-release fertilizers, such as Osmocote and Nutricote, are more expensive than granular fertilizers but feed over a much longer period of time. Slow-release fertilizers allow you to skip the summer fertilizer application since they will still be releasing nutrients 6 to 8 months (or longer) after application.

PESTS

Insects become more common as warmer weather settles in.

Watch for aphids clustering on new growth and flower buds. Spray with insecticidal soap or Ultra-Fine Oil.

The leading pest afflicting **azaleas** is the azalea lacebug. Look for tiny white spots on the upper surface of the leaves. Turn a leaf over and you will see dark brown specks on the back.

Treat promptly before the damage becomes too severe. Once heavily damaged, the foliage will not regain its attractive color. Spray, especially under the leaves, with acephate (Orthene), Malathion, or Ultra-Fine Oil. Make applications every ten days until June.

Caterpillars will chew holes in new foliage.

The damage is generally not serious, but if necessary, treat with Bt, Sevin, or acephate.

Powdery mildew will show up on a variety of shrubs if the weather is warm and dry. Look for a fine, white powdery coating on the foliage. Spray with chlorothalonil, thiophanate methyl, or sulfur (Hi-Yield Wettable Dusting Sulfur).

PRUNING

Prune spring-flowering shrubs any time after they finish flowering. Unless you are creating special shapes, such as clipped hedges or topiary, try to work with and preserve the natural form of the shrub when you are pruning. This can be best accomplished by using hand pruners (preferably bypass-type) rather than shears. When used repeatedly, shears turn shrubs into mounds, boxes, spheres, and other geometrical shapes. Unless this is how you want your shrubs to look, don't use them.

MAY

SHRUBS

PLANNING

We often think of May as late spring, but it is really quite hot and summery this month. If the winter was mild, **oleanders** will begin to enliven landscapes with clusters of red, pink, white, or rose flowers. One of the most fragrant flowers, the **gardenia,** opens white flowers that perfume the air and fade to a buttery yellow. **Hydrangeas** brighten shady plantings with cotton-candy heads of blue, pink, rose, or lavender flowers. Careful planning shows in how well shrubs thrive, fit in their location, and provide needed color, privacy, screening, or beauty.

Shrubs are a long-term commitment in the landscape; mistakes will not just go away. Constantly evaluate how well shrubs are living up to your expectations, and plan on changes to refine shrub plantings. Most of us inherit a landscape when we purchase a home. Spend a year getting to know your site and the existing plant materials. If shrub plantings do not function the way you want, if the previous owner made mistakes (you know, the giant azalea hiding the picture window), or if there are shrubs that are not doing well, feel free to make the changes needed to create the landscape you and your family want.

PLANTING

Although planting shrubs from containers may continue, increasingly stressful weather conditions mean that extra care will be needed. The chance of problems with newly planted shrubs increases as the weather gets hotter. If you do plant shrubs now, do not disturb the root system, even if it is rootbound. Shrubs will not tolerate damage to their root systems when it is hot.

CARE

In an effort to make a planting look full from the beginning, shrubs are often planted too close together. Even professionals are guilty of this. Eventually, the shrubs begin to crowd one another. Overcrowding creates stress through competition and increases insect and disease problems. In extreme cases, it might be necessary to remove some of the shrubs to make room for the rest. Sometimes regular pruning can keep things from getting out of hand. Avoid this problem by spacing shrubs properly at the beginning, even if the bed doesn't look full.

WATERING

As temperatures rise, shrubs absorb water faster from the soil. Enough rain usually falls to meet the needs of established shrubs. Shrubs planted within the last six months, however, need to be watered once or twice a week whenever beds are dry and rainfall is scarce.

FERTILIZING

Acid-loving plants can develop a disease called iron chlorosis, caused by a deficiency of iron. The symptoms are found mostly in new growth. Leaves turn a yellow-green color, while the veins of the leaves stay dark green. **Azaleas, gardenias, roses, blueberries,** and **banana shrubs** are a few plants in which this condition occurs, especially when they are grown in alkaline soil. Treat with a fertilizer rich in chelated iron (like Liquid Iron), following label directions, and acidify the soil with sulfur, copperas, aluminum sulfate, or a liquid soil acidifier.

 PESTS

Continue to spray for azalea lacebugs. Watch for signs of other pest problems. Identify the problem, and use the appropriate pesticide, if necessary. This sounds vague, but there are so many types of pests and so many types of shrubs. Fortunately, gardeners can go for years without seeing a major outbreak of pests on their shrubs. If you need help identifying a problem, contact your local parish agent, talk to local nursery staff, or use another reference. I have found the *Southern Living Garden Problem Solver* to be very helpful.

 PRUNING

This is a major month to prune spring-flowering shrubs that need it. About the only shrubs you wouldn't prune now are those that bloom in summer. Prune with a definite vision of what you are trying to accomplish. Ask, and fully answer, two questions before pruning begins:

1. Why, specifically, do I feel this plant needs to be pruned? (Or, what specific goal do I want to accomplish; what problem do I need to correct?)

2. How do I need to prune this plant to accomplish the goal?

There are two basic techniques we use to prune shrubs: heading back and thinning out.

Heading back involves shortening shoots or branches. It stimulates growth and branching. Heading back is often used to control the size of shrubs, encourage fullness, rejuvenate older shrubs, and maintain specific shapes, as with topiary and espalier. Shearing is a form of heading back. Often overutilized by gardeners, careless shearing can destroy the natural form of a plant.

Thinning out removes shoots or branches at their point of origin, either back to a branch fork or the main trunk. Thinning cuts can control the size and shape of a plant while doing a better job of maintaining its natural shape. Thinning cuts do not stimulate growth and often work more with the plant's natural growth patterns to correct problems.

Heading Back

There are two main types of pruning:
heading back and thinning out.

Thinning Out

JUNE

SHRUBS

PLANNING

Keeping records about plants in your landscape is a great way to learn from past experiences. Shrubs aren't as finicky as other types of plants and are long-lived when selected and cared for properly. You might think that keeping records is not very important, but pest problems, treatments that were effective or ineffective, blooming times, when shrubs were planted, and where they were purchased are all valuable bits of information. Keep a notebook handy to jot down quick observations. As time goes by, you'll be surprised at how helpful your notes can be.

PLANTING

The intense heat of the next three months will make it more difficult for shrubs planted now to survive and become established. If at all possible, avoid this hottest time of the year for planting shrubs and wait for cooler weather this fall.

Transplanting shrubs should not be attempted. Plants use water faster when it is hot and they are in active growth. To damage the roots now would reduce the plants' abilities to absorb water just when they need it most.

CARE

Most summer-flowering shrubs bloom over a relatively long period, compared to spring-flowering shrubs. Faded flowers often linger as new ones are being produced, detracting from the attractiveness of the display. Pull off or trim faded flowers as they occur. In the case of **dwarf crape myrtles, oleanders,** and others, trimming off the faded flowers will encourage more blooms to form.

Hot weather makes it less pleasant to be outside. Use the early morning or early evening hours to walk around the landscape and check out your shrub plantings. Look for plants that need to be pruned, pest problems getting started, weeds that need to be pulled, and other assorted jobs. All gardeners eventually learn that these problems are much easier to deal with if handled sooner rather than later.

WATERING

Watch carefully for drought stress on shrubs planted within the last six months, especially those planted after March. Symptoms to look for include wilting, scorched leaf edges, or dull, brown, or dropping leaves. Water deeply and thoroughly once or twice a week when adequate rain does not fall.

Ironically, you may be watering properly but your shrubs are still showing signs of drought stress. Newly planted shrubs have a restricted root system that has not grown extensively into the soil of the bed. A shrub can pull all the water out of its rootball and get desperately thirsty even when the soil of the bed feels moist. Stick your fingers directly into the rootball under a shrub rather than in the soil of the bed to see if it is dry.

If you see drought symptoms even though you are watering, turn a hose on trickle and lay it at the base of each shrub for about ten minutes to provide water directly to the shrub's roots where it is needed. Drought symptoms are generally more common when sprinklers are used to irrigate and less of a problem when soaker hoses are used.

 ## FERTILIZING

Most spring-flowering and other shrubs have finished their primary growth period, and the fertilizer provided in March was sufficient. Unless you cut them back, little or no growth will occur throughout the rest of the summer. Fertilizing established shrubs that are about as big as you want them to be is of little benefit. If you have problems controlling the size of shrubs in your landscape, fertilizing them will just make matters worse.

Young shrubs, in their second year after planting, may be fertilized in June or July to encourage additional growth. Use about the same rate you did in the spring, or less. Generally, avoid fertilizing shrubs planted in the past eight months. They should not be pushed to grow while they are establishing.

 ## PESTS

Control powdery mildew on **Chinese mahonia, dwarf crape myrtle, euonymus,** and others with benomyl, Daconil, or other fungicides labeled to control powdery mildew on ornamentals.

Control whiteflies that may appear on citrus.

Control whiteflies on **gardenias** and **dwarf citrus trees** with Ultra-Fine Oil sprayed under the leaves. Make three applications ten days apart, and spray during the cooler early morning hours.

 ## PRUNING

You should finish any extensive pruning that needs to be done on spring-flowering shrubs this month, or by early July at the latest.

JULY
SHRUBS

PLANNING

Is there a bland sameness to your shrub plantings? Many shrubs have a medium texture that can look uninteresting if there are no contrasts nearby. Plant shrubs with a variety of textures (coarse-textured plants have large leaves, fine-textured plants have small or thin leaves, and medium-textured plants fall somewhere in between) and growth habits (upright, bushy, mounding) to create interest and contrast. Groups of herbaceous perennials, annuals, bulbs, and ornamental grasses can also be included in shrub plantings. Make plans to plant or rearrange shrubs this fall if needed.

PLANTING

Although planting can continue through the summer with container-grown shrubs, think carefully before you decide to plant now. It is far better to wait for the weather to cool.

If you are in a new house without any landscaping and need to do something, plant beds of heat-tolerant blooming plants now instead of shrubs. Good choices are **pentas, lantana, blue daze, coleus, dusty miller, purslane, periwinkle, torenia, melampodium,** and **salvia** for sunny areas, and **impatiens** and **begonias** for shade. These plants will grow, bloom, and thrive in midsummer heat through November. At that time they can be pulled up and replaced with permanent shrub plantings.

CARE

Shrubs should not require a great deal of care in your landscape. Other than occasional pruning, watering, and dealing with infrequent pest problems, shrubs do not demand a lot of time. Shrubs that always seem to have something wrong or need constant work to be kept attractive may not have been good choices for your landscape. Decide if there is a problem that can be corrected, or replace those shrubs with lower-maintenance types this fall.

WATERING

Even well-established shrubs will need to be watered if rain does not occur for ten days. Intense heat stresses shrubs, and they need an adequate supply of water to deal with it. On the other hand, frequent rains may occur, particularly in south Louisiana, making irrigation unnecessary. Watch the weather and water when needed. **Azaleas** are shallow-rooted and one of the most drought-vulnerable shrubs we grow.

A soaker hose, mulch, and a rain guage will be your helpers in the fight against drought.

 FERTILIZING

You may fertilize established shrubs that were last fed in March. This is recommended for shrubs that you want to grow as much and as fast as possible. This is not recommended for shrubs that have already out-grown their space and have to be cut back frequently. Use an all-purpose granular fertilizer appropriate for your area at the rate recommended on the label (or less).

Apply a fertilizer containing chelated iron to acid-loving plants such as **azaleas, gardenias, blueberries,** and others that show an iron deficiency. Young leaves will appear yellow-green with dark green veins. Apply a soil acidifier to lower the pH and make iron more readily available.

 PESTS

A black deposit on foliage is a fungus called "sooty mold" that indicates the presence of sucking insects. It is not attacking the shrub but living off sugary excretions produced by the sucking insects. Sucking insects that commonly produce this sugary substance (called honeydew) include aphids, whiteflies, and scales.

All can be controlled with applications of Ultra-Fine Oil (spray in the early morning) or a systemic insecticide such as acephate (Orthene), or imidacloprid (Merit).

Caterpillars and beetles can chew holes in shrub leaves.

Control with Sevin.

Rainy weather encourages leaf spot diseases, but they rarely warrant spraying. Generally, by the time you notice the spots, the damage is already done.

Wet soil also encourages root rot diseases in late summer. Established shrubs that are otherwise healthy may show dead or wilted branches. Fungal infections have generally killed the portion of the root system that provided water to that section of the shrub. A shrub may wilt completely and die. Often only one or a few shrubs in a planting are affected.

There is little that can be done. Pull back the mulch and loosen the soil slightly to increase air spaces and allow soil to dry out. To avoid the problem, make sure beds drain well when they are being prepared.

 PRUNING

Finish pruning spring-flowering shrubs early this month. Do not prune **sasanquas** or **camellias;** their buds for fall and winter bloom are already set. Prune hedges as needed to keep them neat and thick. Remember that the base of the hedge should be slightly wider than the top. This prevents lower portions of the hedge from being shaded and thinning out.

AUGUST

SHRUBS

PLANNING

These last hot weeks of a long, hot summer are particularly stressful to shrubs in the landscape (as well as to the gardener). Carefully chosen shrubs, well adapted to our climate and planted in the proper growing conditions, however, should have no difficulty getting through this most trying time of the year.

The planting season begins in a couple of months, and it's not too soon to make plans. Check out local botanical gardens and gardens open to the public, as well as local nurseries. Shrubs that are thriving in the heat of August make good choices for your landscape. Shrubs in public gardens and nurseries are generally well labeled, so it is not as difficult to identify a shrub you are not familiar with. Once a shrub catches your eye, spend some time researching the plant.

PLANTING

This is not a good month for planting or transplanting shrubs in the landscape. The intense heat of this month is hard enough for an established shrub to endure. New plantings are especially vulnerable. If you do plant, proper watering is crucial.

CARE

Late-summer stress can occasionally cause shrubs to drop some of their older leaves. This is generally not a major problem and no cause for alarm.

Keep beds well mulched. Not only does this help control weeds and conserve soil moisture, but it also helps prevent the soil from building up so much heat. In older plantings where the shrubs have grown enough to shade the soil of the bed, this is less critical. But in new plantings where the ground is still exposed, a 2- to

There are many types of mulch available to the gardener, either free or for purchase.

3-inch layer of mulch is very beneficial.

Choose a mulch that suits your taste, but try to use what is available for free. Pine straw, shade tree leaves (saved from the fall), dry grass clippings, and partially finished compost are all excellent. You may also purchase mulch such as pine bark or pine straw.

WATERING

August can be very hot and dry. Provide deep, thorough irrigation with sprinklers or soaker hoses. Water once or twice a week if rain has not occurred in the last five to seven days for new plantings, in the last ten days for established plantings.

FERTILIZING

No fertilizer is needed for the rest of the growing season. Late applications of fertilizer may reduce the hardiness of your shrubs. Fertilizing now may stimulate shrubs to grow during our mild to warm fall when shrubs should be slowing down and getting ready for winter.

PESTS

Spider mites can be a problem on shrubs such as **azaleas, junipers, camellias,** and **hollies** during hot, dry weather. Spider mites are generally too tiny to see without magnification, but the foliage will become faded and tan as they feed.

Control with insecticidal soap, Ultra-Fine Oil (spray during the early morning), or Malathion. Spray under the leaves.

Azalea lacebugs become more active in the late summer and fall.

Watch for new damage and spray with Malathion or Ultra-Fine Oil as needed.

Continue to treat for caterpillars and beetles, which chew holes in the leaves of a variety of shrubs.

If the damage is light, spraying is not necessary. Sevin will control both pests.

PRUNING

Finish shearing hedges or pruning shrubs not grown for flowers. Pruning after August will stimulate new growth which will not have time to harden off before winter, making the plant susceptible to freeze injury.

If you prune spring-flowering shrubs this month or later, you will remove flower buds from next year's display.

SEPTEMBER

SHRUBS

PLANNING

This month usually brings some relief from the heat. **Sweet olives** will often burst into bloom with the first cool front. The small, inconspicuous, creamy-white flowers produce one of the most delightful fragrances of any shrub. Fragrance is an often overlooked aspect of flowering shrubs, but it can add so much to the enjoyment of our gardens. Plan to include some fragrant shrubs in your landscape. Good choices include **butterfly bush** (*Buddleia*), **sweet shrub** (*Caly-canthus*), **sasanqua, gardenia,** **Virginia willow, winter honey-suckle** (*Lonicera fragrantissima*), **star magnolia** (*Magnolia stel-lata*), and **native azalea** (*Rhodo-dendron canescens*).

Planning on planting some shrubs this fall? If we do get some beautiful cool weather and you feel like digging in the garden, go ahead and start preparing beds now for plant-ing shrubs next month.

PLANTING

Wait until next month to begin planting. The weather will be more pleasant for you to get out and dig beds, and the shrubs will appreciate the cooler tem-peratures.

CARE

Now that the hottest weather is coming to an end, take time to evaluate the shrubs growing in your landscape. What would you do differently regarding pest control? Sometimes we decide to let a problem go untreated, then regret the decision when a lot of damage occurs. Make a note to treat if the problem should show up again next summer. You might decide to prune some

Butterfly Bush

shrubs differently. Perhaps you should have cut them back sooner or later, more than you did or less.

If we do not take the time to look at what we have done and remember the results, we may continue to make the same mistakes or forget something that worked well. Take some time to make a few notes in your garden journal.

WATERING

Although September temperatures may become milder, the weather can also be sweltering and dry. If your new shrub plantings are still alive, you've been doing an excellent job of watering. Keep up the good work.

FERTILIZING

No fertilizers are needed for the rest of the year.

PESTS

The same pests that have been around all summer continue this month. Insect pests to control include whiteflies (especially on **gardenias**), lacebugs (especially on **azaleas**), scales (especially on **camellias, banana shrub, hollies,** and **euonymus**), and aphids (especially on **oleanders**).

All can be treated with Ultra-Fine Oil or Orthene.

Disease problems generally begin to diminish as weather grows cooler, especially if September is relatively dry. If the summer has been very wet, root rot may have taken its toll on some shrub plantings.

Wait until fall to replace dead shrubs. Before planting new shrubs, dig generous amounts of organic matter into the area. Plant the shrubs slightly higher to ensure better drainage.

If you have let weeds get the upper hand during the hot weather of summer, get out on cooler days and try to get them under control.

Pull, dig, or spot-treat with herbicides such as Roundup or Finale. Although you can use them very close to desirable plants, do not allow either of these herbicides to get on the foliage or stems of your shrubs. Use a piece of cardboard as a shield, cover nearby shrubs with plastic bags, or otherwise prevent spray from getting on the shrubs. Fusilade and Vantage are selective herbicides that will kill grassy weeds, but not the ornamentals listed on the label. These products may be helpful in situations where it would be impossible to spray the weed without getting the herbicide on the shrub. Both work best when the grass is young.

PRUNING

The only pruning that would be appropriate from now on would be thinning (see the May pruning information, page 171). Since thinning does not stimulate growth, it may be done just about anytime. Remember: spring-flowering shrubs and **gardenias, hydrangeas, sasanquas,** and **camellias** have already set their flower buds. Any pruning now will remove flower buds and reduce the display.

OCTOBER

SHRUBS

PLANNING

Shrub planting can begin this month, but there is no hurry. If you need to plant a new landscape or extensively redesign an existing one, take some time to think about what you want to plant and where it will be located. An attractive, functional landscape doesn't just happen. You cannot go to the nursery one Saturday morning, buy a bunch of shrubs that catch your eye (or happen to be on sale), bring them home, plant them here and there, and expect the landscape to turn out the way you wanted. But you probably know better than that by now.

Take time to consider your needs and develop a plan for a landscape that will be attractive, functional, and successful. See "Planning the Garden" (page 11) for more information on how to do this, and the introduction to this chapter (pages 159-160) for information on how to select shrubs. You have plenty of time to do this—the planting season runs from now until March. November through early December, however, is a particularly good time for landscape installation.

It may be helpful to outline possible new beds with lime or flour so you can "see" it first.

PLANTING

It's still too early to transplant, but you can begin to plant container-grown shrubs. Proper bed preparation is the first step to growing shrubs successfully.

Follow the steps below for bed preparation:

1. Remove unwanted vegetation from the bed area. Weeds or turfgrass may be removed physically or killed with a herbicide such as glyphosate (follow label directions carefully) and turned under.

2. Turn the soil to a depth of at least 8 to 10 inches with a shovel, spade, or garden fork.

3. Spread any desired amendments over the turned soil. You should always add about 4 inches of organic matter such as compost, sphagnum peat moss, rotted manure, or finely ground pine bark. Sprinkle a general-purpose granular fertilizer over the area next. Use a 1:1:1 ratio fertilizer (such as 8-8-8 or 13-13-13) if your soil is low in phosphorus, a 3:1:2 ratio fertilizer (such as 15-5-10) if your soil is high in phosphorus. Have your soil tested through the parish LSU AgCenter Extension office to determine other amendments to add.

4. Thoroughly incorporate the amendments into the soil of the bed, rake smooth, and shape the edges. The level of the soil in the bed will be higher than it was before. This is good, as it will improve drainage.

If you don't intend to plant right away, apply a 2- to 4-inch layer of mulch over the prepared bed. This will keep the soil loose and prevent weeds from growing until you plant. At that time you can pull off the mulch, plant, then replace it, or simply plant through the existing mulch.

 WATERING

Although cooler, October can be one of our driest months. Established shrubs probably will not need attention, but continue to water shrubs planted in the past year if regular rainfall does not occur.

 FERTILIZING

Apply fertilizer during bed preparation, but no fertilizer should be applied to existing shrub plantings this month.

 PESTS

Azalea lacebugs will be active through November. These insects feed from the underside of the leaves, causing small, white dots on the upper side of the leaves and dark-brown spots on the back.

Do not let a lot of damage occur before you treat. Once the damage occurs, the leaves will not turn green again, even if you control the lacebugs. Spray under the leaves with Orthene, Malathion, or Ultra-Fine Oil every ten days, or as needed.

 PRUNING

This is not a good time of the year to prune shrubs. If absolutely necessary, thinning may be used to correct problems that can't wait.

NOVEMBER

SHRUBS

PLANNING

Despite gardening in the Deep South, Louisiana gardeners still have a hard time resisting the feeling that this is the end of the gardening year—that it's time to put up the tools, watch the plants go dormant, and wait for a blanket of snow to cover the landscape. This is not the end (and we rarely get snow). In fact, it's a prime time for planting in our state. So much can be planted now, including shrubs.

Although the ideal planting season for shrubs runs from now through March, planting in November and early December is particularly recommended. The weather is generally mild and pleasant, and shrubs planted in late fall and early winter benefit in several ways:

• The plants are dormant during this time and therefore less likely to suffer transplant shock.

This is especially important for balled-and-burlapped shrubs.

• The mild weather and regular rainfall typical of our winters allow the new plantings to settle in and adjust with little stress (and less work for you).

• Planting shrubs now also allows them to become well established prior to spring growth and the intense heat of summer.

Research shows that the roots of plants can continue to grow and develop during our mild winters, even though the top is dormant. Shrubs planted now will develop well-established root systems better able to absorb water than spring-planted shrubs. This increases their ability to survive that first stressful summer after planting.

If you were looking for a break, think again. It's time to get out your shovels and start planting.

PLANTING

A huge advantage of planting shrubs during this time of year is that the nurseries are much less busy than they are in the spring, when most people head to the nurseries. Now that you know better, enjoy the time and attention that nursery staffs can give you as you make your shrub purchases.

Plant shrubs in well-prepared beds. Avoid preparing beds and planting if the soil is wet. Wait a couple of days after a heavy rain before digging in the soil. Working wet soil damages its structure and can lead to soil compaction.

1. Place shrubs in their containers on top of the soil where they will be planted. Make sure the spacing and arrangement are proper before going on to the next step.

2. Push down slightly on a pot to make a shallow depression, and set the shrub—in its container—aside.

3. Dig a hole into the depression deep enough to accommodate, and a little wider than, the rootball.

4. Remove the shrub from the container. If the roots are tightly packed in a solid mass, cut into the ball in several places or pull apart the root system somewhat. This will encourage the roots to grow into the surrounding soil.

5. Place the shrub's rootball into the hole. It is critical for the top of the rootball to be level with or slightly above the soil surface of the bed.

6. Use your hands to push and firm soil into the space between the rootball and the sides of the hole.

7. After planting all the shrubs, water them in thoroughly by hand to finish settling the soil around their roots.

8. Finally, mulch the bed.

You can follow the same procedure for balled-and-burlapped shrubs. Larger-sized shrubs are sometimes sold that way. After you set the rootball into the hole, remove any twine, nails, or wire securing the burlap. Pull down or remove the burlap (use a knife or scissors), being careful not to break the rootball. (The "burlap" may actually be a synthetic material that resists decay. If you're not sure if the wrapping is true burlap that will rot or is the look-alike material, remove it completely from the hole.)

WATERING

Established shrubs should not need to be watered during this time of the year. Water-in newly planted shrubs thoroughly, watering occasionally thereafter if the weather is mild and dry.

FERTILIZING

No fertilizer should be applied to shrubs this month.

PESTS

Few pest problems will plague your shrubs from here on out. If you notice scale on **camellias, hollies, euonymus,** or other plants, the cool season is an ideal time to treat with oil sprays. During cooler temperatures, heavier oils (such as Volck Oil Spray) are safe to use, or you can continue to use Ultra-Fine Oil.

PRUNING

Be very cautious about what you prune and how. November can be relatively mild, and shrubs often do not get a strong signal to go dormant. Shearing or heading back shrubs might still stimulate growth, which is not a good idea just before winter. Spring-flowering shrubs have set their buds and should not be pruned extensively until after they bloom next spring. Light, selective pruning may be done if absolutely necessary. Try to use thinning cuts, which do not stimulate new growth, to correct any problems.

You can use heavier oil during cool months to combat scale.(Scale enlarged for detail.)

DECEMBER

SHRUBS

PLANNING

Although gardeners usually purchase shrubs from local nurseries, they are also available through mail-order companies. They often have more unusual cultivars that are not available locally. Be cautious and selective. Try new cultivars of a shrub you already know will do well in Louisiana.

PLANTING

If planted now, shrubs will have about five months to get established before dealing with high temperatures next May. This makes them better prepared to survive their first summer in the ground.

Transplanting or moving shrubs in your landscape to a new location can also begin now. If you plan on moving a deciduous shrub, wait until it has dropped its leaves to move it. Transplanting may be done from now until the end of February.

When transplanting, dig the shrub with as much of the root system as you can manage. Roots spread out more than they grow down, so it is more important for you to take a rootball that is wider than it is deep. Replant shrubs immediately in holes you have already dug and prepared. It is very important for the roots not to dry out once the shrub is out of the ground. Wrap in plastic or place in a container if the shrub cannot be replanted immediately. Water-in thoroughly once planted, and water during the winter if needed. Continue to treat the transplanted shrubs as new plantings next summer, and pay careful attention to water needs.

CARE

In south Louisiana, gardeners often plant various tropical shrubs in their landscapes. The chance of severe injury or loss during cold winters makes it generally unwise to include too many tropicals in landscape plantings. For more information on protecting tender plants during the winter, see pages 16–17.

WATERING

Cool to cold weather and generally abundant rainfall make watering established shrubs this month unnecessary. Water newly planted shrubs and those that have been transplanted if the weather turns dry and mild.

FERTILIZING

Fertilizer should not be applied to shrubs this month.

PESTS

Other than applying oil sprays for scale, little pest control is necessary in December.

PRUNING

By mid-December, shrubs are pretty much dormant, and pruning them now will not stimulate new growth. Feel free to trim hedges and other shrubs, unless they bloom in the spring.

HELPFUL HINTS

Did you ever stop to think that outdoor plants make good Christmas gifts? Since this month is an excellent planting month, drop a few hints to family members or friends about the kind of shrubs you would like in your landscape. Growing plants continue to increase in value with proper care, and a plant received as a gift can make a lasting impression.

TREES

Trees are a vital part of most landscapes. They provide shade, privacy, windbreaks, fruit or nuts, and flowers, and can increase real-estate value as well. Select them carefully. They will be around for a long time. Proper placement is very important, as mistakes are not easily corrected later on when trees are large.

PLANNING

There is no one perfect tree for Louisiana. All trees have advantages and disadvantages, depending on their planting locations and desired characteristics. Here are some points you need to consider:

1. Select a tree that will mature at a size right for its site. I cannot stress this too much. Planting trees that will grow too large for their locations is one of the most common mistakes people make (along with planting too many trees). Generally, small trees are those that grow from 15 to 25 feet tall, medium-sized trees grow from 30 to 55 feet tall, and large trees are those that grow 60 feet or taller.

2. Think about the purpose of the tree and why you feel it is needed. This will help you determine what characteristics the tree should have, such as its shape, size, and rate of growth. Ornamental features such as flowers, attractive berries, brightly

colored fall foliage or unusual bark should also be considered.

3. Decide if you want a tree that retains its foliage year-round (evergreen) or loses its leaves in the winter (deciduous). Deciduous trees are particularly useful where you want shade in the summer and sun in the winter.

4. Choose trees that are well adapted to our growing conditions. They must be able to tolerate long, hot summers and mild winters. A number of northern species of beech, maple, conifers, and others you might see in catalogs are unsuitable for our state. Trees that are not completely hardy are not good choices either. The beautiful golden raintree (*Koelreuteria bipinnata*), for instance, is too susceptible to freeze injury to make it a good choice.

5. Check the location of overhead power lines, and if you must plant under them, use small, low-growing trees. Consider underground water lines and septic tanks as well as walks, drives, and paved surfaces that may be damaged by the roots of large trees. Locate large trees at least 15 to 25 feet away from your house.

PLANTING AND TRANSPLANTING

Planting trees properly can make the difference between success and failure. Whether the tree is balled and burlapped or container grown, dig the hole at least twice the diameter of the rootball, and no deeper than the height of the rootball.

Remove the tree from the container and place it gently in the hole. A rootball tightly packed with thick, encircling roots indicates a rootbound condition. Try to unwrap or open up or even cut some of the roots to encourage them to spread into the surrounding soil. Once the tree is in the hole, remove any nylon twine or wire supports that may have been used, and fold down the burlap from the top of the rootball. The top of the rootball should be level with or slightly above the surrounding soil. It is critical that you do not plant the tree too deep.

Thoroughly pulverize the soil dug out from the hole and use this soil, without any additions, to backfill around the tree. Add soil around the tree until the hole is half full, then firm the soil to eliminate air pockets—but do not pack it tight. Finish filling the hole, firm again, and then water the tree thoroughly to settle it in. Generally, we do not add fertilizer to the planting hole. The use of a root-stimulator solution is optional.

If the tree is tall enough to be unstable, it should be staked; otherwise, it's not necessary. Do not drive the stake into place directly against the trunk and tie the tree to it. Two or three stakes should be firmly driven into the ground just beyond the rootball. Tie cloth strips, old nylon stockings, or wire (covered with a piece of garden hose where it touches the trunk) to the stakes and then to the trunk of the tree. Leave the support in place no more than nine to twelve months.

CARE FOR YOUR TREES

Keep the area one to two feet out from the trunk of a newly planted tree mulched and free from weeds and grass. This will encourage the tree to establish faster by eliminating competition from grass roots. It also prevents lawn mowers and string trimmers from damaging the bark at the base of the tree, which can cause stunting or death. The mulch should be about 4 inches deep and pulled back slightly from the base of the tree.

People tend to think of established trees as almost indestructible. Trees do not need a great deal of care compared to other plants in the landscape, but they do occasionally need water, fertilizer, and pest control.

Perhaps the greatest threat to trees is people. A common misconception is that tree roots are located deep in the soil and so are well protected from damage. Actually, tree roots are remarkably shallow. The majority of the root system responsible for absorbing water and minerals is located in the

upper 12 inches of soil, and it spreads out at least twice as far as the branches.

As a result, many people damage or kill their trees in a variety of ways. Tree roots are vulnerable to damage from soil compaction caused by excessive foot traffic or vehicular traffic. Whether building a new home on a lot with existing trees, an addition to an existing home, or a new patio, construction work kills lots of trees. Even repairing driveways, streets, and sidewalks may cause extensive damage to tree roots. In some parts of the state, soil subsidence makes occasional filling needed. If filling is necessary, no more than 2 inches of fill per year should be spread over a tree's root system.

WATERING

Water a newly planted or transplanted tree whenever the weather is dry. This is the single most important thing you can do to ensure its survival, especially during the first summer after planting. To properly water a tree its first year, turn a hose on trickle and lay the end on top of the ground within a few inches of the trunk. Let the water trickle for about twenty minutes. This should be done once or twice a week during hot, dry weather.

A bucket with holes in the bottom also works well. Use a 3- to 5-gallon bucket (for example an old kitty litter container, 5-gallon paint bucket, etc.) Make 5 to 10 holes with a hot metal skewer on one side of the bottom of the bucket. Place the bucket with the holes next to the trunk. Fill the bucket twice a week during hot, dry weather.

Older, established trees rarely have to be watered, but exceptionally dry weather during the months of June, July, August, and September may place enough stress on trees to make watering necessary. Lawn sprinklers are the best devices for watering the expansive root systems of established trees. Set the sprinkler to apply about an inch of water, and water about once a week until sufficient rain occurs.

FERTILIZING

In the first five to ten years after planting, young trees can be encouraged to grow significantly faster if fertilized annually. Older trees can be fertilized less often. In fact, for older trees with good vigor, color, and rate of growth, fertilization is not needed.

Trees are generally fertilized in late January or February in anticipation of growth beginning in February or March.

PEST CONTROL

Although they require less pest control than other plants in the landscape, trees do occasionally have pest problems that need to be controlled. The best trees are relatively free from pest problems or will not be badly damaged or killed by pests that do attack them. This is fortunate, as the average gardener does not have the proper equipment to spray a large tree.

When selecting a tree for your landscape, be sure you are familiar with its potential pest problems: how serious they tend to be and how often they are likely to occur.

PRUNING

For a variety of reasons, virtually all trees must be pruned at some time. Lower branches are gradually removed from a young, growing tree to lift its canopy to an appropriate height. Dead or diseased branches must occasionally be removed. Fruit trees are pruned in a variety of specialized forms. Problems with poorly placed branches or an unattractive shape may need to be fixed.

Pruning needs to be done correctly. Except for certain types of fruit trees, pruning is generally kept to a minimum but should certainly not be avoided when necessary.

JANUARY
TREES

PLANNING

Determining the selection and placement of trees in your landscape are some of the most important decisions you will make. No other plant material is as long-lived or will have as profound an effect on its surroundings. No other plant materials can create the major problems that poorly selected or improperly placed trees will. The most common mistakes are:

• planting too many trees
• planting trees that grow too large for their site
• planting trees not well adapted to Louisiana
• planting trees too close to the house
• planting tall trees under power lines

Remember that the trees you plant will grow much larger than the saplings you purchase and bring home from the nursery. It is tempting to plant more trees than you really need, and it's common to realize years later that you made a terrible mistake. Cutting down a tree is never an easy decision, so it is better not to put yourself (or whoever owns the property later) in that situation.

PLANTING

January is an excellent month to plant trees. The third Friday in January is Arbor Day in Louisiana.

Deciduous trees are leafless at this time of the year, so when you go to the nursery to make your selection, expect to see bare branches. Don't be afraid to purchase and plant these trees. Their dormancy makes this a great time to get them into the ground, especially balled-and-burlapped specimens. Evergreen species will, of course, have foliage.

Select the right location for the tree in your landscape. To get a feel for how well the tree will fit in the spot you have selected, try this exercise:

• Place the tree where you intend to plant it.

• Look up the expected spread of the branches (use the Tree Planting Chart on pages 272-275 or another reference such as *Southern Plants* by Odenwald and Turner).

• Divide the expected spread by two, and cut a piece of twine or string that many feet long.

If, for instance, the expected spread is 40 feet, cut a piece of string 20 feet long.

• Tie one end of the string to the tree trunk, stretch out the string to its full length, and walk in a circle around the tree.

I can't think of a more effective way for you to really see how much space the tree will occupy.

CARE

Trees require little care in the middle of the winter while they are dormant. Winter storms may damage trees by breaking branches. Ice storms in north Louisiana sometimes create heavy ice build-up on branches, causing them to break. Either prune off ragged stubs yourself or have a professional arborist do it.

WATERING

Water-in newly planted trees thoroughly. Newly planted deciduous trees generally will not need to be watered again this time of the year. Newly planted evergreen trees should be watered as needed if the weather is mild and dry. Established trees will not need to be watered this month.

FERTILIZING

Trees can be fertilized in late January. Newly planted trees should not be fertilized. Established trees in their first five to ten years after planting can be encouraged to grow faster with moderate annual fertilization. For older trees in good health with good color and growth rate, fertilization is optional. Fertilization is recommended for older trees that show nutrient-deficiency symptoms or have been damaged.

Use a granular fertilizer with a 3:1:2 ratio such as 15-5-10. The amount of fertilizer to use is determined by the size of the tree. In the past, the amount to use was based on the diameter of the trunk. One pound of 15-5-10 was applied for each inch of diameter of the trunk. New recommendations are based on the square footage of the root system.

To determine the square footage of the root system of a tree, measure the distance from the trunk to the outer tips of the branches (called the "dripline"). Multiply that number by two (since roots reach out about twice as far as the branches). Multiply that number by itself, and then by 3.14 to determine the square footage. Apply 20 pounds of 15-5-10 per thousand feet of root area.

Example: It is 10 feet from the trunk to the dripline.

10 × 2 = 20

20 × 20 = 400

400 × 3.14 = 1256 square ft.

So, at 20 pounds of 15-5-10 per 1000 square feet, about 25 pounds of fertilizer would be applied to the tree.

Apply the fertilizer in holes 1 to 2 inches wide and about 12 inches deep, spaced 2 to 3 feet apart (use a piece of pipe to make the holes). Make the holes in a doughnut-shaped area centered on the dripline, and fill each hole with fertilizer to within about 2 inches of the top. If some of the area cannot be fertilized because of concrete surfaces or buildings, reduce the amount of fertilizer applied.

There are other fertilizer methods available. Tree fertilizers may be purchased in compressed spikes that are driven into the ground. Follow the manufacturer's recommendations on the number to use. Devices that hook up to a garden hose are available at nurseries. These inject a fertilizer solution through a metal probe inserted in the soil. Tree-care companies will fertilize your trees for a fee. They frequently use a system that injects a fertilizer solution into the soil.

PRUNING

Shade trees may be pruned just about any time. January is an appropriate month to prune most fruit trees such as apples, pears, peaches, and plums. Pruning fruit trees is rather specific. For more detailed information, contact your local LSU AgCenter Extension office for a free copy of "The Louisiana Home Orchard" brochure.

Do not prune spring-flowering trees now. Some of the earliest-flowering trees, such as **Taiwan flowering cherry, Drummond red maple,** and **oriental magnolia,** will often begin to bloom in late January, especially in southeast Louisiana.

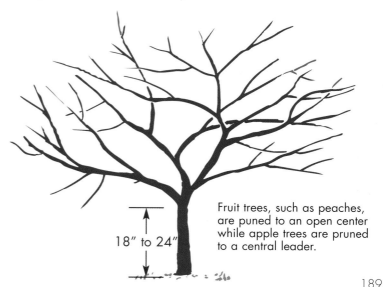

18" to 24"

Fruit trees, such as peaches, are puned to an open center while apple trees are pruned to a central leader.

FEBRUARY

TREES

PLANNING

We are approaching the end of the ideal planting season for trees in Louisiana, especially those that are balled and burlapped. Finalize your decisions on tree planting soon. Trees are often planted for shade. If your patio is too hot and sunny to use during the summer, consider planting a small to medium-sized tree to the south or southwest of the patio to provide cooling shade. Select a deciduous tree that will drop its leaves in the wintertime and allow sunlight to reach the patio when its warmth is welcome. Since the tree will be close to an outdoor living area, consider other features such as flowers, fragrance, and interesting bark. If the tree will overhang the patio surface, remember that flowers or fruit dropping can be messy.

PLANTING

Finish transplanting trees this month. Gardeners rarely transplant trees. By the time you realize a mistake has been made, a tree is generally too large to move. On occasion, trees will grow from seeds that fall in flower beds or along fences. If you recognize the tree as a type you would like to grow in your yard and you have a suitable location for it, dig it up and transplant it now while it is dormant. This is generally most successful with young saplings that have trunk diameters of one inch or less.

Continue to plant container-grown or balled-and-burlapped shade trees, flowering trees, and fruit trees while they are still dormant and the weather is cool.

CARE

Stake newly planted trees if they seem unstable once planted. Drive two 2x2 inch wooden stakes or metal pipes firmly into the ground beyond the rootball of the tree. Tie cloth strips, strips of old nylon stockings, or wire (covered with a piece of garden hose where it touches the trunk) to the stakes and then to the trunk of the tree. There should be a little slack in the lines connecting the tree to the stakes. This will allow the trunk to sway slightly and help make it strong. Leave the support in place no more than nine to twelve months.

WATERING

Other than newly planted trees, no watering is necessary this month.

FERTILIZING

Finish fertilizing most trees in February. It is important for the nutrients to be available to a tree as it begins spring growth. See pages 188-189 or Fertilizing in January) for directions on tree fertilization.

PESTS

Some pest problems must be dealt with before they occur. **Oaks,** especially **water oaks** (*Quercus nigra*), are susceptible to a fungus disease called oak leaf blister. Symptoms of this disease (light-green blistered areas on leaves that eventually turn brown and cause leaf drop) show up in early summer, but by then it is too late to do anything.

If your oaks have had heavy infections of oak leaf blister in the past, spray them with Daconil, Bordeaux mixture, or mancozeb (or have a tree care company do it if the tree is large) just as the dormant buds swell and begin to grow. Although the infected leaves are unattractive and leaf drop during the summer is a nuisance, the disease is not fatal.

Magnolias are commonly infested with oyster scale, which looks like small white bumps on the foliage. Light infestations are not a problem, but high popula-

HELPFUL HINTS

Although considered evergreen, **live oaks** drop some, most, or all of their leaves in late February and early March. Almost immediately, new growth, often with a reddish tint, appears to replace the lost leaves. The amount of leaf drop can vary from year to year but is no cause for alarm. Rake up the leaves and use them as mulch, put them in your compost pile, or store them in plastic bags for later use.

Notice the attractive, burgundy, boomerang-shaped fruit clustered along the branches of female **swamp red maples** in February and March.

---

tions should be controlled. Trees may be treated with an oil spray now.

Spraying for most fruit trees begins this month. Never use insecticides on fruit trees when they are in bloom. Most are pollinated by insects, and the use of insecticides will interfere with pollination. Fruit trees are sprayed according to specific schedules depending on the type of tree.

Use an oil spray on magnolias this month to prevent an infestation of oyster scale.

Contact your parish LSU Ag-Center Extension office to obtain spray schedules for all of the most commonly grown fruit trees.

Live oaks are often attacked by buck moth caterpillars. These large, black, spiny caterpillars begin to hatch in late February and early March from eggs laid in December. Trees can be sprayed now with an oil spray to suffocate and kill the eggs. Thorough coverage is critical.

If the tree is large, have a tree care company do the work. Buck moth caterpillars can deliver painful stings to people who come into contact with them.

 PRUNING

If you haven't pruned your fruit trees, do so now. It is important to know how to properly prune the type of fruit trees you are growing. Pruning fruit trees is generally done to strict guidelines, beginning about a year after planting and continuing through the life of the tree. Check references on growing fruit trees for specific recommendations (get a free copy of "The Louisiana Home Orchard" brochure from your parish LSU AgCenter Extension office).

Continue to do needed pruning on trees in your landscape. Now is the best time to prune summer-flowering trees.

MARCH

TREES

PLANNING

Spring-flowering trees bloom from late January through mid-April. The relatively small size of most spring-flowering trees makes it fairly easy to find room for them. Study your landscape carefully for appropriate locations. Make sure the spot you choose to plant a spring-flowering tree fits into the existing landscape in an attractive and appropriate way. Will the color of the tree's flowers blend with the flowers of other plants in the area that bloom at the same time? Make your decisions and

get the tree planted as soon as possible. If you really don't have room to plant one, enjoy the ones you see in other yards.

PLANTING

This is the last month of the ideal planting season, and the last month when balled-and-burlapped trees should be purchased and planted. Spring fever is spreading with warmer weather, and many gardeners are finally getting to the nurseries to purchase trees for their landscapes.

Plant trees, using these steps:

1. Dig the hole two to three times the diameter of the rootball, and no deeper than the height of the rootball.

2. Remove a container-grown tree from the container. If the rootball is tightly packed with thick encircling roots, try to unwrap, open up, or even cut some of the roots to encourage them to spread into the surrounding soil. Place the rootball in the hole.

3. Place a balled-and-burlapped tree into the planting hole, remove any nails, nylon twine, or wire basket, and fold down the burlap from the top half of the rootball. The top of the rootball should be level with or slightly above the surrounding soil. Do not plant trees too deep.

4. Thoroughly pulverize the soil dug out from the hole and use this soil, without any additions, to backfill around the tree. Add soil around the tree until the hole is half full, then firm the soil to eliminate air pockets—but do not pack it tight. Finish filling the hole, firm again, and water the tree thoroughly to settle it in.

5. It is not recommended that you add fertilizer to the planting hole, although you may apply some slow-release fertilizer in the upper few inches. The use of a root-stimulator solution is optional.

6. Stake the tree if it is unstable—otherwise, it's not necessary. Two or three stakes should be firmly driven into the ground just

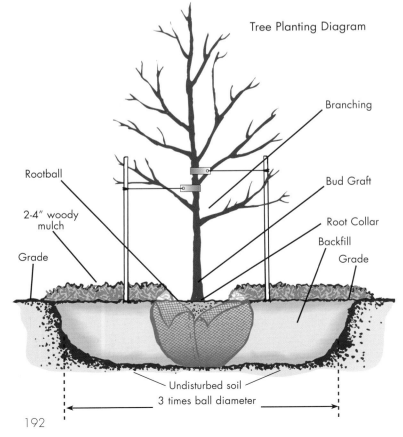

Tree Planting Diagram

Branching

Rootball

Bud Graft

2-4" woody mulch

Root Collar

Backfill

Grade

Grade

Undisturbed soil

3 times ball diameter

beyond the rootball. Use strips of cloth or old nylon stockings or wire (covered with a piece of garden hose where it touches the trunk) tied to the stakes and then to the trunk of the tree. Leave the support in place no more than nine to twelve months.

CARE

Keep the area 1 to 2 feet out from the trunk of a newly planted tree mulched and free from weeds and grass. This will encourage the tree to establish faster by eliminating competition from grass roots. It also prevents lawn mowers and string trimmers from damaging the bark at the base of the tree, which can cause stunting or death. The mulch should be about 4 inches deep and pulled back slightly from the base of the tree.

People are often tempted to plant a small flower bed around a newly planted tree—but just leave the area mulched. The young tree will not appreciate your digging around it every few months to replant bedding plants.

WATERING

There is no need to water established trees. If the weather is mild and dry, water newly planted trees thoroughly once a week.

FERTILIZING

Fertilize trees as soon as possible if you didn't last month. Trees that leaf out late, such as **pecans** and **Chinese pistachios,** can be fertilized this month. Trees that are likely candidates for fertilization include those in their first five years after planting (if accelerated growth is desired), those that are suffering from nutrient deficiencies, those that have sustained damage, and those that are in low vigor. For established trees that seem healthy and vigorous and have good color and growth, fertilization is not needed.

PESTS

Spray **oak** trees for buck moth caterpillars in mid-March if you had a bad outbreak last year. All the eggs will have hatched, and the young caterpillars are easily controlled. Spray with Sevin, Orthene, or Bt. Have the tree sprayed professionally if it is too big for you to handle.

Continue to spray trees infested with scale, such as **magnolias, Chinese parasol tree, hollies,** and **Taiwan flowering cherry.** Use horticultural oil sprays, making two or three applications spaced ten days apart.

Follow spray schedules for fruit trees faithfully. It is too late to do anything when your ripe peaches have worms in them. Fruit trees are sprayed to prevent problems.

Aphids may show up on the new growth of **maples** and **birches.** Spray with Malathion or Orthene.

Evergreen trees such as **hollies, cherry laurels,** and others will yellow and drop numerous leaves in spring. This is just the older foliage being shed; it's natural and no cause for alarm.

PRUNING

Do not prune newly planted trees unless it is to remove dead or broken branches. Young trees need all of their foliage to create the food required to establish a strong root system. Identify problems such as poorly placed branches or low forks, and make plans to correct those by pruning some time next winter.

Trees planted a year or more generally need some pruning. As the trees grow, gradually prune off the lowest branches on the trunk. Based on the height of the tree, about half the height should be bare trunk and half the height foliage. As the tree grows taller, continue to remove the lowest branches until the canopy is the desired height from the ground.

Do not prune **pines** in March or April, as they tend to bleed more this time of the year.

APRIL

TREES

PLANNING

Keeping simple records about your trees can be very helpful. Record such information as when trees are planted, their names, where they were purchased, what kind of pest problems occur (including when they occur and what treatments are used), and other information you think will be helpful.

PLANTING

Container-grown trees can, technically, be planted throughout the year. But planting trees when the weather is hot puts them at much greater risk for problems. If you still need to plant trees, it would be better to do so now.

CARE

When building on a lot with existing trees, plan carefully for how to preserve the trees during construction. Consult with an arborist to identify healthy trees worth saving. Work with the architect to create a design that will preserve desirable trees. Decide which trees can be saved. Generally, you will need

to remove any trees that will be within five feet of the new house. Communicate effectively with the contractor and make it clear how important protecting trees on the site is to you.

• Create barriers around selected trees with bright-orange temporary fencing material.

The barriers should be placed well beyond the reach of the branches. This area should be strictly OFF LIMITS to construction activity.

• Roots can be damaged by filling.

Most trees will not tolerate more than a few inches of filling over their roots.

• Roots can be damaged by trenching for underground utilities.

Move trenches away from trees, or tunnel under roots.

• Roots can be damaged by soil compaction.

Route heavy equipment traffic away from tree roots.

• Avoid scrapes on the trunk and broken branches—the barrier will help. Do not allow equipment to be cleaned or chemicals to be dumped under trees.

Continue to emphasize to the architect, contractor, crew foremen, and anyone else concerned that protecting the trees is not optional, it is a critical part of the process.

WATERING

The weather is still relatively mild, but sunny warm days and dry weather can mean you need to water. The most effective way to water a newly planted tree is with a trickling hose or a dripping bucket. See Watering on page 187 for how to do this. Do this for each newly planted tree about once a week if needed.

FERTILIZING

You can still apply fertilizer, though it will not be as beneficial when applied this late.

Iron deficiencies can show up on certain trees growing in alkaline soils. Several types of **oaks** and **pines** are often affected. Symptoms include yellowing of the foliage, especially the newer leaves. Generally, you will see a pattern of green veins on a yellow-green background. Treat the tree with chelated iron now if symptoms are noticed. Apply sulfur or copperas to the area where the roots are located to help acidify the soil.

PESTS

If your **oak** tree is infested with buck moth caterpillars, have it sprayed before the caterpillars start to move to the ground. Once on the ground, they crawl everywhere and pose a significant risk of stinging you and your family. Professional arborists can use insecticides which will effectively and quickly control the large caterpillars.

The tiny, gall-forming insect called pecan phylloxera causes green, round swellings (galls) to form on leaves.

Spray pecans with Malathion as buds begin to swell and grow. When you see the galls later in the summer, it's too late to do anything.

Small birds called sapsuckers peck holes in neat rows. The holes just penetrate the bark and cause sap to bleed from them. Later, the sapsuckers return to feed on the sugary sap and any insects that may have been attracted to it. The damage is generally minor, but tightly spaced holes in several rows completely encircling a branch may girdle the branch and, on rare occasions, kill it.

Control is generally not necessary, but when damage begins, you can wrap the trunk and lower branches with black plastic, aluminum foil, or burlap for a few weeks while the sapsuckers migrate through your area.

PRUNING

Prune spring-flowering trees this month and next month if needed. Have a definite purpose in mind before pruning. Does the tree need shaping, or lower branches removed? Does it have branches that are poorly placed or blocking a view or a walkway?

Prune off any freeze damage that may have occurred to tender trees such as **citrus, golden rain-trees, orchid trees** (*Bauhinia*), and **camphor trees.** It is best to wait until new growth has begun and you can clearly see what is dead and what is still alive. Their susceptibility to cold damage must be taken into consideration before deciding to include tender trees in your landscape.

Continue to study all of your trees for problems that can be corrected by pruning such as low branches, low branches over the roof of the house, dead or rotten branches, branches obstructing views, and branches blocking paths or sidewalks or interfering with vehicular traffic. Prune as needed.

Have a specific purpose in mind before picking up pruning tools. Before pruning, choose the branches that, once removed, will accomplish your goal. Have a specific purpose in mind.

MAY

TREES

PLANNING

Take some time to note important information in your journal about the spring season. What pest problems occurred on which trees, and what was done to control them? Should anything be done differently next year? When did spring-flowering trees bloom, and how well did they combine with other plants blooming around them?

Now is a good time to make plans for summer tree care. Newly planted trees will need regular watering throughout the summer. Identify pruning that needs to be done, and decide what you can do yourself and what needs to be taken care of professionally. Remember pest problems that you had last summer, and make plans to spray this year if necessary.

PLANTING

You may continue to plant container-grown trees this month, but they are at a great disadvantage to trees planted earlier. Do not disturb the roots of container-grown trees planted this late, even if they are rootbound. Pay careful attention to watering late-planted trees.

Plant **palm trees** now. The best planting season for palms runs from May to August. Palms are tropical and do best planted during the summer. Like traditional trees, palms are also sold container grown or balled and burlapped. Larger sizes are generally sold balled and burlapped. Plant them following the recommendations given for planting trees in March (pages 192-193).

CARE

Promptly remove any branches that begin to hang too low over public sidewalks or streets. Individuals may be tempted to pull and break branches over sidewalks, and vehicles can break or rip away branches as they drive by. In either case, the tree could be damaged with ragged stubs or bark stripped off the trunk. Prune these branches properly to get them out of harm's way and prevent damage to the tree.

WATERING

As the weather heats up, it will become increasingly important for you to water newly planted trees if sufficient rain should not fall. Whenever a good rain ($1/2$ to 1 inch) does not fall for a week, run a hose out to the newly planted tree, lay the end a few inches from the base of the tree, and turn the water on trickle. Let the water run for twenty minutes to thoroughly soak the rootball. Do this once or twice a week until a good rain occurs.

Magnolias are one of the most drought-susceptible of the trees we commonly grow. As they come into bloom in May, they will appear wilted (the leaves will hang down somewhat) if the weather is dry. In addition, magnolias shed their oldest leaves in late spring and early summer, so numerous, yellow, dropping leaves may also be observed. Put out a sprinkler and water the roots if the weather is dry. Don't worry about the yellow, dropping leaves.

FERTILIZING

Fertilizers will not be as beneficial applied this late, but if you needed to fertilize a tree and didn't, you still may. How vigorous was the growth of trees in your landscape? If more than 6 inches of new growth is apparent, fertilization is optional or not needed. If the growth is between 2 to 6 inches, consider fertilization. If only 2 inches or less of new growth occurred, the tree should be fertilized. Follow direc-

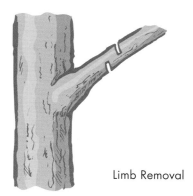

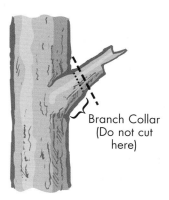

Limb Removal

Branch Collar
(Do not cut
here)

tions given in the month of January (pages 188-189). Make a note of which trees should be fertilized next year.

PESTS

When they are building nests, squirrels chew off small branches to use in the construction. The trouble is that they don't use all of the branches they chew off—lots of them get dropped to the ground. If you find a lot of small branches (about the size of your finger) with green leaves under your shade tree, do not be concerned. The damage squirrels cause is generally minor.

PRUNING

If you need to cut branches from your trees, you must do it correctly, especially if the branches are over 1 inch in diameter. Use a pruning saw especially made for pruning plants. These saws have narrow blades for maneuverability and special teeth for efficient cutting. Make three cuts to remove a branch:

1. The first cut is made about 6 to 8 inches out from the trunk. Position the saw under the branch and cut upward about $1/4$ of the way through the branch.

2. With the saw positioned on top of the branch a few inches out from the first cut, saw downward until the branch falls away.

3. The final cut to remove the stub is very important and must be made properly. Locate the ridge of bark that runs at an angle from where the branch joins the trunk. Position your pruning saw just to the outside of the bark ridge and saw downward at a 45-degree angle from it. As you near the end of the cut, slow down, and support the stub with your other hand. It is important to prevent the bark from pulling away from the trunk as you finish your cut.

This method of cutting preserves a layer of protective chemicals located at the base of the branch, which helps prevent fungal infections and decay. You do not need to apply pruning paint to the fresh cut.

JUNE
TREES

 PLANNING

June marks the beginning of hurricane season. Trees, in particular, are at risk from the high winds that accompany these massive storms. If you live in the southern part of the state, plan now to take care of your trees in order to minimize possible problems. Do not wait until storms begin to threaten.

Trees that have large dead branches or are totally dead should be dealt with as soon as possible. Dead branches should be pruned off and dead trees completely removed.

Look at the overall condition of your trees. A tree that is sickly, low in vigor, and shows significant signs of decayed areas or termites in the trunk may need to be removed if it poses a threat to buildings.

Trees that are very one-sided or leaning significantly may also need attention. Selective pruning can relieve the weight on the heavier side, balancing out the weight distribution of the canopy. After the prolonged rain associated with hurricanes, the soil is often so soft that trees may topple if their weight is not properly proportioned.

Thinning the canopy reduces the wind resistance of the tree and reduces the chances of the tree blowing over or of branches breaking.

Look for branches that hang over the house near the roof. Although the branches may not be touching the roof under normal conditions, the high winds of hurricanes can cause trees to bend a little and branches to flail around considerably. These branches can cause extensive damage to the roof and should generally be removed.

Remember, now is the time to do these chores.

 PLANTING

Due to extreme heat, the next several months are particularly bad for planting trees in your landscape, even from containers. Wait at least until October, if at all possible.

Because of their tropical nature, **palms** are best planted in summer, between May and August.

 CARE

Bald cypress is a popular yard tree. It rarely produces knees (roots protruding from the ground) in home landscapes, but occa-

Bald cypress

sionally does. If they are a problem, use a saw to cut the knees off just below the soil surface. This will not injure the tree.

WATERING

If it has not rained for several weeks, use lawn sprinklers to apply 1 inch of water to your established trees. The root system of these trees extends well beyond the reach of the branches. The most important area to apply water to is at the dripline (the area under the ends of the branches) at the edge of the canopy.

Recently planted trees should be thoroughly watered anytime rain does not occur for five to seven days—continue this practice for the rest of the summer.

FERTILIZING

Trees often send out a second flush of growth in mid- to late summer. Older, established trees do not need to be fertilized again if you fertilized last spring. But young trees you are trying to encourage to grow or trees in low vigor may benefit from a second fertilizer application this time of year. Use half the rate that was applied in January or February. For complete direc-

tions on fertilizing trees, see January (pages 188-189).

PESTS

Watch for signs of pest problems on your trees. Identify the problem and use the appropriate pesticide if necessary. This sounds vague, but there are so many types of pests and so many types of trees. Fortunately, gardeners can go for years without seeing a major outbreak of pests on their trees, so generally it's not that bad. If you need help identifying a problem, contact your local parish agent, talk to local nursery staff, or use a reference. I have found the *Southern Living Garden Problem Solver* to be very helpful. It is a reference book that contains lots of good pictures and information to help gardeners diagnose various pest and cultural problems.

In areas of the state where there are a lot of **pine trees,** watch for signs of southern pine beetles. These beetles bore into the trunk of pine trees and feed under the bark. A heavy infestation can quickly kill a tree. Look for holes in the trunk, often with sap coming out of them. Needles may rapidly turn brown. Once a tree is infested, little can be done for it. Trees not infested can be

protected by spraying their trunks with approved insecticides.

For preventative treatment, spray in early spring or when threat of attack exists. Have infested trees cut down promptly and removed.

PRUNING

The type of pruning that may be necessary to correct problems before hurricanes is often best handled by professional arborists.

Arborists (individuals trained in the care of trees) and tree removal services that can do this work are listed in the Yellow Pages under "Trees." Get several estimates for the work. Talk to company representatives thoroughly about the work you see needs to be done and work they see needs to be done. Come to a clear agreement on what the job will entail. A written contract is always best.

Make sure the company you choose is licensed by the Louisiana Department of Agriculture and Forestry and is fully insured (ask to see a copy of their license and proof of insurance). Check with the Better Business Bureau before you make your final decision. It is always a good idea to be present when tree pruning is being done.

JULY
TREES

 PLANNING

Although not extremely demanding, trees do need occasional attention. Regular, timely care is the best way to handle them. Observe your trees regularly and make plans to take care of problems at appropriate times. (If you see pecan phylloxera now, for instance, it is too late for any control. Mark your calendar, make an entry in your garden journal, and plan on spraying the tree next April if you want to control this pest.) This is a great month to walk around your landscape and see where additional shade is needed.

 PLANTING

The intense heat of the next few months makes this a stressful, undesirable time to plant trees in the landscape. It will be easier on you and the trees if you can wait for the weather to cool this fall before you plant. The exception is **palm trees,** which should be planted between May and August.

Do not dig up and transplant trees now. The chances of their surviving are poor.

 CARE

Filling is necessary in areas of the state where soil subsidence is a problem; it is fairly common in the New Orleans area. Trees will tolerate some fill placed over their root systems, but generally no more than 2 inches a year is considered safe. If you cover only part of the root system, the tree may tolerate deeper fill. Remember, tree roots spread out 2 times the reach of the branches. Leaving a small area around the trunk without fill will do no good whatsoever.

The roots that absorb water and minerals for the tree are located primarily in the upper 12 inches of soil. They need oxygen and grow close to the surface where oxygen is readily available. When excessive amounts of fill is placed over these roots, they suffocate and die. With its roots dead or badly damaged, the tree will die or go into decline. Don't risk a valuable tree. Consult with an arborist or parish agent before extensive filling.

 WATERING

If it has not rained for several weeks, apply 1 inch of water to the roots of trees once every two weeks until it rains. Use lawn sprinklers to water your established trees. The most important area to apply water is the dripline (the area under the ends of the branches) at the edge of the canopy.

For the rest of the summer, recently planted trees should be thoroughly watered anytime rain does not occur for five to seven days. Lay the end of a hose within a few inches of the trunk and let it trickle for twenty minutes.

 FERTILIZING

Older established trees do not need to be fertilized again if you fertilized last spring. But young trees, trees in stress, or trees in low vigor may benefit from a second fertilizer application this month. Trees often send out a second flush of growth in mid- to late summer. Use $1/2$ the rate that was applied in January or February. For complete directions on fertilizing trees, see January (pages 188-189).

 PESTS

Large, established trees are rarely badly damaged by insects or disease. Young trees, however, do not have as many leaves to lose to insects or fungal infections. Caterpillars can easily eat half the leaves off a young tree in just a few days. Pay more attention to pest control on trees the first five years after planting.

Webworms attack a wide variety of trees but seem especially fond of pecans. These caterpillars create large nests of silk at the ends of branches. Their feeding inside the nest causes the leaves enclosed to turn brown.

Although it looks terrible, the damage webworms cause is generally not significant. There are multiple generations through the summer, so it would require repeated spraying (Sevin, Bt) from midsummer to fall to control these pests. If the nest is low enough, prune it off.

Hot, dry weather is just what spider mites love. Conifers such as the **Eastern red cedar** and **bald cypress** are particularly vulnerable, although spider mites will attack a wide variety of other trees including **oaks**. Look for needles or leaves in the interior of the tree to fade and turn brown, gradually extending toward the ends of the branches.

HELPFUL HINTS

During the first several years after planting a young tree, keep an area at least 1 foot out from the trunk mulched. Young trees do not have well-developed bark, and the base of the trunk is easily damaged by mowers and string trimmers. Use a herbicide like Roundup occasionally if weeds or grass start to grow through the mulch, or pull them by hand. Young trees grow faster when grass is not allowed to grow close to them.

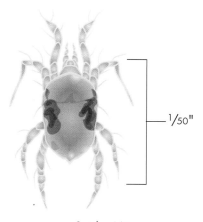

1/50"

Spider Mite

Trees that are in stress are more susceptible, so keep trees well watered, especially those recently planted. Spray with Ultra-Fine Oil, Kelthane, or Malathion.

To prevent peach tree borers, spray the trunks of peaches, nectarines, and flowering cherries with Thiodan. If you see gelatinous sap oozing from spots on the trunk, you know they have attacked.

Make one application each month through October.

 PRUNING

Suckers are vigorous, fast-growing shoots that originate low on the trunk or at soil level. Some trees, such as **crape myrtle, wax myrtle, yaupon,** and **Bradford pear,** are worse about suckering than others. Remove suckers promptly as they appear. Prune them off flush with the trunk or at their point of origin (even if it's below ground). It you leave a stub, it will resprout.

AUGUST

TREES

PLANNING

Now is an excellent time to evaluate your landscape and determine where more shade is needed. Energy bills soar right along with the temperatures, but shade trees in your landscape can help you keep cooler and lower your utility bills.

Trees that shade the house during the summer can lower air-conditioning bills by blocking the sun from the windows, exterior walls, and roof. Research reports show that shade trees can reduce heat gains by 40 percent to 80 percent, depending on their placement and density. Deciduous trees are generally the best choice. They let the sun shine on the house in the winter when the sun's added warmth is welcome, and provide shade during the summer when it is needed.

Trees should be planted on the southwestern and western side of a house to be most effective. Planting trees to the south and east will also help shade the house.

Plant trees the proper distance from the house and away from concrete-surfaced areas such as sidewalks and driveways. The recommended distances generally depend on the mature size of the tree. Larger trees, such as

oaks, should be planted at least 15 feet away from sidewalks, driveways, and the house.

Decide on other areas where shade is necessary or desirable. Outdoor living areas such as patios are unusable here in the summer without some sort of shade. Choose small-growing trees for planting close to patios, as they are more in scale and

are less likely to damage surfacing materials.

This month is the time to make decisions on where shade is needed and where to plant shade trees, but the ideal tree-planting season is October through March.

Trees that shade the house alleviate high energy bills in summer's heat.

 PLANTING

Finish planting **palms** this month. They will need the remaining warm weather to become established before winter. If the palm tree is tall, it will generally need to be staked. The supports should be strong enugh to hold the weight of the palm.

The weather is still too hot for this to be a good time to plant other types of trees in the landscape.

 CARE

Even with good care and regular watering, recently planted trees may look stressed at this time of the year. The foliage may be pale, leaf edges may appear brown and scorched, and little growth may have occurred during the summer. This is not unusual, and you should not be overly alarmed. Keep up good care. Until these trees establish a good root system, they may continue to show late-summer stress for the next several years.

 WATERING

Whenever a good rain (at least 1/2 to 1 inch) does not fall for five to seven days, run a hose out to the newly planted tree, lay the end a few inches from the base of the tree, and turn the water on trickle. Let the water run for twenty minutes to thoroughly soak the rootball. Do this twice a week until it rains.

Older, well established trees rarely need to be watered. Watch the lawn. Whenever the lawn looks drought-stressed, it's time to water shade trees as well. Using a lawn sprinkler, apply about an inch of water over the area of the tree's root system.

 FERTILIZING

Fertilizer containing nitrogen should not be applied to trees for the rest of the year. Late fertilization may stimulate late growth during the mild to warm fall season—this will reduce the hardiness of a tree and promote winter injury.

Iron deficiencies can show up on certain trees growing in alkaline soils. Several types of **oaks** and **pines** are often affected.

Symptoms include yellow foliage, especially the newer leaves. Generally, you will see a pattern of green veins on a yellow-green background. Treat the tree with chelated iron now since it will not stimulate growth. Apply sulfur or copperas to the area where the roots are located to help acidify the soil.

 PESTS

By this late in the year, it is questionable whether spraying a pest is worth it. Use your best judgment, but be aware that leaves of deciduous trees often begin a slow decline this month anyway, and they generally start to fall in November.

 PRUNING

Trim faded flower heads off **crape myrtles** and **vitex** to stimulate another flush of flowers. Spring-flowering trees have set their flower buds for next year and should not be pruned. Promptly prune any broken branches or damage caused by hurricanes.

SEPTEMBER

TREES

PLANNING

Trees often live longer than we do, but age will eventually take its toll on trees as it does with every other living organism. Different trees have different life expectancies. Short-lived trees, such as **flowering cherries**, will typically live for fifteen to twenty years. Many trees will live for fifty to eighty years, and the longest-lived trees, like **live oaks**, will live well over one hundred years.

As trees age, they lose vigor. Decay will often develop in the trunk and major branches as a tree's natural resistance weakens. Large dead branches, weaker growth, and overall decline are signs an old tree is reaching the end of its life. Before they actually die, they become a hazard and will need to be removed. Large, dead branches can drop or the entire tree can blow over (September is generally our most active hurricane month). If you are fortunate enough to have old, mature trees in your landscape, appreciate them. But plan to watch them carefully over the years for signs of decline.

PLANTING

Hold off on planting trees until the weather begins to cool down next month.

CARE

Summer thunderstorms can damage trees with high, gusty winds and lightning. Storm-damaged trees often need pruning. This should include sawing off damaged limbs immediately after damage occurs. See page 197 for the proper way to cut the branch. Cuts should not be made flush with the trunk as this removes the tree's natural defenses against decay. Pruning paints are not necessary.

Lightning strikes are not uncommon. As soon as they occur, take pictures and contact your homeowner's insurance company. Trees damaged by acts of nature are usually covered by insurance policies. Lightning can kill a tree, damage it severely, or cause minor damage. If the tree is going to die as a result of the lightning strike, it will generally do so in a matter of a few weeks. Wait at least four weeks after the strike to have any repair work done. Repair work usually means trimming off any loose bark and broken branches. Make a note to fertilize the tree next January.

Watch short-lived trees, such as flowering cherries, carefully over the years for signs of decline.

 WATERING

Although September temperatures may become milder, the weather can also be sweltering and dry. If your new tree plantings are still alive, you've been doing an excellent job of watering. Keep up the good work.

 FERTILIZING

No fertilizer is needed by trees for the rest of the year.

 PESTS

Watch over newly planted trees. It is unlikely that pest control will be necessary this late in the year, but young trees need as much foliage for as long as possible to get established. Control pest problems promptly. Contact your parish LSU AgCenter Extension office for help with the diagnosis of any problems.

 PRUNING

As trees in the landscape mature and grow large, the shade they create will quite often not allow grass to grow well. If you are trying to deal with this sort of situation, here are some things you can do:

• The amount of sunlight reaching the turf can be increased by selective pruning. The lower branches and some of the inner branches may be pruned to allow more light to reach the lawn below.

• Raising and thinning the canopy on older, mature trees is best done by a professional arborist who can determine which branches can be removed without harming the tree.

After this is done, the existing grass will (we hope) do better, or if the grass has died out in the area, you can lay new sod and see if it will take. Remember, this is a temporary solution, as the trees will continue to grow over the years and shade will once again become a problem.

If after these efforts you still can't get grass to grow under your tree, it's time to accept the situation (as we gardeners often must do), and stop wasting your effort and money trying to make grass grow where the shade of the tree simply won't allow it to. Unless cutting down the tree is an option, your next step is to look at the area as an outstanding opportunity to plant a shade-tolerant ground cover or create a new garden with shade-loving plants.

The most important thing to remember when creating landscaped areas under a tree is to respect the root system of the tree itself. Avoid severing any roots larger than 1 inch in diameter. Use a gardening fork, rather than a shovel or spade, to turn the soil under the tree since the fork will damage fewer roots. If you need to bring in extra soil to create the planting area, use as little as possible—preferably no more than 2 to 4 inches. Do not pile several inches of soil up around the base of the trunk of the tree as this can lead to decay. If you intend to fill over an area that will cover a large part of the tree's root system (which extends out well beyond the reach of the branches), do not apply more than 2 inches of soil.

OCTOBER

TREES

 PLANNING

The fall planting season gets started this month. You may have already made your decisions on the types of trees you would like to plant. If you haven't done this yet, now is the time to begin. Take your time and select just the right tree for each situation. The ideal planting season runs from this month through March.

Visit local nurseries and look at what is available. Ask what other types of trees they will get in later, what sizes will be available, and the prices. If you are planning on purchasing a large tree, you should check on delivery and installation prices since it may be too big for you to handle. Shop around.

 PLANTING

It is still too early to transplant trees, but if you have identified a tree you want to move, root pruning it now is a good idea. By cutting some of the long roots this month, new fibrous ones are formed closer to the trunk within the area of the soil to be moved with the plant.

Push a sharp-bladed shovel straight down, then pull straight out of the soil, forming a circle of connected cuts around the tree. The circle should be cut within the size of the rootball you intend to dig up when transplanting the tree later. If you plan to dig a rootball 1 foot out from the trunk, for instance, make your root pruning cut 8 to 10 inches out from the trunk. The size of the rootball a tree should be moved with is determined by adding 9 inches to the rootball for every inch diameter of the tree's trunk. Using this rule, a tree with a trunk diameter of 2 inches would need an 18-inch-diameter rootball. Dig and transplant a root-pruned tree in early to mid-December.

You can begin to plant trees into the landscape this month.

 CARE

Trees in areas that have a lot of foot traffic or those trees that cars are allowed to park under may eventually begin to suffer root damage due to soil compaction. You will notice low vigor, die-back, and an unusual number of dead branches in the tree.

Talk to a professional arborist about injecting water under high pressure into the soil of the root zone to loosen it and improve air content (in the spring a fertilizer solution should be used). Do not allow cars to park on the ground under trees. To alleviate a problem with foot traffic, apply a thick layer (4 to 6 inches) of shredded bark or composted wood chips under the tree—as far out as the branches reach, if possible. Keep the mulch pulled back somewhat from the trunk.

 WATERING

Cooler weather means less stress on trees. Established trees should not need supplemental water for the rest of the year, even if the weather is dry. Continue to water trees planted within the past year as needed. This should be the last month you have to worry about watering them.

 FERTILIZING

Trees should not be fertilized this month with any fertilizer containing nitrogen.

PESTS

Spray **magnolias, hollies,** and other trees that have scale infestations with Orthene or an oil spray. As we move into the fall, do not be concerned about the declining health of deciduous tree foliage. You will begin to see various leaf spot, scorched edges, and other symptoms. The trees are getting ready to shed their leaves, and the spots and blemishes are just part of the process.

PRUNING

Continue to take care of any pruning that needs to be done on trees in your landscape. Avoid heading-back cuts (see Pruning in the Introduction, page 15) that might stimulate late growth. Remember that spring-flowering trees have already set their flower buds for next year.

Holly

NOVEMBER

TREES

PLANNING

When you are looking at the young trees offered by nurseries, you may realize it's hard to know what a tree will look like as it matures. When deciding on which trees to plant in your landscape, try to find specimens of mature trees to observe. Local public gardens, botanical gardens, or arboreta are useful to visit, as the plants are often labeled with their names. Ask friends, neighbors, and relatives what kinds of trees they have in their yards and take a look at them.

PLANTING

November and early December are, perhaps, the best times to plant trees in Louisiana. The soil is still warm from summer, which encourages vigorous root growth. At the same time the weather is cool, and the trees are going dormant which reduces stress. Generous rainfall during the winter makes constant attention to watering unnecessary. Planting at this time is especially beneficial for balled-and-burlapped trees because they lose so much of their root system when they are dug.

Plant trees properly according to these steps:

1. Dig the hole at least twice the diameter of the rootball, and no deeper than the height of the rootball.

2. Remove a container-grown tree from the container. If the rootball is tightly packed with thick encircling roots, try to unwrap, open up, or even cut some of the roots to encourage them to spread into the surrounding soil. Place the rootball in the hole.

3. Place balled-and-burlapped trees into the planting hole, remove any nails, nylon twine, or wire basket that has been used to secure the burlap, and fold down the burlap from the top half of the rootball. The top of the rootball should be level with or slightly above the surrounding soil. It is critical that you do not plant trees too deep.

4. Thoroughly pulverize the soil dug out from the hole and use this soil, without any additions, to backfill around the tree. Add soil around the tree until the hole is half full, then firm the soil to eliminate air pockets—but do not pack it tight. Finish filling the hole, firm again, and then water the tree thoroughly to settle it in.

5. Generally, don't add fertilizer to the planting hole, although some slow-release fertilizer could be added in the upper few inches. The use of a root-stimulator solution is optional.

6. Stake the tree if it is tall enough to be unstable; otherwise, it's not necessary. Two or three stakes should be firmly driven into the ground just beyond the rootball. Use strips of cloth or old nylon stockings or wire (covered with a piece of garden hose where it touches the trunk) tied to the stakes and then to the trunk of the tree. Leave the support in place no more than nine to twelve months.

CARE

Have you thanked your trees lately? Trees provide welcome shade, make our houses cooler and outdoor living areas usable during the summer, and help our environment in many ways. Trees help purify the air. They reduce smog and air pollution problems. They provide shelter and food to wildlife. Where dust is a problem, trees can be placed to serve as filters. Their roots stabilize the soil and reduce erosion. Tree plantings can be effective windbreaks during the winter. Noise pollution can be absorbed by tree plantings by as much as 50 percent. And trees tend to increase the value and sales appeal of property. We may be thinking about how we have to care for our trees, but it's good to think of how they care for us as well.

HELPFUL HINT

In mid- to late November, trees begin to show off their fall colors. Although not as spectacular as the fall color up North, there is still enough to appreciate. The following trees are some of the most reliable for fall color (those marked with a plus sign (+) will show good fall color even in the warmest parts of the state): **beech, red oak, willow oak, Shumard oak+, smooth sumac+, flowering dogwood, Japanese persimmon, ginkgo+, sourwood, sassafras, crape myrtle+, Drummond red maple+, sugar maple, 'Bradford' pear, Chinese pistachio+, sweetgum+,** and **Florida maple+**.

Sourwood not only produces flowers to support bees, it also has fantastic fall foliage.

WATERING

Water-in newly planted trees thoroughly, but you should have to do little supplemental watering over the winter. Established trees will not need to be watered this month.

FERTILIZING

No fertilizer needs to be applied to trees this month.

PESTS

Other than scale, few pest problems require treatment now. Deciduous trees drop their leaves this month and into December. Check them and evergreen trees such as **magnolia** and **holly** for signs of scale.

Spray with horticultural oil or Orthene if needed.

Live oaks are one of our favorite trees and are widely planted around the state. They often drop a lot of leaves in November. Look at the leaves and you will see that most of them have a golden-tan fluffy growth on the back. This is called wooly oak gall and is caused by a tiny insect.

Although the leaf drop is a nuisance, the condition is harmless and nothing to worry about. The leaves make excellent mulch or can be placed in your compost pile.

Avoid scraping or damaging the bark at the base of a tree and do not pile mulch or soil several inches thick around it. This can lead to fungal organisms penetrating the wood and can cause decay.

Once decay has started in the trunk of a tree, there is nothing that can be done to stop it if the tree's own defenses fail.

PRUNING

Identify pruning needs and take care of the pruning.

DECEMBER

TREES

PLANNING

Plan on getting out and enjoying the fall color on trees in the area. If fall color is something you want to include in your landscape, note which trees put on the best display in your area and plant them.

Spend some time catching up on journal entries. Record unusual weather, new tree plantings, and anything else you think might be useful later on.

PLANTING

This is the month to start transplanting trees.

1. Dig a hole for the tree in its new location before you dig it up. It's important to replant the tree as quickly as possible. Dig the hole as deep and twice as wide as the rootball you intend to dig with the tree.

2. Dig the tree. Get as much of the root system as you can. On average, dig a rootball about 9 inches across for every inch of diameter of the trunk (a tree with a 2-inch-diameter trunk needs an 18-inch rootball).

3. Do not let the roots dry out before you plant the tree. Wrap them if necessary.

4. Place the tree in the hole at the same depth it was growing. Thoroughly break up the soil removed to make the hole, and use it to fill in around the trees's roots.

5. Water the tree thoroughly.

6. Most trees home gardeners would transplant are small enough not to need staking. If the tree seems unstable, stake it.

Early December is an ideal time to plant trees in your landscape.

CARE

Any recently planted tree whose stakes have been in place for nine to twelve months should have the support removed. If you have newly planted trees that will remain staked, check where the ties come into contact with the trunk and make sure they are not causing damage.

WATERING

Water-in trees as they are planted, and if weather is mild and dry, water occasionally as needed. Established trees will not need to be watered this time of year.

FERTILIZING

No fertilizer should be applied to trees this time of year.

PESTS

If you live in an area where buck moth caterpillars are a problem, you will discover the adult moths emerge, mate, and lay eggs this month. The moths are charcoal gray and creamy white with a dark reddish-orange abdomen. Make plans to have your trees sprayed in mid-March of next year.

Any trees with scale infestations can be sprayed with horticultural oil during the winter for control. Make several applications about ten days apart for effective control. Do not spray immediately before temperatures below freezing are predicted.

PRUNING

Winter is an ideal time to prune trees. Deciduous trees are leafless. This allows you to see more clearly the structure of your trees, and you don't have the weight of the foliage to deal with. Evergreen trees may be pruned this time of the year as well.

VINES, GROUND COVERS, & ORNAMENTAL GRASSES

VINES

No other plants can do what vines can do in the landscape. They are indispensable for growing up a pillar, covering an unattractive fence, softening architectural features, or creating screens. A vine-covered arbor provides a shady retreat.

Vines are a remarkably diverse group of plants. They include annuals and perennials and can be woody or herbaceous, evergreen or deciduous. Perennial vines are the most important group, as they become a permanent part of the landscape. Before you use them (and you really should), there are a couple of things you need understand about vines.

First, they're lazy. Rather than putting the considerable effort it takes into growing a strong stem, they use another plant or structure to provide support. Where does all that unused energy go? Into the fastest-growing plants in your landscape! You must be prepared for the extraordinary rate of growth of which vines are capable, and be willing to control them when necessary.

Second, vines climb in two distinct ways: by twining and by clinging. Twining vines climb by wrapping their stems, leaves, or tendrils around a support. They must have string, wire, latticework, trellises, poles, or other support structures they can twist around. Clinging vines can grow on flat sur-

faces by using roots along their stems or holdfasts. They are useful for covering the sides of buildings or walls without having to build a support. It is very important to know how a vine you want to use climbs.

Vines are grown for their attractive foliage and colorful flowers. Some provide ornamental or edible fruit, and several produce fragrant flowers. When you determine a vine is needed in your landscape, the selection process is the same as for any plant. Decide on the characteristics you would like the vine to have, determine the growing conditions in the area where it will be planted, and choose the vine that most closely fits.

Caring for vines involves controlling and training them more than anything else, as well as watering, fertilizing, and pest control on occasion.

GROUND COVERS

The term ground cover generally refers to low-growing plants, other than turfgrasses, used to cover proportionally large areas of the landscape. Perennial, evergreen plants having a running, sprawling, or spreading habit are generally used. Many have variegated foliage or produce colorful flowers while others are more subdued. Ground covers create an effect or establish a presence in the landscape that provides variation in height, texture, and color that enriches their surroundings. Yet, they require far less maintenance than flower beds or lawns.

In addition to the beauty they provide, ground covers have practical uses as well. Some ground covers are effective in erosion control while others, because they don't have to be mowed, reduce maintenance in problem areas such as on steep slopes or under low-branched trees and shrubs. Where the roots of large trees protrude, ground covers hide the roots and prevent mowing problems. They provide barriers to foot traffic (most people won't walk through them) and can guide traffic movement through a site. Ground covers are probably used most commonly in confined areas where lawn mowing is difficult or in shade where grass will not grow.

When selecting ground covers, it is important to consider carefully the characteristics you would like the ground cover to have (height, texture, color, etc.) as well as the growing conditions where it will be planted, such as sunny or shady, dry or moist.

You should also look at the size of the area to be planted. Only the most reliable, fast-spreading, and reasonably priced ground covers should be considered for large areas. Monkey grass (*Ophiopogon japonicus*) and creeping lily turf (*Liriope spicata*) are good choices for shade to part sun. Asiatic jasmine (*Trachelospermum asiaticum*) is excellent for sun to part shade.

Whatever type of ground cover you choose, proper preparation of the planting area will help ensure good establishment and faster growth. Maintaining ground covers involves some weeding, trimming back, watering, and fertilizing but most are undemanding in the care they require.

ORNAMENTAL GRASSES

Ornamental grasses are an often-overlooked group of herbaceous perennials that thrive in Louisiana gardens and will grow beautifully with minimal effort. The term ornamental grass is applied to grasses and grasslike plants that are used chiefly for their beauty. They are a large and complex group of plants with a wide range of growth habits and culture. This versatile group of plants is becoming increasingly popular all across the United States, but they still deserve to be more widely utilized in Louisiana.

CHAPTER NINE

Some of our worst garden weeds are grasses. Crabgrass, torpedograss, wild bermudagrass, and Johnsongrass are persistent, difficult-to-control pests that many of us are all too familiar with. As a result, many gardeners are reluctant to deliberately plant grasses into flower beds or borders in their landscape.

Ornamental grasses, however, are truly attractive and not rampantly aggressive. Like their weedy cousins, they are tough and susceptible to virtually no insect or disease problems. Ornamental grasses are an excellent choice for gardeners trying to create a landscape that is more self-reliant, requiring less spraying, fertilization, and maintenance.

The strong vertical, mounding, or fountaining form of many ornamental grasses combined with their feathery flower heads make a unique contribution to the landscape.

Grass foliage moves in breezes and catches the light like few other plants. It adds fine texture and colors such as metallic blues, burgundy, white, creamy yellow, and every shade of green imaginable. Grasses also offer an impressive array of flower plumes and seedheads for added interest at various times.

Most ornamental grasses grow best in full to part sun, but they are tolerant of a wide range of growing conditions. If you are planting them into an existing bed, little improvement will be needed. Turn the soil and then incorporate a 2-inch layer of organic matter in the area to be planted. Water them thoroughly once or twice a week until they are established, then just sit back and relax.

Some ornamental grasses are evergreen, but most go dormant for the winter. At some point before the end of February, cut the plants back to within a few inches of the ground. Other than that, occasional watering and fertilizing is all they need.

JANUARY
VINES, GROUND COVERS, & ORNAMENTAL GRASSES

 PLANNING

This rather catchall chapter includes three very useful and interesting groups of plants. There are spots and situations in virtually every landscape where vines, ground covers, or ornamental grasses would provide just the right touch. Many ground covers and vines are quiet, unassuming plants that play a supporting role in the landscape, but they can be flashy focal points as well. Ornamental grasses almost always stand out, but their soft, fine-textured foliage rarely dominates a garden bed.

The plant lists at the beginning of this chapter just scratch the surface of these three remarkable plant groups. Plan on curling up by the fire this winter with a good reference on plant materials for our state, such as *Southern Plants* by Odenwald and Turner or *Louisiana Gardener's Guide* by Gill and White, and learn more about vines, ground covers, and ornamental grasses that will thrive here.

 PLANTING

Virtually all of the hardy perennial vines, ground covers, and ornamental grasses can be planted or transplanted this month.

If needed, now is a good time to transplant or divide your ornamental grasses. Cut back the brown foliage, lift the clump, divide it into 2 to 4 pieces, and replant them into your landscape or share with friends.

Ground covers may also be divided and/or transplanted now. This is a good way to create new areas of ground cover without having to buy any plants. **Liriope, monkey grass, strawberry geranium, ajuga, Japanese ardisia, aspidistra,** and **ferns** can all be divided now.

 CARE

Do not allow your ground cover to stay covered by fallen leaves. Rake out leaves and use them for mulch or put them in your compost pile. Vining ground covers, such as **Asian jasmine** and **English ivy,** catch at the tines of garden rakes and can make raking difficult. Try using a leaf blower to blow out the leaves; many models can also be used to vacuum up the leaves. Consider planting **monkey grass** or **creeping lily turf** in areas under trees where you will need to rake out leaves.

 PESTS

Scale is sometimes a problem on plants like **Japanese ardisia, aspidistra, Carolina jessamine,** and **akebia.** Look over your plants carefully for small white or tan bumps that detach easily when pushed with your thumbnail.

Control with horticultural oil. Make two to three applications ten days apart. Do not spray if sub-freezing temperatures are predicted within twenty-four hours.

 PRUNING

Some ornamental grasses are evergreen, but most go dormant for the winter. At some point before the end of February, cut back the plants to within a few inches of the ground. When you cut them back during the winter depends on whether you like the appearance of the dead foliage or not. Cutting back must, however, be done before the fresh, new growth comes up in spring.

Do not prune spring-blooming vines now or you will reduce or eliminate their flowers. The lovely fall-blooming vine **rosa de montana** dies back during the winter. Remove the dead growth now if you haven't already done so.

FEBRUARY
VINES, GROUND COVERS, & ORNAMENTAL GRASSES

PLANNING

Are there areas where it is difficult to mow or where grass will not grow due to shade? These are ideal locations for ground covers.

PLANTING

Take these steps to prepare an area for planting ground covers.

1. First remove all existing unwanted vegetation such as lawngrass or weeds from the area. This could be done physically, or you can use a herbicide such as glyphosate, but do a thorough job.

2. Next, till the soil to loosen it. When working under a tree, use a turning fork to minimize damage to the tree's roots, and avoid severing roots larger than an inch in diameter whenever possible. Two or 3 inches of additional blended soil mix may be added, if necessary, and incorporated into the existing soil.

3. Spread 2 inches of organic matter (compost, peat moss, or rotted manure) and fertilizer ($1/2$ cup of 15-5-10 per 30 square feet if your soil is high in phosphorus, or 1 cup of 8-8-8 per 30 square feet if your soil is low in phosphorus) over the area, and work it in.

Continue to plant and transplant hardy perennial vines and ornamental grasses.

CARE

Are there perennial beds that require more work than you have time to give? Combined with a few of the perennials you find that relatively care-free, ornamental grasses will create a bed that is interesting and attractive, and requires far less maintenance.

WATERING

Water newly planted, transplanted, or divided vines, ground covers, and ornamental grasses thoroughly when they go in the ground.

FERTILIZING

It is best to to fertilize in March.

PESTS

Keep an eye out for scale insects on various vines and ground covers. Spray with horticultural oil if you find them.

Cool-season weeds will be growing in ground covers this time of year. Weed beds regularly to keep them attractive.

PRUNING

Virtually all of the plants we use as ground covers are evergreen. As time goes by, unattractive old foliage will often accumulate among the healthy leaves, and the planting will need a good shearing back to rejuvenate it. Use hedge shearers, string trimmers, or even your lawnmower adjusted to its highest setting (make sure the blades are sharp and push the mower through the planting slowly). Clipping every two to three years is generally adequate. For several popular ground covers, it is important that this be done before new growth begins next month. Ground covers that are good candidates for trimming now include **monkey grass, creeping lily turf, English ivy, liriope, Asian jasmine, Japanese ardisia,** and **dwarf bamboo.** Use handpruners to selectively prune unattractive leaves from plants such as **aspidistra, autumn fern,** and **holly fern.**

MARCH

VINES, GROUND COVERS, & ORNAMENTAL GRASSES

PLANNING

There are wonderful vines, ground cover plants, and ornamental grasses available by mail that may not be in stock at local nurseries. I prefer to purchase plants at local nurseries whenever possible, but catalogs and the Internet can introduce you to a whole new world of plants. Send off your order now, and specify that you would like it shipped as soon as possible. Mail-order plants are often shipped bare root or are fairly small. They will need time to establish during the relatively mild weather of March, April, and May before intense heat arrives.

PLANTING

Finish up ground cover plantings this month so they will have some time to become established before the fierce heat of summer arrives.

1. Plant the ground cover into well-prepared beds (see February) at the proper spacing. Proper spacing varies with the type chosen, so check with the staff at the nursery or consult references. Planting at the closest recommended spacing will provide quicker coverage, but it will cost you more money.

2. After the area is planted, mulch with 1 or 2 inches of leaves, pine bark, or shredded pine straw. Until the ground cover fills in, weed control is very important. Your best defense is a good layer of mulch. Hand weed regularly as necessary to maintain good weed control. In addition, most ground covers spread faster when mulched.

3. Water the area thoroughly to settle things in, and you are done.

Plant vines this month. Prepare the spot by removing any unwanted plants (weeds or turfgrass), and turn over the soil. Add about 4 inches of organic matter, and thoroughly dig it in. When you plant the vine, make sure the top of the rootball is even with the soil level, firm the soil around it, and water it in. Apply a slow-release fertilizer or a light sprinkling of granular fertilizer, and mulch around the plant to control weeds and conserve moisture.

CARE

When deciding on how far apart to space new ground cover plantings, look at your budget. Planting an area with ground cover is not cheap. Decide on how much you are prepared to spend on the project, purchase as many plants as your budget will allow, and space them evenly throughout the area. You may discover they end up farther apart than recommended—but most of us do not have an unlimited gardening budget. You can wait for those plants to fill in, or when more money becomes available, buy more plants and plant them evenly among the originals. Over time, you will fill up the bed while staying within your budget.

WATERING

Warmer temperatures and active growth make watering increasingly important if regular rainfall does not occur. Newly planted ground covers, vines, and ornamental grasses need the most attention. They are vulnerable to drying out until they have a chance to grow a strong root system into the surrounding soil. Water new plantings once or twice a week as needed, especially those in full sun.

FERTILIZING

Fertilize established ground covers, vines, and ornamental grasses this month. Choose a general-purpose fertilizer appropriate to your area and apply it according to package directions. When fertilizer is sprinkled over ground cover plantings, water immediately afterwards to wash the fertilizer granules off the foliage and onto the soil. It is particularly important to fertilize ground covers that were cut back. Fertilize vines moderately and only if you need to stimulate extra growth. If your ornamental grasses have not yet begun to grow, wait until next month to fertilize.

PESTS

Mild weather is perfect for using horticultural oils. These excellent, low toxicity pesticides will control scale, aphids, spider mites, and various other pests. **Carolina yellow jessamine** will sometimes be attacked by scale.

HELPFUL HINT

After you cut back your ornamental grass, lay the clippings on the lawn and run your mower (with a bag attached) over them. The chopped grass blades make great mulch, or they can be added to your compost pile.

Treat now if you see scale on any of your vines or ground covers.

Caterpillars are an occasional pest for some vines. Look for chewed leaves or holes in the foliage. If the damage is minor, just keep an eye on it.

If the damage warrants spraying the plant, treat with Sevin, Bt, or other insecticides labeled to control caterpillars on ornamental plants.

PRUNING

Carolina yellow jessamine should be finished blooming by now. Trim it back if necessary.

If you have not cut back brown ornamental grass foliage, do so as soon as possible. Don't wait until you see the new growth. If new growth has already started, make your pruning cuts just above it. There's not much you will need to do to ornamental grasses after this for the rest of the growing season.

Carolina yellow jessamine

APRIL
VINES, GROUND COVERS, & ORNAMENTAL GRASSES

PLANNING

Look around your landscape for places where a container of ornamental grass (alone or combined with other plants) would make a nice addition, such as patios, porches, or decks.

PLANTING

Ground covers and vines need to be planted as soon as possible. Grasses are so tough they can be planted throughout the summer, but if you want to transplant or divide some that are already growing in your landscape, do it now.

CARE

Vines tend to grow strongly upwards. If you use a vine to cover a fence or trellis and want it to be full at the bottom, this can be a problem. When you plant the vines, weave the long stems horizontally along the lower portion of the fence or trellis. As the vine grows upwards, continue to weave it back and forth through the support. When a vine reaches the top of its support, don't just cut it off. Take the ends of the vine and weave them back downward. This takes some effort, but the result will be much more attractive and the vine will be fuller from top to bottom.

WATERING

Use a sprinkler to apply 1/2 to 1 inch of water once a week when the weather is dry. Tree roots will compete with the ground cover plants for water. Make sure there is enough water for both.

FERTILIZING

Fertilize this month if you did not do so in March. Apply fertilizer to ground cover plantings in particular, especially those that are still growing to fill an area. Use a general-purpose granular fertilizer appropriate to your area or a 3:1:2 ratio fertilizer such as 15-5-10. Water immediately to wash the fertilizer off the ground cover foliage and down to the soil.

Fertilizing vines is optional and not recommended if they have a history of growing vigorously. Fertilize if you need to stimulate growth, or if the vines are in low vigor or have poor foliage color.

Ornamental grasses are often planted among annuals, perennials, and shrubs and will benefit from the fertilizer scattered throughout the bed for everything else. (Overly generous fertilization of ornamental grasses can produce tall, weak-stemmed plants prone to lying over.)

PESTS

Both cool-season and warm-season weeds are active. Stay on top of weed control by using mulches wherever possible, and handweed where needed. A good, thick stand of ground cover generally prevents many weeds from growing, but some will still occur.

Grassy weeds in ground covers can be controlled with Fusilade or Vantage. Some broadleaf weeds and sedges can be controlled with Image. Read and follow label directions carefully, and make sure the ornamental plants in the bed are listed on the label as tolerant to the herbicide.

PRUNING

Prune spring-flowering vines such as **Carolina yellow jessamine, wisteria,** and **akebia** after they finish flowering. Instead of pruning off long strands, weave them back into the supporting structure to thicken the vine.

MAY

VINES, GROUND COVERS, & ORNAMENTAL GRASSES

PLANNING

Walk through your landscape as often as you can. Carry a shoulder bag with snips, handpruners, a spray bottle of premixed glyphosate, and a 12-inch by 12-inch piece of cardboard or rigid plastic. Stop and lightly prune vines and ground covers; pull a few weeds or spray them with Roundup. Check out insect and disease problems.

PLANTING

Planting ground covers and vines this late means you will have to put extra effort into getting them established in the heat. This primarily means paying careful attention to watering. Ornamental grasses are tougher and can be planted throughout the summer.

CARE

Some ground covers will require occasional pruning. Make a point to look at your vines every week, and tend to the training, weaving, snipping, and pruning it takes to keep them where they belong. Keep an eye out for insect and disease problems.

WATERING

Established vines and ornamental grasses are often included in beds or plantings with other plant materials. If you water the area enough to keep the other plants happy, the vines and grasses will be happy too.

Established beds of ground cover will also need water only when it is unusually hot and dry. Newly planted ground cover will need more attention. Water regularly and thoroughly whenever a week or so goes by without a good rain.

FERTILIZING

To provide the greatest benefit, fertilizer should have been applied last month. If you haven't fertilized ground cover areas, particularly those that are still filling in, do so as soon as possible. Evenly sprinkle a general-purpose granular fertilizer over the area, following package recommendations, and water-in.

Vines and ornamental grasses don't need much fertilizer, but if you are trying stimulate growth, they can be fertilized as well.

PESTS

Watch for insect and disease problems on vines and ground covers. Aphids may show up on the new growth of many kinds of vines. Spray with insecticidal soap, Ultra-Fine Oil, or Malathion to control. Caterpillars are a minor problem. Treat with Bt, Sevin, or other insecticides.

Low-growing ground covers with succulent leaves such as **ajuga, strawberry geranium, lysimachia,** and **hosta** may be attacked by snails and slugs. Treat these areas with snail and slug bait, or set out beer traps.

PRUNING

The best time to do extensive pruning of flowering perennial vines is right after they flower. Lightly prune and train throughout the summer.

Prune off unsightly leaves from **aspidistra, ferns,** and **ligularia** ground covers to keep them looking neat and attractive.

Vines that we use as ground covers (such as **Asian jasmine** and **English ivy**) don't have the good sense to stop at the edge of their bed and will continue to grow out onto areas where they are not wanted. Prune back the edges of those plantings occasionally to keep them neat.

JUNE
VINES, GROUND COVERS, & ORNAMENTAL GRASSES

PLANNING

Your lawngrass is growing vigorously now. This is a good time to identify areas where the grass is not thriving or has disappeared entirely. The most frequent cause of poor growth is too much shade. Plant a shade-loving ground cover in the location and quit fussing with the grass.

PLANTING

Shady areas are less stressful during summer heat. If you don't want to wait until this fall to plant a bare shady area, decide what kind of ground cover you would like and plant it now. Just make sure you keep it well watered and mulched. Tough ground covers, such as **monkey grass, creeping lily turf, liriope,** and **Asian jasmine,** should do okay if planted this late as long as they are kept well watered.

When working under a tree, use a turning fork to minimize damage to the tree's roots, and avoid severing roots larger than an inch in diameter whenever possible. Two or 3 inches of additional blended soil mix (generally called topsoil or garden soil) may be added if necessary and incorporated into the existing soil. Follow the bed preparation steps recommended in February Planting (page 15).

CARE

Evaluate how well vines are growing on the support provided for them. Whether the vine is trained on an arch, fence, pole, trellis, or latticework—is it turning out as you intended? Decide if:

• the vine is too large and rampant and has overwhelmed the support.

• the support is not strong enough to hold up the weight of the vine.

• all of the growth is at the top, and the bottom and middle of the vine is bare.

• the vine does not like the growing conditions and is not doing well.

If there are problems, decide on a solution:

• Replace the vine this fall with one that would be more suitable.

• Replace the support, if practical, with one that is stronger or larger.

• Prune the vine regularly to keep it the size and shape desired.

• Prune the vine so that the structure it is growing on, such as

Wisteria is a very heavy vine; make sure you have adequate support for it.

an arch, column, or building, is not completely covered.

WATERING

Daytime highs in the 90s and nights in the 70s will place tremendous stress on plants in our landscapes over the next three or four months. Plants use water far faster when it is hot. If it has not rained for more than ten days, water established ground cover plantings. Use a sprinkler to apply about an inch of water to the area. Remember, trees' roots will also absorb some of the water. Monitor plantings under trees closely. New plantings should be deeply watered when rain has not occurred for seven to ten days.

Ornamental grasses rarely need to be watered once established. Recently planted grasses should be watered regularly if the weather is dry.

If you are growing any specimens of ornamental grasses, vines, or ground covers as container plants, they may need to be watered every day. Check them often.

FERTILIZING

Fertilizers applied in spring or early summer are sufficient, and none needs to be applied now.

PESTS

Hot, muggy weather and lots of rain make diseases worse this time of the year. Leaf spot diseases caused by various fungus organisms attack **ardisia, Confederate jasmine, dwarf bamboo, liriope,** and **monkey grass.** Trim off any badly damaged foliage and spray with thiophanate methyl or chlorothanonil.

Weeds in ground cover plantings can be quite a nuisance. Nutsedge or cocograss is a diffi-

cult weed with very thin yellow-green leaves and a nutlike bulb. A herbicide called Image has a label for use on several types of ground covers and will do an excellent job of selectively killing the nutsedge. Grassy weeds such as bermudagrass and torpedo-grass also cause problems. Two herbicides, Fusilade and Vantage, will do a good job controlling these weeds and can be used over the top of several commonly used ground covers. Read the labels of these products carefully and use them strictly according to directions.

PRUNING

Other than regular maintenance work on vines, little pruning needs to be done now. Keep beds of **Asian jasmine** edged so they will look neat.

JULY
VINES, GROUND COVERS, & ORNAMENTAL GRASSES

PLANNING

Record information on the performance of plants in your landscape. It is the best way to avoid repeating mistakes and helps you do a better job of caring for your plants. Take some time, while you escape the heat indoors, to make some notes on your ground covers, vines, and ornamental grasses. Important information includes blooming times, when and where various plants were planted, where you got them, when pest problems occurred, and what was done to control them. Photographs or videotapes are excellent for recording how things look and change from season to season.

PLANTING

It's hot. It's very, very hot. Planting of almost all plant materials is difficult this time of the year. If you have to get out and plant in this heat, disturb the roots of the plants as little as possible and keep them well watered. The sturdier ground covers such as **creeping lily turf** and **monkey grass** will tough it out if planted now, and ornamental grasses can be successfully planted now. Regular watering will be the key to success when planting this time of year.

CARE

Keep ground cover beds well mulched, especially those that have not yet filled in. Don't expect recently planted ground covers to fill an area in a single growing season. There is an old saying about the growth of ground covers: The first year they sleep, the second year they creep, and the third year they leap. If your ground cover is not growing as fast as you expected, perhaps your expectations were too high. Let it get established this year, and anticipate more growth next year.

Many ornamental grasses begin to bloom in July. Notice how attractive the plumes are waving above the foliage in different shades of silver, cream, and tan with tints of bronze, burgundy, or gold.

Pampas grass

WATERING

Water is especially critical this time of the year. Most established plantings can get by with an occasional deep watering when the weather is dry. Recent plantings, especially of ground covers, should be watered thoroughly whenever a week passes without rain. Do not be tempted to water every day—you will encourage fungal diseases. It is much better to water deeply and occasionally than lightly every day.

FERTILIZING

Ground cover areas fertilized this spring can be fertilized again this month. Sprinkle a general-purpose granular fertilizer evenly over the area and water it in. One-half cup of 15-5-10 will cover 30 square feet and encourage vigorous growth. This is most important for ground cover plantings that have not yet covered the entire bed. Well-established ground covers that have densely covered their beds do not necessarily need fertilizer beyond the spring application.

PESTS

Ajuga is susceptible to crown rot—plants will suddenly wilt and die even though the soil is moist. The disease can spread rapidly through a planting, wiping out years of growth. Because of this disease, a gardener should really think twice before planting ajuga over large areas.

At the first sign of trouble, drench the bed with Terraclor. Repeat the application every two to four weeks until the weather cools down in October.

Aspidistra is virtually indestructible (hence the common name **cast-iron plant**). It does sometimes become infested with a white scale which occurs primarily on the leaf stems and lower portions of the foliage. Spray with Ultra-Fine Oil during the cooler early-morning hours for control. Leaf spot also will attack aspidistra. Prune out infected leaves.

Spot-treat with glyphosate to control tough weeds. Do not get these herbicides on desirable plants. Keep beds well mulched. Pull weeds promptly when they appear. Grassy weeds can be controlled with Fusilade or Vantage, and some broadleaf weeds and sedges with Image. These herbicides will not hurt ornamental plants listed on the label as tolerant to the herbicide.

PRUNING

Some vines, such as **coral honeysuckle,** bloom sporadically throughout the summer. The more you snip on these, the fewer flowers you will have. Rather than trimming off long shoots, try weaving them back into the main part of the vine or the support.

AUGUST
VINES, GROUND COVERS, & ORNAMENTAL GRASSES

 PLANNING

August is a popular month for family vacations. If you are going to be gone for more than a few days, ask a friend or neighbor to water outside containers for you. Ground covers planted in the ground this spring or early summer will also need watering if it doesn't rain. Before you leave for your vacation:

- water everything thoroughly.
- make sure beds are weeded and mulched.
- edge ground cover plantings that need it.
- trim vines.
- remove spent flowers from vines and ground covers.

 PLANTING

With cooler weather just a couple of months away, it doesn't make much sense to plant during this extreme heat. Containers of ornamental grasses may be available at local nurseries. You can plant them now to fill in gaps in perennial borders, but be prepared to water regularly.

 CARE

Last month I mentioned how ground covers grow slowly the first year after planting and then speed up as they become better established. Vines can be the same way. As you watch the trellis disappear under a mound of green foliage and tendrils are reaching for you as you walk by, it's time to do some serious pruning on established vines.

 WATERING

Proper watering is critical during this time of the year. Do not think that watering beds by hand is adequate. As relaxing and therapeutic as it is for the gardener, it is not good for your plants. Use soaker hoses or sprinklers, and leave them on long enough for the water to moisten the soil down about 4 to 6 inches. Morning is the best time to water so that plants will be well supplied with water going into the hottest part of the day. Late-afternoon or early-evening watering with sprinklers is less desirable.

 FERTILIZING

Spring and midsummer fertilizer applications are all that ground covers need. If you did not fertilize last month, fertilize ground cover plantings now. This second fertilizer application is particularly recommended for plantings that have not yet grown to cover their area fully.

 PESTS

Spider mites thrive in the hot, dry weather of August. **Juniper** ground covers are especially susceptible to spider mites, which cause browning of the needles.

Spray plants with Kelthane or Malathion.

Hostas are often badly damaged by snails and slugs and need particular attention. Continue to use baits and traps to control snails and slugs.

 PRUNING

Finish up major pruning jobs early this month. Vines that bloom in the spring, such as **wisteria, Carolina yellow jessamine,** and **akebia,** need time to grow and set flower buds before winter. Trim back ground covers that have become overgrown. Avoid much pruning after this.

September

VINES, GROUND COVERS, & ORNAMENTAL GRASSES

 **PLANNING**

Now that the summer season is coming to a close, take some time to walk around and evaluate the plantings in your landscape. You will probably see successes and a few failures as well. What worked and what didn't work?

We tend to live with the landscape problems we create (or those that previous owners of the property created for us). If you see a problem, decide on a solution and take action.

 **PLANTING**

It's been a long, hot summer. It is still too hot to transplant anything. It's still too hot to do much planting either. Rest up and save your energy for the planting season that is right around the corner.

 **CARE**

Strong, gusty winds can blow down stalks in clumps of ornamental grasses. The stalks often straighten themselves back up, but sometimes they need a little help. Push the stalks that are lying down back up, and use

HELPFUL HINTS

Flower plumes or seedheads of ornamental grasses can be cut and used in arrangements. Spray with a little clear shellac to keep them from shattering.

green twine in a loop all the way around the plant to hold the stalks in place. If it seems a better solution, cut back the stalks that laid over.

 **WATERING**

September can be hot and dry, so continue to water when necessary. When watering, do a thorough job. Water deeply and occasionally rather than lightly every day.

 **FERTILIZING**

No fertilizer will be required by vines, ground covers, or ornamental grasses for the rest of the year.

 **PESTS**

Pests have had all summer to build up population levels. Inspect plants frequently. To minimize the impact on beneficial insects, spray only infested plants.

Effective low-toxicity insecticides include Bt to control caterpillars, Sevin to control chewing insects (caterpillars and beetles), insecticidal soaps to control soft-bodied sucking insects such as aphids, and Ultra-Fine Oil to control white flies, scale, soft-bodied insects, and insect eggs. Use Ultra-Fine Oil in the very early morning hours to minimize the possibility of its burning foliage.

Rain that occurs soon after insecticides are applied may wash off and reduce the effectiveness of many pesticides. Repeat applications as needed.

 **PRUNING**

Minimize pruning now to limit flushes of new growth. Remove excessively long shoots from vines, but do not shear back the whole plant. Trim the edges of ground covers if needed.

OCTOBER

VINES, GROUND COVERS, & ORNAMENTAL GRASSES

 PLANNING

With careful planning and selection of plants, there can always be something wonderful going on in your landscape. Ornamental grasses are all decked out with feathery plumes in shades of beige, silver, creamy-white, and tan with highlights of bronze, gold, and burgundy. The plumes in combination with the grasses' handsome foliage offer a striking effect.

Antigonon vines are in full bloom. Once you have seen this magnificent vine in bloom, you will want one. The delicate sprays of vivid rosy-pink flowers cover the vine, producing a memorable display.

 PLANTING

October begins the fall planting season, especially for ground covers and hardy perennial vines. When planting ground covers, proper preparation of the planting area will help ensure good establishment and faster growth:

1. First remove all existing unwanted vegetation such as lawngrass or weeds from the area. This could be done physically, or you can use a herbicidesuch as glyphosate or Finale, but do a thorough job.

2. Next, till the soil to loosen it. When working under a tree, use a turning fork to minimize damage to the tree's roots, and avoid severing roots larger than an inch in diameter whenever possible. Two or 3 inches of additional blended soil mix (generally called topsoil or garden soil) may be added if necessary and incorporated into the existing soil.

3. Spread 2 inches of organic matter (compost, peat moss, or rotted manure) and fertilizer ($1/2$ cup of 15-5-10 per 30 square feet if your soil is high in phosphorus, or 1 cup of 8-8-8 per 30 square feet if your soil is low in phosphorus) over the area, and work it in.

 CARE

Mulches in your beds have probably decayed and thinned over the summer, but this is not a bad thing. Organic mulches add organic matter to the soil as they decay. Mulches do, however, lose their effectiveness in controlling weeds when they become too thin. If needed, add new mulch over the old to create a mulch depth of at least 2 inches.

 WATERING

You can generally relax as the weather cools. October may be dry and mild to hot some years, so watch the weather and water if needed.

 PESTS

Preemergence herbicides, also called weed preventers, may be applied to ground cover beds to suppress the growth of cool-season weeds. Common preemergence herbicides are Dacthal, Eptam, Amaze, and Preen.

 PRUNING

Pruning should be kept to a minimum. Any pruning done now to spring-flowering vines will reduce the number of flowers next spring.

Most ground covers should not be pruned. If needed, edge beds of **Asian jasmine** to keep them neat.

NOVEMBER

VINES, GROUND COVERS, & ORNAMENTAL GRASSES

 PLANNING

November weather can run from delightful to downright chilly. Deciduous vines like **wisteria** will begin to look tired, and the foliage will begin to die before it drops. We use very few deciduous ground covers, but **hostas** have become fairly popular. They generally go dormant this month. Mark the location of the plants to avoid damaging them later if you dig in the bed.

 PLANTING

Continue to plant hardy perennial vines and ground covers. They will not grow over the winter, but they will send out new roots and get established. As a result, they will outgrow plants that are planted next spring and not have to be fussed over so much next summer.

You can also dig, divide, and transplant ground covers this month.

 CARE

If you planted one of the more tender tropical vines such as **mandevilla, pandorea,** or **butterfly vine,** you now have two choices. The first is to let winter do what it will. These vines grow rapidly and can be treated as annuals after an entire summer of flowers. Plant new plants next spring if they do not make it through the winter. The second is to mulch them thickly over their roots and lower stem to a depth of about 10 inches. If the tops freeze, the roots have a chance of surviving. For more information, see the section on winter protection in the Introduction (pages 16-17).

 WATERING

Cool to cold moist weather generally makes watering this month unnecessary. Water plants that have just been planted or transplanted if the weather turns mild and dry.

 FERTILIZING

Fertilizing is not necessary now.

 PESTS

Few, if any, pests bother these plants this time of the year.

Weed gardens regularly and maintain a good layer of mulch to keep weeds under control.

If the weather is still mild, some caterpillar damage may occur.

Treat plants with Sevin or Bt.

Check vines and ground covers for the presence of scale insects. They will look like white or tan bumps on leaves or stems that detach easily when pushed with your thumbnail.

Spray plants with horticultural oil (Ultra-Fine Oil, Volck Oil Spray, Summer Oil). Spray the plants thoroughly. Oils kill by suffocating the scale and will not be effective unless the insects are coated with it. Make 2 to 3 applications about ten days apart.

 PRUNING

Pruning should be kept to a minimum. Growth has generally slowed considerably or stopped. If you have kept up with maintaining control during the main growing season, things should be looking just fine now.

DECEMBER
VINES, GROUND COVERS, & ORNAMENTAL GRASSES

 PLANNING

Gardening does not stop in Louisiana during the winter, but it does slow down. This is a good time to go over all of your gardening tools. How many were broken or lost last summer? In what condition are the rest? What needs to be replaced? What needs to be repaired? Are there tools you need that you don't have? With gift-giving season right around the corner, this is a good time to pick out some new tools. A few well-placed suggestions will probably get you what you need.

 PLANTING

You can plant ground covers and hardy perennial vines throughout the winter, but early December is an especially good time. The weather is generally still mild, and the soil is warm from summer. If planted now, plants will make strong root growth and be ready to grow vigorously next spring and summer. The weather conditions over the next several months mean you can just about water them in and walk away.

Ground covers can be dug, divided, and transplanted this month. This is a good time to transplant vines as well.

 CARE

Cut back the dead growth of **antigonon vine** after freezes kill it back. Put some mulch over the roots to protect them from the cold.

 WATERING

Water-in newly planted or transplanted ground covers and vines. Cool weather and regular rainfall make the need for additional irrigation unlikely.

 FERTILIZING

No fertilizer is required by these plants until next spring.

 PESTS

Take a rest. Few pest problems are likely to show up on these plants during the winter. Scales are an exception.

If you see scales on vines or ground covers, spray with a horticultural oil. Make two to three applications ten days apart, and don't spray when a freeze is predicted that night.

 PRUNING

To keep things looking neat, selectively prune out damaged, brown, or diseased leaves from plants such as **aspidistra, ligularia,** and **ferns.** Otherwise, little or no pruning should be done to ground covers or vines this month.

When cold weather browns the foliage of ornamental grasses, you can cut them back immediately or wait. Some gardeners like the way ornamental grasses look when they are dormant—others just think they look like dead grass.

Holly fern

WATER & BOG PLANTS

They are called ponds, ornamental ponds, aquatic features, pond gardens, water features, and aquatic gardens . . . Whatever you call yours, including a water feature in the landscape has gone from being unusual to relatively common. Flexible, durable pond liners and readily available equipment and supplies have made it possible for almost anyone to create an aquatic garden.

There are as many different ways to create an aquatic garden as there are gardeners. Aquatic gardens can be simple enough for an individual to build in an afternoon, or require weeks for a whole crew using heavy equipment to complete the job. In this chapter we will focus on the simpler aquatic gardens: combinations of water, plants, fish, and, perhaps, a recirculating pump to provide the wonderful sound of splashing water.

Relatively care-free (most of the work is in the setup), aquatic gardens do require some maintenance. The plants in them need grooming, fertilizing, dividing, and other care at the proper times.

PLANNING

Setting up an aquatic garden can involve significant amounts of time, landscape area, and investment. Changes later on can be difficult and costly, so thorough planning is essential before you install an aquatic garden. The first decisions you need to make should include the style, location, and size of your aquatic garden.

Aquatic gardens can be formal or naturalistic. Formal styles involve geometric shapes and finished materials such as cast concrete, bricks, or dressed stone. A naturalistic pond would have an

irregular shape and utilize natural materials such as stone. Consider the style of your existing landscape. An irregularly shaped naturalistic pond might look out of place in an otherwise clipped and geometric formal landscape. Since most landscapes tend to be rather informal, the naturalistic style pond is the most popular.

Locate the aquatic garden where you can readily see and enjoy it. Choose a spot near where you sit outside or where it can be seen from indoors. Place it far enough away from a fence or building so that plants can be planted between the pond and the structure.

A spot that gets a minimum of five hours of sun daily will allow you to grow a wide selection of aquatic plants, especially blooming water lilies. But a shady pond will also work, with proper plant selection.

Choose a level site to prevent excessive runoff from entering the pond. If you intend to have pumps, locate the pond near existing ground fault interrupt electrical outlets. Make sure the area is not available to unsupervised children. Trees will drop leaves in the pond, increasing maintenance and blocking sunlight, so locate ponds away from trees.

The size of your aquatic garden should be in scale with its location. Think carefully about the size you want, as it is generally not possible to change it once the aquatic garden is installed. Consider the shape of the pond as well. Formal ponds will have a geometric shape such as a rectangle or circle. Naturalistic ponds will have an irregular shape that can be more precisely determined when the pond is laid out, but try to decide on a general shape beforehand.

Although rigid, preformed plastic or fiberglass liners are available in various shapes, most people choose a flexible liner because it allows more freedom to create a pond of any size and shape.

1. Create the pond outline with a garden hose. Avoid sharp curves, as they will make it more difficult to lay the liner.

2. Once you have the shape to your satisfaction, calculate the size of the liner you will need, and purchase it. The best, most durable liners are made of butyl rubber. The length of the liner will equal the overall length of the pond plus twice the depth plus 3 feet. The width of the liner will equal the overall width of the pond plus twice the depth plus 3 feet.

Liner Length = Pond Length + 2 x (Pond Depth) + 3 ft.

Liner Width = Pond Width + 2 x (Pond Depth) + 3 ft.

3. Dig out the pond to a depth of about 14 to 16 inches. Our mild climate prevents ponds from freezing more than an inch or two deep in the winter, so you can dig a deeper pond if you like, although it is not necessary. The sides should slant slightly away from the center of the pond. Place the soil in a ring a foot or two away from the edge of the pond. It will be used later.

4. Rake the bottom of the pond smooth. Clip off any roots and remove any rocks or debris. Lay a board across the pond and place a level on it. Do this from several directions. The sides of the pond must be level. Smooth the sides and bottom and cover all exposed surfaces with 15-pound roofing felt, which will act as a cushion for the liner.

5. Place the folded liner in the pond and open it up. Spread out the liner over the excavated area and start filling the pond with water. Pleat or fold the liner as the pond fills to make the bottom and sides smooth.

6. When the pond is almost full, place the first layer of flat stones (veneer rocks, available from local stone suppliers) around the sides, overhanging the edge by about 2 inches. You may pile the rocks one or more layers thick depending on how high you wish to raise the level of the pond above ground level. You will need about one ton of 1- to 2-inch-thick flat veneer rocks for a 6-by-10-foot pond. You will need more for a waterfall.

7. Standing inside the pond, grasp the edge of the liner that is outside the pond and pull it over

the first layer of rocks, overlapping about 6 inches (trim off or fold under any excess liner).

8. Place another row of rocks on top, making sure the liner does not show through any cracks (cover cracks with smaller rocks).

9. Finish filling the pond.

10. Rake the excavated soil back to the edge of the rocks to cover the exposed liner, and taper it away from the pond.

11. If the pond water is chlorinated, put dechlorinator (Shieldex, Instochlor) in the water. Now you are ready for plants and fish.

You will have built your pond slightly above the level of the rest of the yard. This will prevent runoff, and the liner will stay in place.

PLANTING

Submerged plants live below the water surface and help keep the pond healthy. They oxygenate the water, prevent algae growth by using up nutrients in the water, and provide shelter for fish.

Floating plants dangle their roots in the water and hold their leaves up in the air. They move freely over the water surface and provide beauty and interest in the aquatic garden.

Planting is quite easy. Simply toss submerged plants into the pond, spreading them around in various locations. Floating plants, which will move around, can be placed into the pond wherever you want them.

Plants that grow in soil are grown in containers filled with heavy garden soil. They include deep-water aquatic plants, shallow-water marginal plants, and moisture-loving bog plants. These types of plants are usually purchased prepotted from local nurseries that carry aquatic plants, and they simply need to be placed in the aquatic garden. Water lilies are sometimes sold bare root, especially when mail ordered. To plant bare-root water lilies or marginals in containers:

1. Fill a container about $1/2$ to $2/3$ full with heavy garden soil. Do not use soilless mixes or soil high in organic matter.

2. Place the rhizome, bulb, or roots in the pot with the tip or crown level with the rim, push fertilizer tablets into the soil (follow package directions for the number to use based on pot size), and fill the pot with soil to within about an inch of the pot rim. The tip or crown should be just exposed.

3. Place a layer of large gravel, sand, or small stones over the soil surface. This keeps the soil in place and reduces damage to plant roots from fish.

4. Water the container thoroughly and gently set it into the pond. Check that the depth of water covering the pot is appropriate for the plant. Boost the pot up with bricks if necessary.

CARE

These are not high-maintenance plants. Regular care means removing faded flowers and dead or unattractive leaves, which keeps the plants looking good and prevents dead vegetation from fouling the water. The exuberant growth of many water and bog plants will occasionally call for trimming back, dividing, and repotting. Floating water plants can grow to completely cover the water surface, and some will have to be removed on occasion. Tropical water lilies may need to be lifted and stored in protected locations in winter.

WATERING

Evaporation and water splashing from fountains or waterfalls will gradually lower the water level. Maintain the water level at the full capacity of the pond. This is important for the health of the plants and the fish. It is better to add a little water frequently than a lot of water occasionally, especially if your water is chlorinated. If you are adding more than an inch of water, use some dechlorinator.

JANUARY
WATER & BOG PLANTS

 PLANNING

This is a great month to plan an aquatic garden. Most gardeners will wait until the weather is more reliably warm to install a pond, but if you have been considering putting a pond in your landscape, start planning for it now. Consider the kind of aquatic garden or pond you want. A half whisky barrel (lined with pond liner) or a large glazed ceramic pot without drainage holes (or seal the drainage holes) would be suitable for a small garden with a few plants and fish—or you may want something large and elaborate.

Make decisions on how large, where, and what style the water garden will be, what type of building materials you will use, and what kind of plants you want to include. Stop by local nurseries that deal in or specialize in aquatic gardens and talk to the staff. They will have great information on aquatic gardening in your part of the state.

Most aquatic plants are dormant during the winter, but you can look at different types of pond liners, pumps, equipment, and supplies that are needed for an aquatic garden. Pick up a reference on aquatic gardens or ponds, and read it to become familiar with what is involved in this fascinating type of garden.

 PLANTING

It is still too early to do much planting or transplanting in the aquatic garden. If the weather is nice and you are in the mood, marginal plants can be divided and repotted this month—but most gardeners wait until February.

 CARE

Most aquatic plants are dormant now, depending on how cold it has been where you garden. If no significant freezes have occurred, some plants may still be green. Winter freezes will damage or kill the foliage of most aquatic plants, but the roots in the pots are reliably hardy. Do not allow the pots to freeze. Lower them deeper in the water if prolonged freezing temperatures are predicted.

Promptly remove any leaves that blow or drop into the pond over the winter.

If a freeze in the mid- to low 20s is predicted, gather a few **water hyacinth** and **water lettuce** plants and put them in a bucket or tub of water placed in a location where the temperatures will stay above freezing. When the weather warms up a few days later, return them to the pond.

Check **tropical water lilies** you may have stored in a frost-free location for the winter. Make sure they stay covered with water in tubs, or, if stored in damp sand, do not allow them to dry out. Light is not necessary for these plants as they are leafless and dormant.

 WATERING

Maintain water levels in your aquatic garden during the winter. Cooler temperatures and rainfall generally mean you won't have to add water as often as in the summer. Do not run your pump when water temperatures approach freezing.

 PRUNING

Trim off cold-damaged foliage. Most aquatic plants can be cut back to within a few inches of the pot after going dormant.

HELPFUL HINTS

When fertilizing plants in an aquatic garden, use slow-release fertilizer tablets specifically made for that purpose. (Other types of fertilizers may raise nitrogen levels of the water and increase problems with algae.) **Water lilies** are especially heavy feeders and will not perform at their highest level without regular fertilization in summer.

FEBRUARY
WATER & BOG PLANTS

 PLANNING

When reading up on water gardens, don't get intimidated by the details. You will read about every possible problem that may occur and think there is no way for you to be successful. But the same can be said of every type of gardening. I have found my aquatic garden to be one of the least labor intensive parts of my landscape, and you probably will, too. Problems will occur (such as green water), but time and experience will enable you to deal with them effectively, just as in the rest of your landscape.

 PLANTING

It is best to clean out smaller aquatic gardens about once a year (although I occasionally skip a year or two), and larger ponds every few years. February is an appropriate time in the warmer sections of the state, but if the weather remains cold, there will be no problem waiting until early March. The temperature of the water should be above 55 degrees Fahrenheit.

Here's the proper way to clean out an aquatic garden:

1. Remove all of the fish and plants (put fish and submerged and floating plants in buckets or tubs filled with water from the pond), and pump out the water from the pond. As the water gets low, catch any fish you missed.

2. Lightly scrub the bottom and sides of the pond with a brush— do not use cleaners or soap. Rinse lightly and pump out the rinsewater.

3. Add new water until the pond is almost full, and put dechlorinator it. Save room to return the water that the plants and fish are now in. It is full of beneficial microorganisms.

4. Put the submerged and floating plants and the water they were stored in back into the pond.

5. Divide and repot containerized water and bog plants (except **Louisiana irises**), and place them back into the pond.

6. Put fish in plastic bags filled with water from the bucket or tub they were held in, and float the bags in the pond for about fifteen minutes or until the water in the bag and the water in the pond are the same temperature. Release the fish.

 CARE

Through the winter, remove any leaves that fall into the pond to keep them from fouling the water.

It is still too early to place **tropical water lilies** back into the aquatic garden. Make sure the sand they are stored in stays wet or the pot is covered by water.

Do not run your pump when water temperatures go below 40 degrees Fahrenheit.

 WATERING

Maintain the water level in your aquatic garden. Water depth is important to provide cold protection to those plants you are overwintering in the pond.

 PRUNING

Even if you decide not to clean out your pond this month, trim off all dead, brown, freeze-damaged leaves and stems from water and bog plants.

HELPFUL HINTS

Do not use chemical pesticides in or around your pond. Bt may be used for caterpillar control, but handpicking is preferred. Aphids can be dislodged with a strong stream of water, and the fish will eat them. Herons, egrets, and other animals may come to dine on your fish and can become pests. Overall, pests rarely create major problems.

MARCH
WATER & BOG PLANTS

PLANNING

Water and bog plants are a beautiful group of plants that provide color, texture, and even fragrance to the landscape. Add to that the reflective qualities of water and the sounds created by fountains and waterfalls, and you will see why these gardens have become so popular. Make plans now for the type of aquatic garden you might want to include in your landscape. Late spring is an excellent time to install one.

PLANTING

Clean out your pond, if you need to, in early March. It is advisable to do this if there is a thick layer of gunk on the bottom. It is best to get it done while the weather is cool, the plants are dormant, and the fish are less active. Pond-cleaning time is the best time to divide and repot water and bog plants. They grow so enthusiastically over the summer, it is a good idea to divide them at least once a year (**Louisiana irises** are divided in September).

To divide **hardy water lilies:**

1. Remove the plant from the pot, and hose soil off the rhi-

Use the manufacturer's label directions when adding aquatic plant fertilizer tablets.

zome to reveal the growing points.

2. Cut the rhizome into sections, each having a growing point with leaves and roots.

3. Fill a container $1/2$ to $2/3$ full of heavy garden soil. Three-gallon black plastic containers work well.

4. Plant the division with the rhizome positioned horizontally and the cut end against the side of the pot.

5. Add more soil to fill the pot to within about an inch of the top. The tip of the growing point should be exposed.

6. Top off with a layer of large gravel or sand.

7. Water the pot to saturate the soil, and gently place the pot in the pond. The rim of the pot should be 6 to 10 inches below the water surface.

To divide marginal or bog plants:

1. Remove the plant from the pot. If it is potbound, you may have to cut the plastic pot to free the plant.

2. Hose off the soil to reveal the root and rhizome structure of the plant.

3. Use a large knife to cut the plant into 2 to 4 pieces.

4. Fill a container $1/2$ to $2/3$ full of heavy garden soil. One- to 3-gallon black plastic containers work well.

5. Plant the division in the middle of the pot.

6. Add more soil to fill the pot to within about an inch of the top. The crown of the plants should be at soil level.

7. Top off with a layer of large gravel or sand.

HELPFUL HINTS

If your pond liner is leaking, it should be repaired during the pond-cleaning process. When all of the water is out of the pond and the liner has been scrubbed, rinsed clean, and the rinsewater removed, dry the liner and locate the leak. Patch kits are available where you purchased your liner and should be used according to directions. To avoid damaging the liner in the future:

1. Do not allow dogs into your pond.

2. Wear rubber sole sneakers when walking in the pond.

3. Make sure tools, such as skimmer nets, do not have sharp edges or points that might damage the liner.

4. Materials used to raise pots closer to the surface, such as bricks or aged concrete blocks, should not have sharp points or edges.

Patch kits are available where you purchased your liner.

8. Water the pot to saturate the soil, and gently place the pot in the pond. The rim of the pot should be no more that 2 to 4 inches below the soil surface. Raise the pot with bricks if necessary.

CARE

If the temperature of the water in your pond is staying at around 60 degrees Fahrenheit, you can place tropical water lilies stored indoors over the winter back into the pond. Otherwise, wait until April.

FERTILIZING

When dividing and repotting plants in February and March, you may or may not need to add aquatic plant fertilizer tablets. Put the appropriate number of tables in each pot according to the manufacturer's directions if the plants are showing signs of growth. Otherwise, you can wait until new growth begins.

PESTS

Pest problems should still be at a minimum, but as the weather warms it is more likely you will see aphids or caterpillars on your plants (or at least the holes caterpillars chew).

PRUNING

Trim back water and bog plants when you divide and repot them, if you haven't already done so. If you choose not to divide now, cut them back to within a few inches of the soil anyway, so the healthy new growth does not get mixed into the old, unattractive foliage.

APRIL
WATER & BOG PLANTS

PLANNING

This is a great month to install a new aquatic garden. Aquatic plants are growing vigorously, and the nurseries carrying these plants should have a wide selection available. Complete any decisions that need to be made before you start the work. Careful planning is critical to achieving the results you want.

Plan to include a few goldfish in your aquatic garden. (Koi are usually too damaging to plants to include them in an aquatic garden.) Put in 1 linear foot of fish for each 25 square feet of pond surface area. For example, if you have 50 square feet of pond, you may have four 6-inch fish or eight 3-inch fish. Do not feed the goldfish. They are an important part of the balanced

ecosystem you are attempting to create. Mosquitoes can breed in aquatic gardens if there are no goldfish in the pond to eat them. Along with eating mosquito larvae, goldfish will graze on algae and submerged plants. Submerged plants will use the nitrogen the fish excrete and grow better, the fish will nibble on the submerged plants (keeping them under control), and the submerged plants will oxygenate the water to the benefit of the fish. Isn't nature incredible?

Would you like to put in more plants? Don't get carried away and overcrowd the pond. The plants should have plenty of room. Ponds with plants crammed together and growing all over each other lose much of their attractiveness. In addition, if you can't see the water any more because it is completely covered by plants, you lose the beauty of the water.

Louisiana irises are in full bloom this month. Enjoy the spectacular colorful flowers of these marvelous natives in your aquatic garden. Don't have any? Go buy some in bloom at local nurseries now. Even if they were not grown in an aquatic situation, just cover the soil with gravel, water thoroughly, and place in your pond.

Simply lower a newly purchased water and bog plant into the pond where you want them to grow.

PLANTING

Place your **tropical water lilies** back into the pond by late April if you stored them inside over the winter. Those stored in sand should be potted in heavy garden soil with the growing point just at the soil surface. Place the pot in shallow water, with about 2 to 4 inches of water over the pot. Give your plants until the end of May to resprout. Sometimes the plants never recover from winter storage and have to be replaced. Tropical water lilies left in the pond may not have survived the winter (they will not tolerate water temperatures much below 50 degrees Fahrenheit), and they will also need to be replaced. Water lily plants are not cheap, but most aquatic gardens include only one or two of these spectacular plants. Given the amazing number of flowers they produce, they are well worth the investment even if they last only one season.

Newly purchased water and bog plants in pots are simply placed in the pond where you want them to grow. I love that. No holes to dig, no beds to prepare, no mulching, watering, or weeding. Who said aquatic gardening is hard? Make sure you still have enough submerged plants, and add more if necessary.

CARE

Green water is caused by the explosive growth of microscopic green plants called algae. It is very common in newly created aquatic gardens and will occasionally show up in established ponds as well. Don't panic. It's not that bad. Abundant algae growth is caused by an excessive amount of nutrients in the water and lots of available sunlight. New ponds are prone to this problem because the new plants are not yet absorbing a lot of the nutrients from the water and have not grown enough to cover 50 to 60 percent of the water surface. The solution is to be patient and wait. As the plants settle in, the problem should clear up. Make sure you have included about one bunch of submerged plants for every square foot of pond surface. When the problem arises in an existing pond, add more submerged plants to absorb the nutrients from the water, and more floating plants to absorb nutrients and block sunlight from reaching the water. Do not use chemicals to control the algae.

HELPFUL HINTS

Check out all equipment before installing it in the pond. Test all pumps, filters, connections, hoses, tubing, and electrical boxes. Make sure electrical outlets used to power pumps are equipped with ground fault interrupt switches. This breaker is extremely sensitive to a change in current and will trip the circuit immediately if anything should go wrong with the pump or its wiring. This will prevent a potentially serious shock in case of a failure of the waterproof seal on the pump motor. Never pull on or lift a pump by its electrical cord, as that is one way to damage the waterproof seal.

WATERING

Make sure the water level of the pond stays full. When adding small amounts of water (10 percent or less), you do not need to add a dechlorinator. If you inadvertently allow the water level to get low and have to add a lot of water, be sure to add a dechlorinator along with it. (If you aren't sure, add the dechlorinator.)

FERTILIZING

Any water or bog plants that were not repotted and fertilized last month should be fertilized this month. This includes just about everything except **tropical water lilies.** Always use fertilizers such as Pondtabb pellets that were especially designed to fer-

tilize aquatic plants. Most plants should be fertilized every four to six weeks during the growing season. **Tropical water lilies** should be fertilized twice a month from May to the first of September.

PESTS

Never use pesticides in or around your aquatic garden. Fish are very sensitive to pesticides. If herons or egrets are eating the fish, cover the pond with chicken wire or bird netting (available at local nurseries) for several days to a week until they move on. Cover whenever necessary during the summer. Losing a few goldfish is no big deal. They are inexpensive and easily replaced.

MAY

WATER & BOG PLANTS

 PLANNING

You do not have to include a pump and moving water in your aquatic garden. The plants and fish will be perfectly happy without it. Moving water is not necessary to oxygenate the water in the pond (submerged plants do that) and will not keep your water clear (once again, the plants do that). The sound and appearance of water running down a waterfall or fountaining up out of the pond is so wonderful, however, that most aquatic gardeners include it at the installation or add it later.

The pumps most often used in small ponds are oil-filled and submersible, and operate on normal 115-volt household current (plug only into a ground fault interrupt outlet).

 PLANTING

Submerged plants, such as **anacharis,** do not necessarily have to be planted in pots. They generally do well simply tossed into the pond. Sometimes, though, they do better when planted in pots. Stick the ends of the plants (usually sold in bundles held together with a rubber band) in

1-gallon pots of soil (cover the surface with pebbles) or pebbles. See which works best for you.

You can continue to purchase and add aquatic plants to your garden all summer.

 CARE

About 50 to 60 percent of the water surface should be covered with floating plants or the foliage of water lilies. If too much sun reaches the water, it will encourage the growth of algae. On the other hand, if the enthusiastic growth of plants covers most or all of the water surface, you lose the wonderful reflective qualities of the water. The aquatic garden will begin to look like just another regular garden bed. Remove excess growth regularly to keep some of the water surface clear of plants. Give the extras to friends who have aquatic gardens, or add them to your compost pile.

Do not allow grass clippings to get in the water when you mow the lawn area around the pond. Grass clippings in the pond look unsightly and will foul the water when they decay. Be especially careful if the grass has been recently sprayed with a pesticide. Avoid using pesticides in

the landscape around the pond, and never use pesticides in the pond unless they are safe for the fish.

 WATERING

Water quality is a major concern in aquatic gardens. Clear water is highly desirable; if it turns green, the attractiveness of the pond is diminished. This condition usually clears up on its own as long as enough submerged plants are placed in the water and enough of the surface is covered. Filters are rarely a necessity.

If you have large Japanese koi, however, you will need a filter because these are active fish and keep things stirred up; they also eat the submerged plants which are needed to keep the water clear. Koi also must be fed and produce a lot of waste that must be removed. If you have koi or a large number of other fish, and you feed them—you will need some kind of filter.

There are many types of filters. Various types of boxes and cylinders are on the market which use some kind of sponge-like pad that trap particles as the water passes through them. Filters must be cleaned regularly—once a

There are various types of filters available to maintain the quality of your pond's water.

month, every week, or even every day depending on the size of the filter, the size of the pond, and the many different conditions that vary from pond to pond. Filter pads are generally replaced once a year.

Large biological filters, which are generally used in larger ponds, are usually comprised of screens, gravel, and coarse sand. They are more expensive than simpler filters but work very well.

FERTILIZING

Fertilize **water lilies** twice a month and other water and bog plants once every four to six weeks. If growth is rampant, feel free to skip fertilization for all except water lilies. Push the tablets of aquatic plant fertilizer deep into the soil of the pot. You may notice the water tends to become green when you fertilize all your plants at the same time; this is due to extra nitrogen leaching from the pots into the water. Stagger your fertilization schedules. Fertilize $1/2$ the plants one month, and $1/2$ the following month.

PESTS

Aphids love to feed on **water lettuce.** Knock them off with a strong stream of water and the fish will eat them. Repeat as necessary. You can also remove and dispose of those plants that are most heavily infested.

PRUNING

Water lily leaves live about three weeks in the summer, then begin to yellow and die. Promptly remove yellowing water lily leaves by reaching in and cutting the stems close to the crown of the plant. Remove faded flowers as well.

Groom marginal or bog plants regularly to remove unattractive or damaged foliage and faded flowers. Aquatic gardens always attract a lot of attention and need to look their best.

JUNE
WATER & BOG PLANTS

PLANNING

Ponds should be beautiful now. The diversity among aquatic plants is astounding. Some have beautiful flowers, others have striking foliage, some are variegated, and all have distinct personalities. It's fun to create a garden when you have so much material to work with.

Have you ever wished you could rearrange a flower garden once it was up and growing? With aquatic gardens you can. Don't get carried away—it does disrupt the pond—but you can move plants around to create a different arrangement if you like. Remember, everything is in pots. Simply lift out the pot and place the plant in its new location.

PLANTING

You can continue to add aquatic plants to your pond all through the summer. Be adventurous; try something new.

Want to have an aquatic garden right up on a patio, balcony, or deck? Nothing could be easier. Line a half whisky barrel with pond liner, or choose any other suitable container that will hold water. Fill it up, add dechlorinator, and place a few aquatic plants in the water. Make sure

you choose one or two plants from each of the major groups: submerged, floating, and containerized (**water lilies** and marginal or bog plants). Only the smallest water lilies can be used, and don't forget that they need about six hours of sun every day to bloom well. Throw in a few goldfish and you're all set.

CARE

At some point you will hear or read about the pH of the water in your aquatic garden. This is not something you need to be overly concerned about. The pH is used to indicate how acid or alkaline the water is. A pH of 7 is neutral, numbers below 7 indicate an acid condition, and numbers above 7 indicate an alkaline condition. Fish and aquatic plants seem to be adaptable to a wide range of pH levels. As a rule, ponds which are clear usually have a pH of 7 or slightly below. Ponds where the water is green with algae have a higher pH. Excess nitrogen from fertilizer, decaying organic matter, and fish waste is converted to ammonia, which is alkaline. The ammonia provides nitrogen for the algae, resulting in green water. The pH is not the cause of the green water, but a symptom. If you have sufficient submerged plants in the pond, they will absorb the extra nitrogen in the water. Less ammonia means a pH closer to 7.

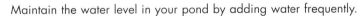

Maintain the water level in your pond by adding water frequently.

WATERING

Maintain the water level in your pond. If you ever need to add more than 10 percent of the amount of water in the pond, add a dechlorinator along with the water. If you aren't sure if you need to use dechlorinator, add the dechlorinator just to be safe.

FERTILIZING

Water lilies are heavy feeders. They really hit their stride this month, but if you want those gorgeous flowers to be produced regularly (most tropicals have at least one flower open every day), they must be fed. Apply one or two pond fertilizer tablets every two weeks through September 1.

Fertilize other pond plants growing in containers once every four to six weeks. If growth is rampant, don't fertilize.

Submerged and floating plants obtain the nutrients they need from the water. Their job is to remove nitrogen from the water that leaches out of pots or comes from fish waste. Never add fertilizer to the water of your pond.

PESTS

Filamentous algae is different from the microscopic plants that

Nymphaea 'St. Louis Gold' is a favorite water lily for summer.

cause green water. It produces threadlike green strands that mat together and look messy and unsightly. The same efforts to control regular algae will also control filamentous algae.

Until it starts to clear up, remove it using a stick or large cooking fork (you can roll it up on the fork much as you would spaghetti). A brush used to clean toilets also works well.

Caterpillars chew holes in a variety of floating and marginal plants as well as water lilies. If the damage is not too bad, no control is necessary. Inspect the plants carefully and handpick caterpillars when you see them.

Bt is not toxic to the fish and may be helpful in controlling a severe outbreak.

PRUNING

The fast, vigorous growth of aquatic plants calls for regular pruning and grooming. Do not let dead leaves and flowers get into the water and decompose. This will add nutrients and can deplete the oxygen level of the water. Prune aquatic plants as necessary to remove yellow leaves and faded flowers.

JULY
WATER & BOG PLANTS

 PLANNING

Summertime and the living is easy—but hot! Nothing makes the garden seem cooler than the sound of water. If you have problems with background noise from a nearby highway or other sources, the sound of water can drown it out with soothing tones. If you plan on adding a pump and fountain to your aquatic garden, it's best if you can hear the sound it will make at the nursery. That's the advantage of purchasing supplies at a nursery that has a variety of ponds set up with various fountains, spouting statues, and nozzles in operation. That way you can pick out just the sound you are looking for.

 PLANTING

If a marginal plant has outgrown its pot, you can divide it now:

1. Remove the plant from the pot. If it is potbound, you may have to cut the plastic pot to free the plant.

2. Hose off the soil to reveal the root and rhizome structure of the plant.

3. Use a large knife to cut the plant into 2 to 4 pieces.

4. Fill a container 1/2 to 2/3 full of heavy garden soil. One- to 3-gallon black plastic containers work well.

5. Plant the division in the middle of the pot.

6. Add more soil to fill the pot to within about an inch of the top. The crown of the plants should be at soil level.

7. Top off with a layer of gravel.

8. Water the pot to saturate the soil, and gently place the pot in the pond. The rim of the pot should be no more that 2 to 4 inches below the soil surface. Raise the pot with bricks if necessary.

 CARE

Deadhead flowers after they have faded to keep them from falling into the water. Remove leaves that turn yellow or are damaged by insects or diseases. This will keep your plants looking their best. Continual care in keeping organic matter out of the water or removing organic debris from the water will help keep the pond clear.

Do not deadhead **lotus** flowers. Let the seedpods develop—they make valuable additions to flower arrangements when they mature.

Use a sharp knife to cut the plant into 2 to 4 pieces.

 WATERING

Hot, dry weather will increase evaporation and lower the pond level. Add water regularly to maintain the level. It is better to add some water every day or so than to let the water get low and have to add a lot. The addition of large amounts of water can hurt the fish by rapidly changing the water temperature and adding chlorine.

 FERTILIZING

Fertilize **water lilies** twice a month with a fertilizer designed to be used on aquatic plants. Follow manufacturer's directions.

 PESTS

Leaf spots and other diseases will occasionally show up on aquatic plants. Promptly prune off infected leaves to keep diseases under control. Most aquatic plants are relatively pest free and grow so fast that any damaged growth is quickly replaced.

HELPFUL HINTS

Don't forget to clean the intake screen on your pump regularly. If you notice the flow of water is diminished, it usually has something to do with the intake screen. The three best ways to destroy a pump are to:
- let the water level drop below the pump.
- lift or pull it by the electrical cord.
- ignore the decrease in water flow which indicates a blocked screen or jammed impeller.

If the pump quits working, remove the screws and open the impeller housing (the impeller is what moves the water and looks like a propeller). Something may have lodged in the impeller, stopping it from turning. If this is the case, remove the debris and see if the pump will work. This is about the only repair you can do for submerged motors. Never try to open the sealed motor housing.

 PRUNING

Don't let the rapid growth of aquatic plants lead to overgrowth. Prune **water lilies** or marginals, or remove some of the submerged or floating plants if they are taking over the pond. It's a water garden, so make sure you can see some of the water.

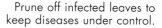
Prune off infected leaves to keep diseases under control.

AUGUST
WATER & BOG PLANTS

 PLANNING

You can still install a pond this month. That's the beauty of aquatic gardening. No matter how hot it is (too hot to plant anything else), you can still create a beautiful aquatic garden. Aquatic gardens take careful planning to be successful. Take a look at the introduction to this chapter to see how to do it (pages 229-231).

 PLANTING

For a garden pond to be successful it should contain fish. Be sure to "plant" some goldfish in your aquatic garden. Adding fish creates a balanced ecosystem with interactions between the plants and the fish. These interactions help ensure proper water conditions. Fish also keep mosquitoes from breeding in the pond.

It's best to add goldfish. Japanese koi are voracious feeders that eat plants—**water lilies**, **water hyacinths**, and submerged plants—and even jump up to feed on plants growing around the perimeter of the pond. If you want an aquatic garden with lots of plants, including floating plants and submerged plants, you cannot have koi.

 CARE

Several animals cause problems in aquatic gardens. Do not allow turtles, crawfish, ducks, or geese in the pond. They will eat your **water lilies** and other water plants. Alligators will eat your fish and are also not compatible with the aquatic garden (not to mention the possibility of their scaring the daylights out of you or your guests).

Frogs and toads are attracted to ponds and are generally welcome. If toads lay a large number of eggs in the pond, the resulting tadpoles excrete a poison that can kill your fish. Scoop out the eggs when you find them. A few tadpoles are okay—thousands are not.

Do not let your dog play in the pond. In addition to disturbing plants and knocking over pots, the dog can damage the pond liner with its toenails, causing leaks.

 WATERING

Add water regularly to keep the pond consistently full.

 FERTILIZING

Fertilize aquatic plants regularly—once a month for **water lilies**, and once every four to six weeks for marginals. Only use fertilizer specifically formulated for use on aquatic plants.

 PESTS

Watch carefully for pests, and take prompt action to control them. Prune off diseased foliage. Remove aphids with a strong stream of water. Pick off caterpillars and drop them in the water for the fish to eat. Remove filamentous algae by rolling it on a stick or large cooking fork like spaghetti.

 PRUNING

Prune as needed to control the growth of overly vigorous aquatic plants. If rampant growth is a big problem, cut back on fertilizer.

Turtles, if not controlled, will eat your water lilies.

SEPTEMBER
WATER & BOG PLANTS

 PLANNING

September is our most active hurricane month. Gardeners who live in the southern part of the state need to know how they will prepare should one of these enormously destructive storms threaten. The only good thing about hurricanes is that we generally have enough advance warning to take action. Here are a few tips for preparing your aquatic garden:

1. Unplug pumps; roll up and stash any electrical cords.

2. Set all aquatic plants growing in containers on the bottom of the pond.

3. Pick up and store indoors any loose objects around the pond.

4. Gather some of your floating plants in a large plastic garbage bag and store inside. High winds will likely take any floating plants left in the pond.

5. High rains will cause the pond to overflow, but there is not much you can do about it. Flooding could wash fish out of the pond. Put them in buckets of pond water, and bring indoors any fish you could not bear to lose.

 PLANTING

You can still purchase and place aquatic plants in the garden. I might not go out and buy **tropical water lilies** now, given there is little of their bloom season left. Wait and buy one next May so you can enjoy the flowers all summer.

This month is the best time to divide and repot your **Louisiana irises** and **calla lilies.**

 CARE

Remove any dead or decaying vegetation regularly so that it does not foul the water.

 WATERING

Add water often to maintain the proper level in your pond. If you find the water level drops constantly and you must add large amounts of water, you may have a leak. If so, you will need to remove the plants and fish, drain the pond, find the leak, and use a patch to fix it. Patch kits for pond liners are available where you purchased the liner.

 FERTILIZING

Although the weather is warm and aquatic plants are still growing, the changing of the seasons is not far off. Stop fertilizing **water lilies** early this month. Most other aquatic plants begin to slow down now. I generally stop fertilizing everything after mid-September.

 PESTS

Raccoons are not uncommon, even in urban areas. They are skillful fishers who can catch and eat fish from your pond. Try placing a chicken wire barrier over the pond at night for a week or so until they move on. If you get desperate, you can try trapping them. Contact your local animal control authorities.

 PRUNING

Continue to remove yellowing water lily leaves regularly.

OCTOBER
WATER & BOG PLANTS

PLANNING

It's time to make winter plans for the aquatic garden. The weather is cool, and summer is finally over. Evaluate the general condition of the garden. Are there plants that did not do well? Try to identify why, and make notes about how to correct the problems next year. Which of the plants are hardy, and which might need winter protection? Will you try to protect the tender plants or just let them take their chances?

PLANTING

With winter on the way, now is not a good time to add aquatic plants to the pond.

CARE

Some trees will begin to drop leaves this month. Keep fallen leaves skimmed off the pond surface or they will sink to the bottom, decay, and foul the water. As organic matter settles to the bottom and starts to decay, it can decrease the oxygen levels of the water, which is not healthy for the fish. Organic matter will also release nutrients as it decays, which can encourage algae growth and cause green water.

WATERING

The weather is beautiful, but October is often dry. While you enjoy this fine time of the year, don't forget to maintain the water level of the pond.

FERTILIZING

No fertilizer will be needed this month or for the rest of the year.

PESTS

Pest problems diminish this time of the year. Do not mistake the slower growth and declining health of aquatic plants as a pest problem. Shorter days and cooler temperatures are signaling many of them to go dormant. Yellow leaves, leaf spots, and brown edges are more probably symptoms of the changing seasons than a disease or insect.

Marginals growing in containers rarely have weeds grow in the pots with them, but some weeds may have found their way in. Look over the marginal plants in your garden, and pull any weeds you find growing in the pots. If they overwinter in the pots, they may be even worse next year.

PRUNING

More and more old, yellow, or brown foliage will begin to show up on **water lilies** and marginal or bog plants. Keep the plants well groomed so they will look as attractive as possible for as long as possible. Continue to regularly deadhead, and remove any old flowers that have dropped into the water.

HELPFUL HINTS

Harvest mature **lotus** pods for flower arrangements. Wait until the seeds are exposed, cut the pods, and hang them upside down to dry.

NOVEMBER

WATER & BOG PLANTS

 PLANNING

The growing season for the aquatic garden winds down this month. Early freezes in north Louisiana will brown back and induce dormancy in aquatic plants, ending the wonderful beauty and pleasure the garden provided this summer. Wasn't the garden beautiful, and aren't you glad you decided to put one in your landscape? Before you forget, take some time to jot down a few notes about the garden. What worked really well, and what was a disappointment? What would you do differently next year? Do this now before you forget.

 PLANTING

Marginals can be divided and repotted before the winter, if you like. There is no hurry. Most gardeners wait and do this in spring.

 CARE

You will notice that **water lily** plants have grown smaller and stopped blooming. Most water lilies would bloom year-round except that winter temperatures are too cold and the days too short. Even if you move yours

HELPFUL HINTS

Lots of shade trees drop leaves this month, and it can get to be a real hassle to keep them cleaned out of the pond. If the pond is not too big, place netting over it to catch the leaves. It is far easier to occasionally dump the leaves off the netting than to skim them off the pond. Put the leaves in your compost pile or use them for mulch. Make sure the edges of the netting are staked down to keep it from blowing off the pond.

into a large tub in a warm greenhouse, they will stop blooming by mid-December because the days are so short. Interestingly, many blue varieties of tropical water lilies will bloom through the winter in a warm greenhouse. These varieties are also the ones that do best in partial shade, and they tend to survive the winter in outside ponds much better than the others.

 WATERING

Water loss from evaporation slows as the weather cools and regular rains occur, but keep an eye on the water level through the winter. Water depth is critical when the weather is cold enough to freeze the surface of the water. Plants and fish need the water to be deep enough that they can stay down in unfrozen water toward the bottom of the pond.

 PESTS

As foliage cover decreases, fish become more vulnerable to animals catching and eating them. I try not to get attached to the goldfish (I never name them). If a few get eaten, they are not expensive to replace. You can, however, place chicken wire or netting over the pond to prevent this. If you lose a few fish, you can wait until spring to replace them.

 PRUNING

When freezes kill back marginals, cut them back close to the soil.

DECEMBER
WATER & BOG PLANTS

PLANNING

Aquatic gardens are certainly not at their most attractive during the winter. Try to tidy things up as much as possible. As long as the weather is mild and the water temperature is above 40 degrees Fahrenheit, you can continue to run the pump. When working in the yard or sitting on the patio, the delightful sound of water can be just as welcome now as it was during the summer. Unplug it during periods of sub-freezing temperatures.

CARE

Tropical water lilies, water hyacinths, water lettuce, and **cyperus** are commonly grown water plants that are not reliably hardy during the winter, particularly in north Louisiana. If temperatures will drop to the mid- to low 20s, bring a few plants of water lettuce and water hyacinth inside and keep them in a plastic bag or float them in a large container. If the freeze gets the ones in the pond, at least you saved a few (and a few is enough). Place them back into the pond after the cold weather passes, and repeat as necessary. Cut back cyperus, bury the pot up to its rim in a garden bed, and

mulch over the plant with several inches of pine straw. Place it back into the pond in the spring.

Most of the other plants in your aquatic garden are hardy. Do not be confused when they go dormant—they are not dead. Cut them back hard, and set the pots on the bottom of the pond if extreme cold is predicted. As long as they stay below the ice, they will be fine. Ice occurs occasionally, if at all, and rarely gets more than an inch or two thick. **Louisiana irises** are in active growth during the wintertime. If you included them in your aquatic garden, you will have at least some green.

Some gardeners grow tropical **water lilies** as annuals and let them take their chances in the pond over the winter. Winters are often mild enough for them to survive in south Louisiana. If you want to hedge your bets, bring the pot inside and submerge it in a bucket of water, or store the roots and crowns in wet sand in an area that will stay between 50 and 60 degrees Fahrenheit. **Hardy lilies** do not need to be brought in. Set the pots on the bottom of the pond as you do the hardy marginals.

There is no need to move goldfish or koi in for the winter, and you do not need to put a heater in the pond. These fish go into a natural semi-hibernation when

water temperatures fall below 45 degrees Fahrenheit. Koi do not need to be fed when temperatures are that low and should be fed sparingly over the winter. Should the pond freeze over, the fish will be fine in the liquid water underneath the ice. Do not strike the ice to break it or you may hurt the fish. Pour boiling water on the ice to open a hole, or place one or two milk jugs about $1/4$ full of water in the pond the night before. Remove them in the morning to create holes. Ice rarely lasts more than a day or two.

WATERING

Check the moisture regularly for the **water lilies** you are wintering indoors. The sand must stay damp or the bucket full of water. Continue to maintain the water level in your pond through the winter. The water depth is necessary to protect your fish and water plants from cold.

PRUNING

As aquatic plants go dormant, cut them back to a few inches above the soil line. Put the prunings in your compost pile.

ABOUT HOUSEPLANTS

What is a "houseplant?" You can look far and wide, and nowhere in the world will you find a plant that evolved inside a house. The plants we use as houseplants are adapted to grow in natural, outdoor conditions similar to those we maintain inside our homes—relatively low light and mild temperatures that range from the 60s to the 80s Fahrenheit year-round. Plants native to shady tropical forests provide many of the common, easily grown houseplants. They often have interesting or beautiful features such as colorful or unique foliage or flowers and adapt well to growing in containers.

PLANNING FOR HOUSEPLANTS

People enjoy the presence of plants indoors—they make us feel comfortable. Just look at the considerable expense that is made to maintain lush indoor landscapes in malls (maybe relaxed people spend more money?).

Growing houseplants successfully starts with understanding their needs. Houseplants contribute to and become part of the interior decor, but they are not furniture or knickknacks. They are alive, and like all living things they have certain needs that must be met for them to remain healthy.

ABOUT HOUSEPLANTS

The most important of these is light. You cannot grow a plant where there is not enough light, no matter how good it looks in the location. Light is the energy plants use to create their food.

Houseplants are often spur-of-the-moment purchases, but planning will produce more consistent and satisfactory results. Walk through your home and think about where plants would be appropriate. Focus particularly on areas where the family spends a lot of time, such as the kitchen or living room. Where is there sufficient light? How many plants do you want and how large should they be? Will they sit on a windowsill or on the floor, or perhaps hang in a basket?

BUYING HOUSEPLANTS

Houseplants are available from a wide variety of sources, from nurseries and flea markets to chain store garden centers and even grocery stores. Quality is of particular importance—the plants should be vigorous and healthy with good color and shape and no insects or diseases.

A plant's overall condition depends on a strong, healthy root system, and I commonly slip a plant out of its pot to look at the roots before I purchase it. The rootball should be full of healthy roots but not completely solid. Look at the foliage carefully. Avoid plants with yellow leaves or brown leaf edges or spots which indicate the plant has been poorly cared for. Are there signs of scale, mealybugs, or mites that could infest your other plants at home?

Make sure there is a tag in the pot with the name of the plant on it. Without a name you cannot look up or ask someone for information about the plant.

GROWING HOUSEPLANTS

Houseplants need light, water, a container, potting soil, and the right temperature.

LIGHT

Houseplants are generally grouped into high light, medium light, and low light categories. These generic terms have no clear meaning to most people. Here are some helpful guidelines:

• High light levels are provided by unobstructed east- and west-facing windows.

• Medium (summer) to high (winter) light levels are provided by unobstructed south-facing windows.

• North-facing windows provide low light levels. Low light levels may also be provided by placing

BROMELIADS

Bromeliads are popular, easy-care houseplants. Once a plant blooms it slowly loses vigor and dies. Don't despair. Before that happens the plant will produce side shoots from its base called "pups." When they reach about 1/3 to 1/2 the size of the original plant, they can be cut from the plant with a knife and potted up. With good care, they will bloom in a year or two.

ABOUT HOUSEPLANTS

plants several feet from east-, west-, or south-facing windows. Light is most often provided by sunlight shining through windows, but artificial light can also be used effectively to grow indoor plants.

Rarely do you have to worry about plants receiving too much light indoors. Within four to six weeks a plant will tell you if there is a problem. If there are no pests present and the plant has been watered properly, a deteriorating condition usually indicates insufficient light. Move the plant to a brighter location.

WATER

For the majority of plants, it is really quite simple. Stick your finger into the pot. If the soil feels wet or moist, don't water. If the soil feels dry, water. Do not allow plants to wilt before you water them. This stresses them and can cause leaf drop, flower bud drop, and brown leaf edges.

Apply water until some runs out of the pot's drainage holes and into the saucer underneath. That way you know that you have moistened the entire rootball. Do not let the pot sit in a saucer full of water. Remove the water in the saucer if it is still there a few hours later.

CONTAINERS

Houseplant containers should have drainage holes. There must be some way for excess water to drain out of the soil. Otherwise, we run the risk of soil staying saturated, drowning the roots, and encouraging root rot. Choose pots you find attractive and that fit in well with your interior decor. Clay, plastic, and other materials are all appropriate as long as they drain.

POTTING SOIL

Select soil that is specifically blended for use in containers, called "potting soil." Do not use topsoil or garden soil products, or soil dug up from outdoor garden beds. Professionals use soil-less potting mixes made up of peat moss, perlite, and vermiculite. Soilless mixes are available under brand names such as ProMix, Jiffy Mix, and Peter's Professional Potting Soil. Make sure that the potting soil or mix is loose, drains freely, and does not pack tightly in the pot.

TEMPERATURE

Since most of the plants grown as houseplants are native to the tropics, they should not be exposed to freezing temperatures. Generally, avoid temperatures below 45 degrees Fahrenheit. Avoid extremely high temperatures as well. The normal temperatures we maintain inside our homes are just fine for most houseplants.

PLANTING

Plants growing in containers eventually need to be repotted. When you purchase a new houseplant, don't be in a hurry to repot it. New plants have enough changes to deal with, without having to cope with the root disturbance involved in repotting.

There are several reasons for repotting houseplants. Over time, roots fill and become tightly packed in the container, causing the plant to lose vigor (plants in this condition are called "potbound"). The plant may grow until its size is out of scale with the pot. Potting mixes degrade over time and may need to be replaced. Sometimes gardeners repot plants simply to change the appearance of the pot.

STEPS FOR REPOTTING HOUSEPLANTS

1. Choose a new pot that is no more than twice as large as the original pot. Generally, 2 to 4 inches larger is recommended.

2. Add a layer of potting mix to the new pot. It should be deep enough so that when the plant is placed into the new pot, the top of the rootball is about 1 inch below the pot rim.

ABOUT HOUSEPLANTS

3. Remove the plant from the old pot. Slide it out, leaving the root system intact. If the roots are tightly packed together, use your fingers to loosen them. Do not tear the root system apart.

4. Place the plant in its new container. If necessary, add more soil underneath the plant or remove some until the plant is positioned properly.

5. Add new potting soil in the space between the rootball and the pot. Use your fingers to firm the soil as you add it, but do not pack it tightly. Fill to within 1/2 to 1 inch of the rim.

6. Water the newly potted plant thoroughly.

FERTILIZING

Plants growing indoors need relatively little fertilizer. Actively growing houseplants that are producing new leaves and/or flowers will benefit from regular, light, fertilizer applications. Most water-soluble or slow-release commercial houseplant fertilizers work well. Houseplants that are not growing or that are doing poorly should not be fertilized.

PEST CONTROL

Pest outbreaks on indoor plants can be devastating. There are no natural predators indoors, and the climate is warm, dry, and favorable for insects to reproduce and spread. Most pests come in with new houseplants. If you can, isolate new houseplants for several weeks to make sure no pest problems develop. Inspect your houseplants regularly and treat pest problems aggressively and promptly.

The major insect pests of houseplants are scales, mealybugs, and spider mites. Infested plants should be placed far away from healthy plants. Always wash your hands after working with an infested plant to avoid spreading the problem.

The easiest way to deal with most of these pests is to use a premixed, ready-to-use houseplant insecticide containing insecticidal soap or pyrethrin. Repeated applications are generally necessary for complete control. Ultra-Fine Oil is also effective for controlling these pests, especially scale insects, which can be difficult to eradicate.

PLANT SELECTIONS

Name	Shape	Light	Water
Aechema fasciata **Chinese Evergreen**	Upright, vase	Medium	Moist; keep cup formed by the leaves filled
Aeschynanthus spp. **Lipstick Vine**	Trailing/vining, basket	Medium to High	Moist, drier in winter
Aglaonema spp. **Chinese Evergreen**	Bushy	Low	Semi-moist
Aloe vera **Aloe, Burn Plant**	Succulent	High	Dry
Aphelandra squarrosa **Zebra Plant**	Bushy	Medium	Semi-moist
Araucaria exelsia **Norfolk Island Pine**	Tree	High	Moist
Asparagus spp. **Asparagus Ferns**	Trailing/vining, basket	High	Moist
Aspidistra elatior **Cast-Iron Plant**	Bushy	Low to Medium	Moist
Beaucarnea recurvata **Ponytail Palm**	Tree	Medium to High	Dry

ABOUT HOUSEPLANTS

PLANT SELECTIONS

Name	Shape	Light	Water
Begonia spp. **Fibrous, Cane, Rex**	Bushy	Medium to High	Moist
Bougainvillea spp. **Bougainvillea**	Trailing, basket	High	Moist; let dry between watering to induce bloom
Brassaia actinophylla **Schefflera**	Tree	High	Moist
Bromeliads (many types)	Generally vase-shaped	Medium	Semi-moist; keep cup formed by the leaves filled
Cactus (many types)	Succulent	High	Dry
Calathea makoyana **Peacock Plant**	Bushy	Medium	Moist, needs high humidity
Chamaedorea spp. **Indoor Palm**	Tree	Low to Medium	Moist
Chlorophytum elatum **Spider Plant**	Trailing, basket	Medium to High	Moist
Cissus rhombifolia **Grape Ivy**	Trailing/vining, basket	Medium	Moist
Codiaeum spp. **Croton**	Bushy	High	Moist
Crassula argentea **Jade Plant**	Bushy succulent	High	Dry
Dieffenbachia spp. **Dumb Cane**	Bushy to tree	Medium	Moist
Dizygotheca elegantissima **False Aralia**	Tree	High	Moist
Dracaena fragrans **Cornstalk Plant**	Tree	Low to Medium	Moist
Dracaena marginata **Dragon Tree**	Tree	Medium	Moist
Episcia spp. **Flame Violet**	Bushy/trailing, basket	Medium to High; keep inside	Moist
Euphorbia spp. **Crown of Thorns, Pencil Plant, others**	Bushy to tree	High	Dry
Ferns, Various **Boston, Bird's Nest**	Bushy to trailing, basket	Low to Medium	Moist, high humidity
Ficus spp. **Weeping Fig, Rubber Tree, Fiddle-leaf Fig**	Tree	Medium to High	Moist
Hedera helix **English Ivy**	Trailing/vining, basket	Medium	Moist
Hibiscus	Bushy, large	High	Moist

PLANT SELECTIONS

Name	Shape	Light	Water
Howea forsteriana **Kentia Palm**	Tree	Low to Medium	Moist
Hoya carnosa **Wax Plant**	Trailing/vining, basket	High	Dry
Maranta leuconeura **Prayer Plant**	Bushy	Medium	Moist
Monstera deliciosa **Split-leaf Philodendron**	Vine	Low to Medium	Moist
Orchids, Various	Bushy	Medium to High	Various
Peperomia spp. **Peperomia**	Bushy to trailing, basket	Medium	Dry
Philodendron Self-heading types	Bushy	Medium	Moist
Pilea cadierei **Aluminum Plant**	Bushy	Medium	Moist
Plectranthus spp. **Swedish Ivy**	Trailing/vining, basket	Medium to High	Moist
Rhapis excelsa **Lady Palm**	Small tree, bushy	Medium	Moist
Saintpaulia **African Violet**	Low rosette	High; do not grow outside	Moist
Sansevieria spp. **Mother-in-law Tongue**	Low rosette, upright	Medium	Dry
Scindapsus or *Epipremnum* **Pothos, Ivy**	Trailing/vining, basket	Low to Medium	Moist
Spathiphyllum **Peace Lily**	Bushy	Low to Medium (no direct sun)	Constantly moist
Syngonium polypodium **Tri-leaf Woner**	Bushy to vining, basket	Low to Medium	Moist
Tradescantia spp. **Wandering Jew**	Trailing/vining, basket	Medium	Moist
Zygocactus hybrids **Holiday Cactus**	Bushy succulent	Medium to High	Moist, dry in fall

LIGHT: Low—North window, 75 to 200 foot-candles, no direct sun outdoors; Medium—South window in summer, 200 to 500 foot-candles, minimal direct sun outdoors (early morning); High—East or West window, South window in winter, 500 to 1000 foot-candles, four to six hours of direct sun outside, preferably morning.

WATER: Moist—allow to dry slightly before watering, feels dry when finger inserted about one inch; Dry—allow soil to dry before watering, pencil or chopstick inserted 2/3 into pot is dry.

LOUISIANA COOPERATIVE EXTENSION SERVICE

a branch of the Louisiana State University Agricultural Center

Phone Numbers for Parish Offices

Acadia Parish	318/788-8821
Allen Parish	318/639-4376
Ascension Parish	504/621-5799
Assumption Parish	504/369-6386
Avoyelles Parish	318/253-7526
Beauregard Parish	318/463-7006
Bienville Parish	318/263-7400
Bossier Parish	318/965-2326
Caddo Parish	318/673-7700
Calcasieu Parish	318/475-8812
Caldwell Parish	318/649-2663
Cameron Parish	318/775-5516
Catahoula Parish	318/744-5442
Claiborne Parish	318/927-3110
Concordia Parish	318/336-5315
DeSoto Parish	318/872-0533
East Baton Rouge Parish	225/389-3056
East Carroll Parish	318/559-1459
East Feliciana Parish	504/683-3101
Evangeline Parish	318/363-5646
Franklin Parish	318/435-7551
Grant Parish	318/627-3675
Iberia Parish	318/369-4441
Iberville Parish	225/687-5155
Jackson Parish	318/259-5690
Jefferson Parish	504/838-1170
Jefferson Davis Parish	318/824-1773
Lafayette Parish	318/291-7090
Lafourche Parish	504/446-1316
LaSalle Parish	318/992-2205
Lincoln Parish	318/251-5134
Livingston Parish	225/686-3020
Madison Parish	318/574-2465
Morehouse Parish	318/281-5741
Natchitoches Parish	318/357-2224
Orleans Parish	504/482-1107
Ouachita Parish	318/323-2251
Plaquemines Parish	504/682-0081 Ext. 2233
Pointe Coupee Parish	504/638-5533
Rapides Parish	318/473-6605
Red River Parish	318/932-4342
Richland Parish	318/728-3216
Sabine Parish	318/256-3406
St. Bernard Parish	504/278-4234
St. Charles Parish	504/783-6231
St. Helena Parish	225/222-4136
St. James Parish	225/562-2320
St. John Parish	504/497-3261
St. Landry Parish	318/948-0561
St. Martin Parish	318/332-2181
St. Mary Parish	318/828-4100 Ext. 300
St. Tammany Parish	504/875-2635
Tangipahoa Parish	504/748-9381
Tensas Parish	318/766-3222
Terrebonne Parish	504/873-6495
Union Parish	318/368-9935
Vermilion Parish	318/898-4335
Vernon Parish	318/239-3231
Washington Parish	504/839-7855
Webster Parish	318/371-1371
West Baton Rouge Parish	225/336-2416
West Carroll Parish	318/428-3571
West Feliciana Parish	225/635-3614
Winn Parish	318/628-4528

PLANTING CHARTS

Warm-Season Annuals

Name	Plant Seed or Transplant
+Angelonia++	March to August
Ageratum	March to October
Amaranthus++	April to August
Balsam++	April to August
+Blue Daze+++	April to Agusut
Celosia	April to August
Cleome++	March to October
+Coleus+++	April to August
Cosmos++	March to August
Dahlberg Daisy++	March to October
+Dusty Miller	March to October
+Four-o'clock++	April to August
Gaillardia	April to August
Gomphrena	April to August
+Impatiens+++	April to August
+Lantana+++	March to September
Marigold++	March to October
Melampodium++	March to August
Narrow-leaf Zinnia	March to August
+Ornamental Pepper	April to September
+Pentas+++	April to September
Perilla	March to August
+Periwinkle	May to August
Portulaca++	April to August
+Purslane	April to August
Rudbeckia	April to August
+Salvia	March to October
+Scaevola+++	April to August
Sunflower++	March to October
Tithonia++	April to August
Torenia	April to August
+Verbena	March to October
+Wax Begonia++	March to August
Zinnia++	March to August

Cool-Season Annuals

Name	Plant Seed or Transplant
Alyssum+	September to February
Annual Baby's Breath	September to February
Annual Candytuft	September to March
Annual Phlox+	September to March
Bachelor's Button+	September to March
Calendula+	September to March
Dahlberg Daisy+	September to March
Delphinium++	September to February
Dianthus	September to March
Dusty Miller	August to April
English Daisy	September to February
Forget-me-not+	September to February
Geranium++	August to March
Hollyhock	August to March
Larkspur+	October to Dec. (direct seed)
Nasturtium+	September to November
	February to March
Nemophila	September to October
Nicotiana	September to March
Nierembergia	September to March
Ornamental Cabbage and Kale	September to February
Pansy++	August to November (seed)
	October to February (trans)
Petunia++	September to March
Poppies+	October to Dec. (direct seed)
Snapdragon	August to March
Statice	September to March
Stock	September to March
Sweet Pea+	October to Dec. (direct seed)
Toadflax	October to March
Virginia Stock+	October to March
Viola	August to November (seed)
	October to February (trans)
Wall Flower	October to March

Warm-Season Annuals:
+   Tender perennials
++   Easily direct-seeded
+++ Best to buy transplants
At the beginning of the planting season, you can plant seed in flats or directly in beds, or you can use transplants. Use transplants if you are planting towards the end of an annual's planting season.

Cool-Season Annuals:
+   Easily direct-seeded
++   Best to buy transplants
At the beginning of the planting season, you can plant seed in flats or directly in beds, or you can use transplants. Use transplants if you are planting towards the end of an annual's planting season.

Although many bedding plants prefer partial sun to full sun (about six to eight hours of direct sun), the following will do well in shade, or even prefer shade or partial shade (about two to four hours of direct sun).

Warm-Season: Balsam•, Cleome•, Coleus•, Four o'clocks•, Impatiens, Pentas•, Salvia•, Torenia•, Wax Begonia; *Cool-Season:* Forget-me-not, Nasturtium•, Nemophila, Nicotiana•, Pansy•, Viola•

•Also will do well in full sun

PLANTING CHARTS

Spring Bulbs

Name	Plant	Depth	Spacing	Blooms
Allium (Flowering Onion)	Sept. to Dec.	2 in. to 4 in.	4 in. to 12 in.	April to May
Anemone	Oct. to early Dec.	1 in.	6 in. to 8 in.	March to May
Arisaema	Oct. to early Dec.	2 in. to 4 in.	8 in. to 12 in.	March to May
Bletilla (Ground Orchid)	Sept. to April	1 in.	6 in. to 8 in.	March to April
Brodiaea 'Koningin Fabiola'	Oct. to early Dec.	2 in. to 4 in.	2 in. to 4 in.	April
Crocus	Oct. to early Dec.	2 in.	2 in. to 3 in.	Feb. to March
Hippeastrum (Amaryllis)	Sept. to Dec. in pots. April in garden.	Neck exposed	8 in. to 12 in.	Nov. to Jan. in pots. April in garden.
Hyacinth	late Dec. to early Jan.	3 in. to 4 in.	4 in. to 6 in.	March
Iris, Dutch (bulbous)	Oct. to early Dec.	2 in. to 4 in.	4 in. to 6 in.	March to April
Iris, Louisiana, Siberian, Japanese, Bearded (rhizomatous)	Sept. to Feb.	Just below soil surface	12 in. to 18 in.	March to May
Leucojum (Snowflake)	Oct. to early Dec.	4 in.	4 in. to 6 in.	April
Lily, Easter	Oct. to early Dec.	4 in.	8 in. to 12 in.	April to May
Muscari (Grape Hyacinth)	Oct. to early Dec.	2 in.	2 in. to 4 in.	March to April
Narcissus (including **Daffodils**)	Oct. to early Dec.	4 in.	4 in. to 6 in.	Jan. to April
Ornithogalum (Star of Bethlehem)	Oct. to early Dec.	4 in.	4 in.	April
Ranunculus	Oct. to early Dec.	1 in.	8 in.	April to May
Scilla peruviana (**Cuban Lily**)	Oct. to early Dec.	2 in. to 4 in.	8 in. to 12 in.	April
Spanish Bluebell (*Hyacinthioides hispanicus*)	Oct. to early Dec.	4 in. to 6 in.	4 in.	April
Sparaxis	Oct. to early Dec.	1 in. to 2 in.	3 in. to 4 in.	April to May
Spring Starflower (*Ipheion uniflorum*)	Oct. to early Dec.	2 in. to 3 in.	3 in. to 6 in.	March to May
Sisyrinchium	Oct. to early Dec.	2 in.	4 in. to 6 in.	April
Tulip	Late Dec. to early Jan.	4 in. to 6 in.	4 in. to 8 in.	March to April
Zantedeschia (Calla Lily)	Sept. to Nov. (bulbs). March to May (plants).	2 in. to 3 in.	12 in. to 18 in.	April to May

Notes: Because they bloom in the spring, **amaryllis, Louisiana iris, calla lily,** and **bletilla** are grouped with the spring bulbs. However, their foliage persists through the summer, and they should be handled as summer bulbs.

The following are some of the spring bulbs that tend to be reliably long-lived here and bloom for several years at least. *Narcissus* cultivars such as **paperwhites, Chinese sacred lily,** 'Soleil d'Or', 'Grand Primo', 'Cheerfulness', **jonquils**, 'Sweetness', 'Trevethian', 'Peeping Tom', 'February Gold', 'Thalia', 'Ice Wings', and 'Petrel'; and larger flowered **daffodil** cultivars such as 'Ice Follies', 'Carlton', 'Fortune', and 'Unsurpassable' (the farther north you garden in Louisiana, the more **daffodil** and **narcissus** cultivars will successfully rebloom). Other reblooming bulbs include **calla lily, snowflake,** some **flowering onions, ground orchid, amaryllis,** Spanish bluebells, spring **starflower,** *Tulipa clusiana* var. *chrysantha*, **Dutch iris, Louisiana iris,** yellow flag, blue flag, lapeirousia, sisyrinchium, *Scilla peruviana*, and **Easter lily**.

PLANTING CHARTS

Summer Bulbs

Name	Plant	Depth	Spacing	Blooms
Achimenes	May to June	1 in.	4 in. to 6 in.	June to Oct.
Agapanthus	March to Aug.	1 in.	8 in. to 12 in.	May to June
Alpinia (Shell Ginger)	March to Aug.	1 in.	1 ft. to 5 ft.	May to June
Belamcanda (Blackberry Lily)	March to April	1 in.	8 in. to 12 in.	June to Aug.
Caladium	April to July	1 in. to 2 in.	6 in. to 12 in.	Foliage May to Oct.
Canna	March to Aug.	1 in. to 2 in.	12 in. to 18 in.	May to Nov.
Clivia	March to Aug.	1 in.	18 in. to 24 in.	March to May
Costus (Spril Ginger)	March to Aug.	1 in.	1 ft. to 2 ft.	June to Oct.
Crinum	March to Aug.	Neck exposed	1 ft. to 3 ft.	April to Oct.
Curcuma (Hidden Lily Ginger)	March to Aug.	1 in. to 2 in.	1 ft. to 2 ft.	May to Aug.
Dahlia	March to May	4 in.	8 in. to 18 in.	May to Oct.
Dietes (African Iris)	March to Sept.	1 in.	1 ft. to 3 ft.	April to June
Elephant Ear (Colocasia, Alocasia)	April to Aug.	Neck exposed	2 ft. to 3 ft.	Foliage spring to frost
Eucomia (Pineapple Lily)	Sept. to Nov.	Neck exposed	18 in.	May
Gladiolus	Feb. to March	4 in. to 6 in.	6 in.	April to June
Globba (Dancing Lady Ginger)	April to Sept.	1 in.	1 ft.	July to Oct.
Gloriosa Lily	March to April	4 in.	8 in. to 12 in.	May to Aug.
Habranthus	Sept. to Dec.	1 in.	8 in.	May to July
Hedychium (Butterfly Ginger)	March to Sept.	1 in.	1 ft. to 2 ft.	May to Nov.
Hymenocallis (Spider Lily)	March to Sept.	Neck exposed	1 ft. to 3 ft.	June to Aug.
Kaempferia (Peacock Ginger)	April to Aug.	1 in.	8 in. to 12 in.	June to Sept.
Iris (Bearded, Siberian)	Oct. to Feb.	1 in.	12 in.	April to May
Lily (Philippine, Formosa, Tiger)	March	4 in. to 6 in.	1 ft.	July to Sept.
Lycoris (Spider Lily, Naked Ladies)	March to Aug.	3 in. to 4 in.	4 in.	Sept. to Oct.
Neomarica (Walking Iris)	March to Aug.	1 in.	8 in. to 12 in.	May
Oxalis (*Oxalis regnellii* and *O. triangularis*)	March to Sept.	1 in. to 2 in.	6 in. to 8 in.	March to Nov.
Sprekelia (Aztec Lily)	March to April	Neck exposed	8 in. to 12 in.	May
Tigridia (Tiger Flower)	March to May	4 in.	8 in.	May to June
Tuberose (Polianthes)	Feb. to April	1 in. to 2 in.	8 in.	June to July
Tulbaghia (Society Garlic)	March to Sept.	1 in.	10 in.	April to Nov.
Zephyranthes (Rain Lily)	Oct. to Feb.	1 in. to 2 in.	2 in. to 3 in.	Spring to fall
Zingiber (Pine Cone Ginger)	March to Sept.	1 in.	1 ft. to 2 ft.	July to Sept.

Note: Plant dormant bulbs, divisions, or container-grown plants early in the planting time given. Later in the planting time given, it's best to choose container-grown bulbs in active growth.

PLANTING CHARTS

Vegetables

Crop	Planting Dates		Seeds/Plants per 50 feet	Inches Between Plants	Days to Harvest
	Spring	Fall			
Asparagus (plants)	1/1 to 3/31	10/1 to 1/1	25	24	
Beans, Snap, Bush	2/15 to 5/15	8/10 to 9/10	1/4 lb.	2 to 3	48 to 55
Beans, Snap, Pole	2/15 to 5/15	8/10 to 8/10	1 oz.	12	60 to 66
Beans, Lima, Bush	3/1 to 5/30	8/1 to 9/1	1/4 lb.	3 to 4	60 to 67
Beans, Lima, Bush	3/1 to 5/30	8/1 to 9/1	1/8 lb.	12	77 to 90
Beets	1/15 to 3/1	8/15 to 11/1	1/2 oz.	2 to 4	55 to 60
Broccoli (seed)	1/1 to 1/31	7/15 to 10/1	1/64 oz.	12 to 24	110 to 130
Broccoli (plants)	2/1 to 3/1	8/15 to 11/1	33 to 25	12 to 24	70 to 90
Brussels Sprouts		8/15 to 11/1	1/64 oz.	18 to 24	130
Cabbage (seed)	12/1 to 1/15	7/15 to 11/30	1/64 oz.	12 to 24	95 to 105
Cabbage (plants)	1/15 to 3/1	9/1 to 1/15	33 to 25	12 to 24	65 to 75
Cantaloupe	3/1 to 5/31	6/1 to 8/1	1/4 oz.	18 to 24	80 to 85
Carrots	1/15 to 3/1	9/1 to 11/1	1/8 oz.	1 to 2	70 to 75
Cauliflower (seed)	1/15 to 2/15	7/15 to 9/15	1/32 oz.	18 to 24	85 to 95
Cauliflower (plants)	2/15 to 3/15	8/15 to 10/15	1/32 oz.	18 to 24	55 to 65
Celery		10/1 to 12/1	1/128 oz.	8 to 12	210
Chard, Swiss	1/15 to 5/1	8/15 to 11/1	1/4 oz.	6 to 12	55
Chinese Cabbage	1/15 to 2/15	7/15 to 10/1	1/64 oz.	12 to 18	90 to 110
Collards	2/15 to 5/31	6/1 to 11/1	1/32 oz.	6 to 12	75
Corn, Sweet	2/15 to 5/15		1.5 oz.	10 to 12	70 to 92
Cucumber	3/1 to 6/1	8/1 to 9/15	1/8 oz.	12 to 18	50 to 65
Eggplant (seed)	1/15 to 6/1		1/64 oz.		140
Eggplant (plants)	4/1 to 8/1		25 to 30	18 to 24	85
Garlic (toes)		10/1 to 11/30	1 pound	4 to 6	210
Kohlrabi	1/1 to 3/31	8/15 to 10/30	1/32 oz.	6	55 to 75
Lettuce	1/1 to 3/1	9/1 to 11/1	1/64 oz.	4 to 12	45 to 80
Mustard Greens	1/1 to 3/15	8/1 to 12/31	1/16 oz.	2 to 6	35 to 50
Okra	4/15 to 5/31	6/1 to 8/1	1/4 oz.	12	60

PLANTING CHARTS

Vegetables

Crop	Planting Dates Spring	Fall	Seeds/Plants per 50 feet	Inches Between Plants	Days to Harvest
Onion, Leek (seed)		9/20 to 10/31	1/16 oz.		135 to 210
Onion, Leek (sets/plants)	12/15 to 1/30	1/30	1/16 oz.	2 to 4 (onion) 6 (leek)	120 to 150
Peanut	4/1 to 7/15		1/4 pound	4 to 8	110 to 120
Peas, English and Snow	12/15 to 2/15	9/1 to 10/1	1 to 2 oz.	2 to 3	60 to 70
Peas, Southern	3/15 to 8/10		2 to 4 oz.	4 to 6	70 to 80
Pepper, Hot (seed)	1/15 to 5/1		1/32 oz.		100
Pepper, Hot (plants)	3/15 to 7/15		33 to 50	12 to 18	40
Pepper, Bell (seed)	1/15 to 2/28	6/5 to 8/5	1/32 oz.		120
Pepper, Bell (plants)	3/15 to 5/15	7/15 to 8/15	33 to 80	15 to 18	70 to 80
Potato, Irish (rubers)	1/20 to 2/28	8/15 to 9/10	5 to 6 pounds	12	90 to 120
Potato, Sweet (slips)	4/10 to 7/1		33 to 40 plants	12	90 to 120
Pumpkin	3/15 to 7/31	8/1 to 9/15	1/4 oz.	36 to 60	90 to 120
Radish	1/15 to 3/31	9/1 to 11/1	1/2 oz.	1 to 2	22 to 35
Rutabaga		7/1 to 2/28	1/32 oz.	4 to 8	50
Shallot (sets)		7/1 to 2/28	100 to 150	12	50
Spinach		10/1 to 2/28	1/8 oz.	3 to 6	45 to 55
Squash, Summer	3/1 to 8/15		1/4 oz.	36	50 to 90
Tomato (seed)	1/1 to 3/15	6/1 to 7/1	1/128 oz.		100 to 115
Tomato (plants)	3/1 to 5/1	7/1 to 8/15	25 to 33 plants	16 to 24	60 to 75
Turnip		8/1 to 2/18	1/16 oz.	2 to 6	40 to 60
Watermelon	3/15 to 8/1		1/8 oz.	48	90 to 110

Information from Louisiana Cooperative Extension publication *Louisiana Vegetable Planting Guide.*

PLANTING CHARTS

Cool-Season Annual Herbs

(Grown from September to June; hardy)

Name	Height (inches)	Spacing (inches)	Cultural Hints	Uses
Anise *Pimpinella anisum*	24	18	Seeds or transplants in fall, transplants in early spring, sun	Leaves and dried seeds provide licorice flavor
Arugula *Eruca versicaria*	12 to 36	12	Seeds or transplants fall to early spring; sun	Leaves and flowers used in salads
Borage *Borago officinalis*	24 to 36	18	Seeds or transplants fall to early spring; sun; reseeds	Attractive, edible blue flowers use in salads and drinks
Chamomile *Chamaemdum nobile*	8	10	Seeds or transplants in fall, transplants in early spring; sun	Flowers used in teas
Chervil *Anthriscus cerefolium*	10	12	Seeds or transplants in fall, transplants in early spring; sun to part shade	Aromatic leaves used in cooking
Coriander/Cilantro *Coriandrum sativum*	12 to 24	12	Seeds or transplants fall to early spring; sun to part shade	Seeds used in confections, leaves in salsas and cooking
Dill *Anethum graveolens*	12 to 36	12	Seeds or transplant fall through late spring; protect if temps. go below the mid 20s; sun to part shade	Leaves and seeds used in flavoring and pickling
Fennel *Foeniculum vulgare*	24 to 48	18	Seeds or transplants in fall through late spring; sun to part shade; may survive more than one season	Anise flavor in leaves and dried seeds; fleshy leaf bases eaten as a vegetable
Parsley *Petroselinum crispim*	12 to 24	12 to 18	Seeds or transplants fall to early spring; sun to part shade	Curly leaf good ornamental, flat leaf more flavorful; culinary

Warm-Season Annual Herbs

(Grown from March to November; tender)

Name	Height (inches)	Spacing (inches)	Cultural Hints	Uses
Basil *Ocimum basilicum*	12 to 36	12 to 18	Seeds or transplants after danger of frost; transplants through Aug.; sun	Foliage and flowers popular culinary seasoning
Perilla *Perilla crispum*	24 to 30	18	Seeds or transplants after danger of frost, transplants through Aug.; reseeds; sun to part shade	Uniquely flavored leaves used in teas, salads and cooking
Sesame *Astragalus sesameus*	30 to 36	12 to 18	Seeds or transplants after danger of frost; sun	Seeds used in baking and cooking
Summer Savory *Satureja hortensis*	18	12	Transplants after danger of frost; short-lived in LA.; sun	Leaves used in salads and cooking

PLANTING CHARTS

Perennial Herbs

(Trees, shrubs, and herbaceous perennials; planted year-round with fall and spring preferred))

Name	Height (feet)	Spacing (feet)	Cultural Hints	Uses
Bay *Laurus nobilis*	15	5	Tree or large shrub; protect below 20 degrees; sun	Leaves used in cooking; good container plant in north LA.
Beebalm *Monarda didyma,* *M. fistulosa*	2 to 3	1	Seeds in spring; transplants any time; divisions fall or spring; spreads rapidly; sun to part sun	Showy flowers, aromatic seed heads; leaves used in tea
Burnet *Poterium sanguisorba*	1/2 to 1	1 to 1/2	Well-drained soil; full to part sun; seeds or divisions in spring	Cucumber-flavored leaves used fresh in salads; attractive evergreen foliage
Catnip *Nepeta cataria*	2	1 to 2	Well-drained soil; seeds, transplants, or divisions; sun to part shade; often short-lived in LA.	Leaves used in teas and seasonings; cats love it
Chives *Allium schoenoprasum*	1	1/2	Seeds, transplants or divisions; divide in fall when overcrowded; sun	Leaves used for mild onion flavor; attractive, lavender, edible flowers
Chives, Garlic *Allium tuberosum*	1	1/2 to 1	Seeds, transplants, or divisions; divide spring or fall; sun to part shade	Leaves used for mild garlic flavor; attractive, white, edible flowers
Geraniums, Scented *Pelargonium* spp.	1 to 2	1 to 2	Well-drained soil; full to part sun; transplants or rooted cuttings; protect below mid 20s; may be short-lived	Aromatic leaves used in jellies, cakes, and potpourri; grow in containers in N. LA.
Horseradish *Armoracia rusticana*	2	1	Rich soil; divided every 1 to 2 years in fall; sun	Roots used for strong, pungent flavor
Lavender *Lavandula* spp.	2	1 to 2	Needs perfect drainage; often more successful in pots, difficult due to hot, humid summers; sun	Flowers dried for sachets and potpourri; some culinary uses
Lemon Balm *Melissa officinalis*	1 to 1 1/2	1 1/2	Easy; seeds, transplants, or divisions; full sun to part shade	Lemon-scented leaves culinary uses as well as teas and potpourri
Lemon Grass *Cymbopogon citratus*	3	2 to 3	Transplants or divisions in spring; protect below low 20s; sun to part sun; good container plant in N. LA.	Lemon-flavored leaf bases used in cooking
Mexican Tarragon, Mexican Mint, Marigold *Tagetes lucida*	2 to 3	1	Transplants after danger of frost; dormant in winter; sun to part sun	Foliage has pungent tarragon flavor; attractive, gold, edible flowers in fall
Mexican Oregano *Poliomentha longiflora*	2 to 3	2 to 3	Transplants any time; shrubby; sun to part sun	Foliage provides pungent oregano substitute

PLANTING CHARTS

Perennial Herbs

Name	Height (feet)	Spacing (feet)	Cultural Hints	Uses
Mints, Various *Mentha* spp. and hybrids	¹/₂ to 2	1	Plant transplants or divisions	Aromatic foliage used for flavorings, teas; spearmint and peppermint most popular
Oregano *Origanum vulgare*	¹/₂ to 2	1 to 1¹/₂	Seeds, transplants, or divisions in spring; sun to part sun	Foliage has many culinary uses; good ground cover
Rosemary *Rosmarinus officinalis*	2 to 3	2	Well-drained, alkaline soil; protect below 20 degrees; transplants or rooted cuttings in spring; sun to part sun	Foliage has many culinary uses; woody shrub
Sage *Salvia officinalis*	1 to 2	1 to 2	Well-drained, alkaline soil; difficult due to hot, humid summers; short-lived; sun	Seasoning for meats and dressings
Sorrel *Rumex acetosa*	1	1	Transplants or divisions in fall or spring; sun	Acidic, sour foliage used in salads
Sweet Marjoram *Origanum marjorana*	1	1¹/₂	Well-drained soil; protect below 20 degrees; transplants or divisions in spring	Foliage has many culinary uses
Tarragon *Artemisia dracunculus*	1 to 2	1 to 2	Plant transplants in fall; will not tolerate summer heat, grow as a cool-season annual; part sun	Foliage has mild anise flavor; has many culinary uses
Thyme *Thymus vulgaris*	¹/₂ to 1	1	Well-drained, alkaline soil; plant transplants in fall; difficult due to hot, humid summers; short-lived; sun to part sun	Foliage has many culinary uses

Information from the Louisiana Cooperative Extension Service *Louisiana Master Gardener Handbook*

PLANTING CHARTS

Perennials

Name	Light	Type and Size	Flowers	Comments
Acanthus mollis **Acanthus**	Part sun to part shade	Dormant in late summer; 24 inches	Erect spike, white and lavender; late spring	Dramatic foliage; needs excellent drainage
Achillea millefolium **Yarrow**	Full sun to part shade	Evergreen in mild winters; 12 inches	Flat clusters of various colors on stalks to 24 inches; early summer	Ferny, aromatic foliage; very easy to grow; flowers dry well; native and non-natives
Acorus gramineus 'Variegatus' **Variegated Acorus**	Part shade to shade	Evergreen; 12 inches	Not significant	Does well in poorly drained soil; attractive grass-like foliage
Artemisia ludoviciana *A.* 'Powis Castle' **Artemisia**	Full to part sun	Semi-dormant in winter; 2 to 3 feet	Not significant	Outstanding silvery foliage; cut back winter/spring
Asarum spp. **Wild Ginger**	Part shade to shade	Evergreen; 6 to 8 inches	Small brown, not significant	Shiny kidney-shaped dark green leaves
Asclepias curassavica *A. tuberosa* **Butterfly Weed**	Full to part sun	Dormnt in winter; 1 to 3 feet	Showy orange flowers in summer	Excellent nectar food for butterflies, larval food for Monarchs; native
Asparagus densiflorus 'Sprengeri' **Asparagus Fern**	Full sun to shade	Evergreen, dormant if low 20s occur; 1 to 2 feet (zone 9 only)	Tiny, white to pale pink, summer; scarlet pea-size fruit	Tough, indestructible in the garden or in containers; mulch crown in winter
Aspidistra elatior **Cast-iron Plant**	Shade to full shade	Evergreen; 2½ feet	Not significant	Prune out unattractive leaves as necessary; tough; easy to grow
Aster spp. and hybrids **Aster**	Full to part sun	Dormant in winter; 1 to 5 feet, depending on type	Showy, daisy-like in clusters, many colors; late summer, fall	Excellent for late-season color; cut back hard after bloomings; native and non-natives
Chlorophytum comosum 'Variegatum' **Spider Plant**	Part shade to full shade	Evergreen, dormant if low 20s occur; 1 foot (zone 9 only)	Not significant; remove flower stalks to keep the plants looking neat	Normally thought of as a houseplant; the roots will survive the low teens
Coreopsis lanceolata **Coreopsis; Tickseed**	Full to part sun	Dormant in winter; 24 inches	Yellow, gold, mahogany daisy-like flower; early to midsummer	Very showy flowers and easy to grow from seed; native

PLANTING CHARTS

Perennials

Name	Light	Type and Size	Flowers	Comments
Cuphea micropetala **Cigar Plant**	Full to part sun	Dormant after first freezes; 2 to 5 feet	Yellow and red-orange fall to winter, and spring if mild winter; early to midsummer	Cut back hard after freezes brown the foliage; can spread aggressively
Dendranthema x morifolium cultivars **Garden Mums**	Full to part sun	Dormant in winter; 1 to 2 feet	Showy daisy-like flowers in many colors; fall	Cut back hard in winter, divide in early spring
Echinacea purpurea **Purple Coneflower**	Full to part sun	Dormant in winter; 2 feet	Purple or white daisy-like flowers with a prominent cone; summer	Cut back after flowering; easily grown native
Eupatorium coeolestinum **Wild** or **Hardy Ageratum**	Full sun to part shade	Dormant in winter; 2 to 3 feet	Soft lavender-blue fluffy flowers, primarily in fall; some blooms in early summer	Spreads rapidly; native; Joe-Pye Weed (*E. maculatum* and *E. purpureu*m) are also good
Hemerocallis hybrids **Daylily**	Full to part sun	Semi-dormant in winter; 1½ to 3 feet in bloom	Larger flowers on stalks in many colors; early to late summer	Reliable, easy perennial; divide in Sept. or Oct.
Hibiscus moscheutos **Hardy Hibiscus**	Full to part sun	Dormant in winter; 2 to 4 feet	Very large plate-sized blooms in white, pink, or red; early to late summer	Reliable; spectacular in bloom; easy to grow from seed; cut back in fall
Hosta spp. and hybrids **Hosta; Plantain Lily**	Part shade to shade	Dormant in winter; 6 to 24 inches	Lavender or white, bell-shaped flowers on stalks to 3 feet, some fragrant; summer	Excellent for shady areas; snails and slugs may be a major problem
Leucanthemum x superbum **Shasta Daisy**	Full sun to part shade	Dormant in winter; 24 inches in bloom	White daisy flowers with yellow centers; spring	Problems with rotting out in summer increase closer to the coast; provide good drainage
Farfugium japonicum **Ligularia**	Part shade to shade	Evergreen; 18 inches	Clusters of 1-inch yellow daisy-like flowers; late summer to fall	Excellent texture plant for shady beds; leaves look like lily pads

LIGHT REQUIREMENTS:
FULL SUN: Eight hours or more of direct sun
PART SUN: About six hours of direct sun
PART SHADE: About four hours of direct sun
FULL SHADE: Little or no direct sun
SHADE: About two hours of direct sun

PLANTING CHARTS

Perennials

Name	Light	Type and Size	Flowers	Comments
Monarda fistulosa *M. didyma* **Beebalm**	Full to part sun	Dormant in winter; 2 to 3 feet	Flower heads in various colors; summer	Cut back hard after flowering for repeat bloom; aromatic foliage
Phlox divaricata **Blue Phlox** or **Louisiana Phlox**	Full sun to part shade	Dormant in winter; 12 inches	Lavender-blue to purple flower clusters; spring	Flowers occur about four weeks; trim back when finished
Phlox paniculata **Garden Phlox** (Summer or Border)	Full to part sun	Dormant in winter; 2 to 3 feet	Various colors; early to late summer; most varieties will not thrive here in zones 8 and 9	Those with magenta flowers, such as 'Robert Poore', are most reliable
Physostegia virginiana **Obedient Plant**	Full to part sun	Dormant in winter; 2 to 3 feet	Spikes of rosy purple or white; midsummer	Staking is recommended; spreads rapidly
Rudbeckia hirta 'Angustifolia' **Black-Eyed Susan**	Full to part sun	Dormant in winter; 2 feet	Golden daisies with dark brown centers; midsummer	Reliable, long-lived, and easy; cut back after flowering; native
Ruellia brittoniana **Ruellia; Summer** or **Mexican Petunia**	Full sun to part shade	Dormant after first freezes; 1 to 5 feet, depending on cultivar	Lavender, purple, or pink; blooms spring to early winter	Very easy and reliable; self-seeds readily; new cultivars include dwarfs and variegated foliage; native and non-natives
Salvia spp. and hybrids **Salvia; Sage**	Full sun to part shade	Evergreen in some areas if winter is mild; 1 to 6 feet, depending on type	Spikes in various colors, especially purples, reds, and blues; spring, summer, and especially fall	A large group that includes many excellent plants for Louisiana gardens; trim in late summer and cut back in late winter; native and non-natives
Saxifraga stolonifera **Strawberry Begonia**	Shade	Evergreen; 4 inches	Airy panicles of small white flowers; spring	Attractive foliage dark green with silver veins
Sedum spp. **Sedum; Stonecrop**	Full to part sun	Usually evergreen succulent; 4 to 12 inches	Various colors of star-shaped flowers generally in clusters	Many types; some do better than others; needs well-drained soil
Solidago spp. and hybrids **Goldenrod**	Full to part sun	Dormant in winter; 2 to 6 feet, depending on type	Spikes of golden yellow; late summer to fall	Does not cause hayfever; excellent tough natives for late-season color
Spigelia marilandica **Indian Pink**	Part shade to shade	Dormant in winter; 12 to 18 inches	Clusters of red and yellow tubular flowers; spring	Delightful native for shady areas

PLANTING CHARTS

Perennials

Name	Light	Type and Size	Flowers	Comments
Stokesia laevis **Stokes' Aster**	Full to part sun	Dormant in winter; 1 to 2 feet in bloom	Showy lavender-blue flowers in early summer	Reliable, easy, long-lived native
Tradescantia virginiana **Spiderwort**	Full sun to part shade	Dormant in winter; 1 to 2½ feet	Clusters of purple, blue, rose, or pink; spring/early summer	Native wildflower tolerates damp conditions; easy and reliable
Veronica spicata **Veronica; Speedwell**	Full to part sun	Dormant in winter; 1 to 2 feet	Spikes of purple, blue, or rose in early to midsummer	Cut back faded flower spikes to encourage more bloom
Viola odorata **Violet**	Part shade to shade	Evergreen; 4 inches	Small, fragrant purple flowers; spring	Nice for edging or detail planting shady beds

LIGHT REQUIREMENTS:
FULL SUN: Eight hours or more of direct sun
PART SUN: About six hours of direct sun
PART SHADE: About four hours of direct sun
FULL SHADE: Little or no direct sun
SHADE: About two hours of direct sun

PLANTING CHARTS

Types of Roses

MODERN ROSES

(Types developed after 1867, the year the first hybrid tea was introduced.)

HYBRID TEA Large, exquisitely shaped flowers (generally produced singly on long stems) and an amazing range of colors are the hallmarks of hybrid teas. The flowers of many cultivars are richly fragrant. The plants range in size from 3 to more than 6 feet and can be leggy and awkward in appearance. Some cultivars may be highly susceptible to blackspot; these roses generally require regular spraying and pruning to remain healthy and vigorous. Repeat-flowering.

POLYANTHA Excellent in landscape plantings, polyanthas are vigorously growing, bushy plants that produce small flowers in large clusters or sprays. Most are relatively disease resistant, and they are some of the more reliable and easy-to-grow roses in our state. Many cultivars are fairly small, staying around 3 feet, while others can get quite a bit larger. Repeat-flowering.

GRANDIFLORA Tall plants (up to 7 feet) produce hybrid tea–like flowers singly or in clusters on long stems. Comparable to hybrid teas, they may also require similar care. Repeat-flowering.

FLORIBUNDA A useful type of rose for landscape planting, the floribunda's shrubby growth is less ungainly than that of hybrid teas. The flowers are small, often brightly colored, and produced in clusters. Fragrance is light or lacking entirely. Repeat-flowering.

CLIMBERS AND **RAMBLERS** Many types of roses will produce long canes that can be tied or trained on a support. Some roses have been bred to climb while others are vigorous mutations of bush roses. Climbing roses generally do not "climb" the way vines do and must be tied or woven onto supports.

MINIATURES Tiny to small bushes generally under 2 feet, miniature roses are delightful in containers. They are very hardy and will easily tolerate winter weather when planted in the ground. On a small scale (less than an inch), the flowers are similar to hybrid teas and come in many colors. Repeat-flowering.

SHRUB ROSES A catchall name for roses that tend to be bushy and useful for landscape planting. Includes English roses, ground cover roses, landscape roses, hedge roses, and others. Repeat-flowering.

OLD GARDEN ROSES

(Types developed before 1867. The term "old garden rose" is used for many distinctly different types, and some types and varieties grow better in Louisiana than others. The following are just a few of the many types.)

CHINA The first repeat-blooming roses, the flowers are produced constantly and have thin, delicate petals. The foliage is neat, dark green, pointed, and rarely bothered by blackspot. These roses have a bushy, twiggy growth habit that fits in well with other landscape plantings. Repeat-flowering.

TEA Wonderful roses for Louisiana, teas produce relatively large flowers in pastel shades and light reds. The fragrant flowers are produced continuously on robust bushes that are rugged and disease resistant. Repeat-flowering.

NOISETTE Mostly climbers, although a few are robust shrubs, these roses thrive in the Deep South. The pastel-colored flowers are fragrant and produced in clusters that hang down from the canes. Repeat-flowering.

BOURBON Though more susceptible to blackspot than the previously mentioned old garden roses, many of the Bourbons will thrive in our climate. The flowers are usually quite fragrant and produced on large, robust shrubs. Many are repeat-flowering.

NOTEWORTHY SPECIES ROSES

(The following once-blooming species roses are excellent, tough roses for Louisiana landscapes.)

Lady Banks Rose (*Rosa banksiae*, white; *R. banksiae* 'Lutea', yellow);
Cherokee Rose (*Rosa laevigata*); **Swamp Rose** (*Rosa palustris scandens*);
Chestnut Rose (*Rosa roxburghii*); **Mccartney Rose** (*Rosa bracteata*); **Musk Rose** (*Rosa moschata*)

PLANTING CHARTS

Shrubs

Name	Size (H × W) and Type	Light	Flowers and Comments
American Beautyberry *Callicarpa americana*	6 by 4 feet; deciduous	Full to part sun	Native shrub suitable for relaxed landscape styles; purple berries in clusters along stems in late summer
Aucuba *Aucuba japonica* 'Variegata'	5 by 3 feet; evergreen	Shade	Dark green and yellow variegation; coarse texture; looks tropical but is quite hardy
Azaleas *Rhododendron* spp. and cultivars	2 by 2 to 10 by 10 feet, depending on cultivar; mostly evergreen	Part shade to sun, depending on cultivar	Many different cultivars of this very popular spring-flowering shrub exist; Indica types are largest and easy to grow! azalea cultivars that bloom at times other than spring are becoming more popular
Banana Shrub *Michelia figo*	15 by 6 feet; evergreen	Full sun to part shade	Very fragrant, banana scented, creamy yellow flowers in April
Butterfly Bush *Buddleja alternifolia* *B. davidii*	6 by 6 feet to 10 feet by 10 feet; deciduous	Full to part sun	Long summer blooming season; spikes of fragrant purple, pink, or white flowers are attractive to butterflies; tends to be short-lived
Camellia *Camellia japonica*	12 by 8 feet; evergreen	Part sun to part shade	Large flowers of striking beauty in shades of red, pink, or white December to March; acid-loving
Chinese Holly *Ilex cornuta* and many cultivars	3 by 3 to 12 by 10 feet, depending on cultivar; evergreen	Full sun to part shade	Most cultivars produce bright red berries fall to spring; leaves are prickly; watch for white scale insects, especially on the back sides of leaves
Chinese Mahonia *Mahonia fortunei*	3 by 3 feet; evergreen	Part morning shade to shade	Excellent small shrub for shady areas; flowers are not significant
Cleyera *Ternstroemia gymnanthera*	8 by 5 feet; evergreen	Morning sun to part shade	Slow growth; good for a hedge in part shade; new growth is burgundy; flowers not significant; best in acidic soils
Dwarf Yaupon *Ilex vomitoria* 'Nana'	3 by 3 feet; evergreen	Sun to part shade	Tough, widely planted shrub with small leaves and a neat growth habit; no berries are generally produced
Fatsia *Fatsia japonica*	5 by 4 feet; evergreen	Part shade to shade	Large tropical leaves on a plant hardy to the mid- to low teens; striking large clusters of small white flowers in early December
Flowering Quince *Chaenomeles speciosa*	8 by 6 feet; deciduous	Full to part sun	Showy flowers in shades of red, pink, or white produced in late winter/early spring before the foliage

PLANTING CHARTS

Shrubs

Name	Size (H × W) and Type	Light	Flowers and Comments
Gardenia *Gardenia jasminoides*	6 by 5 feet; evergreen	Morning full to part sun	Very fragrant, white flowers in May; some flowers in fall; acid-loving; watch for whiteflies
Glossy Abelia *Abelia × grandiflora*	3 by 3 to 10 by 10 feet, depending on cultivar; semi-evergreen	Full to part sun	Long summer blooming season, small white flowers in clusters; pest-free; evergreen in all but the coldest winters
Hydrangea *Hydrangea macrophylla*	4 by 4 feet; deciduous	Part shade to shade; no afternoon sun	Large, showy flower clusters in shades of blue, lavender, or pink in May; prune before the end of July; blue in acidic soils, pink in alkaline soils
Indian Hawthorne *Raphiolepsis indica*	2 by 2 to 5 by 4 feet, depending on cultivar; evergreen	Part sun to full sun	Clusters of pink or white flowers in April; white cultivars generally more more resistant to fireblight; watch for scale
Japanese Viburnum *Viburnum japonicum*	12 by 6 feet; evergreen	Full sun to part shade	Excellent hedge plant; watch for thrips during summer; flowers not significant.
Japanese Yew *Podocarpus macrophyllus*	15 by 6 feet; evergreen	Full sun to part shade	Useful as a hedge or screen; grows well in part shade; flowers not significant
Junipers *Juniperus* spp. and cultivars	1 by 3 to 10 by 10 feet, depending on type; evergreen	Full sun	Large group of plants of various sizes and growth habits; full sun and good drainage are important; spider mites are common
Loropetalum *Loropetalum chinensis*	8 by 6 feet; evergreen	Full sun to part shade	Excellent fast-growing shrub; popular cultivars have bronze to purple foliage and rosy pink flowers
Mock Orange *Philadelphus coronarius*	10 by 6 feet; deciduous	Full sun to part shade	Large, arching branches produce showy fragrant, white flowers in late spring
Nandina *Nandina domestica*	2 by 2 to 6 by 4 feet, depending on cultivar; evergreen	Full sun to part shade	Tough, adaptable shrub that is essentially pest-free
Oakleaf Hydrangea *Hydrangea quercifolia*	8 by 5 feet; deciduous	Part sun to part shade	Large spikes of white flowers in early summer age to old rose by fall; beautiful bark shows well during the leafless winter period; native
Oleander *Nerium oleander*	15 by 10 feet; evergreen	Full to part sun	Large shrub with a long summer blooming season, flowers red, pink, white, or peach; watch for aphids and scale; subject to freeze injury injury by temperatures in low 20s Fahrenheit

PLANTING CHARTS

Shrubs

Name	Size (H × W) and Type	Light	Flowers and Comments
Pineapple Guava *Feijoa sellowiana*	10 by 8 feet; evergreen	Full to part sun	Attractive white and red flowers in early summer followed by green, edible fruit ripening in September
Pittosporum *Pittosporum tobira*	12 by 10 feet; evergreen	Full sun to part shade	Often planted where a smaller shrub would be more appropriate; very fragrant creamy white flowers in early summer; dwarf cultivars are susceptible to root rot
Pomegranate, Dwarf *Punica granatum* 'Nana'	3 by 2 feet; deciduous	Full sun to part shade	Bright orange double flowers in early to midsummer, attractive fruit; the standard pomegranate grows to 10+ feet and the cultivar 'Wonderful' produces edible fruit
Pyracantha *Pyracantha coccinea*	12 by 10 feet; evergreen	Full to part sun	Showy white flowers in spring, bright orange-red fruit in fall and winter; very thorny; prone to a variety of insect and disease problems
Rose of Sharon, Althea *Hibiscus syriacus*	10 by 5 feet; deciduous	Full sun to part shade	Showy flowers like small hibiscus in white, pink, rose, or lavender in summer over several months; tall upright shrub; easily trained into a small tree form
Sasanqua *Camellia sasanqua*	10 by 8 feet; evergreen	Full sun to part shade	Showy, fragrant flowers in October through December; good for hedges or screens
Sweet Olive *Osmanthus fragrans*	15 by 10 feet; evergreen	Full sun to part shade	A "must have" for gardeners looking for fragrance; will slowly grow into a small tree; tiny, creamy white flowers are produced from fall to spring
Spirea, Bridal Wreath *Spirea × vanhoutei*	6 by 5 feet; deciduous	Full to part sun	Often planted where a smaller shrub would be a better choice; beautiful fountain of white flowers in April
Virginia Willow *Itea virginica*	5 by 4 feet; deciduous	Full sun to part shade	Spikes of small white flowers in late spring and outstanding burgundy red fall foliage make this native shrub worth planting
Wax-leaf Ligustrum *Ligustrum japonicum*	15 by 10 feet; evergreen	Full sun to part shade	Fast-growing shrub popular for hedges and screens; clusters of fragrant white flowers in summer

PLANTING CHARTS

Trees

Name	Type	Height × Width	Comments
American Holly *Ilex opaca*	Evergreen	40 to 50 by 15 to 30 feet	Excellent medium-sized tree; red berries on females in winter are eaten by birds; native; 'Savannah' is a popular smaller-growing hybrid cultivar; native
Bald Cypress *Taxodium distichum*	Deciduous	50 to 100 by 20 to 50 feet	Narrow cone shape when young; knees rarely produced in cultivation, remove if desired; an unusual conifer that drops its needles in winter; native
Bradford Flowering Pear *Pyrus calleryana* 'Bradford'	Deciduous	30 to 50 by 20 to 40 feet	Narrow upright growth when young becomes broader as trees age; white flowers in spring and brilliant fall foliage not as prominent in warmer portions of the state; older trees prone to branch splitting; 'Aristocrat' and other cultivars are available
Cabbage Palm *Sabal palmetto*	Evergreen	25 by 6 feet	Hardy throughout the state; may be damaged or killed by temperatures below 15 degrees; slow rate of growth
Canaert Red Cedar *Juniperus virginiana* 'Canaertii'	Evergreen	20 to 40 by 20 by 30 feet	Attractive fine-textured conifer; trunk with peeling bark has great character; good source of wildlife food; spider mites and bag worms may occur; native
Cherry Laurel *Prunus caroliniana*	Evergreen	25 to 10 feet	Fast-growing small tree; well-drained soil; good for small areas; spikes of tiny white flowers in spring; purple-black fruit eaten by birds; can be messy; excellent screen or hedge; native
Chinese Parasol Tree *Firmiana simplex*	Deciduous	35 by 15 feet	Large leaves and a smooth, green trunk make this tree distinctive; appropriate for use fairly close to buildings and patios; unusual seedpods; prone to white scale
Chinese Pistachio *Pistacia chinensis*	Deciduous	25 to 40 by 20 by 35 feet	Brilliant orange-red to gold fall color; excellent shade tree; leafs out relatively late—early to mid-April; a different species from the one that produces edible nuts
Crape Myrtle *Lagerstroemia indica* and *L. indica* x *fauriei*	Deciduous	15 to 10 feet up to 25 by 15 feet	Outstanding and popular small tree; blooms over long summer season in shades of red, pink, white, and purple; smooth bark and attractive growth habit; often grown as a multitrunked tree; aphids, powdery mildew and leaf spot may occur
Deodar Cedar *Cedrus deodara*	Evergreen	40 to 60 by 20 to 30 feet	Looks like it belongs up North but does very well in in Louisiana; silvery-green needles; branches form graceful tiers; pyramidal shape more irregular with age
Dwarf Palmetto *Sabal minor*	Evergreen	6 by 5 feet	Small palm, more like a shrub; very hardy throughout the state; native

PLANTING CHARTS

Trees

Name	Type	Height × Width	Comments
Flowering Dogwood *Cornus florida*	Deciduous	20 to 30 by 25 feet	Beautiful spring flowers before the foliage in shades of white, pink, or rose; prefers some shade; best used where there is excellent drainage and acid soils; prone to several pests; native
Fringe Tree *Chionanthus virginicus*	Deciduous	20 to 25 by 15 to 20 feet	Also called grancy graybeard; greenish-white fringe-like flowers in spring as foliage emerges; excellent small ornamental tree; native; Chinese fringe tree (*C. retusa*) also recommended; the white flowers are more showy
Ginkgo *Ginkgo biloba*	Deciduous	50 to 70 by 20 to 50 feet	Attractive fan-shaped foliage reliably turns a beautiful yellow in fall; plant grafted males to avoid undesirable fruit; slow rate of growth; tough tree with no problems
Green Ash *Fraxinus pennsylvanica*	Deciduous	40 to 70 by 30 to 50 feet	Excellent fast-growing shade tree; yellow fall color in north Louisiana; native
Japanese Maple *Acer palmatum*	Deciduous	2 to 20 by 3 to 20 feet	Graceful, tiered growth habit; many, many cultivars with various leaf shapes and colors (yellow-green, green, bronze, burgundy); excellent specimen tree; small and relatively slow growing; prefers some afternoon shade
Lacebark Elm *Ulmus parvifolia*	Deciduous to semi-evergreen	40 to 60 by 30 to 50 feet	Very fast-growing shade tree; vase to umbrella shaped; attractive trunk with peeling bark; reliable and relatively pest-free; leafless for a short time in late winter
Loquat *Eriobotrya japonica*	Evergreen	15 by 10 feet	Attractive dark green relatively large leaves; produces edible pale orange fruit in warmest sections of state; if winter is mild; blooms in fall with fruit ripening in spring; can be messy
Needle Palm *Rhapidophyllum lystrix*	Evergreen	6 by 6 feet	Very hardy palm throughout the state; rounded mound of foliage is shrub-like; native to Southeast United States
Oriental Magnolia *Magnolia x soulangiana*	Deciduous	25 by 15 feet	Large, pinkish-purple to white flowers in late winter to early spring before the foliage, fragrant; often grown multitrunked; numerous cultivars available; scale an occasional problem
Parsley Hawthorn *Crataegus marshallii*	Deciduous	15 to 30 by 15 to 20 feet	Clusters of white spring flowers and red fruit in the fall are outstanding features of this small flowering tree; thorny when young; birds eat the fruit; excellent in small areas; native

PLANTING CHARTS

Trees

Name	Type	Height × Width	Comments
Pecan *Carya illinoiensis*	Deciduous	60 to 125 by 40 to 100 feet	Edible nuts; choose 'Melrose', 'Sumner', 'Elliot', or 'Candy' for home plantings; large trees need a lot of room; brittle wood very prone to breakage; prone to webworms; native
Pines *Pinus* spp.	Evergreen	20 to 125 by 15 to 70 feet	Various species including short leaf pine, loblolly pine, slash pine; tall trees that are best planted in areas with sandy, acid soils; Southern pine borer can be problems; native
Redbud *Cercis canadensis*	Deciduous	15 to 30 by 15 to 25 feet	Small pinkish-purple flowers in great profusion in spring before the foliage emerges; attractive heart-shaped leaves turn yellow before dropping; needs excellent drainage; native
Shumard Oak *Quercus shumardii*	Deciduous	80 to 100 by 50 to 60 feet	Relatively fast growth, especially if fertilized when young; shiny, dark-green foliage turns red in fall; excellent large shade tree; strong wood resists wind damage; native
Silver Bell *Halesia diptera*	Deciduous	25 by 20 feet	Bell-shaped, white flowers in spring just as the foliage emerges; adaptable and easy; often used as a substitute where dogwoods do not thrive; good for small areas; native
Southern Live Oak *Quercus virginiana*	Evergreen	50 by 80 feet	An outstandingly beautiful but very large tree; popular, but often planted where a smaller species would be more appropriate; destructive roots; best adapted to south Louisiana; salt tolerant; native
Southern Magnolia *Magnolia grandiflora*	Evergreen	50 to 100 by 30 to 50 feet	Beautiful tree with dark-green shiny foliage; fragrant, white flowers in May and June; considered messy because of leaf drop; numerous pests; scale is common; difficult to grow plants underneath due to heavy shade; destructive roots; native
Spruce Pine *Pinus glabra*	Evergreen	50 by 30 feet	Short, twisted needles on a lower growing pine tree; dense, low branching makes this tree excellent for use as a large screen or noise baffle; better adapted to alkaline soils than other pines; native
Swamp Red Maple *Acer rubrum* var. *drummondii*	Deciduous	50 to 60 by 40 to 50 feet	Excellent fast-growing shade tree; tolerant of poor drainage; females produce attractive burgundy flowers and fruit in February; better adapted to Louisiana than northern red maples; native
Sweet Bay Magnolia *Magnolia virginiana*	Semi-evergreen	20 to 40 by 15 to 25 feet	Generally does not lose all leaves in winter; striking silvery backed foliage; fragrant flowers resemble Southern magnolia but smaller; upright form; tolerates poor drainage; native

PLANTING CHARTS

Trees

Name	Type	Height × Width	Comments
Sweet Gum *Liquidambar styraciflua*	Deciduous	45 to 50 by 40 to 60 feet	Upright pyramidal shape when young, broader with age; star-shaped leaves very reliably turn purple, orange, burgundy, or yellow in fall; prickly fruit can be a nuisance; native
Taiwan Flowering Cherry *Prunus campanulata*	Deciduous	15 by 10 feet	Blooming in late January and early February, the flowers are subject to freeze injury in north Louisiana; magenta flowers appear in great numbers along the branches before foliage; most reliable flowering cherry for south Louisiana
Vitex, Chaste Tree *Vitex agnus-castus*	Deciduous	9 to 15 by 10 to 15 feet	Spikes of lavender-purple in early summer, reblooming in late summer; attractive star-shaped foliage drops early; excellent fast-growing, small ornamental tree
Willow Oak *Quercus phellos*	Deciduous	80 to 100 by 40 to 60 feet	Excellent, fast-growing upright oak with narrow leaves; deserves more use; good for urban sites; leafless for brief period in late winter; native
Windmill Palm *Trachycarpus fortunei*	Evergreen	20 by 6 feet	Beautiful palm with a hairy trunk; good in small areas; reliably hardy in north Louisiana
Yaupon *Ilex vomitoria*	Evergreen	25 to 15 feet	Translucent red berries that glow in sunlight distinguish this small holly; small leaves without spines; grow single or multiple trunk; suckers at base can be a nuisance; native

Vines

Name	Size/Type	Light	Flowers and Comments
Carolina Yellow Jessamine *Gelsemium sempervirens*	to 20 feet; Evergreen, twining	Full sun to part shade	Yellow, fragrant flowers in late winter to early spring; one of the best vines; vigorous; prune regularly to control; native
Chinese Wisteria *Wisteria sinensis*	to 50 feet; Deciduous, twining	Full to part sun	Dangling clusters of fragrant lilac-purple flowers in March–April; vigorous, rampant vine that must be carefully controlled; keep away from trees and houses
Confederate Jasmine *Trachelospermum jasminoides*	20 to 60 feet; Evergreen, twining	Full sun to part shade	Very fragrant clusters of white flowers in early summer; may be severely damaged or killed by temperatures in the mid- to low teens; usually hardy in zones 8b and 9
Coral Honeysuckle *Lonicera sempervirens*	15 to 20 feet; Evergreen, twining	Full to part sun	Clusters of tubular coral red flowers in spring to early summer and scattered through the year; attractive blue-green foliage; easy to control; native

PLANTING CHARTS

Vines

Name	Size/Type	Light	Flowers and Comments
Crossvine *Bignonia capreolata*	to 50 feet; Semi-evergreen, twining	Part sun to part shade	Showy clusters of large tubular yellow and red flowers; large vine not suitable for a small trellis; native; 'Tangarine Beauty' is an outstanding cultivar
English Ivy *Hedera helix*	to 60 feet; Evergreen, clinging	Part sun to shade	Excellent clinging vine; flowers insignificant; many cultivars with different leaf shapes, sizes, and variegations; root rot can be a problem in poorly drained locations
Five-leaf Akebia *Akebia quintana*	to 25 feet; Evergreen; twining.	Full to part sun	Vigorous vine with clusters of fragrant dusky purple flowers in April and scattered blooms through the summer
Rosa de Montana *Antigonon leptopus*	30 to 40 feet Dies back in winter; twining.	Full sun to part shade	Sprays of rosy pink flowers in late summer and fall; useful in covering an arbor for summer shade; winter sun; dies back in winter but returns from roots in spring

Ground Covers

Name	Height	Light	Comments
Asian Jasmine *Trachelospermum asiaticum*	12 to 16 inches	Full sun to part shade	Excellent fast-growing vine for covering large areas; shear back to 4 to 6 inches annually; edge sides of bed as needed; evergreen or semi-evergreen
Aspidistra, **Cast Iron Plant** *Aspidistra elatior*	2 feet	Shade to full shade	Tall ground cover for deep shade; sword-shaped dark-green leaves; evergreen
Autumn Fern *Dryopteris erythrosora*	12 to 18 inches	Shade to full shade	Attractive new growth has a coppery-red tint; tough, reliable evergreen fern
Creeping Juniper *Juniperus horizontalis*	18 inches	Full sun	Needs excellent drainage and air circulation; good for hot, dry, sunny areas; watch for spider mites
Creeping Lily Turf *Liriope spicata*	8 to 10 inches	Shade to part shade	Grasslike foliage; reliable for large areas, better than *L. muscari* as a ground cover since it spreads faster; evergreen
Dwarf Bamboo *Arundinaria pygmaca*	12 to 15 inches	Full sun to part shade	Fast spreading tough plant for sunny areas; cut back foliage in late winter each year
English Ivy *Hedera helix*	8-inch-deep mat	Shade to part sun	Useful for covering large areas and slopes; may be damaged by root rot; use vigorous, fast-growing cultivars as ground cover; evergreen
Holly Fern *Cyrtomium falcatum*	12 to 20 inches	Shade to part sun	Bold, coarse texture almost shrublike; tolerates drier soil than most ferns; evergreen or semi-evergreen

PLANTING CHARTS

Ground Covers

Name	Height	Light	Comments
Japanese Ardisia *Ardisia japonica*	10 inches	Shade to part shade	Bright red berries in winter, but few in number; choose plain green cultivars for ground cover planting; evergreen
Monkey Grass *Ophiopogon japonicus*	8 to 10 inches	Shade to part sun	Grassy appearance; thin dark-green leaves; one of best for planting large areas; evergreen
Strawberry Geranium *Saxifraga stolonifera*	4 inches	Shade to part shade	Delightful plant for small detail planting; round dark-green leaves with silver veins; stalks of small white flowers in spring; evergreen

Ornamental Grasses

Name	Size	Light	Comments
Acorus *Acorus gramineus*	6 to 12 inches	Part shade to shade	Small grasslike plant excellent in moist to wet area; effective as a ground cover or detail planting; evergreen
Fountain Grass *Pennisetum alopecuroides*	10 inches to 3 feet, depending on variety.	Full to part sun	Fine-textured grass, not too large; dwarf cultivars such as 'Hamelin' are only 18 inches; attractive plumes in midsummer; hardy in zones 8 and 9 to statewide, depending on variety
Giant Reed Grass *Arundo donax*	10 to 15 feet	Full to part sun	Large, coarse-textured upright grass suitable for accent or screen; cut back if damaged by winter freezes; produces 2-foot tan plumes in late summer
Lindheimer's Muhly *Muhlenbergia lindheimeri*	3 to 4 feet	Full to part sun	Very attractive dome of fine-textured leaves are bluish-gray-green in color; flower plumes appear in fall
Pampas Grass *Cortaderia selloana*	8 to 10 feet	Full to part sun	Large, mounding fine-textured grass suitable for accent or screen; cut back if damaged by winter freezes; produces attractive creamy white to silvery plumes in late summer; hardy in zones 7, 8, and 9
Variegated Japanese Silver Grass *Miscanthus sinensis* 'Variegata'	5 to 6 feet	Full sun to part shade	Mounding fine-textured grass with creamy white variegated foliage; outstanding specimen or accent; pinkish-tan plumes in midsummer; there are many outstanding cultivars of this grass species; hardy statewide
Zebra Grass *Miscanthus sinensis* 'Zebrinus'	5 to 6 feet	Full sun to part shade	Upright to mounding medium-textured grass; blades are striped horizontally with pale yellow bands; attractive plumes in late summer; cut back in February; hardy statewide

PLANTING CHARTS

Submerged Plants

Name	Size	Flowers	Comments
Hornwort *Ceratophyllum demersum*	1 to 2 feet	Insignificant	Useful in shady ponds; whorls of stiff, slender dark green, forked leaves about 1 inch long crowded toward the tips
Parrot's Feather, Milfoil *Myriophyllum* sp.	1 to 3 feet	Insignificant	Very finely divided foliage looks feathery; excellent and generally available; grows up out of the water as well as underwater
Pondweed, Anacharis *Elodea canadensis*	1 to 3 feet or longer stems	Small creamy white; summer	One of the most widely available and easily grown; thin out and remove excess as needed
Washington Grass, Cabomba *Cobomba caroliniana*	1 foot	Tiny white or purple; summer	Fan-shaped, deeply divided, lacy leaves on long stems; attractive and a favorite spawning place for fish

Floating Plants

Name	Size	Blooms	Comments
Ivy-leaved Duckweed *Lemna trisulca*	Tiny leaves; ½ inch	Insignificant	Does not spread as fast as common duckweed which may also be used; skim off excess as needed
Frogbit *Hydrocharis morsus-ranse*	Leaves about 1 inch; spreading growth	Small white	Round, shiny leaves attractively veined; overwinters as turions on pond bottom
Water Hyacinth *Erichhornia crassipes*	Individual plants 6 to 12 inches across	Showy, spikes of large lavender blue flowers with yellow eye	**Caution:** These plants are on Louisiana's Invasive Plant Species list; do not use these in your aquatic garden; do not allow them to spread into natural bodies of water
Water Lettuce *Pistia stratiotes*	Individual plants 4 to 5 inches across	Insignificant	**Caution:** These plants are on Louisiana's Invasive Plant Species list; do not use these in your aquatic garden; do not allow them to spread into natural bodies of water

Water Lilies

Name	Size	Flowers	Comments
Hardy Water Lilies *Nymphaea* sp.	Spread 2 to 3 feet or more	Summer; many colors; sit on surface of water	Many cultivars that grow various sizes; choose types that are the right size for your pond; need 6 to 10 inches of water from pot rim to surface
Tropical Water Lilies *Nymphaea* sp.	Spread 3 to 6 feet	Summer; many colors; held well above surface of water; day bloomers and night bloomers	Many cultivars that grow various sizes; choose types that are the right size for your pond; need 6 to 10 inches of water from pot rim to water surface; may need to store in a frost-free location during winter, especially in north Louisiana

PLANTING CHARTS

Water Lilies

Name	Size	Flowers	Comments
Lotus *Nelumbo nucifera*	3 to 8 feet	Summer; many colors; large and fragrant	Many cultivars; at least 10 inches from pot rim to water surface; attractive foliage held up out of water; large plants suitable for larger ponds; may need to store in a frost-free location during winter, especially in north Louisiana

Marginal or Bog Plants
(pot rims about 2 to 3 inches below water surface))

Name	Size	Flowers	Comments
Arrow Arum *Peltandra sagittifolia*	18 to 36 inches	Yellow; summer	Large arrowhead-shaped leaves; vigorous growth
Arrowhead *Sagittaria sagitttifolia*	18 to 24 inches	White; summer	Easily grown plants with arrowhead-shaped leaves; attractive flowers
Cattail *Typha* sp. and hybrids	2 to 6 feet	Brown spikes; summer	Upright plants spread rapidly; several cultivars including dwarf and variegated types; can be invasive
Louisiana Iris *Iris* sp. and hybrids	2 to 3 feet	Very showy in many colors; April	Wonderful native does very well in aquatic gardens
Pickerel Weed *Pontederia cordata*	1 to 2 feet	Spikes of bluish-purple; summer; long bloom period	Vigorous and easy native plant; elongated heart-shaped, shiny green leaves
Rushes *Scirpus* sp.	1 to 6 feet	Interesting to insignificant; brown in summer	Upright plants with narrow, cylindrical leaves; several interesting species and cultivars
Thalia *Thalia* sp.	4 to 6 feet	Dangling purple flowers on long thin stems in summer	Large upright plants for the background; lush tropical appearance
Umbrella Plant, Papyrus *Cyperus* sp.	1 to 6 feet	Insigificant to interesting, but not showy	Round stems bear a cluster of narrow leaves at tips

SUMMARY OF PEST CONTROL OPTIONS

Insect Pests

Name	Controls	Plants Affected	When Pest Active
Ants and fire ants	*See below for control details	Few if any plants are affected; nuisance to people	Year-round, especially in warm seasons

*Baits—Hydramethylnon (amidinohydrazone) and sulfluramid (n-ethyl perfluorooctanesulfonamide); Avermectins (abamectin); Spinosyns (spinosad); Insect Growth Regulators (fenoxycarb, methoprene, pyriproxyfen).

*Contact Insecticides—Botanicals (d-limonene—a citrus oil extract, pyrethrum, pyrethrin, rotenone, pine oil, turpentine); Derivatives of Pyrethrin (allethrin, resmethrin, sumithrin, tetramethrin); Carbamates (bendiocarb, carbaryl); Organophosphates (acephate, dichlorvos, fenthion, isofenphos, malathion, propetamphos, propoxur, trichlorfon); Inorganic Compounds—Boric acid, Diatomaceous earth products (D.E., silicone dioxide).

Name	Controls	Plants Affected	When Pest Active
Aphids	acephate, azadirachtin (neem), bifenthrin, cyfluthrin, deltamethrin, esfenvalerate, fluvalinate light horticultural oils, imidacloprid, insecticidal soap, permethrin, pyrethrin, pyrethrum	Any plant with tender new growth	Year-round when plants are actively growing
Armyworms	acephate, bifenthrin, *Bacillus thuringiensis* (Bt), carbaryl, cyfluthrin, esfenvalerate, permethrin, pyrethrin, pyrethrum, spinosad	Lawngrasses	Usually summer; may occur spring and fall
Bagworms	Same as armyworms	Cedar, juniper, and arborvitae	Usually in active growing season; remain year-round if not physically removed
Beetles	acephate, azadirachtin (neem), bifenthrin, cyfluthrin, deltamethrin, esfenvalerate, fluvalinate, light horticultural oils, imidacloprid, permethrin, pyrethrin, pyrethrum	Vegetables, some trees, and flowers	Usually in warm seasons
Billbugs	acephate, bifenthrin, cyfluthrin, fluvalinate	Plants with tender shallow root systems, usually annuals	Year-round; most active in warm, moist times
Borers, Woody Plants	bifenthrin, imidacloprid, thiodan	Trees and old large shrubs	Most active in spring and summer
Caterpillars	Same as armyworms	Many plants with tender growth, vegetables, and annuals	Most active in spring; also active through fall
Chiggers	fluvalinate, malathion	None; nuisance to people	Warm seasons
Chinch bugs	acephate, bifenthrin, carbaryl, cyfluthrin, fluvalinate, isofenphos	Lawngrasses	Hot, dry summers

SUMMARY OF PEST CONTROL OPTIONS

Insect Pests

Name	Controls	Plants Affected	When Pest Active
Crickets (common and mole)	carbaryl, isofenphos, pyrethrin, resmethrin	Mole: any plants they cut the roots of; Common: nuisance to people	Warm and especially moist seasons
Cutworms	acephate, bifenthrin, carbaryl, cyfluthrin, esfenvalerate, pymethrin pyrethrin, pyrethrum, spinosad	Vegetable transplants most affected	Most active in spring
Earwigs	propoxur, malathion, metaldehyde baits, resmethrin, pyrethrin	Plants not normally affected; nuisance to people	Year-round; most active in warm seasons
Fleas	bifenthrin, carbaryl, pyrethrin, propoxur	None; nuisance to people and pets	Year-round; most active in warm seasons
Fungus gnats	Bt/H-14, malathion pyrethrum, pyrethrin	Usually not harmful to plants; most often found in houseplants; may be a nuisance to people	Year-round; most active in growing season
Grasshoppers	acephate, bifenthrin, carbaryl, pyrethrin	Almost any plant	Summer, especially when hot and dry
Grubs	isofenphos, imidacloprid, ethoprop	Lawngrasses	May be active year-round; most damage in cool seasons
Lacebugs	acephate, fluvalinate, light horticultural oil, imidacloprid, malathion	Ornamental shrubs, such as azaleas and pyracanthas	Summer
Leaf cutter bees	carbaryl, malathion, propoxur, pyrethrum, resmethrin	Any plant in the landscape with relatively tender leaves	Warm seasons
Leaf hoppers	acephate, bifenthrin, carbaryl	Vegetables and ornamentals, including roses	Warm active growing season
Leaf miners	acephate, malathion, spinosad	Trees to vegetables	Active growing season
Leaf rollers	Same as armyworms	Various plants in the garden, including cannas	Active growing season
Mealybugs	acephate, light horticultural oils, malathion, pyrethrum, pyrethrin	Any tender plant; houseplants	Year-round indoors; active growing season outdoors
Millipedes and centipedes	carbaryl, bifenthrin, pyrethrin, resmethrin	None; nuisance to people	Year-round; most active in warm, moist seasons
Pecan nut casebearer	*Bacillus thuringiensis* (Bt), carbaryl, malathion	Pecans and hickory	Active growing season
Pecan phylloxera	dormant oils, malathion	Pecans and fruits	Active growing season

SUMMARY OF PEST CONTROL OPTIONS

Insect Pests

Name	Controls	Plants Affected	When Pest Active
Plant bugs	acephate, azadirachtin (neem), bifenthrin, carbaryl, cyfluthrin, permethrin, pyrethrin	Vegetables	Active growing season
Scales	acephate, bifenthrin, dormant horticultural oil, light horticultural oil, imidacloprid	From trees to houseplants	Year-round; most active in growing season
Scorpions	propoxur, malathion, pyrethrin	None; nuisance to people	Warm, moist seasons
Slugs and snails	Various traps (beer), copper metal strips, iron phosphate baits (Sluggo), metaldehyde baits.	Young tender shallow-rooted foliage plants, including hosta	Warm growing season
Sod webworms	Same as armyworms	Lawngrasses	Summer heat
Sowbugs/pillbugs	bifenthrin, carbaryl, fluvalinate	Annuals and vegetables	Warm, moist seasons
Spider mites	bifenthrin, imidacloprid, kelthane, light horticultural oil, malathion, pyrethrin	From trees to houseplants	Year-round indoors; hot, dry times outdoors
Spiders	No control is normally needed; bifenthrin, pyrethrin, resmethrin	None; nuisance to people	Year-round indoors; most active in growing season
Squash bug	pyrethrum, pyrethrin, carbaryl, rotenone	All types of squash	Warm growing season
Squash vine borer	*Bacillus thuringiensis* (Bt), carbaryl, spinosad	All types of squash	Warm growing season
Stinkbugs	rotenone/pyrethrum combination, malathion, carbaryl	Primarily vegetables, including squash	Warm growing season
Thrips	acephate, azadirachtin (neem), bifenthrin, carbaryl, cyfluthrin, permethrin, pyrethrin	Roses are main plants affected	Active growing season
Ticks	bifenthrin, carbaryl, pyrethrin, propoxur	None; nuisance to people and pets	Year-round; primarily in warm seasons
Wasps, hornets, and yellow jackets	permethrin, pyrethrin, resmethrin, carbaryl	None; nuisance to people	Warm seasons
Webworms, fall and tent caterpillars	acephate, bifenthrin, *Bacillus thuringiensis* (Bt), carbaryl, cyfluthrin, esfenvalerate, permethrin, pyrethrum, spinosad	Trees and shrubs sometimes; Lawn grasses	Warm seasons

SUMMARY OF PEST CONTROL OPTIONS

Insect Pests

Name	Controls	Plants Affected	When Pest Active
Whiteflies	acephate, bifenthrin, light horticultural oil, malathion, pyrethrin	Primarily ornamentals, including gardenia and lantana	Warm growing season
Woolly oak galls	No control is necessary	Oak trees	Year-round

Insect Pest Bio-Control Options

Bacillus thuringiensis (Bt): A specific control for several larvae/caterpillars/worms.

Green lacewings: Their larvae feed on numerous insect pests.

Ladybugs/beetles: They prefer certain sucking insect pests, including aphids, mealybugs, and spider mites.

Natural insecticides: Diatomaceous earth (DE), neem, nicotine, pyrethrum, rotone, and sabadilla are used to control insect pests.

Nosema Locustae: A protozoan spore specifically utilized for grasshopper control.

Praying mantis: Prefers grasshopers, crickets, bees, wasps, and flies as their food sources.

Trichogramma wasp: A miniature wasp that attacks the eggs of 200+ insect pests.

Disease Pests

Name	Controls	Plants Affected	When Pest Active
Anthracnose	benomyl, mancozeb, thiophanate methyl, zineb	Trees, vegetables, lawn-grasses, and berries	Spring
Bacteria	streptomycin sulfate, lime and copper sulfate, tribasic copper sulfate	Pears, pyracanthas, and apples, Indian hawthorn	Spring and summer
Blackspot	azoxystrobin, benomyl, calcium polysulfide, captan, chlorothalonil, copper hydroxide, copper oleate, mancoeb, maneb, myclobutanil, propiconazole, sulfur, thiophanate methyl, thiophanate methyl/ mancozeb; triforine	Roses	Active growing season
Brown patch	azoxystrobin, chlorothalonil, iprodione, mancozeb, mancozeb/myclobutanil, PCNB, propiconazole, thiophanate methyl, thiophanate methyl/ mancozeb, triadimefon	Lawngrasses	Usually spring and/or fall

SUMMARY OF PEST CONTROL OPTIONS

Disease Pests

Name	Controls	Plants Affected	When Pest Active
Cotton root rot	No controls available; plant resistant varieties	Trees, especially dogwood; shrubs, especially wax ligustrum	Year-round; most active in warm seasons
Crown rot	benomyl, etridiazole, metalaxyl, PCNB, propamocarb hydrochloride, thiophanate methyl	Any plant especially those rosette form	Year-round; most likely in warm, moist seasons
Downy mildew	chlorothalonil, fixed copper, maneb, maneb + Zn; mancozeb	Vegetables	Active growing season
Fruit rot	benomyl, captan chlorothalonil, sulfur, lime + copper sulfate	Stone fruits	Throughout fruiting seasons
Gray mold (Botrytis)	benomyl, mancozeb, thiophanate methyl	Annuals and perennials, especially amaryllis, carnations and geraniums	Active growing season
Gray leaf spot	azoxystrobin, chlorothalonil, mancozeb, myclobutanil, propiconazole, thiophanate methyl, triadimefon	Lawngrasses	Warm, moist seasons
Leaf spots	benomyl, copper sulfate, chlorothalonil, mancozeb, thiophanate methyl	Flowers, especially roses; shrubs, especially red tips; trees, especially redbud	Warm growing season
Oak leaf blister	chlorothalonil, lime + copper sulfate, mancozeb	Primarily water oak	Spray just as buds swell in spring
Phytophora	Good cultural practices, chlorothalonil, thiophanate methyl, rotate crops	Annual vinca, petunias, and other annuals	Warm growing season
Powdery mildew	benomyl, myclobutanil, sulfur, thiophanate methyl, thiophanate methyl/mancozeb, triadimefon, triforine	Roses, crape myrtles, and vegetables	Warm growing season, especially with humid conditions
Pythium blight	azoxystrobin, clorneb, etridiazole, mancozeb, mefenoxam, propamocarb	Lawngrasses	Warm growing season

SUMMARY OF PEST CONTROL OPTIONS

Disease Pests

Name	Controls	Plants Affected	When Pest Active
Root rot	Provide proper drainage, do not over water; aluminum tris etridiazole, etridiazole/thiophanate methyl, iprodione, PCNB, thiophanate methyl	Any plant	Primarily during hot, wet weather in mid to late summer
Rusts	azoxystrobin, mancozeb, maneb, myclobutanil, sulfur, triadimefon, triforine	Vegetables, roses, and lawngrasses	Warm growing season
Rhizoctonia	benomyl, captan, thiophanate methyl, PCNB	Vegetables	Active growing season
Scab	captan, chlorothalonil	Pecans	Spring, summer, and fall
Stem canker	No controls available; remove infected small plants and dead parts of large plants	Roses and trees	Year-round
Stem rot	Good cultural practices; benomyl, thiophanate methyl	Plants with herbaceous stems	Warm growing season
Take-all patch	azoxystrobin, propiconazole	Lawngrasses	Fall and winter
Viruses	No controls available; plant resistant varieties	All plant groups	Year-round; most active in warm growing season

GLOSSARY

Aeration: tines are driven into soil to introduce air and relieve compaction.

Alkaline soil: soil with a pH greater than 7.0. It lacks acidity, often because it has limestone in it.

All-purpose fertilizer: powdered, liquid, or granular fertilizer with a balanced proportion of the three key nutrients—nitrogen (N), potassium (P), and phosphorus (K). It is suitable as maintenance nutrition for most plants.

Annual: a plant that lives its entire life in one season. It is genetically determined to germinate, grow, flower, set seed, and die the same year.

Arborist: an individual trained in the care of trees. In Louisiana, professional arborists must be licensed by the Louisiana Department of Agriculture and Forestry. Hire only licensed arborists.

Balled and burlapped: describes a tree or shrub grown in the field whose soilball was wrapped with protective burlap and twine when the plant was dug up to be sold or transplanted.

Bare root: describes plants that have been packaged without any soil around their roots. (Often young shrubs and trees purchased through the mail arrive with their exposed roots covered with moist peat or sphagnum moss, sawdust, or similar material, and wrapped in plastic.)

Berm: a narrow raised ring of soil around a tree, used to hold water so it will be directed to the root zone.

Biennial: a plant that grows for two growing seasons, then dies after flowering and setting seed.

Bole: the trunk of a tree.

Bolting: the sending up of a flower stalk by a leafy vegetable. It generally signals a decrease in quality and the end of the productive season.

Bract: a modified leaf structure on a plant stem near its flower that resembles a petal. Often it is more colorful and visible than the actual flower, as in dogwood.

Broadcasting: a type of direct seeding. Seeds are scattered evenly over a bed area and covered to the proper depth. Two to three times as many seeds are planted as actual plants that will be needed. When the seed comes up, the extras are thinned out so that the remaining plants are at the proper spacing.

Bromeliads: popular, easy-care houseplants that slowly lose vigor and die after blooming but can be regrown from side shoots, or pups.

Bud union: the place where the top of a plant was grafted to the rootstock; usually refers to roses.

Canopy: the overhead branching area of a tree, usually referring to its extent including foliage.

Chelated iron: iron in a form immediately available to plants; a component in fertilizers used to treat iron deficiencies in plants.

Clinging: describes vines that can grow on flat surfaces by using roots along their stems. They can cover the sides of buildings or walls without requiring a support to be built.

Cold hardiness: the ability of a perennial plant to survive the winter cold in a particular area.

GLOSSARY

Compost: organic matter that has undergone progressive decomposition by microbial and macrobial activity until it is reduced to a spongy, fluffy texture. Added to soil of any type, it improves the soil's ability to hold air and water and to drain well.

Corm: the swollen energy-storing structure, analogous to a bulb, under the soil at the base of the stem of plants such as crocus and gladiolus.

Cormels: small buds that can develop around the base of a corm.

Cropping: a harvesting practice. Only the lower leaves of leafy vegetables are regularly harvested, so the plant will continue to produce.

Crown: (1) a rosette of leaves on a short stem. (2) the base of a plant at, or just beneath, the surface of the soil where the roots meet the stems.

Cultivar: a CULTIvated VARiety. It is a form of a species that has been identified as special or superior and is purposely selected for propagation and production.

Deadhead: a pruning technique that removes faded flower heads from plants to improve their appearance, abort seed production, and stimulate further flowering.

Deciduous: describes trees and shrubs that, unlike evergreens, lose their leaves in the fall.

Desiccation: drying out of foliage tissues, usually due to drought or wind.

Desucker: to remove side shoots, or suckers.

Diatomaceous earth: a light-colored porous rock (composed of the shells of one-celled algae) that can be placed in a ring around a plant. Snails and slugs do not like to crawl across the tiny sharp particles, and they tend to leave those plants alone.

Direct-seeding: planting seeds directly into the garden.

Division: the practice of splitting apart perennial plants to create several smaller-rooted segments. The practice is useful for controlling the plant's size and for acquiring more plants; it is also essential to the health and continued flowering of certain ones.

Dormancy: the period, usually the winter, when perennial plants temporarily cease active growth and rest. Dormant is the verb form, as used in this sentence: Some plants, like spring-blooming bulbs, go dormant in the summer.

Drilling: a type of direct seeding. Seeds are planted in straight lines at the proper depth, but two to three times closer than the plants ultimately will be spaced. When the seeds come up, the extras are thinned, leaving behind seedlings at the proper spacing. This technique is good if you don't know what the seedlings of the vegetable or flowers you are planting look like. The seedlings are in the drills—the weeds are in between.

Dripline: a ring-shaped area on the ground defined by how far out a tree's branches reach.

Dry soil conditions: the soil is allowed to dry (pencil or chopstick inserted 2/3 into pot is dry) before watering.

Epiphytic: describes a plant that grows on another plant, depending on it for mechanical support but not for nutrients.

Established: the point at which a newly planted tree, shrub, or flower has grown a strong root system into the surrounding soil.

Evergreen: describes perennial plants that do not lose their foliage annually with the onset of winter. Needled or broadleaf foliage will persist and continue to function on a plant through one or more winters, aging and dropping unobtrusively in cycles of three or four years or more.

Fertilizer: a substance added to the plant's environment that provides one or more essential elements.

GLOSSARY

Filling: building up the level of low-lying land with material such as earth or gravel, sometimes necessary to combat soil subsidence.

Floret: a tiny flower, usually one of many forming a cluster, that comprises a single blossom.

Flower scape: a leafless flower stalk that grows directly from the soil, such as a tulip.

Foliar: of or about foliage—usually refers to the practice of spraying foliage, as in fertilizing or treating with insecticide; leaf tissues absorb liquid directly for fast results, and the soil is not affected.

Germinate: to sprout. Germination is a viable seed's first stage of development.

Graft union: the point on the stem of a woody plant with sturdier roots where a stem from a highly ornamental plant is inserted so that it will join with it. Roses are commonly grafted.

Hardscape: the permanent, structural, nonplant part of a landscape, such as walls, sheds, pools, patios, arbors, and walkways.

Herbaceous perennials: plants that live from year to year without producing woody stems.

Herbaceous: plants having fleshy or soft stems; the opposite of woody.

High light: for houseplants, east or west window, south window in winter, 500 to 1,000 foot-candles, or outdoors, 4 to 6 hours of direct sun, preferably morning.

Hills: raised mounds formed in a type of direct-seeding. They are planted with several seeds per hill.

Hybrid: a plant that is the result of intentional or natural cross-pollination between two plants of the same species or genus that are distinctly genetically different.

Impeller: the part of a water pump that moves the water, looking like a propeller.

Intercropping: a way of maximizing production from vegetable beds. Vegetables that are spaced relatively far apart such as broccoli, cauliflower, cabbage, and brussels sprouts do not fully occupy the bed early in their season. The bed space between the plants can be used to grow a quick-maturing crop such as radishes or lettuce which will be harvested and gone by the time larger plants begin to cover those spaces.

Iron chlorosis: a disease in acid-loving plants, caused by a deficiency of iron. Leaves turn a yellow-green color, while the veins of the leaves stay dark green.

Low light: for houseplants, north window, 75 to 200 foot-candles, or outdoors, no direct sun.

Medium light: for houseplants, south window in summer, 200 to 500 foot-candles; or outdoors minimal direct sun (in the early morning).

Melting out: a condition in which herbaceous plants suddenly collapse, wither up, and die. Sometimes the dead tissue is slimy to the touch.

Moist soil conditions: the soil is allowed to dry slightly (feels dry when finger inserted about 1 inch) before watering.

Mulch: a layer of material over bare soil to protect it from erosion and compaction by rain, and to discourage weeds. It may be inorganic (gravel, fabric) or organic (wood chips, bark, pine needles, chopped leaves).

Naturalize: (a) to plant seeds, bulbs, or plants in a random, informal pattern as they would appear in their natural habitat; (b) to adapt to and spread throughout adopted habitats (a tendency of some nonnative plants).

Nectar: the sweet fluid produced by glands on flowers that attract pollinators such as hummingbirds and honeybees for whom it is a source of energy.

GLOSSARY

Organic material, organic matter: any material or debris that is derived from plants. It is carbon-based material capable of undergoing decomposition and decay.

Peat moss: organic matter from peat sedges (United States) or sphagnum mosses (Canada), often used to improve soil texture. The acidity of sphagnum peat moss makes it ideal for boosting or maintaining soil acidity while also improving its drainage.

Perennials: plants that live for three seasons or longer. Unlike annuals and biennials, perennials do not die after flowering and setting seed. Technically, trees, shrubs, lawngrasses, and bulbs are all perennials, but gardeners use the term "perennial" as an abbreviation for "hardy, herbaceous perennial"—a group of nonwoody, hardy plants grown for their attractive flowers or foliage. Some herbaceous perennials are evergreen and never go completely dormant, while others go dormant, lose their leaves, and essentially disappear at certain times of the year, usually winter.

pH: a measurement used to indicate the acidity or alkalinity of water or soil. A pH of 7 is neutral, numbers below 7 indicate an acid condition, and numbers above 7 indicate an alkaline condition.

Photosynthesis: a process plants use to create carbohydrates from carbon dioxide and water. The energy source is sunlight.

Pinch: to remove tender stems and/or leaves by pressing them between thumb and forefinger. This pruning technique encourages branching, compactness, and flowering in plants.

Pollen: the yellow, powdery grains in the center of a flower. A plant's male sex cells, they are transferred to the female plant parts by means of wind or animal pollinators to fertilize them and create seeds.

Preemergence herbicide: a chemical substance applied to beds before plants sprout. It will suppress the growth of weeds and is sometimes called "weed preventer."

Pups: the side shoots on a bromeliad. They can be used for propagating the plant.

Raceme: an arrangement of single stalked flowers along an elongated, unbranched axis.

Rhizome: a swollen energy-storing stem structure, that lies horizontally in the soil, with roots emerging from its lower surface and growth shoots from a growing point at or near its tip, as in bearded iris.

Root flare: the transition at the base of a tree trunk where the bark tissue begins to differentiate and roots begin to form just before entering the soil. This area should not be covered with soil when planting a tree.

Rootbound (or potbound): the condition of a plant that has been confined in a container too long, its roots having been forced to wrap around themselves and even swell out of the container. Successful transplanting or repotting requires untangling and trimming away of some of the matted roots.

Scion: the upper portion of a grafted plant.

Self-seeding: the tendency of some plants to sow their seeds freely around the yard. It creates many seedlings the following season that may or may not be welcome.

Semi-evergreen: tending to be evergreen in a mild climate but deciduous in a rigorous one.

Shearing: the pruning technique whereby plant stems and branches are cut uniformly with long-bladed pruning shears (hedge shears) or powered hedge trimmers. It is used when creating and maintaining formal hedges and topiary.

GLOSSARY

Slow-acting fertilizer: fertilizer that is water insoluble and therefore releases its nutrients gradually as a function of soil temperature, moisture, and related microbial activity. Typically granular, or coated prills, it may be organic or synthetic.

Sooty mold: a black fungal deposit on foliage. It indicates the presence of sucking insects.

Stock: the part of a plant that provides the roots for a grafted plant. It should never be allowed to sprout and grow.

Subsidence: sinking or settling to a lower level. Soil subsidence is a common problem in some areas of the state, including the New Orleans area.

Succulent growth: the sometimes undesirable production of fleshy, fast-growing leaves or stems that results from overfertilization.

Sucker: a vigorous, fast-growing shoot, often undesirable. Underground plant roots produce suckers to form new stems and spread by means of these suckering roots to form large plantings, or colonies. Some plants produce root suckers or branch suckers as a result of pruning or wounding.

True bulb: consists of a compressed stem and a growing point or flower bud enclosed with thick, fleshy, modified leaves.

Tuber: a type of underground storage structure formed from stem tissue, analogous to a bulb (example: caladium).

Twining: describes vines that climb by wrapping their stems, leaves, or tendrils around a support.

Variegated: having various colors or color patterns. The term usually refers to plant foliage that is streaked, edged, blotched, or mottled with a contrasting color, often green with yellow, cream, or white.

BIBLIOGRAPHY

Adams, William D. and Thomas LeRoy, *Common Sense Vegetable Gardening for the South,* Taylor Publishing Company, 1995.

Beales, Peter, *Classic Roses,* Henry Holt and Company, 1997.

Bender, Steve, editor, *Southern Living Garden Book, The,* Oxmoor House, 1998.

Bender, Steve, editor, *Southern Living Garden Problem Solver,* Oxmoor House, 1999.

Brickell, Christopher, editor, *American Horticultural Society Encyclopedia of Garden Plants, The,* Macmillan Publishing Company, NY, 1993.

Courtier, Courtier and Graham Clarke, *Reader's Digest Indoor Plants,* Reader's Digest, 1997.

Druitt, Liz, *Organic Rose Garden, The,* Taylor Publishing Company, 1996.

Gill, Dan and Joe White, *Louisiana Gardener's Guide,* Cool Springs Press, 1997.

Greenlee, John, *Encyclopedia of Ornamental Grasses, The,* Rodale Press, 1992.

Hill, Madalene and Gwyn Barclay, *Southern Herb Growing,* Shearer Publishing, 1987.

McDonald, Elvin, *New Houseplant, The,* Macmillan Publishing Company, 1993.

Odenwald, Neil and James Turner, *Identification, Selection and Use of Southern Plants for Landscape Design,* Claitor's Publishing Division, 1987.

Ogden, Scott, *Garden Bulbs for the South,* Taylor Publishing Company, 1994.

River Oaks Garden Club, *Garden Book for Houston and the Gulf Coast, A,* Pacesetter Press, 1979.

Seidenberg, Charlotte, *New Orleans Garden: Gardening in the Gulf South, The,* University Press of Mississippi, 1993.

Wasowski, Sally, *Gardening with Native Plants of the South,* Taylor Publishing Company, 1994.

Welch, William, *Perennial Garden Color,* Taylor Publishing Company, 1989.

BOTANICAL NAME
INDEX

Artemisia 'Powis Castle', 264
Abelia × grandiflora, 270
Acanthus mollis, 264
Acer palmatum, 273
Acer rubrum var. drummondii, 274
Achillea millefolium, 264
Acorus gramineus, 264, 277
Aechema fasciata, 252
Aeschynanthus spp., 252
Aglaonema spp., 252
Akebia quintana, 276
Allium schoenoprasum, 262
Allium tuberosum, 43, 262
Aloe vera, 252
Alpinia, 41
Anethum graveolens, 261
Anthriscus cerefolium, 261
Antigonon leptopus, 276
Aphelandra squarrosa, 252
Araucaria exelsia, 252
Ardisia japonica, 277
Arisaema, 42
Armoracia rusticana, 262
Artemisia dracunculus, 263
Artemisia ludoviciana, 133, 264
Arum italicum, 43
Arundinaria pygmaca, 276
Arundo donax, 277
Asarum spp., 264
Asclepias curassavica, 133, 264
Asclepias tuberosa, 264
Asparagus densiflorus, 264
Asparagus spp., 252
Aspidistra elatior, 252, 264, 276
Aster spp. and hybrids, 264
Aucuba japonica, 269
Bauhinia, 195
Beaucarnea recurvata, 252
Begonia spp., 253
Bignonia capreolata, 276
Bletilla, 42
Borago officinalis, 261

Bougainvillea spp., 253
Brassaia actinophylla, 253
Buddleia, 178
Buddleja alternifolia, 269
Buddleja davidii, 269
Calathea makoyana, 253
Callicarpa americana, 269
Calycanthus, 178
Camellia japonica, 269
Camellia sasanqua, 271
Carya illinoiensis, 274
Cedrus deodara, 272
Ceratophyllum demersum, 278
Cercis canadensis, 274
Chaenomeles speciosa, 269
Chamaedorea spp., 253
Chamaemdum nobile, 261
Chionanthus virginicus, 273
Chlorophytum comosum, 264
Chlorophytum elatum, 253
Cissus rhombifolia, 253
Cobomba caroliniana, 278
Codiaeum spp., 253
Colchicum, 54, 58
Coreopsis lanceolata, 264
Coriandrum sativum, 261
Cornus florida, 273
Cortaderia selloana, 277
Cosmos bipinnatus, 27
Cosmos sulphureus, 27
Costus, 41
Crassula argentea, 253
Crataegus marshallii, 273
Cuphea micropetala, 265
Curcuma, 41
Cymbopogon citratus, 262
Cyperus sp., 279
Cyrtomium falcatum, 276
Dendranthema × morifolium cultivars, 265
Dieffenbachia spp., 253
Dizygotheca elegantissima, 253
Dracaena fragrans, 253
Dracaena marginata, 253

Dryopteris erythrosora, 276
Echinacea purpurea, 265
Elodea canadensis, 278
Epipremnum, 254
Episcia spp., 253
Erichhornia crassipes, 278
Eriobotrya japonica, 273
Eruca versicaria, 261
Eupatorium coeolestinum, 265
Euphorbia spp., 253
Farfugium japonicum, 265
Fatsia japonica, 269
Feijoa sellowiana, 271
Ficus spp., 253
Firmiana simplex, 272
Foeniculum vulgare, 261
Fraxinus pennsylvanica, 273
Gardenia jasminoides, 270
Gelsemium sempervirens, 275
Ginkgo biloba, 273
Halesia diptera, 274
Hedera helix, 253, 276
Hedychium, 41
Hemerocallis hybrids, 265
Hibiscus, 253, 254
Hibiscus moscheutos, 265
Hibiscus syriacus, 271
Hosta spp. and hybrids, 265
Hyacinthioides hispanicus, 257
Hydrangea macrophylla, 270
Hydrangea quercifolia, 270
Hydrocharis morsus-ranse, 278
Hymenocallis, 43
Ilex cornuta, 269
Ilex opaca, 272
Ilex vomitoria, 269
Ipheion, 41
Ipheion uniflorum, 257
Iris sp. and hybrids, 279
Itea virginica, 271
Juniperus horizontalis, 276
Juniperus spp. and cultivars, 270
Juniperus virginiana, 272
Kaempferia, 41

BOTANICAL NAME INDEX

Koelreuteria bipinnata, 186
Lagerstroemia indica, 272
Lagerstroemia indica ×
    fauriei, 272
Laurus nobilis, 262
Lavandula spp., 262
Lemna trisulca, 278
Leucanthemum ×
    superbum, 265
Leucojum, 41
Ligustrum japonicum, 271
Lilium formosanum, 58
Lilum lancifolium, 58
Liquidambar styraciflua, 275
Liriope spicata, 212, 276
Lonicera fragrantissima, 178
Lonicera sempervirens, 275
Loropetalum chinensis, 270
Lycoris, 41, 54, 63
Magnolia grandiflora, 274
Magnolia × soulangiana, 273
Magnolia stellata, 178
Magnolia virginiana, 274
Mahonia fortunei, 269
Maranta leuconeura, 254
Melissa officinalis, 262
Mentha spp. and hybrids, 263
Michelia figo, 269
Miscanthus sinensis, 277
Monarda didyma, 262, 266
Monarda fistulosa, 262, 266
Monstera deliciosa, 254
Muhlenbergia lindheimeri, 277
Myriophyllum sp., 278
Nandina domestica, 270
Narcissus cultivars, 257
Nelumbo nucifera, 279
Neomarica, 41
Nepeta cataria, 262
Nerium oleander, 270
Nymphaea sp., 278
Ocimum basilicum, 261
Oenothera speciosa, 127
Ophiopogon japonicus, 116,
    212, 277
Origanum marjorana, 263
Origanum vulgare, 263
Osmanthus fragrans, 271
Oxalis regnellii, 258
Oxalis triangularis, 258
Pelargonium spp., 262
Peltandra sagittifolia, 279
Pennisetum alopecuroides, 277

Peperomia spp., 254
Perilla crispum, 261
Petroselinum crispim, 261
Philadelphus coronarius, 270
Philodendron, 254
Phlox divaricata, 266
Phlox paniculata, 266
Physostegia virginiana, 266
Pilea cadierei, 254
Pimpinella anisum, 261
Pinus glabra, 274
Pinus spp., 274
Pistacia chinensis, 272
Pistia stratiotes, 278
Pittosporum tobira, 271
Plectranthus spp., 254
Podocarpus macrophyllus, 270
Poliomentha longiflora, 262
Pontederia cordata, 279
Poterium sanguisorba, 262
Prunus campanulata, 275
Prunus caroliniana, 272
Punica granatum, 271
Pyracantha coccinea, 271
Pyrus calleryana, 272
Quercus nigra, 190
Quercus phellos, 275
Quercus shumardii, 274
Quercus virginiana, 274
Raphiolepsis indica, 270
Rhapidophyllum hystrix, 273
Rhapis excelsa, 254
Rhododendron canescens, 178
Rhododedron spp. and
    cultivars, 269
Rosa banksiae, 268
Rosa bracteata, 268
Rosa laevigata, 268
Rosa moschata, 268
Rosa palustris scandens, 268
Rosa roxburghii, 268
Rosmarinus officinalis, 263
Rudbeckia hirta, 266
Ruellia brittoniana, 266
Rumex acetosa, 263
Sabal minor, 272
Sabal palmetto, 272
Sagittaria sagitttifolia, 279
Saintpaulia, 254
Salvia 'Indigo Spires', 132
Salvia coccinea, 132
Salvia farinacea, 132
Salvia gregii, 132

Salvia guaranitica, 132
Salvia leucantha, 132
Salvia madrensis, 132
Salvia miniata, 132
Salvia officinalis, 263
Salvia spp. and hybrids, 266
Sansevieria spp., 254
Saxifraga stolonifera, 266, 277
Scilla peruviana, 257
Scindapsus, 254
Scirpus sp., 279
Sedum spp., 266
Solidago spp. and hybrids, 266
Spathiphyllum, 254
Spigelia marilandica, 266
Spirea × vanhoutei, 271
Stokesia laevis, 267
Syngonium polypodium, 254
Tagetes lucida, 262
Taxodium distichum, 272
Ternstroemia gymnanthera, 269
Thalia sp., 279
Thymus vulgaris, 263
Tigridia, 41
Trachelospermum
    asiaticum, 212, 276
Trachelospermum
    jasminoides, 275
Trachycarpus fortunei, 275
Tradescantia spp., 254
Tradescantia virginiana, 267
Tricyrtis, 136
Tulbaghia violacea, 43
Tulipa clusiana var.
    chrysantha, 257
Typha sp. and hybrids, 279
Ulmus parvifolia, 273
Veronica spicata, 267
Viburnum japonicum, 270
Viola odorata, 267
Vitex agnus-castus, 275
Wisteria sinensis, 275
Zantedeschia, 257
Zephyranthes, 41
Zingiber, 41
Zygocactus hybrids, 254

COMMON NAME INDEX

abelia, glossy, 270
abelmoschus, 34
acanthus, 119, 121, 124, 134, 264
achimenes, 17, 43, 50, 51, 56, 61, 258
acorn squash, 91
acorus, 277
  variegated, 264
African
  iris, 258
  violet, 254
agapanthus, 17, 41, 43, 50, 52, 258
ageratum, 34, 256
  hardy, 265
  wild, 133, 136, 265
ajuga, 214, 219, 223
akebia, 214, 218, 224
  five-leaf, 276
allium, 41, 257
alocasia, 258
aloe, 252
alpinia, 43, 50, 54, 258
alstroemeria, 42
alternathera, 34
althea, 167, 271
aluminum plant, 254
alyssum, 22, 24, 38, 64, 256
amaranthus, 32, 34, 256
amaryllis, 17, 41, 51, 64, 65, 66, 257
American
  beautyberry, 269
  holly, 272
anacharis, 238, 278
anemone, 257
angelonia, 34, 256
anise, 261
  sage, 132

annual
  baby's breath, 256
  candytuft, 256
  phlox, 22, 25, 27, 38, 256
  ryegrass, 95
antigonon vine, 226, 228
aralia, false, 253
ardisia, 221
  Japanese, 214, 215, 277
arisaema, 257
arrow arum, 279
arrowhead, 279
artemisia, 264
arugula, 75, 79, 261
arum, 50
  arrow, 279
ash, green, 273
Asian jasmine, 109, 212, 214, 215, 219, 220, 221, 226, 276
asparagus, 259
  fern, 119, 125, 252, 264
aspidistra, 109, 214, 215, 219, 223, 228, 276
aster, 125, 264
  Stokes', 267
aucuba, 269
autumn
  fern, 215, 276
  sage, 132
azalea, 26, 161, 162, 168, 169, 170, 175, 177, 179, 269
  native, 178
Aztec lily, 258
baby's breath, annual, 256
bachelor's button, 25, 27, 38, 256
bald cypress, 198, 201, 272
balsam, 32, 34, 256

bamboo, dwarf, 215, 221, 276
banana, 9
  shrub, 170, 179, 269
bare-root rose, 142
basil, 71, 78, 82, 88, 261
  purple leaf, 34
bay, 71, 75, 82, 262
bean, 68, 79, 81
  bush, 259
    snap, 88
  lima, 76, 78, 80, 86, 259
  pole, 88, 259
    snap, 9, 74, 76, 78, 80, 81, 82, 86, 88, 259
bearded iris, 41, 43, 257, 258
beautyberry, American, 269
beebalm, 71, 262, 266
beech, 186, 209
beet, 72, 74, 76, 77, 88, 90, 92, 94, 259
begonia, 174
  cane, 253
  fibrous, 253
  rex, 253
  strawberry, 139, 266
  tuberous, 41, 50
  wax, 34, 256
belamcanda, 43, 50, 258
Belize sage, 132
bell pepper, 76, 78, 81, 82, 86, 260
bentgrass, creeping, 95
bermudgrass, 96, 104, 109, 110, 111, 113, 114
  common, 95, 96, 97, 102, 103
  hybrid, 95, 96, 97
bindweed, 59
birch, 193

COMMON NAME INDEX

bird's nest fern, 253
bird-of-paradise, 17, 41
blackberry lily, 44, 258
black-eyed Susan, 266
bletilla, 43, 50, 257
blue
   daze, 9, 34, 174, 256
   flag, 43, 257
   phlox, 121, 124, 126,
     127, 266
   star, 121, 124
bluebell, Spanish, 257
blueberry, 170, 175
bluegrass
   Kentucky, 95
   rough, 95
borage, 71, 79, 261
Boston fern, 253
bougainvillea, 253
Bourbon rose, 268
Bradford flowering pear, 201,
   209, 272
bridal wreath spirea, 271
broccoli, 9, 72, 73, 74, 77,
   84, 86, 88, 89, 90, 91, 92,
   94, 259
brodiaea, 41, 257
bromeliad, 250, 253
bronze fennel, 93
brunfelsia, 165
brussels sprouts, 68, 84, 86,
   90, 94, 259
bulbing onion, 72, 88
bunching onion, 72, 74, 84,
   86, 88
burn plant, 252
burnet, 71, 262
bush
   bean, 259
   rose, 144
   sage, Mexican, 132
   snap bean, 88
butterfly
   bush, 178, 269
   ginger, 258
   vine, 227
   weed, 34, 124, 125, 136,
     137, 138, 264

butternut squash, 91
cabbage, 9, 22, 68, 72, 73,
   74, 84, 86, 88, 89, 90, 91,
   92, 94, 259
   Chinese, 72, 75, 79, 84,
     86, 88, 90, 94, 259
   ornamental, 27, 256
cabbage palm, 272
cabomba, 278
cactus, 253
   holiday, 254
caladium, 42, 43, 45, 47, 50,
   51, 56, 63, 258
calendula, 22, 25, 27, 38, 256
calla lily, 17, 41, 46, 47, 58,
   60, 63, 245, 257
camellia, 161, 163, 165, 175,
   177, 179, 184, 269
camphor tree, 195
Canaert red cedar, 272
candytuft, annual, 256
cane begonia, 253
cane, dumb, 253
canna, 17, 34, 41, 43, 50,
   51, 52, 53, 58, 258
cantaloupe, 76, 78, 80, 81,
   82, 84, 90, 259
Carolina
   jessamine, 214
     yellow, 217, 218,
       224, 275
carrot, 68, 72, 74, 76, 77, 88,
   90, 92, 94, 259
cast-iron plant, 109, 223, 252,
   264, 276
cat's claw, 59
catnip, 71, 88, 262
cattail, 279
cauliflower, 72, 73, 74, 84, 86,
   88, 89, 90, 91, 92, 94, 259
cayratia, 59
cedar
   Canaert red, 272
   Deodar, 272
   Eastern red, 201
celery, 71, 72, 79, 90, 92,
   94, 259
celosia, 29, 34, 256

centipedegrass, 95, 96, 97,
   101, 103, 104, 107, 108,
   109, 111, 113, 114
chamomile, 71, 79, 261
chard, 68
chaste tree, 275
Cherokee rose, 268
cherry
   flowering, 204
   Taiwan flowering, 8, 189,
     193, 275
cherry laurel, 193, 272
chervil, 71, 75, 79, 261
chestnut rose, 268
China rose, 149, 268
Chinese
   cabbage, 72, 75, 79, 84,
     86, 88, 90, 94, 259
   evergreen, 252
   ground orchid, 42
   holly, 269
   mahonia, 161, 173, 269
   parasol tree, 193, 272
   pistachio, 193, 209, 272
   sacred lily, 257
   wisteria, 275
chives, 71, 262
   garlic, 41, 43, 50, 71,
     82, 262
chrysanthemum, 38, 133, 136
cigar
   flower, 34
   plant, 119, 133, 136, 138,
     139, 265
cilantro, 71, 75, 79, 261
citrus, 195
   tree, dwarf, 173
cleome, 24, 34, 256
cleyera, 163, 269
climber, 141, 144, 145, 148,
   151, 153, 157, 268
   repeat-blooming, 145
climbing okra, 80
clivia, 17, 41, 43, 50, 52, 258
coleus, 34, 174, 256
collards, 72, 73, 74, 75, 76,
   78, 80, 82, 84, 86, 88, 90,
   91, 92, 94, 259

COMMON NAME INDEX

colocasia, 258
common bermudagrass, 95, 96, 97, 102, 103
coneflower, purple, 125, 265
Confederate jasmine, 221, 275
container rose, 142
copper leaf, 34
coral honeysuckle, 223, 275
coreopsis, 125, 264
coriander, 71, 261
corn, 68, 74, 76, 78, 80, 82
    sweet, 81, 259
cornstalk plant, 253
cosmos, 24, 27, 32, 34, 256
    dwarf, 34
costus, 43, 50, 58, 258
crape myrtle, 201, 203, 209, 272
    dwarf, 167, 172, 173
creeper, Virginia, 59
creeping
    bentgrass, 95
    juniper, 276
    lily turf, 212, 214, 215, 220, 222, 276
crinum, 17, 41, 43, 44, 50, 52, 56, 258
crocosmia, 41, 43, 44, 50
crocus, 41, 46, 257
    fall, 54, 58
crossvine, 276
croton, 253
crown of thorns, 253
cucumber, 9, 68, 74, 76, 78, 79, 80, 81, 82, 84, 86, 88, 259
cucuzzi, 76, 78, 80, 82
curcuma, 43, 50, 54, 258
curly
    leaf mustard, 93
    parsley, 93
cushaw, 78
cyperus, 248
cypress, bald, 198, 201, 272
daffodil, 257
Dahlberg daisy, 24, 34, 256
dahlia, 42, 43, 50, 52, 54, 258

daisy
    Dahlberg, 24, 34, 256
    English, 23, 256
    gerbera, 34
    Shasta, 124, 265
daisy shrub, 160
dancing lady ginger, 258
daylily, 121, 125, 134, 265
delphinium, 20, 23, 256
Deodar cedar, 272
dianthus, 9, 22, 24, 25, 27, 38, 256
dietes, 41, 43, 50, 52, 258
dill, 71, 75, 79, 261
dogwood, flowering, 209, 273
dragon tree, 253
Drummond red maple, 189, 209
duckweed, ivy-leaved, 278
dumb cane, 253
dusty miller, 23, 34, 174, 256
Dutch iris, 257
dwarf
    bamboo, 215, 221, 276
    citrus tree, 173
dwarf cosmos, 34
dwarf crape myrtle, 167, 172, 173
dwarf gomphrena, 34
dwarf melampodium, 34
    palmetto, 272
    pentas, 34
    pomegranate, 271
    yaupon, 269
early narcissus, 46
Easter lily, 49, 51, 58, 60, 63, 257
Eastern red cedar, 201
eggplant, 68, 72, 74, 76, 78, 80, 81, 82, 83, 85, 86, 88, 259
elephant ear, 17, 258
elm, lacebark, 273
English
    daisy, 23, 256
    ivy, 214, 215, 219, 253, 276

pea, 72, 88, 91, 94, 260
    rose, 140
eucomia, 258
eucomis, 43, 50
euonymus, 163, 173, 179, 184
evergreen, Chinese, 252
fall crocus, 54, 58
false
    aralia, 253
    indigo, 121
fatsia, 269
fennel, 71, 261
    bronze, 93
fern, 109, 214, 219, 228
    autumn, 215, 276
    bird's nest, 253
    Boston, 253
    holly, 215, 276
fescue, 95
feverfew, 71
fibrous begonia, 253
fiddle-leaf fig, 253
fig
    fiddle-leaf, 253
    weeping, 253
five-leaf akebia, 276
flag
    blue, 43, 257
    yellow, 43, 257
flame violet, 253
floribunda, 140, 141, 142, 145, 146, 154, 268
Florida maple, 209
flowering
    cherry, 204
        Taiwan, 8, 189, 193, 275
    dogwood, 209, 273
    onion, 257
    pear, Bradford, 201, 209, 272
    quince, 163, 165, 269
forget-me-not, 22, 256
Formosa lily, 58, 258
forsythia sage, 132
fountain grass, 277
four-o'clock, 34, 256
foxglove, 20, 23, 27

COMMON NAME INDEX

freesia, 41
French tarragon, 68, 71
fringe tree, 273
frogbit, 278
gaillardia, 32, 34, 256
garden
 mum, 265
 phlox, 266
gardenia, 161, 170, 173, 175, 178, 179, 270
garlic, 77, 88, 90, 91, 92, 94, 259
 society, 41, 43, 50, 52, 56, 258
garlic chives, 41, 43, 50, 71, 82, 262
geranium, 256
 scented, 71, 262
 strawberry, 214, 219, 277
gerbera daisy, 34
giant reed grass, 277
ginger, 9, 17, 41, 43, 44, 52, 54, 56, 58
 butterfly, 258
 dancing lady, 258
 hidden lily, 52, 258
 peacock, 52, 56, 258
 pine cone, 258
 shell, 52, 258
 spril, 258
 wild, 264
ginkgo, 209, 273
gladiolus, 41, 43, 45, 47, 50, 52, 54, 55, 56, 258
globba, 43, 50, 58, 258
gloriosa lily, 42, 43, 44, 50, 52, 54, 56, 258
glossy abelia, 270
golden raintree, 186, 195
goldenrod, 125, 136, 138, 266
gomphrena, 256
 dwarf, 34
grandiflora rose, 140, 141, 142, 145, 146, 153, 268
grape
 hyacinth, 257
 ivy, 253

graptophyllum, 34
grass
 fountain, 277
 giant reed, 277
 monkey, 109, 116, 212, 214, 215, 220, 221, 222, 277
 pampas, 277
 variegated Japanese silver, 277
 Washington, 278
 zebra, 277
green ash, 273
ground orchid, 257
 Chinese, 42
guava, pineapple, 271
habranthus, 43, 50, 258
hardy
 ageratum, 265
 hibiscus, 34, 265
 water lily, 234, 278
hawthorn, parsley, 273
hawthorne, Indian, 270
heather, Mexican, 34, 165
hedychium, 43, 50, 54, 58, 258
hibiscus, 9, 165
 hardy, 34, 265
hidden lily ginger, 52, 258
hippeastrum, 257
holiday cactus, 254
holly, 163, 177, 179, 184, 193, 207, 209
 American, 272
 Chinese, 269
holly fern, 215, 276
hollyhock, 20, 23, 27, 256
honeydew, 78
honeysuckle
 coral, 223, 275
 winter, 178
hornwort, 278
horseradish, 71, 262
hosta, 56, 118, 123, 129, 219, 227, 265
hot pepper, 68, 80, 82, 260
hubbard squash, 91

hurricane lily, 54
hyacinth, 41, 42, 44, 49, 60, 62, 64, 66, 257
 grape, 257
 water, 232, 244, 248, 278
hybrid
 bermudagrass, 95, 96, 97
 tea rose, 140, 141, 142, 145, 146, 153, 154, 268
hydrangea, 161, 167, 170, 179, 270
 oakleaf, 270
hymenocallis, 17, 41, 43, 50, 258
impatiens, 34, 174, 256
Indian
 hawthorne, 270
 pink, 121, 124, 266
indigo, false, 121
indoor palm, 253
iris, 50, 53
 African, 258
 bearded, 41, 43, 257, 258
 Dutch, 257
 Japanese, 41, 257
 Louisiana, 41, 43, 46, 47, 49, 50, 58, 60, 61, 63, 134, 234, 236, 245, 248, 257, 279
 Siberian, 41, 43, 52, 257, 258
 walking, 41, 43, 50, 52, 258
Irish potato, 72, 74, 81, 86, 88, 260
ivy, 254
 English, 214, 215, 219, 253, 276
 grape, 253
 poison, 59
 Swedish, 254
ivy-leaved duckweed, 278
Jack-in-the-pulpit, 42
jade plant, 253
Japanese
 ardisia, 214, 215, 277
 iris, 41, 257

COMMON NAME INDEX

magnolia, 8
maple, 273
persimmon, 209
silver grass, variegated, 277
viburnum, 270
yew, 270
jasmine, Confederate, 221, 275
jessamine
    Carolina, 214
        yellow, 217, 218,
            224, 257
jonquils, 257
Joseph's coat, 34
juniper, 177, 270
    creeping, 276
kaempferia, 43, 50, 258
kale, 27, 72, 75, 79, 88, 90,
    91, 92, 94
    ornamental, 22, 256
kentia palm, 254
Kentucky bluegrass, 95
kohlrabi, 72, 74, 76, 88, 90,
    92, 94, 259
lacebark elm, 273
Lady Banks' rose, 149, 268
lady palm, 254
landscape rose, 140, 149
lantana, 9, 34, 174, 256
lapeirousia, 41, 257
larkspur, 27, 38, 256
laurel, cherry, 193, 272
lavender, 68, 71, 79, 88, 262
leaf lettuce, 75
leek, 72, 77, 88, 90, 92,
    94, 260
lemon balm, 71, 78, 82, 262
lemongrass, 71, 82, 262
lettuce, 9, 68, 72, 73, 74, 76,
    79, 84, 88, 90, 91, 92,
    94, 259
lettuce, water, 232, 239,
    248, 278
leucojum, 257
ligularia, 136, 138, 139, 219,
    228, 265
ligustrum, wax-leaf, 271
lily, 41, 43, 50, 51, 54
    Aztec, 258

blackberry, 44, 258
calla, 41, 46, 47, 58, 60,
    63, 245, 257
Chinese sacred, 257
Easter, 49, 51, 58, 60,
    63, 257
Formosa, 58, 258
gloriosa, 42, 43, 44, 50,
    52, 54, 56, 258
hardy, water, 234, 278
hurricane, 54
peace, 254
Philippine, 56, 58, 258
pineapple, 258
plantain, 265
rain, 41, 52, 258
spider, 41, 43, 54, 63, 258
tiger, 58, 258
toad, 136
tropical water, 231, 232,
    233, 236, 237, 245,
    248, 278
water, 230, 231, 232, 239,
    240, 241, 243, 244,
    245, 246, 247, 248
lily turf, creeping, 212, 214,
    215, 220, 222, 276
lima bean, 76, 78, 80,
    86, 259
Lindheimer's muhly, 277
lipstick vine, 252
liriope, 109, 214, 215,
    220, 221
live oak, 101, 191, 204, 209
    Southern, 274
loosestrife, purple, 133
loquat, 273
loropetalum, 270
lotus, 246, 279
Louisiana
    iris, 41, 43, 46, 47, 49, 50,
        58, 60, 61, 63, 134,
        234, 236, 245, 248,
        257, 279
    phlox, 124, 266
luffa, 78, 80, 82, 84
lycoris, 58, 258
lysimachia, 219

magnolia, 163, 190, 193,
    196, 207, 209
    Japanese, 8
    oriental, 189, 273
    Southern, 274
    star, 165, 178
    sweet bay, 274
mahonia, Chinese, 161,
    173, 269
Malabar spinach, 78
mallow, 34, 125, 127
mandevilla, 227
maple, 186, 193
    Drummond red, 189, 209
    Florida, 209
    Japanese, 273
    red, 8
    sugar, 209
    swamp red, 191, 274
marigold, 9, 24, 29, 32, 34,
    38, 256, 262
    Mexican mint, 262
marjoram, 71
    sweet, 263
Mccartney rose, 268
mealycup sage, 132
melampodium, 34, 174, 256
    dwarf, 34
Mexican
    bush sage, 132
    heather, 34, 165
    mint marigold, 262
    oregano, 82, 262
    petunia, 266
    primrose, 127
    sunflower, 34
    tarragon, 71, 82, 262
milfoil, 278
miniature rose, 141, 145,
    155, 268
mint, 71, 75, 78, 82, 263
    marigold, Mexican, 262
mirliton, 76, 78, 80, 93
mock orange, 270
monarda, 125
monkey grass, 109, 116,
    212, 214, 215, 220, 221,
    222, 277

COMMON NAME INDEX

mother-in-law tongue, 254
muhly, Lindheimer's, 277
mum, 138
    garden, 265
muscari, 257
musk rose, 268
mustard, 68, 72, 74, 75, 76,
    79, 86, 88, 90, 91, 92,
    94, 259
    curly leaf, 93
    red leaf, 93
myrtle
    crape, 201, 203, 209, 272
        dwarf, 167, 172, 173
    wax, 201
naked lady, 54, 258
nandina, 270
narcissus, 41, 257
    early, 46
    paperwhite, 49, 65, 66, 257
narrow-leaf
    sunflower, 136, 138
    zinnia, 34, 256
nasturtium, 22, 27, 256
native azalea, 178
needle palm, 273
nemophila, 256
neomarica, 258
nicotiana, 38, 256
nierembergia, 256
noisette rose, 145, 149, 268
Norfolk Island pine, 252
oak, 190, 193, 194, 195, 201
    live, 101, 191, 204, 209
    red, 209
    Shumard, 209, 274
    Southern live, 274
    water, 190
    willow, 209, 275
oakleaf hydrangea, 270
obedient plant, 127, 266
okra, 68, 78, 80, 81, 82, 84,
    85, 88, 89, 90, 91, 259
    climbing, 80
old garden rose, 141, 145,
    153, 154
oleander, 167, 170, 172,
    179, 270

olive, sweet, 178, 271
onion, 72, 77, 88, 90, 92,
    94, 260
    bulbing, 72, 88
    bunching, 72, 74, 84,
        86, 88
    flowering, 257
orange, mock, 270
orchid, 254
    Chinese ground, 42
    ground, 257
orchid tree, 195
oregano, 71, 75, 263
    Mexican, 82, 262
oriental magnolia, 189,
    273
ornamental
    cabbage, 27, 256
    kale, 22, 256
    pepper, 34, 256
    sweet potato, 34, 42, 54
ornithogalum, 257
oxalis, 41, 43, 50, 52, 56,
    59, 258
palm, 196, 198, 200
    cabbage, 272
    indoor, 253
    kentia, 254
    lady, 254
    needle, 273
    ponytail, 252
    windmill, 275
palmetto, dwarf, 272
pampas grass, 277
pandorea, 227
pansy, 9, 22, 23, 24, 25, 27,
    38, 64, 256
paperwhite narcissus, 49, 65,
    66, 257
papyrus, 279
parasol tree, Chinese, 193,
    272
parrot's feather, 278
parsley, 71, 75, 79, 261
    curly, 93
parsley hawthorn, 273
pea, 81
    English, 72, 88, 91, 94, 260

podded, 91, 94
    snow, 72, 73, 75, 88, 91,
        94, 260
    Southern, 68, 76, 78, 80,
        82, 83, 84, 86, 90, 260
    sweet, 9, 25, 27, 38, 256
peace lily, 254
peacock
    ginger, 52, 56, 258
    plant, 253
peanut, 80, 82, 84, 260
pear, Bradford flowering, 201,
    209, 272
pecan, 193, 274
pencil plant, 253
pennyroyal, 71
pentas, 9, 174, 256
    dwarf, 34
peperomia, 254
pepper, 9, 72, 74, 76, 78, 80,
    83, 84, 85, 86, 88, 91
    bell, 76, 78, 81, 82,
        86, 260
    hot, 68, 80, 82, 260
    ornamental, 34, 256
    sweet, 82
perennial
    ryegrass, 95
    salvia, 132
    verbena, 34
perilla, 34, 71, 78, 82,
    256, 261
periwinkle, 9, 29, 34,
    174, 256
persimmon, Japanese, 209
petunia, 9, 34, 38, 256
    Mexican, 266
    summer, 266
    wild, 125
Philippine lily, 56, 58, 258
philodendron, 17
    split-leaf, 254
phlox
    annual, 22, 25, 27,
        38, 256
    blue, 121, 124, 126,
        127, 266
    garden, 266

COMMON NAME INDEX

Louisiana, 124, 266
pickerel weed, 279
pine, 193, 194, 199, 274
    Norfolk Island, 252
    spruce, 274
pine cone ginger, 258
pineapple
    guava, 271
    lily, 258
pistachio, Chinese, 193, 209, 272
pittosporum, 162, 271
plantain lily, 265
podded pea, 91, 94
poison ivy, 59
pole bean, 88, 259
polianthes, 258
polyantha, 141, 149, 268
pomegranate, dwarf, 271
pondweed, 278
ponytail palm, 252
poppy, 27, 38, 256
portulaca, 32, 34, 256
potato, Irish, 72, 74, 81, 86, 88, 260
pothos, 254
prayer plant, 254
primrose, Mexican, 127
privet, 163
pumpkin, 68, 76, 78, 80, 81, 82, 84, 90, 260
purple
    coneflower, 125, 265
    leaf basil, 34
    loosestrife, 133
purslane, 34, 174, 256
pyracantha, 271
quince, flowering, 163, 165, 269
radish, 68, 72, 74, 76, 77, 88, 90, 91, 92, 94, 260
rain lily, 41, 52, 258
rambler, 141, 144, 148, 151, 153, 157, 268
ranunculus, 42, 257
red cedar
    Canaert, 272
    Eastern, 201

leaf mustard, 93
maple, 8
    Drummond, 189, 209
    swamp, 191, 274
oak, 209
sage, 132
redbud, 274
reed grass, giant, 277
repeat-blooming climber, 145
rex begonia, 253
rosa de montana, 214, 276
rose of Sharon, 271
rose, 12, 170
    bare-root, 142
    Bourbon, 268
    bush, 144
    Cherokee, 268
    chestnut, 268
    China, 149, 268
    container, 142
    English, 140
    grandiflora, 140, 141, 142, 145, 146, 153, 268
    hybrid tea, 140, 141, 142, 145, 146, 153, 154, 268
    Lady Banks', 149, 268
    landscape, 140, 149
    Mccartney, 268
    miniature, 141, 145, 155, 268
    musk, 268
    noisette, 145, 149, 268
    old garden, 141, 145, 153, 154
    shrub, 141, 145, 268
    swamp, 149, 268
    tea, 145, 149, 268
rosemary, 71, 75, 78, 82, 263
rough bluegrass, 95
rubber tree, 253
rudbeckia, 24, 34, 125, 256
ruellia, 119, 133, 136, 138, 139, 266
rush, 279
rutabaga, 72, 74, 77, 86, 88, 92, 94, 260
ryegrass, 98, 99, 111, 112, 113, 114

annual, 95
perennial, 95
sacred lily, Chinese, 257
sage, 68, 71, 75, 79, 88, 263, 266
    autumn, 132
    Belize, 132
    forsythia, 132
    mealycap, 132
    Mexican bush, 132
    red, 132
    Texas, 132
salvia, 34, 119, 125, 132, 133, 136, 138, 139, 174, 256, 266
    perennial, 132
sasanqua, 175, 178, 179, 271
sassafras, 209
savory
    summer, 71, 261
    winter, 71
scaevola, 34, 256
scented geranium, 71, 262
schefflera, 253
sedum, 266
sesame, 71, 78, 82, 261
shallot, 72, 74, 77, 84, 86, 88, 90, 92, 94, 260
Shasta daisy, 124, 265
shell
    flower, 41
    ginger, 52, 258
shrimp plant, 34
shrub rose, 141, 145, 268
Shumard oak, 209, 274
Siberian iris, 41, 43, 52, 257, 258
silver
    bell, 274
    grass, variegated
        Japanese, 277
sisyrinchium, 257
smooth sumac, 209
snap bean, 9, 74, 76, 78, 80, 81, 82, 86, 88, 259
    bush, 88
snapdragon, 9, 22, 25, 27, 38, 256

COMMON NAME INDEX

snow pea, 72, 73, 75, 88, 91, 94, 260
snowflake, 41, 257
society garlic, 41, 43, 50, 52, 56, 258
sorrel, 71, 263
sourwood, 209
Southern
  live oak, 274
  magnolia, 274
  pea, 68, 76, 78, 80, 82, 83, 84, 86, 90, 260
Spanish bluebell, 257
sparaxis, 41, 109, 257
speedwell, 267
spider
  lily, 41, 43, 54, 63, 258
  plant, 119, 139, 253, 264
spiderwort, 125, 267
spinach, 72, 75, 79, 92, 94, 260
  Malabar, 78
spirea, bridal wreath, 271
split-leaf philodendron, 254
sprekelia, 52, 258
spril ginger, 258
spring starflower, 41, 257
spruce pine, 274
squash, 9, 76, 78, 79, 80, 81, 82, 84, 86
  acorn, 91
  butternut, 91
  hubbard, 91
  summer, 76, 91, 260
  winter, 76, 81, 191
St. Augustinegrass, 95, 96, 97, 98, 100, 103, 108, 111, 112, 113, 114
star
  magnolia, 165, 178
  of Bethlehem, 257
starflower, spring, 41, 257
statice, 23, 256
stock, 256
  Virginia, 38, 256
Stokes' aster, 267
stokesia, 127
stonecrop, 266

strawberry
  begonia, 139, 266
  geranium, 214, 219, 277
sugar maple, 209
sumac, smooth, 209
summer
  petunia, 266
  savory, 71, 261
  squash, 76, 91, 260
sunflower, 32, 34, 256
  Mexican, 34
  narrow-leaf, 136, 138
swamp
  red maple, 191, 274
  rose, 149, 268
Swedish ivy, 254
sweet
  bay magnolia, 274
  corn, 81, 259
  gum, 209, 275
  marjoram, 263
  olive, 178, 271
  pea, 9, 25, 27, 38, 256
  pepper, 82
  potato, 78, 80, 82, 84, 90, 260
    ornamental, 34, 42, 54
  shrub, 178
Swiss chard, 72, 74, 75, 76, 78, 80, 82, 86, 88, 90, 92, 94, 259
Taiwan flowering cherry, 8, 189, 193, 275
tarragon, 71, 79, 263
  French, 68, 71
  Mexican, 71, 82, 262
tea rose, 145, 149, 268
Texas sage, 132
thalia, 279
thryallis, 165
thyme, 68, 71, 75, 79, 88, 263
tibouchina, 165
tickseed, 264
tiger
  flower, 258
  lily, 58, 258
tigridia, 43, 50, 258

tithonia, 34, 256
toad lily, 136
toadflax, 256
tomato, 9, 68, 72, 74, 76, 78, 79, 80, 81, 82, 83, 84, 86, 88, 91, 260
torenia, 174, 256
tri-leaf woner, 254
tropical water lily, 231, 232, 233, 236, 237, 245, 248, 278
tuberose, 41, 258
tuberous begonia, 41, 50
tulbaghia, 258
tulip, 41, 42, 44, 49, 60, 62, 64, 66, 257
turnip, 9, 68, 72, 74, 75, 77, 86, 88, 91, 92, 94, 260
umbrella plant, 279
variegated
  acorus, 264
  Japanese silver grass, 277
verbena, 256
  perennial, 34
veronica, 267
viburnum, Japanese, 270
viola, 22, 23, 27, 38, 64, 256
violet, 267
  African, 254
  flame, 253
Virginia
  creeper, 59
  stock, 38, 256
  willow, 178, 271
vitex, 203, 275
walking iris, 41, 43, 50, 52, 258
wall flower, 256
wandering Jew, 254
Washington grass, 278
water
  hyacinth, 232, 244, 248, 278
  lettuce, 232, 239, 248, 278
  lily, 230, 231, 232, 239, 240, 241, 243, 244, 245, 246, 247, 248
    hardy, 234, 278

COMMON NAME INDEX

tropical, 231, 232, 233, 236, 237, 245, 248, 278
oak, 190
watermelon, 76, 78, 80, 82, 84, 90, 260
wax
begonia, 34, 256
myrtle, 201
plant, 254
wax-leaf ligustrum, 271
weeping fig, 253
wild
ageratum, 133, 136, 265
ginger, 264
petunia, 125
willow oak, 209, 275
willow, Virginia, 178, 271

windmill palm, 275
winter
honeysuckle, 178
savory, 71
squash, 76, 81, 91
wishbone flower, 34
wisteria, 218, 224, 227
Chinese, 275
yarrow, 125, 264
yaupon, 201, 275
dwarf, 269
yellow
flag, 43, 257
jessamine, Carolina, 217, 218, 224, 257
yesterday-today-and-tomorrow, 160
yew, Japanese, 270

zebra
grass, 277
plant, 252
zephyranthes, 43, 50, 258
zingiber, 58, 258
zinnia, 9, 32, 256
narrow-leaf, 34, 256
zoysiagrass, 95, 96, 97, 103, 108, 113, 114
zucchini, 85

MEET THE AUTHOR

Dan Gill

Dan Gill is an Associate Professor of Consumer Horticulture with the LSU AgCenter in Baton Rouge. Gill teaches, gives lectures, and writes articles and publications on gardening. Known to New Orleans area listeners as the popular radio host of the *WSMB Garden Show*, Gill is also featured weekly in gardening segments on television stations around the state. He writes a weekly gardening column for *The Times-Picayune* in New Orleans, and his "South Louisiana Region Report" and "Gill's Garden" columns appear monthly in the *Louisiana Gardener Magazine*.

The author received his bachelor's and master's degrees in horticulture from Louisiana State University. In addition, Gill is a member of many groups including the Louisiana State Horticulture Society and the Metro Area Horticulture Foundation, and he is the Director of Research and Education on the Board of the Louisiana Nursery and Landscape Association.

Gill lives and gardens on three acres in Prairieville, Louisiana.

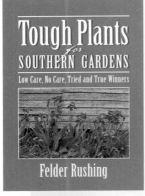
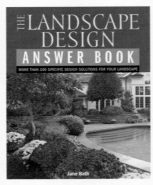
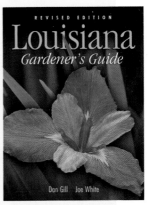

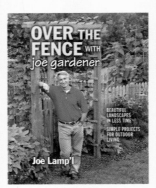